The Brick Reader

Works of art are of an infinite loneliness
and with nothing to be so little appreciated
as with criticism. Only love can grasp
and hold and fairly judge them.
– *Rainer Maria Rilke*

The Brick Reader

**Edited by Linda Spalding
and Michael Ondaatje**

With illustrations by David Bolduc

Coach House Press

Toronto

"From *Letters to Olga*" by Vaclav Havel, trans. P. Wilson © 1983 by Vaclav
Havel, © 1984 by Rowalt Taschenbuch Verlag, Translation © 1988
by Paul Wilson. Reprinted by permission of Alfred A. Knopf, Inc.

"Keeping a Rendez-Vous" by John Berger © 1991 by John Berger. Reprinted by permission of Pantheon Books, a division of Random House, Inc.

Published with the assistance of the Canada Council
and the Ontario Arts Council.

Canadian Cataloguing in Publication Data

The Brick reader
Excerpts from: Brick: a literary journal.
ISBN 0-88910-422-0

1. Canadian literature (English) - History and criticism.*
2. American literature - History and criticism.
3. English literature - History and criticism.
I. Ondaatje, Michael, 1943-   . II. Spalding, Linda.

PN151.B7 1991   820'.9   C91-094970-0

Contents

RUSSELL BANKS

Introduction

irst off, let's say what it's not. *Brick* (subtitled, until #33, "A Journal of Reviews," after that simply "A Literary Journal") is not the *Toronto Review of Books*. We sigh with huge relief. Surely, after having at last made the world safe for academic parochialism and post-Algonquin table-talk, the *New York Review of Books* needs no northern imitators. *Brick* is also not the *Toronto Literary Supplement*, which is to say, its pages are refreshingly free of donnish condescension and garrulousness.

On the other hand (despite its in-your-face name) *Brick* is not one of those funky, hand-crafted, programmatically anti-establishment journals of authenticity — shaggy, humourless, sincere, and Jungian — that in the sixties and seventies we published in our garages and our best friends read the next afternoon in coffee shops. And it's not a "quarterly," one of those inch-thick, perfect-bound tomes sponsored by a university literature department for the purposes of faculty recruitment and promotion, unreadable, theoretically correct, and too expensive to subscribe to except for the tax write-off.

Well, what is it, then? Simply, *Brick* is one of the best, if not the best, journals of ideas published in the English-speaking world — a gathering of literary and (increasingly in recent years) political ideas, put forward, not by academic specialists or political ideologues, but by writers who think and thinkers who write. Its contributors are Canadian, American, British, South African, and Irish; they are poets and novelists, essayists and critics; for the most part they address books and issues from a position slightly left-of-centre, from a multi-cultural, pan-national perspective, in familiar (and popular) genres — the old-fashioned book review, the personal essay and memoir, the interview, letters, and even the obituary. It does not bring news of the literary world to Canada or news of Canada to the literary world; it's more genuinely cosmopolitan than that, more presumptuous and even a bit bumptious, a much-needed corrective to London and New York provincialism. It's *sui generis*.

Founded in London, Ontario in the late 1970s by Stan Dragland and Jean McKay, mainly to review books of fiction and poetry from Canadian small presses, it ran for 24 issues, when in 1985 the journal was taken over by novelist Linda Spalding, who brought novelist-poet Michael Ondaatje in as contributing editor. In Spalding's hands, the lens opened and the focus shifted: the magazine became more deliberately international in its literary interests and more politically engaged, without at the same time giving up its commitment to small presses in general and Canadian writers in particular. That centre has held, expressing the editors' belief that the work being done by Canadian small presses and writers only gathers significance when seen in a larger literary and political context. For theoretical clarification, read here John Ralston Saul's brilliant (and astonishingly brief) essay on Canadian fiction and the larger context. And for practical demonstration, read Geoffrey York's essay, "Oka," on the Mohawks *versus* the rest of Canada, and by implication all of the aboriginal people on the continent *versus* the rest of North America. Or take a look at Derek Cohen's fine piece, "Athol Fugard and the Liberal Dilemma," which, while barely mentioning Canada or the United States, speaks directly nonetheless to several of our most painful and perplexing political dilemmas.

I have read in the pages of *Brick* (and happily find reprinted here) interviews with writers rarely (or not so well) interviewed elsewhere, such as Don DeLillo, Grace Paley, Kazuo Ishiguro, and Alice Munro. And the pairing of writers on writers has been intelligent and imaginative, often as revealing of the essayist as of the subject. Consider Robert Stone on Stephen Crane, and Edmund White on Genet. I particularly like reading the unconventional forms that flourish in *Brick* — the remarkable letters, for example, from writers as different as Vaclav Havel and Saint-Denys Garneau; the tributes and obituaries, like Sarah Sheard on Barrie Nichol and Ken Adachi; and the "talks," like Russell Hoban's reflections on extending reality.

It seems to me, however, that a special strength of *Brick,* amply demonstrated here, has been that sadly neglected form, the personal essay. Witness Marilynne Robinson on her childhood, Paul Wilson on translating Josef Skvorecky, and John Berger on just about everything. The essay by the Irish poet, Eavan Boland, "Outside History," nicely illuminates the intricate, often painful relationship between language, gender, and nationalism, and one doesn't have to be anglophone, female, or Irish to get it. Lawrence Garber writes of his lifelong attachment to James Jones, and you don't have to share that attachment to appreciate its enduring intelligence. (We've all been in love like that.) In recent decades, economic and academic strictures have all but eliminated publication of reflections and ruminations like these and consequently have made the personal essay, that loveliest, most intimate of narrative forms, practically extinct, and we readers and writers very much the poorer for it. The editors of *Brick* are nearly alone in their dedication to this form, and we can only hope that other editors take note and wise up.

At this point, it's only fitting and proper that I get out of the way and let you move on to these excerpts from *Brick.* But first let me compliment editors Spalding and Ondaatje and designers Gordon Robertson and David McFadden for the *look* of the journal, because in some issues I have been as pleased by the layout, photographs, and drawings as by the text they accompany, possibly because they are more than merely illustrative. Chosen with care, wit, and not a little irreverence, the pictures become frame and gloss; they add to the text a voice and intelligence that personalize the journal as a whole, adding to its contents a distinctive tone that is strictly derived from the editors' joint sensibility. Or, as my mother, with undisguised fear, used to say of some of my more vivid friends, their *character* (as in, "Your friend is quite a character!"). In that sense, and in all the more sober senses described above, *Brick,* indeed, has character. Of what other contemporary literary journal can you say that?

That said, however, please, dear reader, read on.

MARILYNNE ROBINSON

When I Was a Child

hen I was a child I read books. My reading was not indiscriminate. I preferred books that were old and thick and hard. I made vocabulary lists.

Surprising as it may seem, I had friends, some of whom read more than I did. I knew a good deal about Constantinople and the Cromwell revolution and chivalry. There was little here that was relevant to my experience, but the shelves of northern Idaho groaned with just the sort of old dull books I craved, so I cannot have been alone in these enthusiasms.

Relevance was precisely not an issue for me. I looked to Galilee for meaning and to Spokane for orthodonture, and beyond that the world where I was I found entirely sufficient.

It may seem strange to begin a talk about the West in terms of old books that had nothing western about them, and of naïve fabrications of stodgily fantastical, authoritative worlds, which answered only to my own forming notions of meaning and importance. But I think it was in fact peculiarly western to feel no tie of particularity to any single past or history, to experience that much underrated thing called deracination, the meditative, free appreciation of whatever comes under one's eye, without any need to make such tedious judgements as "mine" and "not mine."

I went to college in New England and I have lived in Massachusetts for twenty years, and I find that the hardest work in the world — it may in fact be impossible — is to persuade Easterners that growing up in the West is not intellectually crippling. On learning that I am from Idaho, people have not infrequently asked, "Then how were you able to write a book?"

Once or twice, when I felt cynical or lazy, I have replied, "I went to Brown," thinking that might appease them — only to be asked, "How did you manage to get into Brown?" One woman, on learning of my origins, said, "But there *has* to be talent in the family *some*where."

In a way *Housekeeping* is meant as a sort of demonstration of the intellectual culture of my childhood. It was my intention to make only those allusions that would have been available to my narrator, Ruth, if she were me at her age, more or less. The classical allusions, Carthage sown with salt and the sowing of dragon's teeth which sprouted into armed men, stories that

Ruthie combines, were both in the Latin textbook we used at Coeur d'Alene high school. My brother David brought home the fact that God is a sphere whose centre is everywhere and whose circumference is nowhere. I never thought to ask him where he found it. Emily Dickinson and the Bible were blessedly unavoidable.

There are not many references in *Housekeeping* to sources other than these few, though it is a very allusive book, because the narrator deploys every resource she has to try to make the world comprehensible. What she knows, she uses, as she does her eyes and her hands. She appropriates the ruin of Carthage for the purposes of her own speculation. I thought the lore my teachers urged on me must have some such use.

Idaho society at that time at least seemed to lack the sense of social class which elsewhere makes culture a system of signs and passwords, more or less entirely without meaning except as it identifies groups and subgroups. I think it is indifference to these codes among Westerners that makes Easterners think they are without culture. These are relative differences, of course, and wherever accident grants a little reprieve from some human folly it must be assumed that time is running out and the immunity is about to disappear.

As an aspect of my own intellectual life as a bookish child in the far West I was given odds and ends — Dido pining on her flaming couch, Lewis and Clark mapping the wilderness — without one being set apart from the other as especially likely to impress or satisfy anyone. We were simply given these things with the assurance that they were valuable and important in no specific way. I imagine a pearl diver finding a piece of statuary under the Mediterranean, a figure immune to the crush of depth though up to its waist in sand and blue with cold, in tatters of seaweed, its eyes blank with astonishment, its lips parted to make a

sound in some lost dialect, its hand lifted to arouse a city long since lost beyond indifference.

The diver might feel pity at finding so human a thing in so cold a place. It might be his privilege to react with a sharper recognition than anyone in the living world could do, though he had never heard the name of Phidias or Myron. The things we learned were, in the same way, merely given, for us to make what meaning we could of them.

This extended metaphor comes to you courtesy of Mrs. Bloomsburg, my high-school Latin teacher, who led five or six of us through Horace and Virgil and taught us patience with that strange contraption called the epic simile, which, to compare great things with small, appears fairly constantly in my own prose, modified for my own purposes. It was also Mrs. Bloomsburg who trudged us through Cicero's vast sentences, clause depending from clause, the whole cantilevered with subjunctives and weighted with a culminating irony. It was all over our heads. We were bored but dogged. And at the end of it all, I think anyone can see that my style is considerably more in debt to Cicero than to Hemingway.

I admire Hemingway. It is simply an amusing accident that it should be Cicero, of all people, whose influence I must resist. This befell me because I was educated at a certain time at a certain place. When I went to college in New England I found that only I and a handful of boys prepared by Jesuits shared these quaint advantages. In giving them to Ruth I used her to record the intellectual culture of the West as I experienced it myself.

The peculiarities of my early education are one way in which being from the West has set me apart. A man in Alabama asked me how I felt the West was different from the East and the South, and I replied that in the West "lonesome" is a word with strongly positive connotations. I must have phrased my answer better at the

time, because both he and I were struck by the aptness of the remark, and people in Alabama are far too sensitive to language to be pleased with a phrase like "strongly positive connotations." For the moment it will have to serve, however.

I remember when I was a child at Coolin or Sagle or Talache, walking into the woods by myself and feeling the solitude around me build like electricity and pass through my body with a jolt that made my hair prickle. I remember kneeling by a creek that spilled and pooled among rocks and among fallen trees with the unspeakably tender growth of small trees already sprouting from their backs, and thinking, there is only one thing wrong here, which is my own presence, and that is the slightest imaginable intrusion — feeling that my solitude, my loneliness, made me almost acceptable in so sacred a place.

I remember the evenings at my grandparents' ranch, at Sagle, and how in the daytime we chased the barn cats and swung on the front gate and set off pitchy, bruising avalanches in the wood shed, and watched my grandmother scatter chicken feed from an apron with huge pockets in it, suffering the fractious contentment of town children rusticated. And then the cows came home and the wind came up and Venus burned through what little remained of atmosphere, and the dark and the emptiness stood over the old house like some unsought revelation.

It must have been at evening that I heard the word "lonesome" spoken in tones that let me know privilege attached to it, the kind of democratic privilege that comes with simple deserving. I think it is correct to regard the West as a moment in a history much larger than its own. My grandparents and people like them had a picture in their houses of a stag on a cliff, admiring a radiant moon, or a maiden in classical draperies, on the same cliff, admiring the same moon. It was a specimen of decayed Victorianism. In that period mourning, melancholy, regret and loneliness were high sentiments, as they were for the Psalmist and for Sophocles, for the Anglo-Saxon poets and for Shakespeare.

In modern culture these are seen as pathologies — alienation and inauthenticity in Europe, maladjustment and depression in the United States. At present they seem to flourish only in vernacular forms, country-and-western music being one of these. The moon has gone behind a cloud, and I'm so lonesome I could die.

It seems to me that, within limits the Victorians routinely transgressed, the exercise of finding the ingratiating qualities of grave or fearful experience is very wholesome and stabilizing. I am vehemently grateful that, by whatever means, I learned to assume that loneliness should be in great part pleasure, sensitizing and clarifying, and that it is even a truer bond among people than any kind of proximity. It may be mere historical conditioning, but when I see a man or a woman alone, he or she looks mysterious to me, which is only to say that for a moment I see another human being clearly.

I am praising that famous individualism associated with western and American myth. When I praise anything, I proceed from the assumption that the distinctions available to us in this world are not arrayed between good and bad but between bad and worse. Tightly knit communities in which members look to one another for identity, and to establish meaning and value, are disabled and often dangerous, however polished their veneer. The opposition frequently made between individualism on one hand and responsibility to society on the other is a false opposition as we all know. Those who look at things from a little distance can never be valued sufficiently.

But arguments from utility will never produce true individualism. The cult of the individual is properly aesthetic and religious. The significance of every human destiny is absolute and equal. The transactions of conscience, doubt, acceptance, rebellion, are privileged and unknowable. Insofar as such ideas are accessible to proof, I have proved the truth of this view of things to my entire satisfaction. Of course, they are not accessible to proof.

Only lonesomeness allows one to experience this sort of radical singularity, one's greatest dignity and privilege. Understanding this permits one to understand the sacred poetry in strangeness, silence and otherness. The vernacular form of this idea is the western hero, the man of whom nothing can ever really be known.

By this oblique route I have arrived at the question of the frontier, which, I would propose, was neither a place nor a thing, neither a time nor an historical condition. At the simplest level, it amounted to no more than the movement of European-origin people into a part of the world where they had no business being. By the mid-nineteenth century, this was very old news. The same thing had happened on every continent, saving Antarctica.

In this context it is best that I repeat my governing assumption, that history is a dialectic of bad and worse. The history of European civilization vis-à-vis the world from the fifteenth century to the present day is astounding and terrible. The worst aspects of settlements were by no means peculiar to the American

West, but some of its better aspects may well have been. For one thing, the settlement was largely done by self-selecting populations who envisaged permanent settlement on land that, as individuals or communally, they would own outright. The penal colonies and pauper colonies and slash-and-burn raids on the wealth of the land which made the history of the most colonized places so unbelievably desolate were less significant here. On the other hand, there was a Utopian impulse, the hope to create a model of a good human order, that seems to have arrived on the Mayflower, and which flourished through the whole of the nineteenth century. By the standards that apply to events of its kind, the western settlement had a considerable positive content.

I have read fairly extensively over the last few years nineteenth-century writing about American social and political issues. Whether or not the West would be settled was clearly not in doubt. The question was how, and by whom. It appears to me that the Homestead Act was designed to consolidate the Northern victory in the Civil War by establishing an economy of small-holder farming, of the kind that prevailed in the North, as opposed to plantation farming on the Southern model. English agriculture was very close to the kind practised in the South, with the exception that the gangs of English farm labourers, though so poor they were usually called "wretches," were not technically slaves or chattels. In attempting to give the western lands over to the people in parcels suitable to making individual families the owners of the means of their subsistence — and the language I am using here is nineteenth-century and American — Lincoln contained, more or less, the virtual slavery that followed actual slavery. In the terms of the time, as things go in this world, the policies that opened the West were sophisticated, considered and benign. No wonder such hope attached to them.

The American frontier was what it was because it expressed a considerable optimism about what people were and what they might become. Writers of the period assumed that human nature was deformed by drudgery, poverty, contempt and self-contempt. They were obsessed with the fact that most people in most places — including American Blacks on plantations and American whites in city slums — lived lives that were bitterly unworthy of them.

So it is not surprising that their heroes lived outside society, and neither did nor suffered the gruelling injuries that were the stuff of ordinary life. In Whitman the outsider is a visionary. In Thoreau he is a critic. In the vernacular tradition of western myth he is a rescuer and avenger. In every version he expresses discontent with society. So it is not surprising that he is the creation of generations that accomplished more radical reforms of society than had ever been attempted anywhere before.

This brings me around again to an earlier point, that there is no inevitable conflict between individualism as an ideal and a very positive interest in the good of society.

Obviously I have an axe to grind here. My one great objection to the American hero was that he was inevitably male — in decayed forms egregiously male. So I created a female hero, of sorts, also an outsider and a stranger. and while Sylvie obviously has her own history, to the degree that she has not taken the impress of society she expresses the fact that human nature is replete with nameless possibilities, and, by implication, that the world is accessible to new ways of understanding.

Perhaps it was a misfortune for us that so many interesting ideas were associated with access to a habitable wilderness. The real frontier need never close. Everything, for all purposes, still remains to be done.

I think it is a universal sorrow that society, in every

is a regime of small kindnesses, which, together, make the world salubrious, savoury and warm. I think of the acts of comfort offered and received within a household as precisely sacramental. It is the sad tendency of domesticity — as of piety — to contract and of grace to decay into rigour, and peace into tedium. Still it should be clear why I find the Homestead Act all in all the most poetic piece of legislation since Deuteronomy, which it resembles.

Over years I have done an archeology of my own thinking, mainly to attempt an escape from assumptions that would embarrass me if I understood their origins. In the course of this re-education I have become suspiciously articulate and opinionated about things no doubt best left to the unselfconscious regions of the mind. At the same time, I feel I have found a place in the West for my West, and the legitimation of a lifelong intuition that the spirit of this place is, as spirits go, mysterious, aloof, and rapturously gentle. It is, historically, among other things, the orphan child of a brilliant century.

I think it is fair to say that the West has lost its place in the national imagination, because by some sad evolution, the idea of human nature has become the opposite of what it was when the myth of the West began, and now people who are less shaped and constrained by society are assumed to be disabled and dangerous. This is bad news for the American psyche, a fearful and anti-democratic idea, which threatens to close down change. I think it would be a positively good thing for the West to assert itself in the most interesting terms, so that the whole country must hear, and be reanimated by dreams and passions it has too casually put aside and too readily forgotten.

form in which it has ever existed, precludes and forecloses much that we find loveliest and most ingratiating in others and in ourselves. Rousseau said men are born free, yet everywhere they are in chains. Since the time of the Hebrew prophets it has been the role of the outsider to loosen these chains, or lengthen them, if only by bringing the rumour of a life lived otherwise.

That said, I must say too how beautiful human society seems to me, especially in those attenuated forms so characteristic of the West — isolated towns and single houses which sometimes offer only the merest, barest amenities; light, warmth, supper, familiarity. We have colonized a hostile planet, and we must staunch every opening where cold and dark might pour through and destroy the false climates we make, the tiny simulations of forgotten seasons beside the Euphrates, or in Eden. At a certain level housekeeping

VACLAV HAVEL

From *Letters to Olga*

Translated and Introduced by Paul Wilson

t five o'clock in the morning of May 29, 1979, the Czechoslovak State Security Police began arresting members of the Committee to Defend the Unjustly Prosecuted, otherwise known by its Czech acronym, VONS. Fifteen people were rounded up and ten of these, including Vaclav Havel, were detained in Ruzyně prison and later indicted under Article 98 of the Criminal Code for "subversion," a crime against the state that carries a maximum sentence of ten years.

VONS had been formed a year earlier as a direct outgrowth of Charter 77, the Czechoslovak human-rights movement, and its purpose was, in the words of its first official document, "to monitor the cases of people who have been indicted or imprisoned for expressing their beliefs, or who are victims of abuses by the police and the courts." The members of VONS gathered information and circulated typewritten reports of their findings both to official institutions and to the public. By the time of the arrests, 155 of these reports had been issued. They comprised the only hard evidence in the state's case against VONS.

By the time the trial of VONS was held in October 1979, four of the original ten detainees had been dropped from the indictment, leaving, besides Havel, Otta Bednářová, a former television journalist; Václav Benda, a mathematician and prominent Catholic layman; Jiří Dienstbier, a former foreign correspondent; Dana Němcová, a child psychologist; and Petr Uhl, an engineer and revolutionary socialist who had spent four years of the last decade in prison. Even by Czech standards the trial was a travesty of judicial procedure. The state made no effort to prove that subversion, motivated by "hostility" towards society, had actually taken place and the defense attorneys offered only the most cursory arguments for their clients' innocence. Benda's lawyer even congratulated the prosecutor on the indictment and apologized for having to enter a plea of not guilty. In his final statement to the court, Havel concluded by mentioning an odd circumstance that undercut the state's position: "Two months ago, while in prison," he said, "I was asked whether I would not consider accepting an invitation I'd received for a working visit to the United States. I don't know what might have happened had I accepted that offer but I cannot exclude the possibility that I might have been sitting in New York at this very moment. If I am standing in this courtroom now, it is quite possibly by my own choice, a choice which certainly does not suggest that I am hostile towards this country."

The appeal was quashed on December 20, 1979, and soon afterwards the five VONS members who had received "straight" sentences (Dana Němcová's sentence of two years was suspended) were sent under escort from Ruzyně to their various prisons. Otta Bednářová went to serve her three years in the Opava women's prison; Petr Uhl was sent to a maximum-security prison in Mírov; and the remaining three — Dienstbier, Benda and Havel — against all expectations and for reasons no one quite understands, were all assigned to the same prison, Heřmanice, in Ostrava, a large mining and steel-manufacturing city in Northern Moravia, close to the Polish border.

Because of the strict censorship, Havel's letters contain almost nothing about his everyday life in prison. Even after his release he remained reluctant to talk about it, not because the experience had been too harrowing but because he felt that the real meaning of his imprisonment could not be conveyed by mere facts. Nevertheless from what his fellow prisoners have said, from things Havel revealed later, and even from the letters themselves, we can surmise something of what life was like.

November 22, 1980

Dear Olga:
Rereading my last letter I was slightly taken aback to realize that I wrote nothing about what would seem to be the most important loss of all — my opportunity to write. This compelled me to think about myself a little. I shall try, succinctly (and as usual, in a very simplified way), to communicate to you the results of my thinking.

First, although I've been writing ever since I was about six, or rather since I learned the alphabet, I have never (unlike many other writers) felt writing in itself as a physical craving so intense I couldn't live without satisfying it. In my case, the whole matter is somewhat more complicated: as silly as it may sound, I would say that I simply enjoy creating, that I enjoy inventing things (mostly what are called works of art, but not them alone, and if so, then not because they are called art but because that is what the ways of seeing, looking at things and thinking that are nearest to mine are called). If I could have freely chosen my education when I was young, I might have become a film director instead of a writer: my longing to invent and create and thus to say something about the world and myself might have found a more appropriate outlet in the directing of films. There are several reasons for this, including the fact that I am a sociable creature and the less solitary genres suit me more; and since I've already taken up something as solitary as writing, then at least I write plays, which bring me close to the theatre, a "nonsolitary" institution.

Naturally, I'm used to making notes and lists and dealing with all kinds of things in writing (as you know, I'd even note down my intention to have a haircut or buy peppers) and with this possibiltiy denied I feel almost as though I'd lost an arm (to pick up on the simile of the one-legged man in my last letter). So I do miss that aspect of writing, every day and almost biologically, but of course it's not the main thing. Literary creation as such, the actual writing of plays — and this may surprise some — is not something I miss very acutely. Even on the outside, after all, I could go for long periods without writing.

There are several reasons for this, one of which is the following: I enjoy writing only when I know it's just right, when it flows, when I have a decent idea (which seldom happens in my case, because very little seems to suit my rather special approach), when the thing "writes itself," as they say. At such times I enjoy writing perhaps more than anything else. When it doesn't flow, or when I feel it isn't exactly right — that is when it doesn't precisely suit my poetics — then not only do I not enjoy writing, it actually repels me. (I am not the kind of author who can write on demand or on commission, in any style, about anything at all; or rather I might find it possible, but only by constantly suppressing myself.) In other words: "writing per se," any kind of writing at all, is not something I miss nor could I, since I don't need it in the slightest. I would probably miss playwriting very badly only if I had a surefire idea and someone were preventing me from realizing it.

In my case, however, such ideas usually come to me in the act of writing (I think something up and write it down, or in fact, think about it by making notes or thinking about my notes). If I don't have a specific and sufficiently attractive idea and moreover, if my opportunities to work out such an idea are severely limited, there is no reason why I should miss writing.

This doesn't mean, of course, that I don't miss what for me is the main aspect of writing, the concrete expression of "thinking and creating." Naturally I feel that loss a great deal. But the need — if it can be called a "need" at all — is so abstract, so vague, so lacking in particular roots (in one or another sphere of the body or soul), that for the most part I don't tangibly suffer from the lack of it — as something definite and nameable — and I am scarcely aware of it in any precise or permanent sense (for instance I can hardly imagine myself sitting unhappily in the corner of the room because I'd suddenly been overwhelmed by a longing for lost creativity). At the most, one feels that one has been living a long time without a sense of hearing, without substance, without meaning (hence, too, that constant speculation about the "meaning" of it all!), but one would feel that anyway, even without being a writer. That specific lack has been so "absorbed" into the general joylessness of being here that without some finely-tuned skills in self-awareness, one would scarcely be aware of it at all. Moreover, precisely because of this abstractness (inventing and creating relate to everything, but to nothing in particular; you realize yourself through them, and in general they elevate you as a person, but satisfy no particular impulse), the lack of opportunity to write cannot be directly associated with any part of the "particular horizon." Self-realization "as a creator," or rather, the potential for such self-realization, is something diffused throughout the entire horizon, an integral part of it, though it can never be seen there as a visible object. You may miss actresses or ballet dancers, the atmosphere backstage, the chance to miss something as indefinite as "inventing and creating." Of course I'm used to the occasional twinge of longing to write for the theatre (I'd lost that possibiltiy long before coming here, after all), and it would therefore be illogical to write about that in relation to my stay here; and the second and more essential thing — which, though curtailed, I had not really lost until coming here — cannot very well be related to any particular aspect of my lost home. In any case, it's not something "over and done with," something I had once and now have no longer. It is rather something from the realm of possibility, of what I might do or a way I might be (not in the sense of a profession, or of reputation, but in the existential sense). That is, from a realm I deliberately avoided getting into in my last letter (as I made clear) because I had not yet sufficiently recognized or understood my position in it, or because I was simply unable, thus far, to define it notionally. The point is that creation is related to freedom, and the loss of either is similar: for the most part we do not feel a general lack of freedom directly and tangibly, what we feel is only a lack of particular things, which we would choose if we had the freedom to do so.

ROSEMARY SULLIVAN

The Centric and Eccentric Debate

irginia Woolf once wrote: "Great works of art are not single and solitary births; they are the outcome of many years of thinking in common, of thinking by the body of people, so that the experience of the mass is behind the single voice." Her words assume a particular resonance for a Canadian, because the long-view of our literature describes this slow cumulative process by which the thinking, over years, by the body of people has only recently begun to cohere in works that are identifiably, indigenously Canadian, works that speak to the experience of the mass. (To understand why this has been a slow process, I have to take you back to the beginning.)

Of course, literature in Canada has ancient roots, the oral myths and legends of the first peoples, the myths that named and shaped the psychological landscape of the continent long before the Europeans arrived. And there is the literature of the first explorations, the journals of the pragmatic adventurers with their mapping expeditions, their religious crusades, and their records of entrepreneurial ventures, marking the first impact of the European mind. But *"belles-lettres,"* the effort to create a self-conscious literature with journals, publishers, and all the paraphernalia of literary culture begins in English Canada in the early nineteenth century. What you have then is a new literature evolving in a colonial context. I begin here because colonialism has left its imprint on our Canadian minds; it defines who we are.

I speak for only one-half of the culture — English Canada. Perhaps this already alerts you to the fact that what you have in Canada is the evolution of two national literatures, two national cultures, developing autonomously, even oppositionally, with mostly formal dialogue between them. But the evolution of each literature, I would argue, follows an identifiable dynamic.

There's a book that I've always found helpful in understanding my own cultural context. It's Louis Hartz's *The Founding of New Societies: Studies in the Histories of the U.S., Latin America, South Africa, Canada, and Australia*. Hartz insists that the New World societies are peculiar cultural entities. Before such cultures can know who they are, they must first un-invent themselves. The problem is they begin in *medias res*, European transplants, fragments from the larger whole of

Europe struck off during the course of the revolution which brought the West into the modern world. Being part of a whole is psychologically tolerable; being merely a part isolated from the whole is not. In the new colony, cultural identity is confused. The writers must engage in an act of deconstruction and reinvention, stripping down the old European identity, creating a spiritual cartography of place, defining a new psyche rooted in the new landscape.

The new colonial literature always begins in a state of adolescent dependency, trying simply to imitate European culture, usually because it is the transplanted elites who are doing the writing. Thus you find Byron in the back woods of Canada writing unintended parody, Child Roland to the dark maple came. Or, as Northrop Frye said, you have the phenomenon of culture in the bush garden — a literature of European drawing rooms encircled by a wilderness that is alien, a hostile savage territory. But inevitably a period of schizophrenia sets in. The colonial is no longer European but he does not yet feel at home in the new space; it is too large to occupy psychologically. The

need for a national literature, a national identity reflected in literature, plagues him. But he also suffers from a despair rooted in a colonial inferiority complex that gives rise to terrible confusions about identity. The Logos, he feels, is housed elsewhere. Can anything ever be done here? An aggressive nationalism is the only antidote. Each of the New World cultures has hit this moment at a different stage in its development, dependent on the particular blend of European national tradition, racial encounter, and perhaps most important, the kind of political revolution that led to independence, allowing a social imagination to take root and lay the first foundations of a tradition.

As a Canadian listening to endless cultural debates about the lack of a Canadian identity, I always took a peculiar satisfaction in the American example. In the nineteenth century you could find American writers writing: "Have we national traits sufficiently developed to define what we are as Americans? — while we do have Niagara Falls, we have no customs or habits of thought peculiar to ourselves." Melville, trying to convince his countrymen that literature was possible in the U.S., could advise them: — "Shakespeare, had he been born in America might have spoken more frankly. The Declaration of Independence makes a difference." Or reading Octavio Paz on the history of Mexican colonialism, asking all my questions. In 1961, he speaks of Mexico in the 1940s as an adolescent culture obsessed with its identity. He dramatizes the colonial cringe — "an inferiority complex influenced our preference for analysis and our meagreness of creative output was due to our instinctive doubts about our abilities." He speaks of the Mexican imagination vacillating in a labyrinth between solitude and violence.

A colonial culture lives with a sense of cultural domination imposed by an outside influence. The Logos has been kidnapped and it takes a long time to believe it can breathe freely in native air. A period of national articulation is necessary. While I have been stretching a model to accommodate similarities, there are also profound differences, and these are political. Colonialism can be a mental occupation; it can also be an economic, or military subjugation. But in either case, a struggle to recover wholeness, however different the process, is necessary. English-Canadian writers have often envied Quebec since the enemy there seems so obvious. It is the Anglais. But it wasn't the Logos they kidnapped; it was economic power. The writer could have a sense of constructive nationalism, a conviction of a past and a valid historical project, giving memory and intention. In English Canada assertion of wholeness has been slower, more ambiguous. It has been a quiescent process because, like the sibling rival to the older brother, English-Canadian writers have turned, within the parameters of their own language, first to the British as models and then to the Americans, with an exaggerated deference masking hostile insecurity. But with the cumulative impact of the last forty years things have changed in English Canada; the literary culture has passed through its identity crisis.

At some level we all believe that nations are generalized personalities. We speak (somewhat loosely to be sure) of a national psychology, a national consciousness (that is most readily reflected in the art, in the literature). Certain writers manage to touch the nerve pulse of the culture, assume its particular national gaze. The writer who manage this are usually themselves obsessed with national identity. There is one book that I feel cuts to the core of the English-Canadian psyche — Robertson Davies's *Fifth Business,* published in 1970.

When asked what he was doing in *Fifth Business,* Davies said: "I was trying to record the bizarre and passionate life of the Canadian people." "Fifth Business" is a term Davies borrows from opera. In opera there are five characters: the hero, the heroine, the female rival, the villain, and Fifth Business. Fifth Business is the peripheral character who never initiates action; he is the facilitator, the broker, who assists when necessary in the progress of the plot. It is a wonderful metaphor for Canada's perception of itself. Dunstan Ramsey, who plays Fifth Business is, for Davies, an archetypal English-Canadian; a Scots-Presbyterian from a small town in Ontario. He begins the book as an emotional colonial in the territory of consciousness. He grows up with one version of himself — the man of moral rectitude who does his duty. But the novel is Jungian — in the crisis of the novel, Dunstan, at fifty, must confront the revenge of the unlived life.

Davies has said that America is a Freudian culture, with a kind of Manichean view of the psyche; in American ideology and experience what really appeals is the stress between the good guy and the bad guy, the ego and the id, and the intellectual ferocity of issues in the U.S. comes from this black-white tension. The English-Canadian temperament is Jungian — we are the great withholders who hide behind a careful appearance. Dunstan must confront the fact that he has lived life as a spectator sport: out of his fear of exposure rooted in an ingrained sense of inferiority, he has refused to risk himself. Being Canadian he has assumed himself excluded from any of the great spiritual adventures. Amusingly, he has to discover that he is a lot more interesting than the persona he presents to the world. Always acting responsibly, never crossing the boundaries of propriety for fear of censure, he has directed his passions into manageable eccentricities, into hobbies. He has never assumed the moral authority, the nerve, to be fully himself. Davies sends his character to Mexico and Europe, in a reinvention of Henry James's colonial drama. He meets a wild magician who turns out to be a friend from his Canadian childhood, a kind of alter-ego, and the adventure he

undertakes with this shadow self brings him through a necessary Jungian integration. He becomes a formidable character indeed.

This is a Canadian cultural autobiography. It describes the process of breaking out of the self-rehearsals rooted in colonial insecurity. When you do that, you simply acknowledge that you work with what you are. Now we have a new phase in Canadian literature. We've had works that have located us in a Canadian landscape that is evocative, identified the ancestral mosaic that created us, explored the temperamental reticence and failure of nerve that have plagued us. In more recent literature there is a sense of homecoming, a sense that the national consciousness is now lived in.

The novels that have been written in the past fifteen years are pioneering novels, novels of family or cultural history, and the poems are often documentary narratives recording responses to place or local history. Some works lament the loss of cultural memory in gestures of love and longing and yet try to establish continuities. In the works of writers like Margaret Laurence and Rudy Wiebe there is the need to explore the paradox of spiritual homecoming. Writers have a sense of homecoming because for the first time, they can locate their own tradition with confidence. They have the assurance of writing out of an imaginative continuum that stretches over generational barriers.

What I look for today are the works that are written powerfully, eloquently out of this new authority, understanding that Canadian literature is not hived-off from world culture but a necessary voice within it. In my own drama of understanding what this means I have been pushed by a wonderful essay — Carlos Fuentes's "Centric and Eccentric Writing."

Being Mexican, Fuentes also grew up believing that the Logos was housed elsewhere, and that he was condemned to exile on the periphery of world literature. As a diplomat's son he was educated in the "severe English schools" of Santiago de Chile and Buenos Aires, and British literature was his first imaginative territory, peopled, of course, by the Aztec gods of his native Mexico. These two worlds seemed to divide him irreconcilably, indeed schizophrenically, until, as he explains, he found the key to integration. He admits, given his Mexican machismo, it's hard to confess that two women, Jane Austen and Emily Brontë, altered his perception of literature. Austen identified the impasse he confronted; hers was the voice that excluded him. She writes, he explains, as if she represents a "fixed, universal, and eternal human nature." Behind her stands the weighty conviction that "human nature is always one and the same, although imperfectly developed, as Locke put it, in children, madmen, and savages; and that this true human nature is to be found permanently fixed, in Europe and the European elites." This is the presumptive voice of Centric culture. But even within its borders was to be found the voice of the rebel, of the eccentric. Emily Brontë, for Fuentes, is "the bearer of the tragic oppositions, the secret dreams, the dark follies and lost innocence, the outlawed loves." Hers is the voice of rebellion against the Centric culture's monopoly of power and pre-eminence. She demonstrates that literature is capable of receiving the eccentric contributions of our total humanity. Finally he discovered that literature makes eccentrics of us all. And that the writer's mission is always and everywhere to extend the limits of the real, to fracture and reinvent language so that it is capable of carrying our unique experience. His personal dialogue with Brontë, he insists, gave him the authority to understand that only in independence do we find interdependence.

And this reminded me that Canadian literature also participates in the eccentric dialogue from its own outside perspective. We make up a unique literary cartography. The literature is regional, concerned with the articulation of a local life. We can speak of a Prairie identity, a West Coast or Maritime or Ontario identity, all under the loose umbrella of the Canadian complex. And new immigrant writers — Chilean, Czech, Indian — are widening the perspective. The dialogue with Quebec is strengthening, and English-Canadian writers are now curious to participate more aggressively in international culture. Canadian literature as a literature that has rejected cultural colonialism and is exploring the meaning of indigenous identity in its physical, cultural and spiritual aspects has an interesting perspective to offer in the struggle against the homogenizing pressures of technological mass culture. As a country, we are eccentrics, outside witnesses to the centrist dialogue of power. This is the gaze the writers inherit and it's not a bad position for the writer to be in. All writing is eccentric, committed to charting a centrifugal course against reductive forces that would have us live anonymous, acquiescent lives.

HOLLEY RUBINSKY

An Interview With Alistair MacLeod

n November 27, 1976, in a piece for the Toronto *Globe and Mail*, Alistair MacLeod wrote:

> From time to time there are writers who come riding out of the hinterlands of this country called Canada. And they are writing about a life that they really know down to its smallest detail. And it is a life that is fierce and hard and beautiful and close to the bone. They are not fooling around, these writers, not counting their phrases, not being coy. And they have not returned from an aimless walk through a shopping plaza "looking for something to write about." They both know what they want to say and how to say it and they go at their task with the single-mindedness of the Ancient Mariner encountering the wedding guest. "Look," he says, "no wedding for you today because I am going to tell you a story. And I am going to hold you here and not with my hand nor with my 'glittering eye' but by the very power of what I have to tell you and how I choose to tell it. I am going to show you what I saw and heard and smelled and tasted and felt.

> And I am going to tell you what it is like to be abandoned by God and by man and of the true nature of loneliness and of the preciousness of life. And I am going to do it in such a way that your life will never again be the same."

MacLeod was writing — not about his own work, of course, although it seems to me it could be — but of how often in Canada the most powerful short stories originate from, or draw power from, the regions — small towns, rural areas. MacLeod's own stories are set in the Maritimes, Nova Scotia particularly, rooted in fishing, mining, rural traditions. His writing — described by *Publishers Weekly* as being "raw and brutal, sweet and tender" — isn't for everyone: many modern readers won't have the patience for it, because patience it does require: MacLeod's stories aren't "fast reads" and they are not decadent, new-age, minimalist or postmodern.

In 1969 his story "The Boat" was included among the year's twenty best in *Best American Short Stories*; it wasn't until 1976 that "The Boat" and six other stories were collected in his first published book, *The Lost Salt Gift of Blood*. After ten years, in 1986, McClelland and Stewart published MacLeod's second collection, *As*

Birds Bring Forth the Sun, containing seven stories. Much has been noted of his record of producing approximately one story a year, and as we talked he referred to his "slowness," his awareness of it, more than once. His stories, generally about eight thousand words, longer than most short stories, are painstakingly created; you believe that the experiences so lyrically and meticulously described are in some way autobiographical. (In Andrew Garrod's interview in *Speaking for Myself,* MacLeod says when "The Boat" was first published, people were surprised to see his father alive; they thought he should have fallen off the end of the boat, as in the story.)

About the stories there is something solid and unbound by time. They reach into us (some of us, many of us); they pull us from our urban preoccupations back to, or down to, up to, our emotional roots, our basic, human attachments that the twin gods of success and consumerism encourage us to forget, to break with, sneer at, avoid. It's not the personal recognition of place, time, character that resonate in us, because the families in MacLeod's stories aren't yours or mine. His characters are the descendants of immigrant Scots who settled in Nova Scotia two hundred years ago, and their lives are comparatively, deceptively, simple. In MacLeod's families there is no newsworthy abuse, either physical or psychological, no runaway children homeless and prostitute on the streets, no drifters and no drugs. MacLeod writes out of a tradition many of us have forgotten we once came from, or which we never knew but suspect our ancestors (whoever they were) did. The stories deal with universals: attachment to place of origin (however profound the battle away from, or however great the distance run); coming of age (awareness of limitation, in one's parents, oneself, one's environment); ongoing loss (life can't stay the same and change at the same time). There are always roads not taken and those left behind.

This brief and simplistic introduction can't explain, of course, his genius; and genius it is, whether the stories are popularly appreciated, or whether he ever gains more than a side paragraph in papers about Canadian writing. His tack isn't mainstream. I don't think he can be placed in the continuum of the "development" of Canadian writing because no one else writes like he does. Some might call him old-fashioned, although there is nothing remotely Norman Rockwellian about the stories; and while using sophisticated narrative techniques, he aims for the heart and hangs on.

The interview took place on January 23 and 24, 1989 in Windsor, Ontario. The same month, *Publishers Weekly* voted *The Lost Salt Gift of Blood: New and Selected Stories* one of the top paperbacks of the year.

Rubinsky: The title of your novel-in-progress, "No Great Mischief If They Fall," is a quote from Major-General Wolfe. What does it mean?

MacLeod: It's a description that Wolfe used in a letter to his friend Captain Rickson to describe the Highland soldiers he was putting in the front lines at the siege of Quebec. One of the ideas in this projected work is the idea of loyalty. Wolfe distrusts these people, because they have two languages that he does not have: many of them are Gaelic-speaking, and after the 1745 rebellion in Scotland a lot of them went to France and learned French. This is why they're an asset at Quebec. They also represent a kind of threat in the way that anybody who can speak about you behind your back represents; so in his letter to Rickson, he suggests that he's putting these people in the front because they come from a rocky terrain, and they're very good at climbing rocks and they're big and strong and surefooted and all the rest of it. But if they should be killed in going up the cliff of Quebec, no great mischief if they fall.

So he can't lose with these people. I think this is an interesting idea: people are there in the army trying to do the best they can and the commander is writing those kinds of comments about them behind their backs. It raises certain questions, I suppose, about the nature of Canada. Some of these same people were fighting in the American War of Independence and there's a lot of good literature there because Highlanders fought on the American side and some of them fought on the British side and they used to sing songs to one another in Gaelic at night, advocating why the other group was on the wrong side, kind of like Tokyo Rose; because, again, they had language which was not English, the main language of the American Independence fighters and the main language at that time.... I'm dealing in this story with some of the fallout of the Viet Nam War, where those same issues of whether the people who went to fight for the American cause against the Vietnamese were the brave ones or the stupid ones, and if those who came to Canada were the more farsighted or less patriotic. I'm also quite interested in the idea of language and of what it means for people who perhaps are not vocal or perhaps who do not have the right language. There is a tendency for people who have a language to think that all the other people who have the other language, whatever it might be, are speaking in gibberish. This obviously is not true. I come from a Gaelic-speaking background, and when the Highlanders were leaving the Highlands, despite all those things that happened to them, there's no record at all in their own language about what was happening to them, and I find this sort of moving in that the people who were forcing them out were mostly English-speaking people and they referred to the Gaelic language as the Irish tongue, which it is, or as gibberish or jibberish, however you choose to spell it. The interpretation of these peoples' communication with one another was denigrated, because people didn't understand what they were saying. This may be what always happens in terms of conquered peoples. I was reading today a kind of interesting idea in a *New York Times* review of a book called *Bullwhip Days,* about a make-work project in the 1930s. Roosevelt sent interviewers down into the rural south to interview the remnants of people who had been born in slavery. The book is edited by a man named James Mellon and the interesting thing in that book is that slaves never wrote books, never wrote novels; they had, I think he said, "neither language nor leisure." A former slave in the book says, You can never understand it unless you wore the shoe, unless you were in slavery; but where's the novel? There were twelve million people in slavery, but where's their voice? The descriptions are all written by white people because they had the language and the leisure. Who gets to talk, who gets to tell the story: is it just the people with the leisure or just the people with the language?

Rubinsky: In the *Canadian Literature* interview that Colin Nicolson did when you were in Scotland on the Canada–Scotland Writer's Exchange, you could list your ancestors and the places they came from. I looked up the Isle of Eigg and it's a tiny island—

MacLeod: Five miles long. I think that's one of the peculiar accidents of emigration, that there are people who came from Eigg, I don't know how long they were in Eigg although it'll be two hundred years the year after next since they left there — the time of the French Revolution. I know a bit about those people from Eigg. I know who a whole lot of the people were on those ships and where they went. One of the peculiarities of immigration patterns is that no one knows how long those people were there on that island before going to a place like Cape Breton or perhaps P.E.I. They were there another six generations. One can make too much about this business of islands, but

I think if you're an island group of people and then you go to another island, although a bigger one, and you stay there for a long long time and everybody, as far as we can speak of our ancestry, is almost exactly of the same racial stock, it means something. It means a kind of intensification that perhaps not a lot of North Americans have. The Quebec people have been there a long, long time and they've been very much like a French people. Of course the Native peoples are the most obvious. And I'd say the Black settlements in Nova Scotia are the same — Loyalist settlements, having been there in Nova Scotia for two hundred years, with the same family names, staying in the same landscape. Perhaps it does something to your perception, to your interpretation of the world. Perhaps the world stays the same for you longer than it does for people who come into the great melting pot, wherever it might be.

Rubinsky: In "The Closing Down of Summer" the narrator says: "Our sons will go to the universities to study dentistry or law and to become fatly affluent before they are thirty." The main character in "Mischief" is a dentist. I've been wanting to ask you about this obsession.

MacLeod: I don't have an obsession with dentists. I have an obsession with fishermen. I think dentistry's an interesting profession. I'm learning more about dentists because when I go to my dentist, I ask about dental magazines so I can read about what they read. But in this novel I'm interested in people like orthodontists, people who straighten teeth, straighten jaws and so on.

Rubinsky: Why teeth? Why jaws?

MacLeod: It's like plastic surgery, it allows people to appear better than they might otherwise be, but of course it just changes the outside, it doesn't change the inside.

Rubinsky: But why teeth and jaws? You could have chosen to make him a plastic surgeon.

MacLeod: I thought plastic surgery would be a bit too arcane. I tried to think what plastic surgeons would do before they became plastic surgeons but what orthodontists do before they become orthodontists is they become dentists, so it's a step higher. And the other thing that's interesting is that orthodontists and plastic surgeons and people like that only flourish in a rich society and work with rich people. I think that's fine, it's a kind of interesting stratum of society, when you think that in the United States — there are thirty-three million people with no medical care at all, not the most basic thing; well, there they are with their concerns and then there are the people who go to orthodontists. And people who are orthodontists become quite rich. All you have to master, as a dentist, is the intricacies of thirty-two teeth, so I thought that was kind of interesting.

Rubinsky: So you made the son whose parents were killed falling through the ice a dentist.

MacLeod: Well, when people are poor, what do they become when they are no longer poor? How does one become rich?

Rubinsky: What about the three older brothers?

MacLeod: One of them becomes a very good miner. What happens to them is that they never go to school anymore because they're too old and they're too young. And what happens with these people, he and his sister who are three and become raised by their grandparents, is that they become almost like substitute children for the grandparents who have lots of children; so — everything's complicated — in a certain way it's almost to their advantage that this happened, although they don't know that. You never know. What if my mother had lived? What if my father had lived? Would it be better or worse? All they're left with is the way things are; the dead parents are kind of mythical people, because these children only knew

29

them for three years. There are scenes in that novel ... the mother is an only child, but the father's brother talks about the father, and that's kind of an interesting idea, in that he would be with him, the father, for say, forty years, whereas the children would be with their parents for only three and would not know them that well, would not know them as well as the sixteen-year-old knows them. Because of the loss, the parents become magnified. A child looks at their picture and says: If my real mother was here I bet she'd be nice, wouldn't make me put on my snowsuit or whatever the crisis might be. Because of what has happened to these children, they have that wound, and the wound is real, and going out from that wound are all kinds of imaginary things that happen to people when they are hurt. But these children are not really hurt, they actually become more prosperous than almost anybody in their family has ever been. And the orthodontist, he is the royal rich man.

Rubinsky: There's a deep sexuality in your stories that gives them power.

MacLeod: I don't know if I ever thought very much about that, but I know it's there, just part of the world. That's probably not a very good answer. Different people have mentioned this. I don't think of it very much. I know it's there in the same way we're all here because of sexuality, I suppose.

Rubinsky: There are archetypes in "Vision": the witch and the man who isn't what he seems. How conscious are you of that when you're working?

MacLeod: I'm conscious of what I'm doing, but I don't know if I'm really conscious of how other people might label certain things. I was interested in that woman who becomes blind for a number of reasons: how she's very strong-willed, how people sometimes change without realizing they've changed, because obviously you change when you're blind. She and her boyfriend are kind of violent and given to doing things that other people don't do, which may be the basis for a happy marriage, perhaps, I don't know. But then he is asked to give her up as well as the second sight by the clergyman flapping the Bible before his eyes. I don't know if he rejects her in any bitter way, he just says, I'm going to have to stop doing this — and what happens to her is that she flies into a rage, because she did not plan on that. She was willing to be unconventional with him, but then he becomes conventional, a kind of very ordinary man — until the end, in his senility, when he seems to go back to what he was before. So she is not a real witch, she is kind of an extraordinary person, who remains that way, whereas the sister who does marry the man in the end is a very conventional person. And they seem okay.

Rubinsky: All of your narrators are male.

MacLeod: I suppose I'm just more comfortable with that. The last story I did, "Island," is a story about a female.

Rubinsky: But it's done third person.

MacLeod: It's done third person. "The Tuning of Perfection" is done third person, too.

Rubinsky: But all the first-person narrators are male, ten or older.

MacLeod: I think that's just a stylistic decision that one makes, like who gets to tell the story. I'm talking about the point of view now and I think if you're going to use the first person, that's your central consciousness and everything is filtered through him, in my case, through that masculine person; and I think the good news about that is you can go deep. The idea there is that everybody is interested in telling his own story, so if you're going to say, It was dark and stormy when I set out, then you're saying, I'm going to tell about myself, what happened to me. There's a kind of intensity in that. In the "Island" story and in "The Tuning of Perfection" story and in "The Golden Gift of Grey" story, I wanted a larger picture than the central character could have. If you're going to talk about "how I feel," then you're trapped in that point of view; but in the case of "Island" and "The Tuning of Perfection," the way I felt about Archibald or Agnes MacPhedran was that there's a lot happening to them that they perhaps don't understand. So I'm going to do the third person there. I think when you begin to say, I'm going to write a story about a folk singer, about a certain kind of man who wants to do everything right when everybody around him is making all these compromises — he may be done in or not done in by the modern world, but he was the same way in the early world, which is why he and his wife decide to go up the mountain and leave their relatives behind. Then of course when she dies, he's left by himself with the same attitudes but with no one with whom to share these fiercely held ideas. And of course his children become not his children, because they're taken away at three, and he's kind of physically responsible for his children and grandchildren, but they're not being raised by him or his wife; so they become, obviously, more ordinary than he is or than he thinks somebody should be. But I said, Now who's going to tell the story? If Archibald gets to tell this story, he would be so centred in his own consciousness that things are going to be missed by him. So while other people are going to bingo, and they have a great time at bingo, if he got to tell the story, he would say, All those fools going to bingo; he would be too judgmental. I want to back off, so the story is like those doll houses where you can see simultaneously into all the different rooms.

Rubinsky: I thought the use of the third person was interesting in "Island" because you never said she was lonely; yet all of a sudden one day she sees the mackerel fishermen and there's this fantastic scene on the rock, with her trying to become impregnated.

MacLeod: I was interested in that event because it was one of those things that could never happen again. They are kind of crazed by all this sexual imagery — by all the sperm and seed and eggs — highly aroused. By the heat, and the waiting. I did not want to make this like a rape scene, I did not want her to fall in love with the white-haired man; it's just like one of those things that could happen at two o'clock but not at three o'clock, perhaps. But she's very lonely and these people come and they come for something else and then this happens and they just go away and she says, Now, of what I know of this sexual business, this (a pregnancy) is going to happen; but it doesn't happen. What I was dealing with in that story was isolation and what that really means. At the end of her life, it doesn't seem to mean anything much: she's given her life to the lighthouse and then suddenly is replaced by a revolving machine. She falls into that position because of a lot of peculiar circumstances. In her situation, her parents are like her grandparents and almost rickety by the time she's born. In "The Boat," the fact that the boy is the only son and the fact that he's young and that his parents are old, especially the father, means all kinds of things. The age at which people die, the age at which people are born or conceive their children, all these variables create pressures, especially in that culture, of defined roles, cultural roles: women do this and men do that. And I think people of different generations with different concepts are very bothered by things that don't bother us. Illegitimacy, for example, doesn't bother a lot of people at all but it might bother other people and cause all kinds of consternation. Others would say, I don't care who my daughter marries, as long as she's happy, as long as she marries a rich man or she marries someone with perfect teeth.

Rubinsky: Do you work on more than one story at a time?

MacLeod: No. Hardly ever, hardly ever. Nearly

always one at a time. I devote my whole attention to one idea.

Rubinsky: So what's the first thing that comes to you when you're nearing the end of a story? Do you begin then to think of the next one, or have you had a glimmer already?

MacLeod: Perhaps, perhaps. But I don't do three at a time or two at a time. I couldn't bear it. There have been cases where I started things and was interrupted, but I just do one thing at a time.

Rubinsky: So what's the first thing that comes to you when you are about to begin a story? One time at Banff you said one thing would sometimes be the trigger, the thing that kept you on track.

MacLeod: Sometimes it's that and sometimes it's a character in a certain place at a certain time. Quite often it's an idea.

Rubinsky: What do you mean by idea?

MacLeod: I'll write a story about choice, or I'll write a story about isolation or I'll write a story about death or I'll write a story about perseverance or I'll write a story about the loss of innocence or the coming of awareness or loyalty or something like that. I'm interested in how these ideas become activated or influenced by the people that encounter them in the place that the people are and the possibilities — I'm interested in where people are when things happen to them, what those things might be. If your parents die when you're forty or your parents die when you're four, it's not a bit the same.

Rubinsky: Is the idea triggered by something you remember from your past? Your family? Or a setting?

MacLeod: I don't think any of those stories is autobiographical. I'm not an autobiographical writer or anything like that. I don't know where things come from. When we look into ourselves, we find all this hodgepodge of stuff, and memory, memory has to do with remembering certain sights or certain sounds, certain events and so on, and hopefully what the writer does is put these things together in an interesting way.

Rubinsky: Lots of things strike me as perhaps part of your upbringing. But at the same time, I know you didn't even get to Nova Scotia until you were ten. A lot of your narrators are little boys, ten and eleven.

MacLeod: That may be from choosing narrators or remembered narrators who would be interesting for the purpose of the story. The age at which you are when a first-time experience occurs has a great bearing on all kinds of things in your life. The first time things happen to us, they are very, very memorable, because whatever it might be, it's never happened before. In that story "In the Fall," the selling of the horse story, what I was interested in was the fact that as a child you may think you live in sort of a secure world, where your parents have the answer and so on. This is what small children are always doing, when their toy car breaks they come and say, Fix it. I think as a parent you can do this pretty well for awhile, but then suddenly there comes a time when the child realizes that the parents, instead of being wise oracles who know everything, fail in that role, they may also be impotent or incompetent to solve problems that are bothering them.

In "To Everything There Is a Season," my narrator is about eleven and he may be kind of old to still be believing in Santa Claus, but he believes in the belief, and even when that belief is taken away, he's bothered by his own small wound, because his life is never going to be the same again. I'm interested in children of that age, because I think it is a kind of coming of awareness. The central character of "In the Fall" is fourteen, but the betrayal of the horse strikes most powerfully on the younger child. The person who is fourteen is halfway to something, he's not an adult but he's more an adult than a young person. But what he sees in that situation is that there's no way out of that situation, there's no way out of old age; whereas the smaller child says, Oh well, you know what Mother's doing is choosing these chickens over the nice horse, well, I'll show her, I'll kill all the chickens. It's a small child's reaction to adult problems: I'll throw my milk glass on the floor, I'll pull the cat's tail, I'll —

Rubinsky: Take an axe to the chickens.

MacLeod: Chickens are going to be killed anyway. This is just an early step.

Rubinsky: The families in your stories are large, five to eight children, and I assume they're Catholic, although church-going and God aren't mentioned, except incidentally. Can you comment on the place religion holds in the life of your characters?

MacLeod: I don't think it probably plays any conscious part. I have references to clergymen now and then. I try very hard to make the clergymen believe in what clergymen might believe — without saying these people have to be Baptists, these people have to be Presbyterian.

Rubinsky: Then it's part of the universality you're aiming for in your stories.

MacLeod: I'm not particularly interested in religious action. I think it's almost impossible to set your character in any kind of religious environment, without getting into exclusions: all the Anglicans do this or all the Baptists do that. When you get into religion, you begin to make things more narrow, what you're saying seems like, Oh, it's only French Huguenots who have so many children....

Rubinsky: Do you feel that your writing has changed since *Lost Salt?*

MacLeod: I don't think of that consciously at all. I think that maybe it's changed in that the later stories are maybe more thoughtful. They're more layered — some of them aren't and some of them are. I'm not a bit concerned about changing or staying the same, I don't think that matters very much. "The Boat" is twenty years old, and I still like that story very much. It's still a good story. When I finished it, my feeling was, I can't do any more with this, that's the best I can do.

Rubinsky: Have you ever published anything that you thought wasn't finished?

MacLeod: No, I don't think so. Sometimes I have an image or something that I felt wasn't quite right, but generally I don't wish I had them back when they go out. I like to think that if I was left in a dark room with them for two days or two months that I couldn't make them better. Most of them deal with certain ideas, and I think if somebody else was left in a dark room with that idea he or she might do something better or different; when I think it's finished, it's finished as well as I can finish it. This is almost universally so, and it's not vain or anything, I think it's a kind of a defence for my being so slow.

Rubinsky: If there's anything that you feel you have difficulty with in your writing, what might that be?

MacLeod: I don't know how to answer that. I think I do what I do and try to do it as well as I can.

Rubinsky: How aware are you of the potential for sentimentality in your work?

MacLeod: Quite aware. I don't think any of these stories are sentimental, I try hard not to make them sentimental and I think I've been fairly successful. There's a fine line, if you define sentiment as feeling and you define sentimental as having too much feeling. John Ditsky in the *Hollins Critic* says there's an emotional quotient, that is almost, says he, too much to bear if it were not for the dispassionate tone of the style. I was kind of interested to see that. It's like controlled violence, like football; you try to throw as much energy as possible while still staying within the framework of the rules of the game. There is a tension between the material and the artist, or the hopeful artist, and that tension is whether the material's going to control you or whether you are going to control the material; because sometimes the material suggests itself so strongly that it almost says, Put me in, put me in; and you as a writer have to say, almost to your material, No, you can't come in, you can't get on this page now or at all. You feel almost like a lion-tamer, or I do sometimes.

Rubinsky: You work with ballpoint pen and lined paper. When do you type it?

MacLeod: I type it when I get about a page of it.

Rubinsky: And then you edit as you type?

MacLeod: I do most of the editing with the ballpoint pen. I sit and write a sentence and then I write another sentence and then I write another sentence and I work on the individual sentence as I create it and then I type that page. Then I start again with the ballpoint pen. I don't write all the way through as a first draft and then write it again into a second draft or a third draft; I don't work that way. In most cases I just do sentence and sentence, plod, plod, and paragraph. I try to get it right, I try to get the next one right and the next one right.

Rubinsky: Are you able to work during the teaching year?

MacLeod: I find it very difficult. Very difficult because there are very many interruptions. The university has given me a little course release time next year to finish this book, so that may make it better. When I write kind of successfully, my head has to be almost filled all the time with the subject; it's nice if you can just think about it, even if you don't write; if you go and sit for three hours and think about it, and then when you're off doing other things. If it has the dominant place in your mind, things will happen, because you'll be almost subconsciously thinking about how to kill your old woman or whatever you're going to do. I think writing is the thing that will endure the most if one is interested in endurance.

Rubinsky: You can't live your life as though you're going to live forever. You have to decide.

MacLeod: Alice Munro's "Differently" is quite a beautiful story. On the last page the central character, who is a kind of grandmother figure by this time, says to the husband of a couple she used to be friends with long ago something to the effect that they never behaved as if they were going to die; and he says, Oh now; and she says, No, what I mean is we never acted as if any of this would ever end, and he says, Well, how should we have acted? And the best the central character can come up with is "differently." That's how we should have acted. I guess that's what I'm thinking of and what you're suggesting, that things do not go on forever and you cannot forever be Canada's most promising young writer — Canada's most promising geriatric writer — tottering towards Alzheimer's.

Rubinsky: In your stories there's a sense of dissolution, grieving, loss: the culture's coming to an end, the mines are running out, the fishing isn't good anymore, the sons head off to universities.

MacLeod: For people at the edges of whatever it might be, there is always the pull of the centre. There's nothing peculiar about people wanting to go to places where they will get work, because they have to do that. If you are ever on the ferry boats leaving Ireland to go to England, they're all full of people crying. The simple thing would be to think, Well, if you're crying, why don't you stay home, then you won't cry; but it's not that easy, because people are leaving Ireland to go to England because they will get jobs as chambermaids or hod carriers or whatever people from the edges of those kinds of civilizations do.

Rubinsky: And sometimes there's an intellectual need.

MacLeod: Yes, it is an intellectual need. You may love a landscape, you may love a family, but the intellectual,

I don't want to say opportunity, may not be there; and it's very difficult sometimes to make that kind of choice, to follow an intellectual star, at the expense of a lot of other things. That's a kind of tension a lot of people don't understand. They don't understand that maybe this is why fewer people go to university from West Virginia than from a lot of other places; because they can't find their way to university, it's a journey of a lot of miles and a lot of money; it's not that easy.

Rubinsky: I'm thinking of Archibald's granddaughter Sal, in "The Tuning of Perfection," when Archibald asks her if she understands the words to these Gaelic songs, she says, "Oh no, I just make the noises."

MacLeod: She's a kind of type.

Rubinsky: But isn't this what's happening, of necessity what's happening to a certain culture?

MacLeod: It's partially necessity, partially accident, I think. In her case, if you grow up singing Gaelic songs, you don't give much thought to it, you just do it. Then her ability is a chance to get this trip; she can do something that other people can't do, and so she's kind of exotic for five minutes or so. But the conflict there is with her grandfather who is one of those perfectionists who really likes the songs, but the family is kind of fractured, there's a lot of them and so on. In that story the character Carver is of the same generation and he can sing too, but he's got no illusions. He just knows they're for sale. He is, in a way, more sensitive than Sal. He knows he will win since Archibald will not compromise. Some of us are adjustable and some of us are not. People who are adjustable win and Archibald, in today's terms, would be considered a dinosaur, because he doesn't know you can't sing those songs for an hour. So either adjust or die.

Rubinsky: When did you begin to feel confident as a writer?

MacLeod: I was fairly old when I began to do a lot of things and I think that helps. I began to write

seriously when I was in the United States. I spent six years in the United States. When I was at the University of Notre Dame I began to write. I went to Notre Dame partially to study literature, but I also wanted to go to a place where literature was alive and not just a subject for analysis. Lots of people go to a place because they love literature and then they find that literature is being killed by narrow analysis and so on, because it's very often taught by categorizing people. People who teach it are sometimes very unlike people who write it. I think that's a problem today.

One of the reasons I went to Notre Dame was because there was a man there named Frank O'Malley. He was a great writing teacher at the time. He had taught Edwin O'Connor who wrote "The Last Hurrah," so when I was picking a graduate school, Notre Dame seemed a better place to go because that man was there: because what I understood about the place was that there was an appreciation of literature. There was also a great man there named Richard Sullivan. So I went, and while I was doing all my academic work, I took some creative-writing courses which I found were very helpful to me. I wrote "The Boat" in a creative-writing class. I would have been in my late twenties then. Maybe I was beyond the stage of a lot of eighteen-year-old writers, who are still writing about the parts of their bodies that interest them most.

Rubinsky: At Banff you were on the writing faculty for years of what they called W. O. Mitchell's freefall program. I know you liked freefall as a technique for new writers. Why?

MacLeod: I liked it because it answers two questions that bother young people. If you tell them to sit down and pour out what they're most concerned about, that's their subject matter; that's their raw material. It also gets rid of the fear of structure that a lot of new writers have, especially those who have taken a great many English classes, because they get frightened by all of that stuff that's at the back of the *Norton Anthology,* all the literature terminology. They say, Oh my God, rising action, falling action, protagonist, antagonist... Have I got this? Well, no.

Rubinsky: You said that those who teach literature are different from those who write it, and you mentioned that this was a danger. Can you elaborate on that?

MacLeod: I think sometimes there's a kind of antagonism towards living literature, towards living writers, because sometimes people who teach literature are threatened by these people, their presence; it's unfortunate. Sometimes literary criticism becomes a kind of science. I believe that literature comes out of the people and nearly always has and should go back to the people, where they see themselves reflected in the art. I'm very interested in that idea. Robert Kroetsch says, in an interview with Margaret Laurence, that fiction makes us real, that if we do not see ourselves reflected in art, we do not believe that we exist. By that I understand him to mean that if you are living a life and your life has its ups and downs and problems and you look, for example, at American television, "The Cosby Show," for example, and you say, These people have problems but they're not a bit like my problems — you say, Here I am living my life in James Bay or Bella Coola and these people on television don't seem a bit like me: something is either wrong with them or something is wrong with me. It must be with me, because the shows are very glossily produced. Modernistic critics say that they don't believe the author exists or that the author is dead and all there is is text. Maybe, but the danger of being that kind of critic is that you become kind of like the medieval scholastics were, in a small little room with people speaking Latin to one another and meanwhile out there the great unwashed were not speaking Latin,

they were doing whatever they were doing; life was going on. There's a danger, when we get things twisted around, that we think the critic is more important than the producer of the work. This is obviously not so. Nobody who thinks for four minutes could ever be converted to that.

Rubinsky: Your fans insist I ask this, because everyone has a different idea about what "Lost Salt Gift of Blood" means.

MacLeod: Salt is a very ambiguous substance, I suppose, and it's something that adds flavour to food, but if you use too much of it, it can also ruin it. And obviously salt has something to do with the ocean, with salt water, and it's part of folkloric expressions, like rubbing salt in the wound. In a broader sense, gifts that have salt in them can be tasteful or tasteless or burning.

Rubinsky: When we talked about the interview, I thought that since you were taking the time to do it, it would be nice to get the *National Enquirer* interested, and when I wondered what would make them interested, you confessed to me or rather, you confided to me, that Elvis Presley inhabited your body. Is this true?

MacLeod: Oh yes. Elvis Presley inhabited my body and still inhabits my body. Anybody who has seen me dance or heard me sing cannot doubt this indubitable fact.

EAVAN BOLAND

Outside History

ears ago, I went to the Isle of Achill for Easter. I was a student at Trinity then and I had the loan of a friend's cottage. It was a one-storey stone building with two rooms and a view of sloping fields.

April was cold that year. The cottage was in sight of the Atlantic and at night a bitter, humid wind blew across the shore. By day there was heckling sunshine but after dark a fire was necessary. The loneliness of the place suited me. My purposes in being there were purgatorial and I had no intention of going out and about. I had done erratically, to say the least, in my first-year exams. In token of the need to do better, I had brought with me a small, accusing volume of the court poets of the silver age. In other words, those sixteenth-century English song writers, like Wyatt and Raleigh, whose lines appear so elegant, so offhand, yet whose poems smell of the gallows.

I was there less than a week. The cottage had no water and every evening the caretaker, an old woman who shared a cottage with her brother at the bottom of the field, would carry water up to me. I can see her still. She has a tea-towel round her waist — perhaps this is one image that has become all the images I have of her — she wears an old cardigan and her hands are blushing with cold as she puts down the bucket. Sometimes we talk inside the door of the cottage. Once, I remember, we stood there as the dark grew all around us and I could see stars beginning to curve in the stream behind us.

She was the first person to talk to me about the famine. The first person, in fact, to speak to me with any force about the terrible parish of survival and death which the event had been in those regions. She kept repeating to me that they were great people, the people in the famine. Great people. I had never heard that before. She pointed out the beauties of the place. But they themselves, I see now, were a sub-text. On the eastern side of Keel, the cliffs of Menawn rose sheer out of the water. And here was Keel itself, with its blond strand and broken stone, where the villages in the famine, she told me, had moved closer to the shore, the better to eat the seaweed.

Memory is treacherous. It confers meanings which are not apparent at the time. I want to say that I understood this woman as emblem and instance of everything I am about to propose. Of course I did not. Yet even then I sensed a power in the encounter. I knew, without having words for it, that she came from a past which affected me. When she pointed out Keel to me that evening when the wind was brisk and cold and the light was going — when she gestured towards that shore which had stones as outlines and monuments of a desperate people — what was she pointing at? A history? A nation? Her memories or mine?

Those questions, once I began to write my own poetry, came back to haunt me. "I have been amazed, more than once," wrote Helen Cixous, "by a description a woman gave me of a world all her own, which she had been secretly haunting since early childhood." As the years passed, my amazement grew. I would see again the spring evening, the woman talking to me. Above all, I would remember how, when I finished speaking to her, I went in, lit a fire, took out my book of English court poetry and memorized all over again — with no sense of irony or omission — the cadences of power and despair.

I have written this to probe the virulence and necessity of the idea of a nation. Not on its own and not in a vacuum, but as it intersects with a specific poetic inheritance and as that inheritance, in turn, cut across me as woman and poet. Some of these intersections are personal. Some of them may be painful to remember. Nearly all of them are elusive and difficult to describe with any degree of precision. Nevertheless, I believe these intersections, if I can observe them at all properly here, reveal something about poetry, about nationalism, about the difficulties for a woman poet within a constraining national tradition. Perhaps the argument itself is nothing more than a way of revisiting the cold lights of that western evening and the force of that woman's conversation. In any case, the questions inherent in that encounter remain with me. It could well be that they might appear, even to a sympathetic reader, too complex to admit of any answer. In other words, that an argument like mine must contain too many imponderables to admit of any practical focus.

Yet I have no difficulty in stating the central premise of my argument. It is that over a relatively short time — certainly no more than a generation or so — women have moved from being the subjects and objects of Irish poems to being the authors of them. It is a momentous transit. It is also a disruptive one. It raises questions of identity, issues of poetic motive and ethical direction which can seem almost impossibly complex. What is more, such a transit — like the slow course of a star or the shifts in a constellation — is almost invisible to the naked eye. Critics may well miss it or map it inaccurately. Yet such a transit inevitably changes our idea of measurement, of distance, of the past as well as the future. Most importantly, it changes our idea of the Irish poem; of its composition and authority, of its right to appropriate certain themes and make certain fiats. And, since poetry is never local for long, that in turn widens out into further implications.

Everything I am about to argue here could be taken as local and personal, rooted in one country and one poetic inheritance; and both of them mine. Yet, if the names were changed, if situations and places were transposed, the issues might well be revealed as less parochial. This is not, after all, an essay on the craft of the art. I am not writing about aesthetics but about the ethics which are altogether less visible in a poetic tradition. Who the poet is, what he or she nominates as a proper theme for poetry, what self he or she discovers and confirms through this subject matter — all of this involves an ethical choice. The more volatile the material — and a wounded history, public or private, is always volatile — the more intensely ethical the choice. Poetic ethics are evident and urgent in any culture where tensions between a poet and his or her birthplace are inherited and established. Poets from such cultures might well recognize some of the issues raised here. After all, this is not the only country or the only politic where the previously passive objects of a work of art have, in a relatively short time, become the authors of it.

So it is with me. For this very reason, early on as a poet, certainly in my twenties, I realized that the Irish nation as an existing construct in Irish poetry was not available to me. I would not have been able to articulate it at that point, but at some preliminary level I already knew that the anguish and power of that woman's gesture on Achill, with its suggestive hinterland of pain, was not something I could predict or rely on in Irish poetry. There were glimpses here and there; sometimes more than that. But all too often, when I was searching for such an inclusion, what I found was a rhetoric of imagery which alienated me: a fusion of the national and the feminine which seemed to simplify both.

It was not a comfortable realization. There was nothing clear-cut about my feelings. I had tribal ambivalences and doubts; and even then I had an uneasy sense of the conflict which awaited me. On the one hand I knew that, as a poet, I could not easily do without the idea of a nation. Poetry in every time draws on that reserve. On the other, I could not as a woman accept the nation formulated for me by Irish poetry and its traditions. At one point it even looked to me as if the whole thing might be made up of irreconcilable differences. At the very least, it seemed to me that I was likely to remain an outsider in my own national literature, cut off from its archive, at a distance from its energy. Unless, that is, I could repossess it. This essay is about that conflict and that repossession, and about the fact that repossession itself is not a static or single act. Indeed this essay, which describes it, may itself be no more than a part of it.

A nation. It is, in some ways, the most fragile and improbable of concepts. Yet the idea of an Ireland, resolved and healed of its wounds, is an irreducible presence in the Irish past and its literature. In one sense, of course, both the concept and its realization resist definition. It is certainly nothing conceived in what Edmund Burke called "the spirit of rational liberty." When a people have been so dispossessed by event as the Irish in the eighteenth and nineteenth centuries an extra burden falls on the very idea of a nation. What should be a political aspiration becomes a collective fantasy. The dream itself becomes freighted with invention. The Irish nation, materializing in the songs and ballads of these centuries, is a sequence of improvised images. These songs, these images, wonderful and terrible and memorable as they are, propose for a nation an impossible task: to be at once an archive of defeat and a diagram of victory.

As a child I loved these songs. Even now, in some moods and at certain times, I can find it difficult to resist their makeshift angers. And no wonder. The best of them are written — like the lyrics of Wyatt and Raleigh — within sight of the gibbet. They breathe just free of the noose.

In one sense I was a captive audience. My childhood was spent in London. My image-makers as a child, therefore, were refractions of my exile: conversations overheard, memories and visitors. I listened and absorbed. For me, as for many another exile, Ireland was my nation long before it was once again my country. That nation, then and later, was a session of images: of defeats and sacrifices, of individual defiances happening off-stage. The songs enhanced the images; the images reinforced the songs. To me they were the soundings of the place I had lost: drowned treasure.

It took me years to shake off those presences. In the end, though, I did escape. My escape was assisted by the realization that these songs were effect not cause. They were only the curators of the dream; not the inventors. In retrospect I could accuse both them and the dream of certain cruel simplifications. I made then, as I make now, a moral division between what those songs sought to accomplish and what Irish poetry must seek to achieve. The songs, with their postures and their angers, glamourized resistance, action. But the Irish experience, certainly for the purposes of poetry, was only incidentally about action and resistance. At a far deeper level — and here the Achill woman returns — it was about defeat. The coffin ships, the soup queues, those desperate villagers at the shoreline — these things had actually happened. The songs, persuasive, hypnotic, could wish them away. Poetry could not. Of course the relation between a poem and a past is never that simple. When I met the Achill woman I was already a poet, I thought of myself as a poet. Yet nothing that I understood about poetry enabled me to understand her better. Quite the reverse. I turned my back on her in that cold twilight and went to commit to memory the songs and artifices of the very power systems which had made her own memory such an archive of loss.

If I understand her better now, and my relation to her, it is not just because my sense of irony or history has developed over the years; although I hope that they have. It is more likely because of my own experience as a poet. Inevitably, any account of this carries the risk of subjective codes and impressions. Yet, in poetry in particular and women's writing in general, the private witness is often all there is to go on. Since my personal experience as a poet is part of my source material, it is to that I now turn.

I entered Trinity to study English and Latin. Those were the early sixties and Dublin was another world — a place for which I can still feel Henry James's "tiger-pounce of homesickness." In a very real sense it was a city of images and anachronisms. There were still brewery horses on Grafton Street, their rumps draped and smoking under sackcloth. In the coffee bars, they poached eggs in a rolling boil and spooned them onto thick, crustless toast. The lights went on at twilight; by midnight the city was full of echoes.

After the day's lectures, I took a bus home from College. It was a short journey. Home was an attic flat on the near edge of a town that was just beginning to sprawl. There in the kitchen, on an oilskin tablecloth, I wrote my first real poems: derivative, formalist, gesturing poems. I was a very long way from Adrienne Rich's realization that "instead of poems about experience, I am getting poems that are experiences." If anything, my poems were other people's experiences. This, after all, was the heyday of the Movement in Britain, and the neat stanza, the well-broken line, were the very stuff of poetic identity.

Now I wonder how many young women poets taught themselves — in rooms like that, with a blank discipline — to write the poem that was in the air, rather than the one within their experience? How many faltered, as I did, not for lack of answers, but for lack of questions? "It will be a long time still, I think," wrote Virginia Woolf, "before a woman can sit down to write a book without finding a phantom to be slain, a rock to be dashed against."

But for now, let me invent a shift of time. I am turning down those streets which echo after midnight. I am climbing the stairs of a coffee bar which stays open late. I know what I will find. Here is the salt-glazed mug on a table-top which is as scarred as a desk in a country school. Here is the window with its view of an empty street, of lamplight and iron. And there, in the corner, is my younger self.

I draw up a chair, I sit down opposite her. I begin to talk — no, to harangue her. Why, I say, do you do it? Why do you go back to that attic flat, night after night, to write in forms explored and sealed by English men hundreds of years ago? You are Irish. You are a woman. Why do you keep these things at the periphery of the poem? Why do you not move them to the centre, where they belong?

But the woman who looks back at me is uncomprehending. If she answers at all it will be with the rhetoric of a callow apprenticeship: that the poem is pure process, that the technical encounter is the one which guarantees all others. She will speak about the dissonance of the line and the necessity for the stanza. And so on.

"For what is the poet responsible?" asked Allen Tate. "He is responsible for the virtue proper to him as a poet, for his special *arête:* for the mastery of a disciplined language which will not shun the full report of the reality conveyed to him by his awareness."

She is a long way, that young woman — with her gleaming cup and her Movement jargon — from the full report of anything. In her lack of any sense of implication or complication, she might as well be a scientist in the thirties, bombarding uranium with neutrons.

If I try now to analyze why such a dialogue would be a waste of time, I come up with several reasons. One of them is that it would take years for me to see, let alone comprehend, certain realities. Not until the oilskin tablecloth was well folded and the sprawling town had become a rapacious city, and the attic flat was a house in the suburbs, could I accept the fact that I was a woman and a poet in a culture which had the greatest difficulty associating the two ideas. "A woman must often take a critical stance towards her social, historical and cultural position in order to experience her own quest," wrote the American poet and feminist Rachel Blau de Plessis. "Poems of the self's growth, or of self-knowledge, may often include or be preceded by a questioning of major social prescriptions about the shape women's experience should take." In years to come, I would never be sure whether my poems had generated the questions or the questions had facilitated the poems. All that lay ahead. "No poet," said Eliot, "no artist of any kind has his complete meaning alone." In the meantime, I existed whether I liked it or not in a mesh, a web, a labyrinth of associations. Of poems past and present. Contemporary poems. Irish poems.

Irish poetry was predominantly male. Here or there you found a small eloquence, like "After Aughrim" by Emily Lawless. Now and again, in discussion, you heard a woman's name. But the lived vocation, the craft witnessed by a human life — that was missing. And I missed it. Not in the beginning, perhaps. But later, when perceptions of womanhood began to redirect my own work, what I regretted was the absence of an expressed poetic life which would have dignified and revealed mine. The influence of absences should not be underestimated. Isolation itself can have a powerful effect in the life of a young writer. "I'm talking about real influence now," says Raymond Carver. "I'm talking about the moon and the tide."

I turned to the work of Irish male poets. After all, I thought of myself as an Irish poet. I wanted to locate myself within the Irish poetic tradition. The dangers and stresses in my own themes gave me an added incentive to discover a context for them. But what I found dismayed me.

The majority of Irish male poets depended on women as motifs in their poetry. They moved easily, deftly, as if by right among images of women in which I did not believe and of which I could not approve. The women in their poems were often passive, decorative, raised to emblematic status. This was especially true where the woman and the idea of the nation were mixed: where the nation became a woman and the woman took on a national posture.

The trouble was these images did good service as

ornaments. In fact they had a wide acceptance as ornaments by readers of Irish poetry. Women in such poems were frequently referred to approvingly as mythic, emblematic. But to me these passive and simplified women seemed a corruption. Moreover, the transaction they urged on the reader, to accept them as mere decoration, seemed to compound the corruption. For they were not decorations, they were not ornaments. However distorted these images, they had their roots in a suffered truth.

What had happened? How had the women of our past — the women of a long struggle and a terrible survival — undergone such a transformation? How had they suffered Irish history and inscribed themselves in the speech and memory of the Achill woman, only to re-emerge in Irish poetry as fictive queens and national sybils?

The more I thought about it, the more uneasy I became. The wrath and grief of Irish history seemed to me — as it did to many — one of our true possessions. Women were part of that wrath, had endured that grief. It seemed to me a species of human insult that at the end of all, in certain Irish poems, they should become elements of style rather than aspects of truth.

The association of the feminine and the national — and the consequent simplification of both — is not of course a monopoly of Irish poetry. "All my life," wrote Charles de Gaulle, "I have thought about France in a certain way. The emotional side of me tends to imagine France like the princess in the fairy-tale, or the Madonna of the Frescoes." De Gaulle's words point up the power of nationhood to edit the reality of womanhood. Once the idea of a nation influences the perception of a woman then that woman is suddenly and inevitably simplified. She can no longer have complex feelings and aspirations. She becomes the passive projection of a national idea.

Irish poems simplified women most at the point of intersection between womanhood and Irishness. The further the Irish poem drew away from the idea of Ireland, the more real and persuasive became the images of women. Once the pendulum swung back the simplifications started again. The idea of the defeated nation being reborn as a triumphant woman was central to a certain kind of Irish poem. Dark Rosaleen. Cathleen ni Houlihan. The nation as woman; the woman as national muse.

The more I looked at it, the more it seemed to me that in relation to the idea of a nation, many, if not most, Irish male poets had taken the soft option. The irony was that few Irish poets were nationalists. By and large, they had eschewed the fervour and crudity of that ideal. But long after they had rejected the politics of Irish nationalism, they continued to deploy the emblems and enchantments of its culture. It was the culture, not the politics, which informed Irish poetry: not the harsh awakenings, but the old dreams.

In all of this I did not blame nationalism. Nationalism seemed to me inevitable in the Irish context; a necessary hallucination within Joyce's nightmare of history. I did blame Irish poets. Long after it was necessary, Irish poetry had continued to trade in the exhausted fictions of the nation; had allowed those fictions to edit ideas of womanhood and modes of remembrance. Some of the poetry produced by such simplifications was, of course, difficult to argue with. It was difficult to deny that something was gained by poems which used the imagery and emblem of the national muse. Something was gained, certainly; but only at an aesthetic level. What was lost occurred at the deepest, most ethical level; and what was lost was what I valued. Not just the details of a past. Not just the hungers, the angers. These, however terrible, remain local. But the truth these details witness — human truths of survival and humiliation — these also were suppressed along with the details. Gone was the suggestion of any complicated human suffering. Instead, you had the hollow victories, the passive images, the rhyming queens.

I knew that the women of the Irish past were defeated. I knew it instinctively long before the Achill woman pointed down the hill to the Keel shoreline. What I objected to was that Irish poetry should defeat them twice.

"I have not written day after day," said Camus, "because I desire the world to be covered with Greek statues and masterpieces. The man who has such a desire does exist in me. But I have written so much because I cannot keep from being drawn towards everyday life, towards those, whoever they may be, who are humiliated. They need to hope and, if all keep silent, they will be forever deprived of hope and we with them."

This essay originates in some part from my own need to locate myself in a powerful literary tradition in which until then, or so it seemed to me, I had been an element of design rather than an agent of change. But even as a young poet, and certainly by the time my work confronted me with some of these questions, I had already had a vivid, human witness of the stresses which a national literature can impose on a poet. I had already seen the damage it could do.

I remember the Dublin of the sixties almost more vividly than the city that usurped it. I remember its grace and emptiness and the old hotels with their chintzes and Sheffield trays. In one of these I had tea with Padraic Colum. I find it hard to be exact about the year; somewhere around the mid-sixties. But I have no difficulty at all about the season. It was winter. We sat on a sofa by the window overlooking the street. The lamps were on and a fine rain was being glamourized as it fell past their cowls.

Colum was then in his eighties. He had come from his native Longford in the early years of this century to a Dublin fermenting with political and literary change.

Yeats admired his 1913 volume of poetry, *Wild Earth*. He felt the Ireland Colum proposed fit neatly into his own ideas. "It is unbeautiful Ireland," Yeats wrote. "He will contrast finely with our Western dialect-makers."

In old photographs Colum looks the part: curly-headed, dark, winsome. In every way he was a god-send to the Irish Revival. No one would actually have used the term peasant poet. But then no one would have needed to. Such things were understood.

The devil they say casts no shadow. But that folk-image applies to more than evil. There are writers in every country who begin in the morning of promise but by the evening, mysteriously, have cast no shadow and left no mark. Colum is one of them. For some reason, although he was eminently placed to deal with the energies of his own culture, he failed to do so. His musical, tender, hopeful imagination glanced off the barbaric griefs of the nineteenth century. It is no good fudging the issue. Very few of his poems now look persuasive on the page. All that heritage which should have been his — rage robbed of language, suffering denied its dignity — somehow eluded him. When he met it at all, it was with a borrowed sophistication.

Now in old age he struggled for a living. He transited stoically between Dublin and New York giving readings, writing articles. He remained open and approachable. No doubt for this reason, I asked him what he really thought of Yeats. He paused for a moment. His voice had a distinctive, treble resonance. When he answered it was high and emphatic. "Yeats hurt me," he said. "He expected too much of me."

I have never been quite sure what Colum meant. What I understand by his words may be different from their intent. But I see his relation with the Irish Revival as governed by corrupt laws of supply and demand. He could only be tolerated if he read the signals right and acquiesced in his role as a peasant poet. He did not and he could not. To be an accomplice in such a distortion required a calculation he never possessed. But the fact that he was screen-tested for it suggests how relentless the idea of Irishness in Irish poetry has been.

Colum exemplified something else to me. Here also was a poet who had been asked to make the journey, in one working lifetime, from being the object of Irish poems to being their author. He, too, as an image, had been unacceptably simplified in all those poems about the land and the tenantry. So that — if he was to realize his identity — not only must he move from image to image-maker, he must also undo the simplifications of the first by his force and command of the second. I suspect he found the imaginative stresses of that transit beyond his comprehension, let alone his strength. And so something terrible happened to him. He wrote Irish poetry as if he were still the object of it. He wrote with the passivity and simplification of his own reflection looking back at him from poems, plays and novels in which the so-called Irish peasant was a son of the earth, a cipher of the national cause.

He had the worst of both worlds.

Like Colum, Francis Ledwidge was born at the sharp end of history. An Irish poet who fought as a British soldier, a writer in a radical situation who used a conservative idiom to support it — Ledwidge's short life was full of contradiction. He was in his early twenties when he died in World War I.

Despite his own marginal and pressured position, Ledwidge used the conventional language of romantic nationalism. Not always; perhaps not often. But his poem on the death of the leaders of the Easter Rising, "The Blackbirds," is a case in point. It is, in a small way, a celebrated poem and I have certainly not chosen it because it represents careless or shoddy work. Far from it. It is a skillful poem, adroit and quick in its rhythms, with an underlying sweetness of tone. For all that, it provides an example of a gifted poet who did not resist the contemporary orthodoxy. Perhaps he might have had he lived longer and learned more. As it was, Ledwidge surrendered easily to the idioms of the Irish Revival. This in turn meant that he could avail himself of a number of approved stereotypes and, chief among them, the easy blend of feminine and national. Even here he could exercise a choice although, it must be said, a limited one. He could have had the young Queen or the old mother. As it happened, he chose the poor old woman. But we are in no doubt what he means:

The Blackbirds

I heard the Poor Old Woman say
"At break of day the fowler came
And took my blackbirds from their song
Who loved me well through shame and blame.

No more from lovely distances
Their songs shall bless me mile from mile,
Nor to white Ashbourne call me down
To wear my crown another while.

With bended flowers the angels mark
For the skylark the place they lie.
From there its little family
Shall dip their wings first in the sky.

And when the first surprise of flight
Sweet songs excite, from the far dawn
Shall there come blackbirds, loud with love,
Sweet echoes of the singers gone.

But in the lovely hush of eve
Weeping I grieve the silent bills"
I heard the Poor Old Woman say
In Derry of the little hills.

I am not sure this poem would pass muster now. There are too many sugary phrases — "loud with love" and "shame and blame" — evoking the very worst of Georgian poetry. But Ledwidge was young and the impulse for the poem was historical. The 1916 leaders were dead. He was at a foreign front. The poem takes on an extra resonance if it is read as a concealed elegy for his own loyalties.

What is more interesting is how, in his attempt to make the feminine stand in for the national, he has simplified the woman in the poem almost out of existence. She is in no sense the poor old woman of the colloquial expression. There are no vulnerabilities here, no human complexities. She is a Poor Old Woman in capital letters. A mouthpiece. A sign.

Therefore the poem divides into two parts: one vital, one inert. The subject of the poem appears to be the woman. But appearances deceive. She is merely the object, the pretext. The real subject is the blackbirds. They are the animated substance of the piece. They call from "lovely distances"; their "sweet songs" "excite" and "bless." Whatever imaginative power the lyric has, it comes from these birds. Like all effective images, the blackbirds have a life outside the poem. They take their literal shape from the birds we know and to these they return an emblematic force. They continue to be vital once the poem is over.

The woman, on the other hand, is a diagram. By the time the poem is over, she has become a dehumanized ornament. When her speaking part finishes she goes out of the piece and out of our memory. At best, she has been the engine of the action; a convenient frame for the proposition.

The question worth asking is whether this fusion of national and feminine, this interpretation of one by the other, is inevitable. It was after all common practice in Irish poetry: Mangan's Dark Rosaleen comes immediately to mind. In fact the custom and the practice reached back, past the songs and simplifications of the nineteenth century, into the Bardic tradition itself. Daniel Corkery referred to this in his analysis of the Aisling convention in *The Hidden Ireland*. "The vision the poet sees," he wrote, "is always the spirit of Ireland as a majestic and radiant maiden."

So many male Irish poets — the later Yeats seems to me a rare exception — have feminized the national and nationalized the feminine that from time to time it has seemed there is no other option. But an Irish writer who turned away from such usages suggests that there was, in fact, another and more subversive choice.

In the opening pages of *Ulysses,* Joyce describes an old woman. She climbs the steps to the Martello tower, darkening its doorway. She is, in fact, the daily milkwoman. But no sooner has she started to pour a quart of milk into Stephen's measure than she begins to shimmer and dissolve into legendary images: "Silk of the kine and poor old woman, names given her in old times. A wandering crone, lowly form of an immortal, serving her conqueror and her gay betrayer, their common cuckquean, a messenger from the secret morning. To serve or to upbraid, whether he could not tell; but scorned to beg her favor."

The same phrase as Ledwidge uses — "poor old woman" — is included here. But whereas Ledwidge uses it with a straight face, Joyce dazzles it with irony. By reference and inference, he shows himself to be intent on breaking the traditional association of Ireland with ideas of womanhood and tragic motherhood. After all, these simplifications are part and parcel of what he, Joyce, has painfully rejected. They are some of the reasons he is in exile from the mythos of his own country. Now by cunning inflations, by disproportions of language, he takes his revenge. He holds at a glittering, manageable distance a whole tendency in national thought and expression; and dismisses it. But then Joyce is a poetic moralist. Much of *Ulysses,* after all, is invested in Daedelus's search for the ethical shadow of his own aesthetic longings. He has a difficult journey ahead of him. And Joyce has no intention of letting him be waylaid, so early in the book, by the very self-deceptions he has created him to resolve.

It is easy, and intellectually seductive, for a woman artist to walk away from the idea of a nation. There has been, and there must continue to be, a great deal of debate about the energies and myths women writers should bring with them into a new age. Start again, has been the cry of some of the best feminist poets. Wipe clean the slate, start afresh. It is a cry with force and justice behind it. And it is a potent idea: to begin in a new world, clearing the desert as it were, making it blossom; even making the rain.

In any new dispensation the idea of a nation must seem an expendable construct. After all, it has never admitted of women. Its flags and songs and battle-cries, even its poetry, as I've suggested, make use of feminine imagery. But that is all. The true voice and vision of women are routinely excluded.

Then why did I not walk away? Simply because I was not free to. For all my quarrels with the concept, and no doubt partly because of them, I needed to find and repossess that idea at some level of repose. Like the swimmer in Adrienne Rich's poem "Diving into the Wreck," I needed to find out "the damage that was done and the treasures that prevail." I knew the idea was flawed. But if it was flawed, it was also one of the vital human constructs of a place in which, like Leopold Bloom, I was born. More importantly, as a friend and feminist scholar said to me, we ourselves are constructed by the construct. I might be the author of my poems; I was not the author of my past. However crude the diagram, the idea of a nation remained the rough graphic of an ordeal. In some subterranean way I felt myself to be part of that ordeal; its fragmentations extended into mine.

"I am invisible," begins the prologue of Ralph Ellison's novel *The Invisible Man*. "I am invisible, understand, because people refuse to see me. Like the bodyless heads you see sometimes in circus shows it is as though I have been surrounded by mirrors of hard, distorting glass. When they approach me they see only their surroundings, themselves, or figments of their own imagination — indeed everything and anything except me."

In an important sense, Ellison's words applied to the sort of Irish poem which availed of that old, potent blurring of feminine and national. In such poems, the real woman behind the image was not only not explored, she was never even seen. It was a subtle mechanism; subtle and corrupt. And it was linked, I believed, to a wider sequence of things not seen.

A society, a nation, a literary heritage is always in danger of making up its communicable heritage from its visible elements. Women, as it happens, are not especially visible in Ireland. This came to me early and with personal force. I realized when I published a poem that what was seen of me, what drew approval, if it was forthcoming at all, was the poet. The woman, by and large, was invisible. It was an unsettling discovery. Yet I came to believe that my invisibility as a woman was a disguised grace. It had the power to draw me, I sensed, towards realities like the Achill woman. It made clear to me that what she and I shared, apart from those fragile moments of talk, was the danger of being edited out of our own literature by conventional tribalisms.

Marginality within a tradition, however painful, confers certain advantages. It allows the writer clear eyes and a quick critical sense. Above all, the years of marginality suggest to such a writer — and I am speaking of myself now — the real potential of subversion. I wanted to relocate myself within the Irish poetic tradition. I felt the need to do so. I thought of myself as an Irish poet, although I was fairly sure it was not a category that readily suggested itself in connection with my work. A woman poet is rarely regarded as an automatic part of a national poetic tradition; and for the reasons I have already stated. She is too deeply woven into the passive texture of that tradition, too intimate a part of its imagery, to be allowed her freedom. She may know, as an artist, that she is now the maker of the poems and not merely the subject of them. The

critique is slow to catch up. There has been a growing tendency in the last few years for academics and critics in this country to discuss women's poetry as a subculture, to keep it quarantined from the main body of poetry. I thought it vital that women poets such as myself should establish a discourse with the idea of the nation. I felt sure that the most effective way to do this was by subverting the previous terms of that discourse. Rather than accept the nation as it appears in Irish poetry, with its queen and muses, I felt the time had come to rework those images by exploring the emblematic relation between my own feminine experience and a national past.

The truths of womanhood and the defeats of a nation? An improbable intersection? At first sight perhaps. Yet the idea of it opened doors in my mind which had hitherto been closed fast. I began to think there was indeed a connection; that my womanhood and my nationhood were meshed and linked at some root. It was not just that I had a womanly feeling for those women who waited with handcarts, went into the sour stomachs of ships and even — according to terrible legend — eyed their baby's haunches speculatively in the hungers of the 1840s. It was more than that. I was excited by the idea that if there really was an emblematic relation between the defeats of womanhood and the suffering of a nation, I need only prove the first in order to reveal the second. If so, then Irishness and womanhood, those tormenting fragments of my youth, could at last stand in for one another. Out of a painful apprenticeship and an ethical dusk, the laws of metaphor beckoned me.

I was not alone. "Where women write strongly as women," said Alicia Ostriker in her seminal book *Stealing the Language,* "it is clear their intention is to subvert the life and literature they inherit." This was not only true of contemporary women poets. In the terrible years between 1935 and 1940, the Russian poet

Anna Akhmatova composed "The Requiem." It was written for her only son, Lev Gumilev, who at the start of the Stalinist Terror had been arrested, released, re-arrested. Then, like so many others, he disappeared into the silence of a Leningrad prison. For days, months, years Akhmatova queued outside. The "Epilogue to the Requiem" refers to that experience. What is compelling and instructive is the connection it makes between her womanhood and her sense of a nation as a community of grief. The country she wishes to belong to, to be commemorated by, is the one revealed to her by her suffering.

> And if ever in this country they should want
> To build me a monument
>
> I consent to that honor
> But only on condition that they
>
> Erect it not on the seashore where I was born:
> My last links with that were broken long ago,
>
> Nor by the stump in the Royal Gardens
> Where an inconsolable young shade is seeking me
>
> But here, where I stood for three hundred hours
> And where they never, ever opened the doors for me
>
> Lest in blessed death I should ever forget
> The grinding scream of the Black Marias,
>
> The hideous clanging gate, the old
> Woman wailing like a wounded beast.

I am concerned that in the process of summarizing this argument, it may take on a false symmetry. I have, after all, been describing ideas and impressions as if they were events. I have been proposing thoughts and perceptions in a way they did not and could not occur. I have given hard shapes and definite outlines to feelings which were far more hesitant.

The reality was different. Exact definitions do not happen in the real life of a poet; and certainly not in mine. I have written here about the need to repossess the idea of a nation. But there was nothing assured or automatic about it. "It is not in the darkness of belief that I desire you," says Richard Rowan at the end of Joyce's *Exiles,* "but in restless, living, wounding doubt." I had the additional doubts of a writer who knows that a great deal of their literary tradition has been made up in ignorance of their very existence; that its momentum has been predicated on simplifications of their complexity. Yet I still wished to enter that tradition; although I knew my angle of entry must be oblique. None of it was easy. I reached tentative havens after figurative storms. I came to understand what Mallarmé meant when he wrote: "Each newly acquired truth was born only at the expense of an impression that flamed up and then burned itself out, so that its particular darkness could not be isolated."

My particular darkness as an Irish poet has been the subject of this piece. But there were checks and balances. I was, as I have said, a woman in a literary tradition which simplified women. I was also a poet lacking the precedent and example of previous Irish women poets. These were the givens of my working life. But if these circumstances displaced my sense of relation to the Irish past in Irish poetry, they also forced me into a perception of the advantages of being able to move, with almost surreal inevitability, from being within the poem to being its maker. A hundred years ago I might have been a motif in a poem. Now I could have a complex self within my own poem. Part of that process entailed being a privileged witness to forces of reaction in Irish poetry.

Some of these I have named. The tendency to fuse the national and the feminine, to make the image of the woman the pretext of a romantic nationalism — these have been the weaknesses in Irish poetry. As a young poet, these simplifications isolated and estranged me. They also made it clearer to me that my own discourse must be subversive. In other words, that I must be vigilant to write of my own womanhood — whether it was revealed to me in the shape of a child or a woman from Achill — in such a way that I never colluded with the simplified images of women in Irish poetry.

When I was young all this was comfortless. I took to heart the responsibility of making my own critique, even if for years it consisted of little more than accusing Irish poetry in my own mind of deficient ethics. Even now I make no apology for such a critique. I believe it is still necessary. Those simplified women, those conventional reflexes and reflexive feminizations of the national experience; those static, passive, ornamental figures do no credit to a poetic tradition which has been, in other respects, radical and innovative, capable of both latitude and compassion.

But there is more to it. As a young poet I would not have felt so threatened and estranged if the issue had merely been the demands a national program makes on a country's poetry. The real issue went deeper. When I read those simplifications of women I felt there was an underlying fault in Irish poetry; almost a geological weakness. All good poetry depends on an ethical relation between imagination and image. Images are not ornaments; they are truths. When I read about Cathleen ni Houlihan or the Old Woman of the Roads or Dark Rosaleen, I felt that a necessary ethical relation was in danger of being violated over and over again; that a merely ornamental relation between imagination and image was being handed on from poet to poet, from generation to generation; was becoming orthodox poetic practice. It was the violation, even more than the simplification, which alienated me.

No poetic imagination can afford to regard an image as a temporary aesthetic manoeuvre. Once the image is distorted the truth is demeaned. That was the heart of it all as far as I was concerned. In availing themselves of the old convention, in using and re-using women as icons and figments, Irish poets were not just dealing with emblems. They were also evading the real women of an actual past: women whose silence their poetry should have broken. They ran the risk of turning a terrible witness into an empty decoration. One of the ironic purposes of my argument has been to point out that those emblems are no longer silent. They have acquired voices. They have turned from poems to poets.

Writers, if they are wise, do not make their home in any comfort within a national tradition. However vigilant the writer, however enlightened the climate, the dangers persist. So too do the obligations. There is a recurring temptation for any nation, and for any writer who operates within its field of force, to make an ornament of the past; to turn the losses to victories and to restate humiliations as triumphs. In every age language holds out narcosis and amnesia for this purpose. But such triumphs in the end are unsustaining and may, in fact, be corrupt.

If a poet does not tell the truth about time, his or her work will not survive it. Past or present, there is a human dimension to time, human voices within it and human griefs ordained by it. Our present will become the past of other men and women. We depend on them to remember it with the complexity with which it was suffered. As others, once, depended on us.

COLIN TAYLOR

Reading Tutuola

"Has Tutuola anything more than a good imagination and bad grammar?" – *Ama Ata Aidoo*

n 1952, armed only with a pencil and a very tricky thesaurus, Amos Tutuola cranked out *The Palm-Wine Drinkard* in two days, "revised" it over a period of three months, and then packed it off to the "United Society for Christian Literature" in his home region of southwestern Nigeria. At a loss as to what to do with this maniacal manuscript (they were booksellers after all, not publishers) they sent it in a moment of inspired lunacy to Faber and Faber in England. This august publishing house in turn exhibited a highly un-English sense of adventure by releasing the book almost immediately.

The Palm Wine Drinkard became an instant hit; having whirled like a Tasmanian terror onto the "barren" literary landscape of Black Africa, Tutuola found himself, overnight, something of an artistic pioneer, as European critics and readers alike took to his imaginative opus like Berbers to fresh water. Dylan Thomas started the stampede with an enthusiastic review in the

Observer (in which he called the book a "brief, thronged, grisly and bewitching story") and other prominent literary types in England and America, when the book was released there by Grove Press, added to what rapidly became a runaway reputation: in a brief time, Tutuola was established as the first writer from West Africa to have any kind of popular success overseas.

The appeal of Tutuola's book was its potent fusion of strong, suggestive language with subject matters of unsurpassable fantasy and ugliness. But Tutuola's early reputation as a literary radical and a genius arose from the mistaken impression created abroad that he had consciously embarked on a brave experiment with language, and that the book's assortment of wild and woolly ghouls and ghosts was purely of his own imagining.

Later it became widely known that Tutuola was in fact seriously undereducated in the language in which he chose to write. Tutuola is of the Yoruba, the largest ethnic group in Nigeria, and he does most of his talking and thinking in his native tongue. His attempt to translate his thoughts into English without a proper understanding of the syntactic and lexical differences between the two languages accounts for the many unusual constructions ("I ran to his back," "the really road," "my wife was feeling overloading," etc.) that one finds throughout the book, as the syntactic regularity of Yoruba is brought to bear on English.

It also soon became common knowledge that Tutuola drew the incidents and characters in his book directly from the folk-tales, legends and complex integrated mythology of his Yoruba people. Though neither of these revelations was sufficient in itself to deny Tutuola status as a creative writer, they did make his effort seem somewhat less grand than the invention of a world and a language might have been. It wasn't long before he came to be dismissed as a mere collector of folk-tales, and the reaction to his analphabetic arsenal of crazy neologisms, syncopated syntax and sentence fragments, indifferent punctuation and inventive spelling, became one of extreme impatience. Over the course of his next seven literary outings, complaints were raised that Tutuola was repeating himself, that evidently he had nothing of much importance to say, that Faber's continuing to publish him was more a gimmick than the expression of a real commitment to the writer. When *Feather Woman of the Jungle*, Tutuola's fifth book, came out, a writer for the *Times Literary Supplement* hit the nail aggressively on the head when he said: "Increasingly one's reaction is to say 'so what?' in quite the rudest way, and to protest against what is dangerously near a cult of the faux-naif." (This is possibly the same reviewer who, in 1952, had deviated from the norm by referring, in the *TLS*, to *Drinkard* as "a mass of unassimilated material.")

Tutuola's critical rite of passage went in the opposite direction in his native land. At first, the educated élite of Nigeria, knowing from the start the details of Tutuola's limited education as well as the source of his stories, was confused and more than a little upset by the jubilant praise going on outside the country. How could a man with less than seven years of formal education in English (from ages ten to sixteen) be taken for one of its prime innovators? How could a man who had done no more than scribble down, verbatim, stories that were familiar to every boy and girl in Yorubaland, be seen as a visionary? Much scratching of the collective head ensued, and then the answer came: Tutuola was obviously being patronized. As usual, the beady-eyed colonialists were looking (in this case, in Tutuola's chaotic and violent text) for further supporting evidence of the stereotype of Africans as violent and chaotic people. Much of this paranoia was given voice by a certain Mr. Babasola Johnson who, one fine day in 1954, wrote the following letter to the magazine *West Africa*:

> Now let us face facts. *Palm-Wine Drinkard* should not have been published at all. The language in which it is written is foreign to West Africans and English people, or anybody for that matter. It is bad enough to attempt an African narrative in good English; it is worse to attempt it in Mr. Tutuola's strange lingo.

But opinion on Tutuola has come a long way since then. Although he is not everyone's favourite choice for the title of "Father of African Literature" he is at least finally being given the proper respect at home for having braved it alone, and in the process blazing a trail for others like Chinua Achebe, Wole Soyinka, J.P. Clark, Christopher Okigo, T.M. Aluko, and Gabriel Okara. Much attention is now being given to critical study of Tutuola in order to determine the extent of his contribution to the emergence of African literature.

Because Tutuola works primarily with African folk-tales, which belong to an exclusively oral literature, it's not easy to decide how much artistry he brings to his adaptation of them. What one wants to know is: does Tutuola — as he has so often been accused of doing — merely copy down stories as he hears them, without any significant input of imagination and no real sense of craftsmanship? Or does he, as we would expect a creative artist to do, consciously choose from among the many versions of a story the one that best suits his purpose, and then plug this into an all-encompassing conceptual framework? African folk-tales, because they are transmitted orally, maintain their essences but vary significantly in their details from one teller to the next.

The dilemma can be brought into sharper focus with an example. In *Drinkard* the hero, after having travelled for many years to the land of the dead in search of his palm-wine tapster, returns home finally to find his town in the middle of a devastating famine. A former layabout (our intrepid alcoholic had, prior to setting out on his journey, grown accustomed to consuming 225 kegs of palm wine per day), he has been made wise and mature by the many horrific and Herculean ordeals endured on his journey, and feels therefore uniquely qualified, on his return, to save his town from disaster. He decides to offer a sacrifice to the god of heaven, and so asks for a volunteer to transport the gift to the great beyond. A hapless slave, in a desperate bid to be a hero, steps forward. The slave's action is motivated by a desire to gain a fuller acceptance into his community, but unfortunately when he returns from heaven he finds himself even more of an outcast than before; for, even though he has helped to end the famine, the townspeople are afraid that any one of them may be whisked away to heaven by the little fellow and lock their doors to him.

Anyone who has read Chinua Achebe's *Things Fall Apart* will recognize in it another version of this myth. In Achebe's book, it is the hated vulture who volunteers to transport the gift; again, for the same reason as the slave, and again, with the same result. Tutuola's version (as Margaret Laurence pointed out in *Long Drums and Cannons*, her book on Nigerian writers) is undoubtedly the more moving of the two, and can be seen as a parable about the need for human sacrifice in an animistic society. It is a powerful story; but is it Tutuola's?

Consider the implications for Shakespeare's status in our society if we simply *knew* that he took his stories from various sources, but we couldn't get access to these sources in order to see for ourselves the transformations his genius has brought to bear on the raw material.

Amos Tutuola is neither a mere fairy-tale teller, nor the Homer of Africa. He is not a failed novelist, as those who complain of the lack of characterization, dialogue and logical structure in his books would seem to suggest. His glossolalial grammatology does not constitute a new and coherent language. It's a mistake to embark on a reading of Tutuola without keeping those things in mind. Since talk of Tutuola has not actually been raging in the literary salons of Canada, allow me to offer some suggestions as to how to approach the work of the sub-Saharan Dante.

Understanding begins with the realization that Tutuola is exactly the naif-like literary innocent he seems. He is the Douanier Rousseau of world literature. As in the case of that great painter, Tutuola's work is full of ambiguous grey areas that seem to hint at something beyond, something transcendental and profound. They may be there by mistake, and may not even be recognized and understood by the artist himself, but they arise naturally from the vision of an artist of superior intuition, an artist "working by spell and incantation," according to V.S. Pritchett. There are two features that are readily apparent to sensitive readers and that elevate Tutuola above the ranks of the ordinary: the power of his intuition and the Rabelaisian exuberance of his love for storytelling.

Details from a Diego Rivera mural, Mexico City.

Because, let's face it, anyone can transcribe fairy-tales. It takes an artist of high calibre to give them a distinctive voice, and to allow them to transcend themselves. At the time he wrote *Drinkard* Tutuola apparently owned no books. It is purely by intuition that he allows his books a degree of universality by giving them a form familiar to cultures the world over. All his books follow the pattern of a medieval quest or voyage narrative; all of his heroes and heroines undergo a rite of passage, a trial by fire and water, on their way to greater wisdom and harmony with nature. One of Tutuola's best critics, Gerald Moore, situates the books in the tradition of the heroic monomyth, as described by Joseph Campbell in *The Hero with a Thousand Faces*; the books can also be seen as picaresque fictions, minus the rogue element; when viewed as such they make a lot more sense. Gilgamesh, Aeneas, Orpheus's descent into the Underworld, *Pilgrim's Progress*, *Gulliver's Travels*, Odysseus, Heracles — all these are helpful touchstones for a fuller understanding of Tutuola's work.

If we just imagine Tutuola as a gifted camp-fire storyteller who, for whatever idiosyncratic reasons, has chosen instead to write his stories down, and in an unfamiliar language, much of the initially irritating strangeness of his works disappears. His orientation towards oral storytelling accounts for some of the more bizarre linguistic and structural features of his books. Let's take the famous opening paragraph of *Drinkard*.

I was a palm-wine drinkard since I was a boy of ten years of age. I had no other work more than to drink palm-wine in my life. In those days we did not know other money, except COWRIES, so that everything was very cheap, and my father was the richest man in our town.

The way that word, cowries, leaps out at you — like a goof from around a dark corner — is a betrayal of Tutuola's eagerness to communicate directly. Throughout the book, details that MUST NOT BE MISSED are written in bold letters. It is this need (more than simply the absence of proper punctuation) that gives Tutuola's language its high energy and extreme sense of urgency. Another favourite trick of Tutuola's is to appeal directly to the reader in order to drag him or her into the story. In *Drinkard* the hero is called upon to judge two very complicated court cases. Not knowing what to do, he adjourns court for a year (very African, that) and says to the reader:

> So I shall be very much grateful if anyone who reads this story-book can judge one or both cases and send the judgement to me as early as possible, because the whole people in the mixed town want me very urgently to come and judge the two cases.

Like any good storyteller, Tutuola embellishes his tales with a good dose of humour. The drinkard's wife (a non-character, given to oracular speech) gives birth, like Zeus, from an unusual part of her anatomy: her thumb. The offspring is an absolute terror, the most frightful brat imaginable (a kind of Bam Bam Rubble on benzedrine). He lays siege to the town, terrorizes the inhabitants, tortures the parents, and eats all the food in sight. The drinkard, exercising his version of "tough-love," burns the house to the ground, with the sleeping child inside; but the child rises from the ashes and latches on to the wife's head for a few chapters. All this is treated in a disarmingly light manner, the overall effect being both humorous and horrifying:

> This was a wonderful child, because if a hundred men were to fight with him, he would flog them until they would run away. When he sat on a chair, we could not push him away. He was as strong as iron, if he stood on a place nobody could push him off. Now he be-

came our ruler in the house, because sometimes he would say that we should not eat till night and sometimes he would drive us away from the house at midnight and sometimes he would tell us to lie down before him for more than two hours.

This kind of humour is uniquely Tutuola's and can be found on almost every page.

Tutuola is an automatic writer; he claims between three days and three weeks as the average length of time for writing one of his books. He is also an improviser, having admitted in interviews that he makes up much of his material as he goes along. He does not work from a rigid outline, but relates his episodes as they come to his mind; this information he divulged to Geoffrey Parrinder who wrote one of the first profiles of Tutuola (now included as the introduction to *My Life in the Bush of Ghosts*). Tutuola was a messenger for a government firm in Lagos when, out of boredom, he started to jot down stories as he remembered them. He once told an interviewer that "to compose the thing is not hard for me. Even at work I compose, for I cannot be pleased to do nothing, and a messenger does not always have work to do in the office." Perhaps it's the increase in distractions, and the attendant lessening of daily boredom, that accounts for the relative lack of energy and vividness of his later books.

Some disappointment with his work subsequent to *Bush of Ghosts* is justified. I would suggest that this is due to the most clichéd of human experiences, the gradual loss of innocence. As Tutuola is forced by praise and criticism to become more self-conscious, he relies less on intuition and more and more on learned traits and mannerisms. He doesn't quite lose it completely (*Simbi and the Satyr of the Dark Jungle* is just a shade less successful than *Bush of Ghosts* and contains some of his best descriptive passages) until the final book, *The Witch Herbalist of the Remote Town*, which has very little to recommend it.

Some time before writing that book, Tutuola apparently embarked on a lengthy study of the English language. Sadly, the book has all the requisite ghouls and ordeals, but the writing is flat and tortuous. The language fails miserably in terms of its evocative power. Nowhere in this final book can one find such dazzling descriptions as this, taken from *Bush of Ghosts*:

> All kinds of snakes, centipedes and flies were living on every part of his body. Bees, wasps and uncountable mosquitoes were also flying round him and it was hard to see him plainly because of these flies and insects. But immediately this dreadful ghost came inside this house from heaven-knows-where his smell and also the smell of his body first drove us to a long distance before we came back after a few minutes, but still the smell did not let every one of the settlers stand still as all his body was full of excreta, urine, and also wet with the rotten blood of all the animals that he was killing for his food. His mouth which was always opening, his nose and eyes were very hard to look at as they were very dirty and smelling.

If Tutuola's voice in *Bush of Ghosts* is that of "the beginning of man on earth, man emerging, wounded and growing" (Pritchett, for the last time), it's arguable that the man is almost certainly dying in his last work, the victim of English 101.

But anyone who doubts Tutuola's essential seriousness need only give a close read to *Bush of Ghosts*, his most interesting work, by virtue of being his most personal. In it we find a great emphasis on encounters with things repulsive: flies, filth, snakes, spiders, excreta, blood, vomit; it is a sandbox for Jungian analysts. (When the great biography of this writer is finally written, much attention will be given to it in the attempt to understand the nature of his own personal neuroses.) It is an ambitious book, and aspires to be a morality tale; it opens with the exposition of a jealousy scenario, and closes with the line, "This is what hatred did." The psychological complexity of the book's main character is unmatched in Tutuola's other works; the hero, even as he undergoes the most atrocious torments, nevertheless feels a great compulsion to remain in this bush of evil spirits. He reaches heights of great ecstasy, gets stoned often, gets married twice, and stays altogether so long that he begins to feel like a ghost himself, and is reluctant to go home. (It is only after receiving an "Invisible Magnetic Missive" from his parents that he starts to feel homesick.) Such is the intensity of this book that it led Margaret Laurence to conclude: "It is the work of someone who has walked in the pit of hell, and has been courageous enough to open his eyes while he was there."

Tutuola is a supreme surrealist; he outdoes the Dadaists; he is a Heideggerian poet, singing of Being in a peculiar but penetrating language. Though he may not recognize the ontological gap, even if he were to fall headfirst into it, his best works constitute an exploration of this gap — of man's relationship to himself and to his world. All of his heroes (with the exception of the one in *Bush of Ghosts*) make a deliberate quest; they choose to submit to the hardships, in order to feel deserving of the harmony and tranquillity that comes later. In doing so, they reflect an attitude that has a place of very high honour in Yoruban philosophy. Tutuola himself — whose eight books, all published by Faber, are *The Palm-Wine Drinkard* (1952), *My Life in the Bush of Ghosts* (1954), *Simbi and the Satyr of the Dark Jungle* (1955), *The Brave African Huntress* (1958), *Feather Woman of the Jungle* (1962), *Ajaiya and His Inherited Poverty* (1967), *The Witch Herbalist of the Remote Town* (1981), and *Pauper, Brawler and Slanderer* (1987) — has a place among the very best writers in world literature.

JOE ROSENBLATT

The Tip of the Fishing Volcano

avid Profumo — a former deputy editor of *The Fiction Magazine,* short-fiction writer, and reviewer for such publications as the *Times Literary Supplement* and the *Literary Review)* — and Graham Swift — whose third novel, *Waterland,* was nominated for the prestigious Booker Prize in 1983 — have combined their talents in assembling excerpts from the foremost piscatorial writings from antiquity to the present under the seductive title *The Magic Wheel,* taken from a line in Thomas Tod Stoddart's 1835 poem, "The Taking of the Salmon":

With care we'll guard the magic wheel
Until its notes reawaken.

The magic wheel is the fishing reel itself, especially at the magical moment when a trout strikes the artificial fly and that musical wheel pulls in the fish.

The Magic Wheel: An Anthology of Fishing in Literature (1985) is mainly about fresh-water fishing. It embodies the stories, essays, musings or reflections and poems of British anglers, but it is also generously garnished with knowledge from a multi-ethnic palette. There is, for example, the famous quote from the Book of Matthew: "And he saith unto them: Follow me, and I will make you fishers of men." And from the Book of Job: "Canst thou draw out leviathan with an hook? or his tongue with a cord which thou lettest down?"

But Piscatoria Semitica does not overshadow the other lights. Chinese authors knew about fishing, too. Among the Chinese poems in the anthology's first section, "The Ancient Tradition," are Li Yu's "Fisherman's Song" and two poems by Wang Wei — "Taking the Cool of the Evening" and "The Green Stream." Arthur Waley's translation of Po Chü-I's "Fishing in the Wei River," dated 811 A.D. , contains these lines:

In the depths of Wei, carp and grayling swim.
Idly I come with my bamboo fishing-rod
and hang my hook by the banks of Wei stream.

But the first section tends to fill up like an overcrowded fish bowl with too many ancient naturalists possessed of didactic spirits. And this is not ameliorated in the second section, "The Middle Ages," where stern minnows and Scripture become one. I rebel, for instance, against St. Anthony of Padua lecturing to his fish: "Do you think that, without mystery, the first present that God Almighty made to man, was of you, O ye Fishes?"

Despite the often engaging tributes to carp by superstitious medieval man, this reader finds his animistic senses assaulted by far too much human chauvinism. I want to be beamed up into "The Seventeenth Century," and towards a more secular horizon, away from Judaic-Christian piety and its heartburn and guilt. I want less of God's fisherman with all His shiny ectoplasmic bait. In short, I want some real secular fishing. Fortunately the editors have anticipated my need. In "The Ancient Tradition," Herodotus lightens up the surrounding religious fog and, despite the ancient historian Aelian's error in assuming the dear old croc was a type of fish, this is my favourite opening line: "The modes of catching the crocodile are many and varied."

Various descriptions of fishing on the Nile prove unintentionally funny. You will love Aristotle's hangups, for instance. In his *Historia Animalium,* he avers that "eels are not produced from sexual intercourse, nor are they oviparous, not have they ever been detected with semen, or ova...." Herodotus, however, has the last word on eels, stating that they "originate in what are called the entrails of the earth."

Beam in Washington Irving, of "Wilderness Americana" fame, and Canada's own fishing wizard, Roderick Haig-Brown, from "The Later Twentieth Century" and this volume becomes the *pièce de resistance* for every thinking bibliophile in the angling realms.

The Magic Wheel will delight both the secular fisherperson and those "fishers of men" types. Both the rational angler who would tolerate the odd river sprite in the guise of a bluebottle fly and that brooding angler who must see Jesus on the dark side of every gill will find this book a joy, since it is arranged in such a way that each party can thumb his or her way to a favourite poem or essay.

So where is the fly in this fishing ointment? I believe it must lie with the hardcore meat fishperson: There's virtually no bragging about the size of one's lunker. A lack of salmonoid penis envy? The fishing moron whose intellect might range from size A to A-1/4 would be stopped at the shallows long before he arrived at Job. Somehow I can't imagine the average guy (and gal) down at the local Rod and Gun club enjoying the wisdom of Charles Cotton and Izaak Walton. I can almost hear my fishing pal, Moose, frothing around the gills and holding high a beer mug in his hairy hands as he ponders the sun and substance of *The Magic Wheel:* "Who the fuck is this fruitcake ... Pis .. ca ... tor?"

Again, the editors are inscrutably flexible. Their aim is to please some of the macho fish thumpers. The brutes are flushed in the literary blood of the lamb — in this case the fish illuminati — and the volume's literary integrity has not been soiled in the slightest.

I wish I had ingested the wisdom embodied in *The Magic Wheel* — or something else like it — before my first blind date with the Little Qualicum River on Vancouver Island, where I cast my first virgin dryfly. It might have increased my appetite for the spotted fish had I read Aelian's description (in his *De Natura Animaleum*) of the Macedonians discovering the use of an artificial fly after observing bumblebees being summarily executed by trout:

These flies settle on the stream as they seek the food that they like; they can not escape the observations of the fishes that swim below. So that when a fish observes a Hippurus on the surface it swims noiselessly under water for fear of disturbing the surface and to avoid scaring its prey. Then when close at hand in the fly's shadow it opens its jaws and swallows the fly, just as a wolf snatches a sheep from the flock or an eagle seizes a goose from the farmyard.

Hippurus, according to Aelian, is a wasp, but can you trust a bloke who thinks a crocodile is a fish? The insect could as easily have been a honeybee. At least this ancient naturalist, unlike the medieval bestiarist, didn't call his Queen Bee a King Bee.

Aelian goes on to praise the fiendishly clever Macedonian way of imitating life, or wasp: "They wrap the hook in scarlet wool, they attach two feathers that grow beneath a cock's wattles...." Later we learn that the fish is caught when he assumes "that he is going to have a wonderful banquet, opens wide his mouth, is entangled with the hook, and gains a bitter feast, for he is caught."

Does this prove the maxim that trout have more beauty than brain? Trout spook easily if even a shadow crosses their visual range. But a starving being whether it be a trout or a human sometimes thinks with its stomach. And there are heated moments when a fishy *dementia praecox* occurs and the trout give themselves easily to a feeding frenzy in the same way that fervid humans rush about on the floor of the stock exchange lured on by the rise and fall of profits.

The first time I snared a rainbow a fiendish thought flew like a spark across my mind: Trout devour each other not so much because they are prosaically hungry but because they have a pulchritudinous disease: *poetry*. Cannibalism is natural to trout. There is a gastric finality in the act of closing a poem. And if people were the visual equivalent of trout then human cannibalism would be pandemic.

The Magic Wheel closes the ideological gap between the fishers of fish and the fishers of men, for, despite their polarities, here they are drawn together in the general cause of fishing. The adhesive agent is nostalgia and it tugs at the heart valves of even the most cynical spirit.

George Orwell's "Coming Up for Air" (1938), for instance, works its lachrymal magic. The opening line disarms: "I was rather an ugly little boy with butter-coloured hair." The young Orwell then discovers his Shangri-La, an out-of-the-way pool behind "a jungle of blackberry bushes and rotten boughs that had fallen off the trees." He idles away the hours, staring down through fifteen feet of water at carp machining their way around the pool. It is yet an ideal world a few decades away from the slaughters of World War II. The pool is a special hideaway, unique, set apart from other bodies of water:

I knew what had happened. At some time this pool had been connected with the other, and then the stream had dried up and the woods had closed up around the small pool and it had just been forgotten.

The Boy has discovered a treasure, a forgotten pool, a little Eden, and has sworn himself to secrecy. He will tell nobody about the existence of this pool, this Eden, this parent. Orwell says it another way:

Being able to find a quiet pool to sit beside belongs to the time before the war, before the radio, before aeroplanes, before Hitler.... There's a kind of peacefulness even in the names of English coarse fish: Roach, rudd, dace, bleak, barbel, bream, gudgeon, pike, chub, tench.

Often, while gazing at a miniature pool in the Little Qualicum, when the water level drops in July, I realize that the pods of minnows are abiding their time waiting for the rainy season so that they can be joined with others in the mainstream. But the isolated pools with their minnows serve another, higher purpose: the minnows are protected for the time being from cannibals. Nature, again, is a protector as well as a destroyer.

The only pond I was able to find in my youth was artificial. My Uncle Nathan ran a fish store in Toronto's Jewish market, on Baldwin Street, from 1926 until he passed away in 1956. Thousands of carpish monsters passed through his brutal hands. He netted the tribe from one of his many holding tanks which resembled undignified bathtubs, flinging each fish onto a huge butchering block where he bashed each finned fellow on the head with a wooden mallet. Thunk! The poor critters were quickly anaesthetized. In seconds he chopped them into pieces, tossed them into newspaper, and bagged the fractured stiffs for me to take home. Later I'd release the fish parts into a sink filled with cold water and I can still see the pieces moving around furiously, searching for their exiled anatomies. This ritual happened every Friday evening all during my boyhood years. Reading about those boys discovering their private worlds fills me not only with envy but with the hostility I thought had long ago dried up like a riverbed in midsummer. Even at summer camp that private-pond longing could never be satisfied. The collective atmosphere at such a place does not make for any highly individualistic search for a lost pool. I couldn't have found my watery Shangri-La even if the camp itself was surrounded by a large lake. The only thrill I can remember was watching a water snake swallowing a frog very slowly until I nearly fell asleep at the bend of the river where it emptied into the lake. I saw the real side of Eden, and identified strongly with the frog.

I became a convert to the salmon faith when I hooked onto a grinning Tyee in the salt off Qualicum Bay on Vancouver Island. The beast not only attacked my highly decorative and expensive Irish jig but nearly uprooted my arm as he lashed out furiously, repeatedly smashing the side of my twelve-foot aluminum boat.

That mighty salmon appeared to be several feet long and wide as my waist. In less than a minute, the thrashing devil had snapped my forty-pound test line, taking my lure, line, and ego down into thirty feet of water. A leaden silence filled my skull. How many times had Ron Smith, my West Coast publisher and an ace fisherman, spelled out the basics to me? "Play them out, play them out. You got all the time in the world. Don't rush them."

I swear nobody but a fishless eunuch would dismiss the many mouth-watering steaks as thick as your arm that have disappeared into the deep, lost forever. My fish! I would chant a hundred mantras to have straddled and made love to my demoniac animal and kissed those silvery scales off.

Among its many virtues, *The Magic Wheel* has

healing properties, whether the editors intended it or not. Clearly this dignified volume caters to the fishing gimp, to those souls who've snapped their rods apart in anger and frustration, and are still smarting from humiliation. There are essays and poems enough for the fishing basketcases, enough to regenerate some once-healthy piscivorous ego.

There is a strain of fishy poem in this anthology that I could categorize as pacifistic or coitus interruptus, because the poet has only a blur of a suggestion that he or she has actually caught the fish, or that the fish has been dispatched. I refer to Elizabeth Bishop's fish poem with all its polite sublime topsoil. Uncle Nathan covered his kill with sawdust, but he was being purely prosaic. These poets use a different cover. You have to read Bishop's magnificent poem with carboniferous eyes to know if this summery warrior really killed her fish, though the closing of the poem is as sentient as any lake trout, and rightfully deserves its living space in every respectable fishing anthology:

> I stared and stared
> and victory filled up
> the little rented boat,
> from the pool of bilge
> where oil had spread a rainbow
> around the rested engine,
> to the bailer rusted orange,
> the sun-cracked thwarts,
> the oarlocks on their strings,
> the gunnels — until everything
> was rainbow, rainbow, rainbow!
> And I let the fish go.

I suspect those rainbows were more than oilslicks but actual fish scales with their high iridescence. I am sure that Bishop had wiped away the protective mucous membrane, thus the fish would have perished anyway from a hideous fungal infection. My thought impulses reply: "Lady, you should have kept the little beast, eaten the critter."

There are other summery anglers. My favourite is W.B. Yeats, and his poem, "The Song of the Wandering Aengus," from *The Wind among the Reeds* (1899). It tugs my line and the muse's caudal fin brushes up against me: "I dropped a berry in the stream / And caught a little silver trout."

Would you and I have kept a brookie? Yeats is about to kill his trout when it turns into a "glimmering lady." I assumed he tossed his girl back into the drink. The sublime suggests it, but whether he did or not there is a powerful sense of erotic love between the fishermen in this anthology and their quarry. Ted Hughes reverentially refers to pike as "Killers from the egg; the malevolent aged grin. / They dance on the surface among the flies." And only an angler-poet in love with the fish would observe their "gills kneading quietly, and pectorals."

Then why kill fish if you love them? The answer surely must be because we're an omnivorous lot. Hell, why kill a living carrot? Isn't devouring the finality of all consuming love? I'm speaking here metaphorically. I won't refer to the female praying mantis devouring her male lover in that sexual heatwave. Devouring is devouring.

Hughes's pike acknowledges his victor. The animal retreats into the final fog having fought the best fight it had inside its body, and it is a machine that has more than once ignited in a cannibalistic holy frenzy, or dragged a living duck beneath the surface of a pond. The pike is saying with his eyes: "You win, you're the superior pike now. Eat or be eaten. You've won. Turn your face away, and let me die in peace. Don't profane my last moments, you *unterpike*." It is the end of a nasty love affair until, of course, the very next catch.

Anglers, like artists (another dilemma: is the angler

an artist or a technician?), have their tormentors who love to stereotype them. The angler is viewed as a simple-minded soul (possibly retarded?), a silly fishing fool spending far too much time at the stream when there are weightier matters in life, more productive pursuits like making money, or involving one's self in some form of social activism. Alas, the anti-angling lepers have their day in court in this anthology.

Ed Zern, for instance. I detest him for his thin poetic lines (the man has no ear to speak of in poetry), for knocking Izaak Walton, and for laying it generally thick and heavy on the ancient naturalists, and generally taking potshots at the fishing crowd. The nastiest pisciphobe, or really aquaphobe, is none other than the comic genius W.C. Fields (we would bring genius into this anthology to foul hook us), who, when asked about fish and most certainly about water, said he wouldn't drink the stuff because "fish fucked in it." Fair enough. But the phobic types should have been left out of this anthology. Except maybe for Fields, who had nothing against fish themselves, but just didn't care for second-rate water.

The evolved sociological line emphasized in this anthology is that class distinctions at the river have been broken down. I am not speaking here of private fishing clubs leasing sections of a river to its members to catch cloned salmon but to the public sphere (poaching is another delicious morsel in *Wheel*), where an honourable plebe might share a flask of strong rum with an industrial baron. They both will drink the brew to ward off the chills from the fast-running river water. Plebe and brass meet on equal footing but in chestwaders. The pair might even share some vital information as to where the lunkers are congregating and in what hole in what part of the river

system. The editors make their point: a democratization has developed over the centuries. Secular fishing is in. I find this somewhat saddening. Who needs the masses at the stream? We have pollution now, an excess of beer bottles, cigarette packages floating amongst the riffles, and that sort of democratic evil. We also have fished-out rivers. I say screw the masses and democracy at the river. Mass culture kills decent fish and the pleasure of the flesh that is fishing.

The invisibly mended or sculpted prose of Profumo and Swift's introduction to *The Magic Wheel* makes this reader envious. (But that is a good thing. I want my sense challenged if I am to grow.) If this anthology suffers at all it is because it attempts to embrace too many angling centuries in one volume. Also I am sure that a few feminists will knock this anthology because the business of fishing has always been a male preserve generally, and there's little point in dragging in the bones of Dame Juliana Berners and jabbing a proud finger at her masterpiece, *A Treatyse of Fysshynge with an Angle* (from *The Boke of St. Albans*, 1496). The sad fact is that women are under-represented in *The Magic Wheel*. But you can't hang thousands of years of male supremacy onto the shoulders of the editors, or can you? Perhaps *The Invisible Angler* will be written in time.

Fish, I love them. They represent fertility, good luck, Christ, and brain food. Did you know that the Japanese used a single long hair for a flyline? That the Chinese invented the fishing reel at the height of their silk manufacturing when, of course, they needed industrial wheels?

The Magic Wheel is a true live-in companion, something to let your intellect snuggle up against. I've only touched the tip of the fishing volcano.

C D WRIGHT

The Adamantine Practice of Poetry

I am on my yellow moped. Twelve-foot scarf trailing. Pedalling fiendishly over the crests of hill on hill until I join the big wheels on the straightaway to San Francisco State. I am late for work again. Headlamp essential even at eight a.m. I must balance in the gutter to stay in the running. The shield of my helmet is wet; when I reach campus I drip dry. By noon the fog will have burnt off for an hour or so, but by the time I leave the sky will be charcoal and drenching again. Only during lunch hour do I see the beneficent sun. Even in January the campus keeps green with cypress and eucalyptus. The fuchsia blooms gaudily. Bottle brush trees. Calla lilies. Succulents. I am "out there where the plants never die" as Bostonian Fanny Howe describes California, evoking real geographic divisions of poetry, even today in MacAmerica. But on this glorious green, people mingle from literally everywhere — Micronesia, Central America, Papua New Guinea, the Ozark Mountains. Every day an apparent Ethiopian bride sells vials of heavy scents, and Stoney Burke, an improvisational comic, baits the young and complacent. One week a file of low-riders exhibit their cars, next week the makeshift stalls of itinerant craftspeople appear.

Five of us "man" the Poetry Centre. Two in the archives. Three in the main office. We organize talks and readings, then videotape and distribute these events on a lending basis. For student "enrichment" we have audiotapes, three bookcases and a nondescript sofa. Some are regulars: D. F. Brown, a Viet Nam veteran, poet, native of Springfield, Missouri, (seventy-two hilly miles from my home town); Forrest Gander, a Virginia poet, formerly a student of geology. Brown discovered poetry, rather was discovered by poetry, when he was nineteen and a half, in the infantry. Binh Dinh Province. He was a nurse. In the infantry. A man of nineteen. And a half. Boxes of books came to the base camp. For one reason or another Brown was habitually slow reaching the mailroom, the last to rifle the book boxes, poetry the last to be rifled. After everything else, all the serious literature, all the theology, all the pulp and the porn, poetry would remain. On bottom, undisturbed. With little choice and less enthusiasm, he picked up a work by Robert Creeley. Thus one more of us was born: as gravity came to Newton and enlightenment to Siddhartha.

Forrest Gander would graduate from San Francisco State that spring. Gravely personal circumstances had brought him to poetry also. Concentrating both in earth science and English as an undergraduate at William and Mary, smitten with melanoma, spared but chastened, he chose poetry over, let's face it, a gig with an oil company hunting for uranium deposits. Not for the loadstone. Not for the locus Beckett plats for us, "... already old. The ditch is old. In the beginning it was all bright. All bright dots. It does not encroach on the dark. Adamantine darkness of these. As dense at the edge as at the centre...." It wouldn't be in Texaco's interest to locate any position so remote and near as what Beckett described, which could be an acre of hell on earth. Or heaven. The dually maintained residences of poetry. I have never thought it exaggerated to say coming to poetry is a near-death experience. I myself arrived here after a succession of losses. Lastly, after the death by suicide of Frank Stanford, poet from Arkansas. I inherited his small debts, Lost Road Publishers, the book press he started, half the gorgeous corpus of his work (the "adamantine darkness of these"), his devotion to the crooked, humpbacked letters that make up *Mississippi* and the rest of that legendary water's burdensome lexicon. "Horses fuck inside me and a river makes a bend in my shoulder," Stanford wrote. Such was his devotion. I picked up at the bend, but up on the narrow highway, where *83 lives* was scrawled on the rockface. Anonymously. I would go on. This road crooked and steep.

Poet Forrest Gander took his first out-of-college job at the methadone clinic in downtown San Francisco. Something to do with forms. I would hold down the lines at the Poetry Centre a few months longer, filling out papers in quadruplicate for the campus foundation through which every penny awarded our shoestring outfit had to pass and forfeit a percentage. After work Forrest and I would meet for a movie or stir-fried. Or I

would go to the women's gym and he would go home to write or go wherever he went. We lived close by then, but not together.

My roommate was an archivist at the Poetry Centre. And an archivist at home where he collected music, books, magazines. A redheaded fiction writer from Oklahoma. On a visit back to Bartlesville he had taped an electrical storm; when he needed to renew himself he wriggled into his sleeping bag in our dingy apartment on Portrero Hill and listened to the lightning crack through the loudspeakers. I went to the only bar on the hill, played "Wild Horses" on the jukebox, did my laundry or thought about doing laundry, ate a burrito or a piroshki, drank beer. My poems were filled with personal pain. I tried to make them beautiful and interesting. That is, I tried to be artful about my limited but particular experience with pain. Eventually I would modify my goals. Instead of aiming to give beautiful expression to pain, I discharged my wrath less the beauty. Then humour against the wrath. Finally form began to matter, and so to materialize. Not to a terminal pitch. But as a conveyance, an ambulance, to carry the wounded towards some place where we might hope to recover from whatever afflicted us, or at least towards some place where we might rest from the forces. So, you see for me it is not a blasphemy, at least no blasphemy intended, when I say I look to poetry for supernatural help.

Adamant. Carve the mirror with it. If it's the genuine article you should be able to write, "Harlem on my mind" or whatever appears there, on the surface. But it should be immune to being cut with anything other than itself.

The sixteenth-century euphemist John Lilly assigned contradictory properties to its nature: "The Adamant though it be so hard that nothing can bruise it, yet if the warm bloode of a Goat be powred over it, it bursteth."

Increase Mather endowed it with an unusual magnetism: "There is a certain stone called pantarbe which draws gold unto it; so does the adamas hair and twigs." Humble stuff.

After the seventeenth century the confusion of the adamant with the loadstone gave way to its rival identification with the diamond. But first, loadstone or way-stone from the magnet used to guide mariners. Now that so many of us appear in so many ways "lost at sea" perhaps this usage should be revived. The problem with the diamond is cost. The great divide between who mines them and who wears them. Poetry is not that hard.

In the OED, the page following the one featuring loadstone is headed loaf-eater, "one who eats the bread of the master." I would accept poet to be writ here in apposition.

About the rest I remain skeptical, even rhetorically speaking: "That which is impregnable to any application of force; incapable of being broken...." On this "facet," poetry's strength may have been overstated, but one should not admit this in bad company.

The lustre of the adamant may be only an affect, but maintains its appeal. "I just bleed so the stars will have something dark to shine in" wrote the late Frank Stanford.

Practice. By definition practice is distinguished from "profession, theory, knowledge, etc." But what is left once profession, theory, knowledge, etc. are excluded except mechanistic repetition? Leave in, "... exercise in any art for the purpose of, or with the result of attaining proficiency." That's better. For a long time the one poetry broadside in the graduate writing program building at Brown University said simply, "Practice practice put your faith in that," signed W. S. Merwin. After the building was painted, it no longer hung there, and I felt my resolve weaken. "The bringing about" is the plainest, the loveliest utterance allowed. In the Oriental ideal neither practice nor art has been set apart from either living or thinking.

Of poetry. Asking my students what is alien to poetry, the majority said nothing at all. What about evil I asked. What about E-v-i-l. To believe it is capable of staring evil down, you must put poetry forward as innately Utopian. I do.

I further subscribe to the notion it is poetry's immoderate task to save the word, for it is surely going to hell. Any inference here to the strife between non-referentiality and hyper-referentiality is inadvertent. Over these terms debate at least rages. I am more concerned with oxymorons displacing the rightful adjective modifying the rightful noun, i.e. peacemaker missile, with no trace of debate wedged between the two, rendering moot the dispute over the referent, and prompting some poets to write almost entirely in non-words or as a concession in neologisms — starting from a point where the only given is that meaning be meaningless.

Many writers maintain a guarded border between language thick with hair and twigs and the rarefied stuff. No matter which side of the border poets live on they tend to act as if they were being overrun. All I want is a day pass. I like to sleep in my own bed.

Writing leads only to writing according to Colette. I know, I know this much: hair is hair, a beer is a beer is a beer. I know tiger does not eat tiger. And so it seems writing leads only to writing word by word by word. I would like to dedicate each syllable to the countless individuals who have committed the creative, spiritual, intellectual content of their lives to challenging the pugnacious privileges and prerogatives of power. And I would like to register this dedication as a vote against apathy, ignorance, chauvinism, and greed.

Poetry is like food, remarked one of my first teachers, James Whitehead. Freeing me to dislike Rocky Mountain oysters and Robert Lowell. The menu is vast, the list of things I don't want in my mouth quite short.

I know who poetry can't accommodate, the tourist. I don't mean it is necessarily more "highborn" than shell art, though the effort, the ardour of it goes towards being "borne up." But I believe it can't be identified with the compulsion to shop instead of the desire to touch, be touched. *Cables to the Ace:* "How should he (the tourist) realize that the Indian who walks down the street with half a house on his head and a hole in his pants, is Christ? All the tourist thinks is that it is odd for so many Indians to be called Jesus."

Much has been declared about the musicality of poetry. Not so much about the physicality. The adamantine practice of poetry as it pertains to touch — an impression of which can be lifted off the ends of the fingers. These are some of the things I have touched in my life that are forbidden: paintings behind velvet ropes, electric fencing, a vault in an office, a gun in a drawer, my brother's folding money, the poet's anus, the black holes in his heart, where his life went out of him.

"Sometimes art/poetry is like a beautiful sick dog that shits all over the house." Stanford again.

She used language on him, the hill man testified against his wife, as if she had used saltpetre or worse, strychnine. Poetry works. You can use it on folks: "Sty sty leave my eye / go to the next feller passin' by."

What *it* is. A rhomboid. Brilliant. Impenetrable. Which occurs in a pure state. ("As dense at the edge as it is at the centre.") A widely distributed non-radioactive element. Therefore, not to be confused with uranium. What is brought about by some of the most lustrous, least attractive wordsmiths. What cannot be fashioned into prose. Let that go as a very hard and a very cold definition.

When I get off work, run down the unlit stairs swaddled in my twelve-foot, still-damp scarf and swinging my helmet by the strap, my moped is gone. I bought it second hand from a man who bought it for his wife; when she became pregnant he sold it out from under her. Now stolen from under my window at the Poetry Centre. The twenty minutes it took to get back to Portrero Hill turns into an hour and twenty. It's the end of the streetcar line. But I can still meet Forrest for stir-fried, who is already home, working on his breathless poem, "Rush to the Lake." But no, that poem would come later, after we watch the tale end of a silent movie in the lobby of a hotel in Mexico City. "The Last Castrato" would be written there too, the first poem he wrote that I love. Breathless poems. Written in Mexico. Maybe we can take in a nine o'clock movie at the Roxie. I can undo my pack on the ride to my dingy apartment on Portrero Hill, take out a notebook and make an entry.

Psalm to an Old Pear Tree

oy Kiyooka's *Pear Tree Pomes* ("pome" suggesting "pomme," that apple of the western "I") composes a round of "seasonal epiphanies," written meditations on the pear tree outside the poet's window. But Kiyooka in this book is not so eager to rhyme the pear tree's life and fate with his own or to use the pear tree for purposes of self-description. Rather, his writing *becomes* the life of the pear tree. Kiyooka's work in this book corresponds with the concern of Rilke (who is thanked in the book's afterword) that poets should be aware of the old curse that haunts them: using language to describe their sorrows instead of "transforming themselves into hard words as the stone mason of a cathedral obstinately translates himself into the equanimity of the stone." It is not exactly the equanimity of the stone that Kiyooka translates himself into in this book — it is, rather, the complex, thatched and fruitful branches of the pear tree, in which nest singing birds that come and go; its trunk/body cleated, "scarred," "forkt," and "corrugated" with age and use and familiarity; its fruits preserved and eaten, or thrown against garage walls, or enjoyed by the neighbours (in season, one a day for each person who passes by), or rotting in the shade of the tree's branches, forming a midden heap, a rich layered history of pleasure and remembrance. It is a complex, changing, living tree this language becomes — the "pomes" themselves grown from "pears rotting into the ground to nourish the seed of / a small pome."

The "pomes" let in light the way the latticed branches of a pear tree do; their lines trace those branches against a sky momentarily amber. What the pear tree thinks and feels, with the poet sitting in it with or without his Beloved, like an ancient king of Persia enthroned in the equanimity of his garden, is what Kiyooka's beautiful language gives shape to. The poems range in feeling from sorrow to praise and back again. The sorrow comes from their lamenting the loss of a beloved: like a bird from the pear tree, she has flown "to another neighbourhood," leaving the pear tree bereft, birdless, songless, "tongue-tied." Many of the poems seem to be located in the month of October after the pears have fallen and the poet, in his fifty-sixth winter, composes "autumnal silences." There is nothing in the way of self-pity in this book: the poet is addressing the cosmos when he asks the magpie in the

pear tree to be his "unpaid informer," his "unimpeachable i."

The poems turn and turn in a seasonal round. The shape of the pears hanging from the branches is "rotund," learned from the sun. Moon slivers of sliced pear rest in a bowl in winter-time. The correspondence of sun, moon and pear is illustrated in the book by David Bolduc's beautiful watercolours. I had forgotten the pleasure of reading an illustrated book and *Pear Tree Pomes* brought them back to me. Most of the paintings are circular in form, cameos of pear-leaf, pear-core, bowl-with-sliver-of-pear, sliver-of-moon-with-pear-sliver, pear-branches-with-magpie, empty bowl — mandalas of sweetness, ripeness, and rich decay. The drawings also introduce a markedly Japanese or Buddhist aesthetic to the meditative tone of the book, which also engages a thoroughly western eye and ear, with its references to "psychological terrorism" and "baloney sandwiches" and, at times, a language almost Shakespearean in its vowels and rhythms, with its references to "divers tongues" and "winter omen" and "bright gists." In just about any given poem we hear words that would feel at home in a Shakespeare sonnet: compact, votaries, felicitious, awakened.

The illustrations also function as places of silence in the book, where the sounds of words stop and a visual image appears. These images are serene, restful, and dark. They give us pause, for a moment, and then we go on. The poems perform their own circular journey, composing the "dream wheel," "sky wheel," "Chinese chariot wheel" referred to in several poems. The cover illustration shows a mandala of six pear leaves in a circle. "Now the mind lays on its trouble and considers," Wallace Stevens says on the frontispiece. On the same page, Gaston Bachelard speaks of nests, and the poet dedicates the book to the woman and her son whose moving on is part of the occasion of these poems.

The pear tree is the poet's language both in its flowering fruitfulness and in its heaped-up silence: at the end "there are no words left bearing the seasons of a once fruitful tree." Earlier, an "appall'd lover" is bending his ear to the trunk of the pear tree to hear "a lost rhetorick." He remembers a pear tree he knew as a child on the prairies, but in another language, his mother's tongue. "How many languages have i lost losing my childhood pear tree," wonders the poet. "How many languages does a pear tree speak?" asks the poem.

The pear tree becomes the home (home/pome), the abode of the poet in love, in solitude, and in language. This is where the praise comes in. Kiyooka works both with and against the conventions of the genre of the seasonal round to remove the anthropomorphism and to repeat instead an identity (with the verb "to be" often in careful quotation marks) of man, cosmos, and tree. But what may appear to be a lofty subject really isn't lofty at all. In the book, the upper branches of the pear tree are about as transcendent as we get. Kiyooka's language keeps us attached:

language is a fool's fruit
fool-proof pear trees bear the laughter of

and

there are no words left bearing the seasons of
a once-fruitful tree — do you hear me?

and

the old pear tree and i sit quietly
divining the lattices of a frugal winter light

The pears fall to compost the poet's language. He is full of praise for the persistence of the tree, its on-going-ness in the face of use, abuse, condominiums, semiotics, etc. Only an "axeman comin'" could cut it down — and did, apparently, after *Pear Tree Pomes* was published, as Roy Kiyooka told the audience the night he read these poems at R2B2 Books in Vancouver. His extraordinarily rhythmic and pronounced reading of the measures of these poems brought them and the pear tree to life in the crowded little room. We listened to the poet play his dulcimer. We drank his sake. We went home full of praise.

SUANNE KELMAN

Ishiguro in Toronto

azuo Ishiguro won the 1989 Booker Prize for *The Remains of the Day*, a novel narrated by an aging British butler on vacation, reminiscing about his life in service to an aristocrat who flirted with Naziism before World War II.

Like all three of Ishiguro's novels, it is a monologue by a most untrustworthy and emotionally repressed narrator. The Booker judges praised it in these terms: "*The Remains of the Day* renders with humour and pathos a memorable character and explores the large, vexed themes of class, tradition and duty. It was narrowly preferred but universally admired." The prissy tone of this endorsement eerily echoes the butler's own pompous style, which makes *The Remains of the Day* Ishiguro's first funny book.

His first novel, *A Pale View of the Hills*, traces the memories of a Japanese woman, now widowed, being visited by her daughter from her second marriage — to an Englishman — at her home in an English village. A daughter from an earlier marriage in Japan has killed herself some years before.

The narrator's memories return obsessively to her post-war years in Nagasaki, and her friendship with another Japanese woman trapped in a Madame Butterfly relationship with an American. The theme of the suicide or murder of a child runs through the book, evoked by a newspaper item, a dangling rope, or the nightmare story of a madwoman who drowned her baby daughter.

Ishiguro's second novel, *An Artist of the Floating World*, picks up a subplot from *A Pale View of the Hills*. Its narrator, a painter named Masuji Ono, has wholeheartedly supported the rise of militarism and nationalism in Japan in the thirties, to the point of denouncing a rebellious former student to the authorities. The student has spent the war in prison.

In the post-war period, the unrepentant artist is an embarrassment to his remaining family and an obstacle to his second daughter's marriage. Like all of Ishiguro's work to date, *An Artist of the Floating World* is the attempt of an often-deluded character to reconstruct the past, in deep but repressed pain, and with wildly varying degrees of honesty.

Ishiguro has also written television scripts, and has just completed a screenplay for a movie. Called *The Saddest Music in the World*, it is the story of a folk-music contest to determine which tradition can claim the most tragic melody.

Three weeks before he won the Booker, Ishiguro was interviewed in Toronto by Suanne Kelman.

Kelman: *A Pale View of the Hills*, your first novel, is the story of a Japanese woman drifting into an intricate and rather sad, even sinister, relationship with the West. Where did that come from?

Ishiguro: When I was writing it I thought the book was about things like the overturning of social values and parental responsibility. But I think there was a much more emotional motivation behind it that had to do with my personal history. I was born in Japan, in Nagasaki, and I went with my parents to England in 1960 when I was five. It was supposed to be a temporary stay, but it kept getting extended. Almost without deciding to do so, the family remained in England. But as a child, I grew up thinking I was going to return to Japan any day. And so I had this very powerfully imagined country in my head. And by the time I had more or less grown up, I realized that this Japan that existed in my head, and which was very important to me, was a country that no longer existed in reality, if it ever had. I also became aware that as the years passed this place was just fading away in my head, too.

At that point in my life there was a real need to tack it down, to reconstruct this world that I had the most powerful emotional incentives to imagine. I think that had a lot to do with why I turned to novel-writing. It explains something I didn't understand at the time, which was that I wasn't interested in doing research in the conventional sense to fill out my picture of Japan. I was almost defensive about that. I had a Japan inside my head, which I needed to transcribe as accurately as possible.

Kelman: *An Artist of the Floating World* seems very much to come out of that first book, in that one of

the characters from *A Pale View of the Hills* seems suddenly to step on to centre stage. Was that how the second book did start?

Ishiguro: Yes, largely. I think one of the problems about being an inexperienced novelist is that it's difficult to control your work. I was very conscious of certain traps that people fall into when they write their first novel, being too autobiographical or having a certain lack of focus. So I made a big effort to try to be quite clear about what I was trying to do in the book. But nevertheless I found thematic discipline very difficult at that stage. In the first book, a lot of things that I thought were just going to be subplots took over. I would have what seemed to be a good idea, for that moment, for that page, and I would just put it down without thinking where it was going to take me. And before I knew it, I had almost subverted my real intentions. When I finished it, I thought: "Well, the aspect of this book that is most important to me is this bit that has ended up as a subplot," which is a story about this old teacher, whose career has coincided to a certain extent with the rise of militarism in Japan before World War II, and who, after the war, in retirement, finds himself in the awkward position of having to reassess his life's work. I thought I would like to explore that strand much more thoroughly.

It's also to do with the nervousness of the first novelist. I was nervous about fundamental things, that I wouldn't have enough to fill enough pages that it would be called a novel, or that I would lose the reader's attention. I had this rather neurotic urge to throw in everything to keep the thing going. And for the second book I calmed down a little and if ideas — however intrinsically appealing — weren't relevant to the overall design, I developed the discipline to say "No, we don't want this."

Kelman: You seem to enjoy tormenting the reader, dangling some unspecified, upsetting incident for ten or twenty pages, until finally the reader finds out what on earth happened.

Ishiguro: The point is, particularly in the last two books, I haven't structured the novels around a linear plot line. And this does give me tremendous freedom in some senses; I can compose much more freely. Lots of other factors come into why one episode should follow another, if you remove this rather didactic thing, this spine called a plot, which dictates that *y* should follow *x*. But the problem is keeping up some kind of momentum. So I suppose that's just a technical device for providing a certain kind of suspense and structure. It's also important for the reader to consider various things the character is remembering in the light of why he is remembering them, why he is juxtaposing them one alongside another. I wouldn't want to suggest that there's anything particularly deep about this. It's my equivalent to suspense, what's going to happen next.

Kelman: After *A Pale View of the Hills*, it seems almost as if you develop a distaste for dramatic things happening, at least on stage. You use some quite Gothic effects in *A Pale View of the Hills* — morbid and frightening images of murdered children. But in *An Artist of the Floating World*, the hero never confronts the pupil he's wronged. The pupil never takes revenge. When people die, we hear about it months later, when it's been leeched of all emotion.

Ishiguro: It's to do with what you're interested in as a writer, and certainly for those two books I was interested in the justification process that takes place inside people's minds when they try to come to terms with certain things about their past. I wasn't terribly interested in things *happening*. I was interested in all the ways in which people like the painter in *An Artist of the Floating World* or the butler in *The Remains of the Day* fool themselves or hide from themselves. The events, if you like, are to do with that: one side of the person demanding a certain honesty, and the other side demanding some kind of preservation from the truth. And that's the drama that's going on rather than any kind of more plotty things.

Kelman: You said that you don't like to do much research for the novels.

Ishiguro: I do research of a sort. But you see, I think that the research that a novelist does is quite different from what is normally called research. I feel I have to know the fictional landscape in which my novel takes place very well. That's the landscape I have to research, not any actual chunk of history or real country. For *The Remains of the Day* I read accounts written by servants, just to give me props from which I could invent. Similarly, I read a lot of political commentary from that time to try and get a feel for the climate of the debates that were going on. I feel more comfortable if I have some background knowledge and then I know how much licence to give myself.

Kelman: It's hard for someone like me to judge if your Japan is imaginary or not, because it doesn't seem any more jarring than, say, Tanizaki's Japan. But I knew your Britain was imaginary. It seemed a strange Britain for someone of your age to imagine — this strange sort of Wodehouse life.

Ishiguro: That was a conscious decision. I wished to set this book in a mythical landscape, which to a certain extent resembled that mythical version of England that is peddled in the nostalgia industry at the moment. This idea of England, this green, pleasant place of leafy lanes and grand country houses and butlers and tea on the lawn, cricket — this vision of England that actually does play a large role in the political imaginations of a lot of people, not just British people but people around the world.

I think these imaginative landscapes are very important. I felt it was a perfectly reasonable mission on my part to set out to slightly redefine that mythical, cozy England, to say that there is a shadowy side to it. In a way I wanted to rewrite P. G. Wodehouse with a serious political dimension.

Kelman: The great difference is that the butler in P. G. Wodehouse eventually goes downstairs and rolls up his sleeves and flirts with the kitchen maid. That's part of the *Upstairs, Downstairs* vision: that the servants eventually go off duty. I'm interested in the absolute purity of Stevens: a man who wants to lose himself utterly in the dignity of his public person.

Ishiguro: Well, he's a kind of metaphor for something, and as such he's a kind of exaggeration. He's a kind of grotesque. All right, as you say, he wishes to deny this human aspect of himself. It's a story of a man who, misguidedly in my opinion, is so ambitious to achieve a certain ideal that he does so at terrible cost. He actually loses a part of himself that is crucial: that is to say, his capacity to love. That stereotypical figure of the English butler, which is known all round the world, I thought would serve well as some kind of emblem of this terrible fear of the emotional in one's self, and the tendency to equate having feelings with weakness. And this terrible struggle to deny that emotional side that can love and that can suffer. The butler was also a metaphor for me for the relationship ordinary people have to political power. He has these two clear metaphorical functions.

Kelman: In all three books, the characters are very repressed people. Your books seem to me largely built around the things people cannot say to one another, around silences.

Ishiguro: Yes. I think in the last book in particular that has become a much more conscious theme. In the first two books, that just came out stylistically. As you say, the books often work by what is not said as much as by what is said. And the intensity of certain feelings is conveyed by how they are left out, rather than by how they are overtly expressed. I think in the third

book, I was trying to address that condition itself as part of the theme.

Kelman: How are your books received in Japan?

Ishiguro: There's a lot of curiosity about me as a person. There isn't very much interest in my books. The third one may actually have a larger readership, paradoxically, because it is set in the West. The Japanese aren't terribly interested in reading books set in post-war Japan, written by some guy who hasn't lived there in years. This is stuff that they went through many years ago, and they're into something else now.

But they're fascinated with me as a phenomenon. They still like to think there's something unique about being Japanese, and they find the idea that someone could be racially Japanese but partially something else terribly threatening.

Kelman: I don't think there's anything in what we've said so far that would suggest that parts of *The Remains of the Day* are very funny.

Ishiguro: This is the thing that continually distresses me, the tone in which the thing is discussed, which suggests that it's a boring, heavy, depressing work. I'm glad we mentioned people like Wodehouse before, because to a certain extent it was, as I said, an attempt to invade that territory, and that territory includes a light touch and humour.

I suppose there's something funny about people who don't have a sense of humour. Predominantly I think for me what is funny is the same thing as what is tragic. There are a few farce sequences in the book, but the humour that interests me is the humour that arises from the ridiculous and yet sad condition that he is in.

Kelman: Do you read much Japanese literature?

Ishiguro: Only in translation. I can't read *kanji* characters. I'm often as baffled as the average western reader who's been brought up in the western traditions of literature.

People like Mishima and Tanizaki are the people who are most accessible to the West, and that's because they were partly themselves very much influenced by western literature and thought. But traditionalists like Kawabata, who was the only Japanese Nobel Prize winner for literature, I find terribly difficult. We were talking earlier about not depending on plot too much; Kawabata's stuff is sometimes virtually plotless. Obviously one is being asked to appreciate something entirely different. I don't feel that I'm really understanding what he's up to.

Japanese movies are another matter. Almost by definition, Japanese film directors were quite concerned about western influence. Although, having said that, I think Japanese cinema grew up very much in a tradition of its own, alongside the overwhelming Hollywood tradition, and indeed went on to teach Hollywood many things. Particularly directors like Kurosawa and Ozu became people that Hollywood learned from. Some of my very favourite films of all times are Japanese ones.

Kelman: One of the things I noticed in the first two books is the doubling effect, that characters slide in and out of identities — which of two characters actually said this, which child are we watching at this time? In the third book, it becomes time: On which occasion did she say this? There are always echoes and reflections.

Ishiguro: I don't think anything terribly profound is being said there. I'm trying to capture the texture of memory. I need to keep reminding people that the flashbacks aren't just a clinical, technical means of conveying things that happened in the past. This is somebody turning over certain memories, in the light of his current emotional condition. I like blurred edges around these events, so you're not quite certain if they really happened and you're not quite certain to what extent the narrator is deliberately colouring them. And it's convenient. You move from one situation to another by having a character say: "Well, maybe it wasn't that, and maybe it was this." It's just a very easy way of getting from scene *a* to scene *b*.

Kelman: Is there anything you've been dying to be asked — about one of the books or your whole career — that no one's asked?

Ishiguro: No. I do interviews because this is the way publishing has got, now, and that all seems to be part and parcel of my job. But I don't feel an overwhelming need to go around talking about my books. I spend a lot of time getting my books to say just so much. A part of me resists coming back on the stage and saying: "Oh, by the way, during this bit you're supposed to be thinking this."

Kelman: You don't really like it.

Ishiguro: I don't dislike it. Well, I think there's a very interesting side to it, that you do gain quite an insight into your work because of the nature of the questions that are asked. The cumulative effect of a number of people asking questions, if they all zoom in on a particular area that you yourself as a writer hadn't considered to be particularly fertile or contentious, does teach you something about the way the book is being read.

To give an example, with this last book I hadn't been that conscious of, say, the nature of the narrative voice until the book came out, and this was what a lot of the questioning was about, the nature of this narrative voice. Where did you get this funny voice?

The other thing that's interesting is to go to different countries. Quite often there's a difference in emphasis from country to country, and that tells you something about the different respective cultures, because of course the book is the same. It's just being read in different ways.

Kelman: Can you give me an example?

Ishiguro: When I went to Germany with *An Artist of the Floating World,* the questions were overwhelmingly about fascism. They want to make comparisons between the way the Japanese have faced up to their war experience and their militarist/fascist experience and the way Germany has. I don't particularly enjoy talking about my books in Germany because they don't seem to be read as fiction. They seem to be read as a further contribution to some debate.

In England the effect is almost the antithesis. People have not paid much attention to the ideas and just treated it as an exotic kind of little thing, and drawn comparisons to Japanese painting and brushwork, carp splashing about in still ponds. I've had every kind of Japanese cliché phrase — even Sumo wrestling.

Kelman: As you're going through the bookselling machine, lots of people like me are asking you fairly impertinent questions about your life. Does that bother you?

Ishiguro: I've got quite good at not going beyond a certain point. But somehow if you write a book, people think they have a licence to ask you some very intimate things about your past or your feelings about your family. I think a more disturbing tendency at the moment is that a lot of people do interviews and the journalists go away and write up a very scathing, vicious piece.

Kelman: Has that happened to you?

Ishiguro: Not exactly. At the moment I'm somebody who has not been attacked. I'm probably peculiar in not having many enemies in London literary circles. There was a time not so long ago when writers were rather shabby, unglamorous people, who didn't earn very much money. The only people who wanted to interview them were serious literary types. For some reason the perception of the writer has changed, and they've become glamorous people. They've lost the right, along with politicians and actors and other public figures, to be treated with gentleness and respect.

That worries me, because publicity is good for literature in that it sells books and gets books read, but if the tone in which books are sold and talked about actually deteriorates, then we're probably better off not having this publicity at all. It'll get the books to the wrong constituency and the books will be read in the wrong way. It may start to affect the way writers write. I think this is an unhealthy trend.

Now I've often heard writers complain about their time being invaded by doing promotion, spending all their time at literary parties and things. It's very difficult to get yourself into an imaginary world when you keep having to do this. You can actually, if you're not careful, end up becoming a professional conference-attender, a person who goes around talking about books. You can damage whatever got you writing in the first place.

Kelman: Do you think you'll ever write a novel that's not a monologue?

Ishiguro: Oh, I hope so. I think it's important for writers to move on. I think there's a particular danger that if you've been praised by critics for being able to do *x, y, z* well, you can be overcome by a terrible cowardice about leaving territories *x, y* and *z*. I haven't quite decided about the monologue thing, but I do feel I would like to write a book with a different kind of voice, a different tone. I'm at the beginning of my career. I don't want to be forever writing books about old people looking back at their lives in this rather laconic, understated kind of voice.

There are two authors whom I revere. Chekhov on the one hand and Dostoevsky on the other. The books I've written up till now, the last two especially I think, are probably written under the influence of Chekhov. But I think sometimes I would like to write something very messy and jagged and brilliantly imperfect, in the way Dostoevsky has done. That's a side of my writing I'd like to explore further in the future.

Kelman: Do you think you'll ever write a novel in which a character addresses his or her father in the second person rather than the third?

Ishiguro: It depends on what kind of characters we're dealing with. In the Japanese context, it is absolutely natural that people would address their fathers in the third person, there's nothing unusually repressed about that. That's a very western viewpoint to think there's anything terribly odd about this. If you're asking me if there will be a sudden change of tone, will I write a book about an Italian family who scream at each other, I don't know if I would. Obviously what you write comes out of fairly deep things, those things you've inherited as a person. I've grown up with two cultures behind me, the Japanese middle class, or more strictly speaking the Japanese samurai background, and the British middle-class background: Two cultures that both, in a very pronounced way, put a high premium on what in a British context might be

called a stiff upper lip.

It's not just a case of stoicism, it's a different language, a different way of conveying emotion. I enjoy creating effects, emotional intensity and tensions in my writing through what is left out. Or exploring language that hides, rather than language that gropes after something just beyond its diction. Although I enjoy reading the latter kind. There have been some brilliant writers through our history who have tried to bend language around, to go for some things that are just beyond the reach of normal language, everyday language. There's something exciting about that.

But, of course, language also has this other function, which is to conceal and suppress, to deceive one's self and to deceive others. So far, I suppose, I've been involved in exploring that language, particularly the language of self-deception.

Brick readers in Sri Lanka, 1978

GEOFFREY YORK

Oka

n the summer of 1989, I was completing work on a book entitled *The Dispossessed: Life and Death in Native Canada*. As I finished writing, the warning signs were everywhere. The anger and frustration of Canada's aboriginal people was dangerously close to the boiling point. There were bitter protests by Indians who had seen their friends and relatives killed by police bullets or jailed by a discriminatory justice system. There were hunger strikes and sit-ins by Native students whose dreams had been crushed by Ottawa's budget cuts. There were highway barricades and tense confrontations between Indian bands and the oil companies and loggers whose relentless activities were destroying the traditional economy of hunting and fishing. Across the country, from Lubicon Lake to James Bay, from Labrador to Temagami, the pent-up rage of aboriginal people was obvious to anyone who looked.

Canada's elected officials chose to ignore those warning signs. In the spring and summer of 1990, they finally paid the price for their neglect. And the price was steep: the demise of the Meech Lake Accord and the death of a police officer in Oka, Quebec. Because of their failure to understand the anger of aboriginal people, Canada's political leaders were left with a disintegrating nation.

Much of the anger could be traced back to 1987. That was when Canada's first ministers refused to entrench the simple notion of aboriginal self-government in the Canadian Constitution. Just a few weeks later, those same first ministers drafted the Meech Lake Accord, giving Quebec the kind of recognition that was consistently denied to aboriginal people. Meech Lake was the official perpetuation of the myth of "two founding races." It defined Canada as a duality — English and French — and it ignored the people who had lived in Canada for thousands of years before the arrival of the Europeans.

Aboriginal people fought vigorously against the Meech Lake Accord. The politicians gave them a polite hearing — and then the Natives were disregarded. In early June of 1990, when Canada's first ministers held a marathon negotiating session in Ottawa to settle the Meech Lake question, it was again the aboriginal people who were forced to wait outside on the street. They were kept in the dark, locked out of the private negotiations, while their rights were bartered by eleven white men who saw aboriginal issues as just another bargaining chip.

When a deal was struck, it was the aboriginal people who were told to wait for a future bargaining round. The politicians assumed, once again, that the anger in Indian country could be safely ignored. This time, they were wrong.

The supporters of Meech Lake failed to understand the growing strength of the Indian movement. Aboriginal leaders were determined, intelligent, sophisticated and resourceful. On June 12, just three days after the constitutional deal in Ottawa, dozens of Indian chiefs from across Manitoba travelled to Winnipeg to formulate a plan. They mapped out a nine-point strategy to kill Meech Lake.

At first, few people took them seriously. But soon it was clear that the chiefs had adopted a brilliant strategy, exploiting Manitoba's legislative rules and the shortage of time before the June 23 deadline. They hired a procedural expert to determine the best tactics for blocking Meech Lake in the legislature. They recruited thousands of Natives to form a time-consuming parade of speakers at the public hearings that Manitoba was legally required to hold. They hired lawyers to prepare a possible court challenge. And in the most crucial move of all, they persuaded Elijah Harper to spearhead their attack on Meech Lake.

Elijah Harper was the former chief of Red Sucker Lake, an impoverished Ojibway-Cree community in northeastern Manitoba. A quiet but eloquent man who wears his jet-black hair in a long braid, Harper had been the MLA for the vast northern riding of Rupertsland since 1981. Like most aboriginal people, he had nothing to lose in the Meech Lake debate. The threats of separatism in Quebec and instability in the money markets — the pressure tactics that had worked so effectively against every other opponent of Meech Lake — were irrelevant to aboriginal people on reserves where the unemployment rate was ninety per cent. They knew their conditions could not possibly get any worse. It was the anger of these aboriginal communities that fuelled Elijah Harper's decision to fight the Meech Lake Accord.

The top federal officials in Ottawa were baffled by the Manitoba chiefs. For a while, they assumed that the chiefs were simply trying to extract a few concessions from the government. They assumed that the aboriginal leaders would succumb to the pressure-cooker negotiating tactics that had eventually defeated the dissident premiers at the Ottawa bargaining sessions. But the Manitoba chiefs were seeking something more profound: a deep and fundamental shift in Canadian power relationships, forcing the country's political leaders to stop ignoring Indian people.

I remember the frustration and bewilderment on the face of Senator Lowell Murray after his failed efforts to persuade the Manitoba chiefs to accept Meech Lake. He had hoped to establish a negotiating session with the chiefs, allowing him to re-create the same pressure-packed conditions that led to the constitutional deal in Ottawa on June 9. The chiefs, however, had anticipated the federal strategy. After pleading with the chiefs for an hour, Lowell Murray was politely ushered out of the meeting room. For once, the tables were turned. The federal officials were impotent and the aboriginal people held all the power.

The chiefs showed Canadians that power could be exercised in a principled way. By rejecting an offer of minor concessions from the federal government, they proved that their opposition to Meech Lake could not be bought off by short-term rewards. "We're going to put ethics into the political process," a Native lawyer said.

All of the actions of the Manitoba chiefs were formulated in a traditional system of consensus-building and collective decision-making. It was a unique form of democracy, with roots that stretched back for thousands of years. Nobody could impose any decision on the chiefs. Each issue was discussed collectively, with the debate moving around the table until each chief had said as much as he wanted to say. The discussion continued until a consensus emerged. The chiefs continually consulted their elders and the ordinary people in their communities to ensure that their decisions were broadly supported. It was a method that could serve as a model for democracy in Canada.

The successful battle against Meech Lake transformed Elijah Harper into a national hero. It generated a tremendous outpouring of public support for the Indian cause. The Manitoba chiefs received as many as six hundred telephone calls of support per day from non-Native Canadians. And the battle achieved something else: it united Indians from across Canada, pulling them together in an alliance to rally around Elijah Harper. By killing Meech Lake, the aboriginal leaders had put themselves in a much stronger position. They had proven themselves to be powerful, united, tenacious and increasingly capable of winning public support.

On the evening of June 23, when Meech Lake officially died, more than two hundred aboriginal people gathered on the grounds of the Manitoba Legislature to hold a candlelight vigil. It was a solemn and moving ceremony. Elders prayed in the Ojibway language. The Indians sang a Cree song of thanksgiving, and they gathered in a circle to hold their candles silently aloft under the dark prairie sky. "We're here to celebrate the rebirth of our people and the death of Meech Lake," said Phil Fontaine, the calm and dignified leader of the Manitoba Assembly of Chiefs. "It's never going to be the same. There's been a change in the consciousness of the Canadian people. We have a hopeful future now, a bright future."

In the tradition of the aboriginal people, anyone is allowed to speak when the people are gathered in a circle. One of those who stepped forward to speak was Sydney Garrioch, chief of the Cross Lake Band in northern Manitoba. "Next time, we will not be forgotten," he told the gathering. "We went through a hardship, but we never hesitated. We were proud of what we were doing."

The growing unity and strength of Canada's aboriginal people was demonstrated again in the summer of 1990, when the Quebec police attacked a Mohawk barricade in the peaceful town of Oka. The barricade was intended to prevent the expansion of a golf course onto the ancestral land of the Mohawks. At the nearby Kahnawake Reserve, Mohawks blocked the Mercier Bridge, cutting off a major artery to Montreal. In Native communities throughout Ontario and Quebec, aboriginal people organized convoys of food and emergency supplies for the Mohawks. In western Canada and northern Ontario, Indian bands established their own blockades of highways and railway lines to show their support for the Mohawks and to press for a resolution of their own long-standing grievances.

Federal officials and Quebec politicians were quick to accuse the Mohawks of being "criminals" and "terrorists." The Quebec police refused to allow food to be delivered to the Mohawks — even after the food blockade was condemned by human-rights groups. The residents of Chateauguay, unable to tolerate a delay in their commuting to Montreal, went on wild riots and burned the Mohawks in effigy. Media commentators, obsessed by the masks and semi-automatic weapons of the Mohawk warriors, talked incessantly of the need for law and order. But almost everyone ignored the basic underlying issue: Canada's failure to resolve the legitimate land claims of aboriginal people.

For decades, the Mohawks of Kanesatake (the

Native community near Oka) had been crowded onto tiny parcels of land. Convinced that they had been cheated of their rightful land, the people of Kanesatake had tried to follow the official rules to resolve their grievance. They filed a land claim in 1975, but it was rejected by the federal government almost immediately. They filed another land claim in 1977. This time the government delayed its decision for nine years — and then it again rejected the claim. Only after the violence at Oka in 1990 did the government finally take concrete steps to provide the land that the Mohawks so desperately needed.

The delays were typical of Ottawa's handling of land claims across the country. For many Indian bands, justice was almost impossible to obtain. Federal officials have privately admitted that hundreds of Indian bands have a morally valid claim to a larger land base. Virtually every band in the country has suffered the loss of reserve land as a result of railway expropriations, highway construction, urban encroachment, or the simple theft of their land by early settlers. Yet, despite the acknowledged legitimacy of their claims, it can take a decade or longer to resolve a single case.

The government has adopted a rigid and legalistic set of criteria to determine whether a claim should be accepted. Claims are often rejected for technical reasons, even if they are morally legitimate. The federal budget for specific land claims has been steadily reduced (after taking inflation into account). Of the 578 specific land claims that have been filed in the past two decades, only forty-four have been resolved to the satisfaction of the Indian bands. At the current slow pace, it will take another forty years to clear the backlog of land claims. "It seems that the only time real progress is made in claims negotiations is when there is pressure of some kind ... when there is court action or when development is being held up," said Murray Coolican, the former head of a federal task force which reviewed Ottawa's policy on comprehensive land claims.

In 1985, the Coolican task force had recommended a broader and fairer set of criteria for determining whether Indian claims should be accepted. But the government rejected the recommendation. By stifling the legitimate claims of the aboriginal people, Ottawa made it almost inevitable that communities such as Kanesatake would eventually respond with violence. "You close off the channels of peaceful and legal negotiation ... and you provoke violence," said University of Toronto professor Peter Russell, a member of the Coolican task force. He said the government's handling of Indian land claims was "a classic recipe" for violence.

For the governments of Canada and Quebec, the emergence of the Mohawk warriors was a dangerous challenge to the status quo. Because they refused to play by the rules, the warriors were an uncontrolled threat to the established bureaucratic policies for Indian people. Moreover, they were focussing public attention on the weaknesses in federal land-claims policy and the continuing neglect of the legitimate grievance of aboriginal people. Government leaders knew they were suffering a political embarrassment. They responded by treating the Mohawk situation as a public-relations problem. After studying the polls and the advice of media experts, the politicians tried to convince Canadians that the armed standoffs at Oka and Kahnawake were simply a matter of "law and order." And they painted the warriors as unsavoury characters who were motivated by business interests in cigarette smuggling and illegal casinos.

There was a kernel of truth in some of the accusations. A few of the warriors were quick-tempered, vandalized houses and assaulted their enemies. A handful of the older warriors had connections to the cigarette

trade and lucrative bingo halls. But this kernel of information was twisted into a distorted portrait of the Mohawks — a portrait that was widely accepted by Canadians who had little understanding of aboriginal people. This exaggerated caricature of the warriors soon became conventional wisdom, obscuring the reality of Mohawk history and Mohawk beliefs.

The political rhetoric about "the rule of law" failed to acknowledge two central truths. First, the Mohawks are not a lawless people. They have always maintained their own system of justice, their own Great Law of Peace, and their own rules of conduct. By these traditional Mohawk laws, vandalism and assault are illegal. None of the warrior leaders condoned those clear violations of Mohawk law, and indeed they attempted (even under the chaotic conditions of the armed standoffs) to find and punish those who were responsible.

Second, the "rule of law" has consistently been used by Canadian governments to suppress aboriginal people. Laws were created to outlaw Indian spiritual practices, to prohibit Indians from participating in the political system, and to make it illegal for anyone to raise money for Indian land claims. Laws were created to restrict the mobility of aboriginal people and keep them imprisoned on their reserves. Even today, Canadian law still includes the Indian Act, with all of its discriminatory provisions. When the "rule of law" has been regularly exercised by powerful Canadians to stomp out the aboriginal culture, it is hypocritical for politicians to insist that the Mohawks must respect the supremacy of Canadian law. Indeed, it could be argued that Mohawk law has been consistently fairer and closer to natural justice than Canadian law.

The accusations of cigarette and casino influences are similarly distorted. The basic demands of the Mohawk warriors had nothing to do with tobacco and gambling. Anyone who talked to the Mohawks soon discovered the simple truth of the matter: the warriors were motivated by a passionate belief in Mohawk sovereignty and Mohawk nationhood. Even a cursory examination of aboriginal history in Canada provides proof that the Mohawks have always been willing to fight for their sovereignty. Long before the birth of the casinos and the cigarette trade, the Mohawks were fiercely resisting any incursion into their territory.

As far back as the nineteenth century, the Mohawks were defending their land against police attacks. In 1877, for example, the Mohawks of Oka occupied a farm pasture to assert their land rights in the region. In an eerie foreshadowing of the dramatic events of 1990, the Quebec provincial police launched an early-morning raid against the Mohawks. Firing pistols and dragging Mohawks away, the police arrested eight suspects and took them to jail. In retaliation, a crowd of armed Mohawks torched a Catholic church.

The battles at Oka and Kahnawake in 1990 were merely the latest in a long series of clashes between Canadian authorities and Mohawk traditionalists. Many of these historic clashes had a remarkable similarity to the conflicts of today. And yet cigarettes and bingo were never an issue in the battles of the past century. To suggest that the barricades at Oka and Kahnawake were motivated by economic greed is a complete misunderstanding of the entire history of the Mohawk people.

From the late nineteenth century to the present day, federal governments have frequently used violent coercion to force the Mohawks to accept the alien institutions of the European political system. In every case, the Mohawks have resisted. Consider the Mohawk community of Akwesasne, just south of Cornwall on the border between Canada and the United States. In 1899, the federal government sent a team of police officers into Akwesasne to force the Mohawks to accept the federal Indian Act and its model of elective councils. The Mohawks fought back, and there were confrontations and riots. A group of Mohawk chiefs were manacled by the police, and one Mohawk was shot dead by a police bullet.

In 1924, the federal government ordered the RCMP to remove the traditional leadership of the Six Nations Reserve in southwestern Ontario. In an effort to weaken the Mohawks and other Iroquois leaders on the reserve, the RCMP seized the sacred wampum that symbolized the traditional system of government. They expelled the traditional chiefs and imposed a system of elected chiefs. Police remained on the reserve for many years to enforce the rules of the Indian Act.

In the 1940s, the Mohawks continued to insist on their own sovereignty. When the federal government tried to draft Mohawks into the Canadian army, there was strong resistance. The RCMP raided the Kahnawake Reserve and tried to arrest a number of Mohawks, provoking further violent clashes.

Meanwhile, at the Six Nations Reserve, the Mohawks finally marched into their Council House in 1959 and ordered the elected chiefs to leave. The Indians (who, incidentally, called themselves "Mohawk warriors") established their own Iroquois police force to patrol the reserve. A week later, a group of sixty RCMP officers attacked the Council House and tried to arrest some of the key Mohawk leaders. There was a pitched battle between the Mohawks and the RCMP, leading to several injuries and a host of court cases.

Throughout the 1970s, there were similar conflicts. When the Quebec police began to patrol inside Kahnawake in 1973, the Mohawks stubbornly defended their territory, sparking a battle in which several Quebec police cars were damaged. In 1974, a group of Mohawks moved back to their traditional territory in the Adirondacks of northern New York state. There were tense confrontations with the New York state police for many months, until negotiations finally produced a settlement. Another armed standoff erupted in 1979 in Akwesasne when the New York police tried to arrest two Mohawks who had blocked the construction of a fence around the reserve. And there were further barricades and confrontations in the 1980s as a result of police raids at Kahnawake and Akwesasne.

In each case, the Mohawks were motivated by a simple belief: they are a sovereign people who have a legitimate right to govern themselves without foreign interference. Indeed, history confirms that the Mohawks have never signed any agreement to surrender their sovereignty. Moreover, they signed treaties with European countries which clearly recognized their sovereignty. It was not surprising, then, to see the Mohawks resisting another police attack on their traditional territory in the summer of 1990. It was the police who had failed to learn the lessons of history.

Throughout the seventy-eight days of the armed standoff at Oka, politicians begged Canada's aboriginal leaders to condemn the Mohawk warriors. The federal and provincial governments were determined to divide the Indian leadership, to convince Canadians that the warriors were a tiny fringe group with no broad support. But the national aboriginal leaders would not condemn the warriors. Even the moderate leaders were acutely aware that the warriors were expressing the frustrations of generations of aboriginal people. Their viewpoint was simple. Decades of peaceful action had achieved no fundamental justice. They sympathized with any aboriginal person who felt desperate enough to pick up a gun. In fact, some of the leaders had been warning of violence for years. Their refusal to condemn the violence, when it finally came as they had predicted, was a clear indication of the tremendous frustrations of aboriginal people across the country.

The barricades could never have endured for so many weeks if they had not been widely supported by Indian people. The barricade on the Mercier Bridge, for example, was supported by hundreds of Mohawks who were outraged at the police attack on the Mohawks of Oka. At the peak of the confrontation, the Mercier Bridge barricade was actively supported by eighty to ninety per cent of the residents of Kahnawake. It was further proof of the widespread Mohawk belief in sovereignty and nationhood — still the most powerful motivating force among the Mohawks of today.

Canadians often assume that their ancestors conquered the aboriginal people of this country. They assume that the Indians ultimately accepted the power and authority of the Europeans who established governments in Canada. But in reality, the aboriginal people of this country have never been conquered. They have never voluntarily surrendered their nationhood. And so, today, Canadians must face the same question that confronted their ancestors in the nineteenth century. Should the Indians be conquered by brute force and sheer weight of numbers? Or should they be regarded as independent people who can negotiate treaties with the representatives of other nations?

In the nineteenth century, Canadian officials chose to negotiate treaties with the Indians. They implicitly recognized the sovereignty of the aboriginal people. But in 1990, the governments of Canada and Quebec chose a very different course. They resolved the problem of Oka by sending in thousands of heavily armed soldiers in armoured personnel carriers and helicopters. Instead of recognizing Mohawk sovereignty and peacefully negotiating a modern-day treaty, the governments resorted to brute power. By doing so, they virtually guaranteed that the Mohawk rebellions would continue.

At the end of the Oka crisis, Prime Minister Brian Mulroney flatly rejected the most basic aspirations of the Mohawk people. In a speech to the House of Commons, he declared that the concept of aboriginal self-government "does not and cannot ever mean

sovereign independence." In effect, Mr. Mulroney had ruled out forever the fundamental objective of virtually every Mohawk in the country.

The prime minister's speech to the House of Commons was a perfect crystallization of the federal policies that had provoked the Oka crisis in the first place. Mr. Mulroney has never rejected the aspirations of other groups in the country. The Québécois, for example, have clearly enjoyed the right to self-determination, including the right to sovereignty if they choose that path. And yet the Mohawks were told that they were not entitled to the same fundamental rights. It was just another rejection of the goals and beliefs of aboriginal people, and it fuelled the growing sense of anger and grievance of Indians across the country.

The death of Meech Lake and the violent confrontation at Oka were just a foreshadowing of the potential consequences of the anger in Canada's aboriginal community. Ultimately, the frustration and rage of the aboriginal people is the result of centuries of persecution by Canada's official institutions. They have been patient for hundreds of years. As their unity and their determination grows stronger, they will begin to turn their attention to the injustices of recent history. They will seek compensation for the evils of residential schools and the destructive effects of hydro flooding. They will refuse to accept the slum housing and the lack of running water on the reserves. They will demand reforms to the child welfare system and the justice system. And if Canada continues to ignore the warning signs, the anger of the aboriginal people will be felt again.

In the hot days of August, in that eventful summer of 1990, a visitor from South Africa came to a remote Indian reserve in northwestern Ontario. The visitor was Archbishop Desmond Tutu, the anti-apartheid leader who has fought injustice in South Africa for decades. In his eloquent words to the Ojibway people of the Osnaburgh Reserve, he remarked on the similarities between Canada's treatment of its aboriginal people and South Africa's treatment of its Black majority. "When your nation lives a lie, God cannot allow that lie to prevail," he told the Ojibway band. "Because your cause is just, it will prevail. One day, you will be free in the way you want to be free."

When he toured the Osnaburgh Reserve, Tutu saw the same squalor and deprivation that he had seen in the townships and ghettos of South Africa. He saw flimsy shacks of wood and plastic with two or three families crowded into them. He saw the lack of running water and the diseases that resulted from the absence of basic sanitation. The people of Osnaburgh are forced to live "as if they were dirt," he said. "It distresses me. How is it possible anywhere?"

It was extraordinary that the Ojibways could still remain human under those living conditions, Tutu said. Yet the Osnaburgh Reserve is typical of hundreds of Indian reserves across Canada. The aboriginal people of Canada, like the Blacks of South Africa, have always been ignored and neglected by the official institutions of their society. It is a peculiar state of invisibility. "You are there and yet you are not there," Tutu told the Ojibways.

Today, the invisibility of Canada's aboriginal people is finally beginning to end. In this country, as in South Africa, a growing number of the indigenous people are turning to radical and militant tactics. For many, it has become the only way to gain the attention of the government. And the strategy is beginning to succeed. "Even when people have been oppressed and stood upon for years, one day they will stand up and enjoy their freedom," the South African bishop told the people of Osnaburgh. Then he led the Ojibways in a familiar chant — a chant from South Africa. The bishop and the Indians shouted it together: "We will be free."

EDMUND WHITE

Genet's *Prisoner of Love*

hen Jean Genet died in 1986, many people, especially outside France, were surprised to learn he hadn't died years before. Even in France the astonishment mounted when a few months after his death a long posthumous work, *Prisoner of Love*, was published. It was unlike anything Genet had written before and few people had even suspected he remained capable in his seventies of such a sustained effort. It was his first major work to be published in nearly twenty-five years.

The Screens, his last play, had been published in 1961 but it hadn't been staged in Paris until April 21, 1966. Since then Genet had published only a few articles and introductions, among them: the preface to the prison letters of George Jackson, a Black Panther; a notorious defence of the German Red Army faction; and a meditation on the slaughter of Palestinian refugees in Lebanon. He had also written two or three short essays about art, including one on Dostoevsky's *The Brothers Karamazov*.

In the English-speaking world almost nothing had been published by or about Genet in years except for the translation of a long interview that had been conducted by the German novelist Hubert Fichte. Little was known of Genet beyond the legend of the orphan and welfare child who had become a petty thief, jailbird, homosexual prostitute and vagabond and who in the forties had turned himself seemingly overnight into the author of five novels: *Our Lady of the Flowers*, *Miracle of the Rose*, *Funeral Rites*, *Querelle* and the semi-autobiographical *A Thief's Journal*.

This was the man Jean-Paul Sartre had made the subject of a massive "existential psychoanalysis," *Saint-Genet: Actor and Martyr*, a tome (some people said a "tomb") that appeared as the first volume of Genet's "complete works" when Genet was still only in his forties.

After a silence of several years in the late forties and early fifties, Genet reemerged as a playwright. To be sure, the theatre and cinema had been the art forms that had first intrigued him and even during his novel-writing years he'd finished two one-acts, *Deathwatch* and *The Maids*. Now he added to his theatrical œuvre three masterpieces — *The Blacks*, *The Balcony* and *The Screens* — which were played all over the world and which remain, along with the plays of Bertolt

Brecht and Joe Orton, the most substantial theatrical legacy of the post-war epoch.

Following that second burst of creativity Genet sank back into an obscurity he eagerly courted. He resolutely refused to give interviews (with only a few exceptions), to chat on television, to attend opening nights (even of his own plays) or in any other way to lead the life of a professional man of letters, an existence which is busier and more decorous in France than in any other country. As rigorously as the other three great writers living in France during those years — Samuel Beckett, Claude Simon and Julien Gracq — Genet cultivated silence and anonymity. A new portrait emerged in bits and pieces of a writer who was depressed (a suicide attempt was reported in the press), of someone who lived in cheap hotel rooms near train stations, of a man who seldom changed his clothes or bathed, who frequented street kids and fell out with such old literary friends as Cocteau (who'd discovered him) and Sartre (who'd made him famous).

The truth was that Genet *was* depressed in the sixties, especially after the death in 1964 of his lover, Abdallah, a high-wire artist, and Genet subsequently attempted suicide at least once. But in the late sixties and early seventies he took up an entirely new activity that engaged all his energies — backing the political aspirations of marginal groups. *Prisoner of Love* is a record of his years spent with the Black Panthers in the United States and Palestinian soldiers in Jordan and Lebanon. His involvement with the Panthers was substantially over by 1972 but his commitment to the Palestinians continued until his death.

In explaining the title of his book, Genet writes: "When I arrived to an enthusiastic welcome from the fedayeen, I probably wasn't clear headed enough to evaluate the opposing forces or make out the divisions within the Arab world. I ought to have seen sooner that aid to the Palestinians was an illusion. Whether it came from the Gulf or North Africa it was ostentations and declamatory, but flimsy.

"Gradually my feelings changed, especially after the 1973 war. I was still charmed, but I wasn't convinced; I was attracted but not blinded. I behaved like a prisoner of love...." In this passage Genet makes clear that his commitment was based on ties of affection, not ideology, and that not even disillusionment could weaken those ties.

As early as 1974 Genet had said in the Paris newspaper *Le Monde:* "It was completely natural for me to be attracted to the people who are not only the most unfortunate but also crystallize to the highest degree the hatred of the West." Almost ten years later Genet was interviewed by the Austrian journalist Rüdiger Wischenbart, who asked: "What was it that led you to become so deeply involved with the PLO? Previously, with the exception of the Black Panthers in the U.S. and the Red Army factions in West Germany, wasn't it relatively unusual for you to take such a concrete stand for a political group or movement?"

To which Genet replied: "What led me to it first of all is my personal history, which I don't care to go into, which is of no interest to anyone. If you want to know more about it, you can read my books. It's not all that important. But what I will say to you is that the books I wrote previously — I have stopped writing for over thirty years now — were all part of a dream or a day-dream. And since I outlived this dream, this day-dream, I had to take action in order to achieve a sort of fullness of life. You mentioned the Black Panthers, the German Army Faction, and the Palestinians. To be brief about it, I will say that I have immediately gone towards those who asked me to intercede. The Black Panthers came to Paris and asked me to go to the United States, which I did at once. For the Red Army faction, it was Klaus Croissant who came to ask me to intervene in favour of Baader. And ten years ago, it was Leila Shahid [a member of the editorial board of *Revue d'études palestiniennes*] who asked me to go to Beirut. Obviously, I am drawn to peoples in revolt. And this is very natural for me, because I myself have the need to call the whole of society into question."

This response reveals Genet's deliberateness about setting the record straight. He admits that political action filled the void left in his life when he was awakened from his reverie as an artist — a frank acknowledgement of his creative and personal despair, despite a reluctance to discuss it. He then points out that he was *invited* by each group to come to their aid, a point important to clarify lest he be blamed for embracing causes that were not his own. The radical rhetoric of the post-1968 era often rejected the sympathy of outsiders; Genet emphasizes that in each case his help was coherent with his own revolt against established forms of society. As he told Hubert Fichte, he was a Black who might look white or pink, but he was still a Black.

Genet's many imprisonments for "crimes" that never amounted to anything more serious than running away from school, boarding a train without a ticket or stealing a book had made him detest France. When he was only eighteen he'd served in the French army in Damascus, where he'd fallen in love with a younger hairdresser and where he played cards all night with Syrians — and where he first came to despise French colonialism. He'd joined the army in order to cut short the sentence he was serving at Mettray, a reform school near Tours. It didn't require a great leap of the imagination for him to see the link between the oppression he was suffering under French authority and the oppression of colonial peoples (Syria was under French control between the two world wars).

Nevertheless, to regard *Prisoner of Love* as a political tract would be a mistake. As Genet remarked in 1970 in the French periodical *Le Nouvel Observateur:* "I believe that Brecht did nothing for communism, that the revolution was not provoked by Beaumarchais' *The Marriage of Figaro.* The closer a work of art is to perfection, the more it turns in on itself. Still worse, it awakens a taste for the past."

In the same way, one could say that almost any statement about this dense, ambiguous book demands an instant retraction. Just before Genet began *Prisoner of Love* he published a short essay on *The Brothers Karamazov*, which he reads as a giant joke, rife with contradictions — a serious joke. As Genet puts it: "It seems to me, according to this reading, that every novel, poem, painting, piece of music that doesn't destroy itself, I mean that doesn't set itself up as an Aunt Sally in which it is one of the heads, is a fake."

What about the contradictions in his own book? One could say that it is a paean to two virile, male-dominated societies, which for Genet re-create the feudal, all-male worlds of his youth at Mettray, in the army and later in prison, and which gibe well with his persistent fantasies (related in his novels) about pirates, prison colonies, slave galleys, and the German military. It's important, however, to point out right away that *Prisoner of Love* is not an explicitly erotic work, even if nearly every page is warmed by Genet's admiration for these young men's courage, beauty and gaiety and intellectual and verbal inventiveness. His description of a singing contest among the Palestinian soldiers, for instance, in which their voices weave into an intricate, improvised polyphony, is full of love, but a love as chaste as Muslim puritanism might demand. As he writes, he recognizes the erotic waves of "smiling serenity" emanating from the fedayeen without being troubled by them. Perhaps, as he suggests, he is suddenly living amongst teenage men toting weapons and "adorned" with red berets tipped over one eye and leopard uniforms — their fulfillment makes those very fantasies weaken, dissolve: "The sudden appearance of a flock of living, laughing, independent infantrymen left me on the brink of purity. They were like a cloud, a barricade of angels come down to keep me from the edge of an abyss: for I realized at once, with joy, that I was going to be living in a vast barracks."

One night Genet stays awake until dawn debating the existence of God with a squadron of Palestinians. Another evening he has his hair cut in a camp, which serves as the occasion to bring together a group of weary, laughing fedayeen, who tease their elderly French friend in a mixture of literary Arabic, French and English. Genet records the scattered, feeble jokes, then adds in a tone that typifies the simple lyricism of his prose in this book: "They all laughed. And not only my shoulders but my knees as well were covered with snippets of white hair. The first stars came out, timidly in the beginning, then in armfuls all over the still purple sky and everything was more beautiful than I can say. And Jordan is only the Middle East! By now locks of my hair were falling down to my slippers."

But if Genet glorifies such all-male societies (they're the same desert desperadoes William Burroughs conjures up in *The Wild Boys*), he less predictably evidences a new interest in women, especially the noble,

warlike, self-effacing but devious Palestinian peasant women. His affection, to be sure, is directed to mothers, not daughters, but despite such limitations it's a lively enough curiosity, genuine and observant.

The contradictions proliferate. The book was commissioned in a casual way by Yasser Arafat, the head of the Palestinian Liberation Organization, but the text does everything but follow the party line. Genet even compares Arafat to Hitler at one point (only in the sense that every charismatic leader has a symbol, as Hitler his moustache, Churchill his cigar and Arafat his checked headcloth). Genet is also highly critical of the old Palestinian élite. And then in an interview he once went so far as to say: "The day the Palestinians become institutionalized, I will no longer be on their side. The day the Palestinians become a nation like other nations, I will no longer be there."

Such anarchic impulses originate in Genet's own past. He felt himself to be profoundly disinherited and his hatred of France was unrelenting, just as his sympathy for criminals and the outcast was unwavering. In the last incarnation of this Manicheanism, Genet placed on one side Israel, the United States, France and the conservative Arab states and on the other he put himself, the Panthers and the Palestinians.

This dichotomy is not based on anti-Semitism. Genet is clearly anti-Zionist and he sometimes claims that the Israelis are master manipulators of the media as well as of brainwashing techniques, but his objections are political, not racist. He attacks Israeli policies, not "Jewish traits" (the very phrase is racist). Of course many Jews think that no distinction can be made between Jews and Israelis, and such readers will doubtless consider *Prisoner of Love* a monstrous concoction.

Yet for a book about one of the most ideologically heated conflicts of modern times, *Prisoner of Love* is curiously cool and unpolemical. As always, Genet knows how to sink a probe into a politically sensitive area without proposing a cure or a procedure or even an opinion. In his play *The Blacks*, as Jeanette L. Savona points out in her book *Jean Genet*, the interest shifts between the "dreamlike world of the stage" and the "naturalistic backstage world of political action." It's a play that was *perceived* by Black theatrical troupes in the United States as a political statement, although it would be hard to extrapolate a clear directive from the action and dialogue. Similarly, *The Screens* created a violent reaction in the audience when it was first performed in France, since it was perceived as an insult to the French military in Algeria, which it clearly is, but there is no way the play can be fairly read as an endorsement of the Algerian Revolution. Genet was able to have it both ways — he appeared to be politically committed in his writing, but actually he maintained complete artistic independence.

Oddly, this very independence has a source that feminists and gay activists, say, would consider "political" (in the sense of heightened individual consciousness, not group enterprise). When Wischenbart asked Genet if he'd come to the Middle East as a spectator, he replied: "You said to me — and you were right — that very probably I had come as a spectator. When I was very young, I quickly understood that everything in life was blocked for me. I went to school until I was thirteen, to the local primary school. The most I could hope for was to become an accountant or a petty official. So I put myself in a position not to become an accountant, not to become a writer — I didn't know that yet — but to observe the world." Genet's writerly neutrality and acuity, in other words, represent a rejection of *petit bourgeois* values and an affirmation of independence and a passive resistance against the forces of order.

There is also a strictly aesthetic aspect. Genet has a strong sense of where his talent lies, and he knows it is a talent that begins with a rejection of slogans and heroics. In part his caution is due to a fear of unintentionally injuring the Panthers or the Palestinians. He recognizes how susceptible both groups are to misrepresentation in the press. But even deeper is his adherence to his personal skepticism and his original state as a loner and outsider.

Throughout his long career Genet maintained a purported admiration for *treachery* that I've never comprehended. I recognize that a prisoner might be *forced* to betray his friends, but how can one be *proud* of such a failing? Philosophically, Genet was no doubt being systematic in affirming everything that is negative, in reversing all values. But *humanly* what could such a claim mean?

When Genet in his novels insists he admires stoolpigeons and spies or traitors, could he simply be erecting a giant alibi for a strictly personal (and humiliating) lapse of his own? And yet I've never heard of a single charge of betrayal lodged against Genet. He may have broken cruelly with faithful friends, even stolen from them, but no one ever accused him of being an informer or traitor. In *A Thief's Journal* he admits to being an informer, but the confession may be bravado.

Finally I've decided that "treachery" is Genet's code word for the incorrigible subjective voice that can never be factored into the consensus. In *Prisoner of Love* he catches himself using words like "hero" and "martyr" and he admits that the Palestinians are responsible for a debasement of his vocabulary.

A page later Genet finds that the temptation to betray arises when people ignore the "collective emergency" and attend only to private desires. More than in any of his earlier books, Genet seeks in this one to honour the collective emergency, but in the end he remains true to his equally radical (and politically rooted) need for independence. Fidelity to oneself is treachery to the group; artistic quirkiness pokes holes in any political rhetoric.

A recurring theme in *Prisoner of Love* is an old man's longing for a home somewhere on a hill, say, in Cyprus where he can watch in perfect security a distant maritime battle, remote and toylike. At one point Genet daydreams about living in another house he sees in Jordan; when someone tells him he could rent it, the house instantly loses all its appeal. Elsewhere he mentions the house he built in his last years for his Moroccan friend Muhammad El Katrani in Morocco, but he regards it as a gift to the devil.

Of course neither the Panthers nor the Palestinians possess a home, a country. They are people without land, perennial exiles, who set up phantom bureaucracies and shadow administrations but who live in a permanent diaspora. As Genet told Tahar ben Jelloun, the Moroccan novelist: "As you know, I'm on the side of those who seek to have a territory, although I refuse to have one."

One of the repeated images of *Prisoner of Love* is a card game played without cards. Fearing a breakdown in company discipline, a Palestinian officer forbids card-playing. The men, to while away the time, go through the motions of gambling even without cards. At one point Genet even concedes that his having ended up with the Palestinians is the result of purest chance — a stroke of gambler's luck. This theme of absence — an active, organizing absence that takes on moral and aesthetic and psychological weight, like emptiness in Sung landscape painting — moves in every direction. Genet sees Blacks as the letters struck on the empty white page of America. He compares the shapes of his own life to the process of metalworking called "damascening," except in his case no gold has been poured into the hollows gouged out of the baser metal. The card game without cards is linked elsewhere to buffoonish Japanese rituals for propitiating (and amusing) the dead.

At one point Genet begins to wonder why he's been so courted by extremists. They must see him as someone who has suffered as they have. But then Genet asks himself whether he hasn't exaggerated his childhood misery, whether he isn't just a natural sham.

Abysses open up all around him. He wonders if the Palestinians aren't just a media event and the Panthers more an "act" than a real threat to American institutions. He asks: "By agreeing to go first with the Panthers and then with the Palestinians, playing my role as a dreamer inside a dream, wasn't I just one more factor of unreality inside both movements? Wasn't I a European saying to a dream, 'You are a dream — don't wake the sleeper'?"

Such questions "betray" the simple, heroic rhetoric of a revolutionary movement, but they are a way of staying "faithful" to a private, multifaceted vision of truth. They are also a part of Genet's investigation into the nature of propaganda and image-making. At one point Genet humorously remarks that the people we call compulsive liars are just those who fail to project their image with enough force.

All of these ways of "deconstructing" his book point to Genet's fascination with the French philosopher Jacques Derrida, whose book about Genet, *Glas,* imitates one of Genets earlier strategies of printing side by side two entirely different texts.

There are many threads that run through Genet's book, furnishing every page with a surprising toughness — surprising, given that there is no suspense, no plot, little history, and no straightforward chronology.

The characters Genet develops, however, are among his best and very much in his style — larger than life, mythic. Take Mubarak, the lieutenant from the Sudan who speaks French like Maurice Chevalier, who graduated from Sandhurst, whose cheeks are cicatrised with tribal scars, who reads Spinoza, dances to

African rock music and who, when Genet dares to ape him, responds by cruelly imitating Genet imitating him — a *tour de force* as clever as it is unsparing of Genet's age and limp. Curiously Mubarak is also a sort of double for Genet, his younger version, Black, virile, handsome, but just as playful and mercurial, just as cosmopolitan, disabused, philosophical and cultured — a man who strums an imaginary guitar.

But the true continuities of *Prisoner of Love* are the poetic figures that recur — Genet's admiration for those who risk sex-change operations, say. Genet's fluent mind permits him to associate the heroism of sex changes with the suicidal courage of Palestinian soldiers — or with the joy in the face of death expressed by Mozart's *Requiem*.

Death was always one of Genet's great themes. He thought a play should be performed just once, and that one time in a cemetery; he recommended that Giacometti's statues be buried in the ground as offerings to the dead. His first novel, *Our Lady of the Flowers*, ends with the death of Divine, the transvestite hero, and the condemnation to death of Our Lady, a young thug who has murdered an old man. Genet's first published work was a poem, "The Man Sentenced to Death," which he had printed at his own expense while still in prison. All of his other novels celebrate death and murder. In his plays death is staged in many modes. *The Screens*, for instance, ends with most of the many characters, Algerians and French colonials alike, bursting through screens into the afterlife, where they laugh together with eerie complicity. Under the sign of eternity, everything becomes comic. As Genet once remarked, "What is not futile in this world? I'm asking you: what is not futile in the last analysis?"

I've spoken of a few of the many contradictions in *Prisoner of Love*, but perhaps the most obvious one is that it is a religious statement by a non-believer, a bible written by a devil. Genet always pursued his own peculiar destiny as a mystical atheist, a saint complete with miracles, ecstasies, visions and stigmata but no deity and precious few good works. Sartre may tend to dismiss Genet's claims of saintliness, but many pages in *A Thief's Journal* leave little doubt that Genet was perfectly serious:

Though saintliness is my goal, I cannot tell what it is. My point of departure is the word itself, which indicates the state closest to moral perfection. Of which I have known nothing, except that without it my life would be vain. Unable to arrive at a definition of saintliness — no more than of beauty — I want at every moment to create it, that is, to act so that everything I do may lead me to what is unknown to me, so that at every moment I may be guided by a will to saintliness until the time when I am so luminous that people will say, "He is a saint," or more likely, "He *was* a saint." I am being led to it by a constant groping. No method exists. It is only obscurely and with no other proofs than the certainty of achieving saintliness that I make the gestures leading me to it.... Like beauty — and poetry — with which I merge it, saintliness is singular. Its expression is original. Yet it seems to me that its sole basis is renunciation. But I wish to be a saint because, above all, the word indicates the loftiest human attitude, and I shall do all to succeed.

In *Prisoner of Love* there is no statement about saintliness quite so direct, but only because Genet assumes he's already become a saint. He talks of his complete renunciation of things — he aspires to own but one pair of trousers, one shirt, one pair of shoes, nothing more. He experiences a miracle in Istanbul when his body lights up from within. He speaks of himself almost offhandedly in tones usually reserved for God. In referring to why he lives amongst the Palestinians, he writes: "I might as well admit that by staying with them I was staying — I don't know how, how else, to put it — in my own memory. By that rather childish expression I don't mean I lived and remembered previous lives. I'm saying as clearly as I can that the Palestinian revolt was among my oldest memories. 'The Koran is eternal, uncreated, consubstantial with God.' Setting aside the word 'God,' their revolt was eternal, uncreated, consubstantial with me."

Like a *marabout*, a Muslim saint, he seems to expect that his tomb will become an important shrine and he finds nothing odd in a Palestinian soldier's wish to have his bones after his death. Genet imagines his bones will be carried about by the Palestinians until they recapture their homeland and can bury them beside the Dead Sea. (Abdelkebir Khatibi recounts that he once captured Genet's imagination by telling him about the cult of Muslim saints who'd been born Portuguese but who'd betrayed their own people in order to lead the Moroccans against the Christians in the holy wars.)

Elsewhere Genet sees himself as a dwarf shuffling off towards the horizon, a derelict old holy man being absorbed into the elements, an entranced Sufi.

Genet's ideas of sanctity dovetail with his ideas of individual worth. When he first began writing, his sovereign imagination and his brand of Romanticism (a sophisticated and highly philosophical reworking of Decadence) blinded him to the existence of other people except as shadow puppets of desire. As the quotation from *A Thief's Journal* reveals, for the Genet of that period "Saintliness is singular" and its expression original.

Then one day, during a train ride, Genet had a revelation. He was seated in a third-class compartment opposite a dirty, ugly little man — and suddenly Genet felt a strange exchange of personalities with this stranger. Genet flowed into the man's body at the same time as the man flowed into Genet's body. Genet suddenly realized that everyone is of the same value — Raskolnikov's revelation in *Crime and Punishment*. If this insight struck Genet particularly forcefully, perhaps it did so because he'd never previously even considered such a possibility.

In *Prisoner of Love* the tension between the Romantic cult of the unique individual and the Christian faith in spiritual equality is reconciled in the central quest of the book. In the early seventies Genet spent just twenty-two hours in the house of a Palestinian soldier named Hamza and his mother. Ever after he was haunted by thoughts of them — of Hamza going off in the night on a mission, of the mother coming to Genet's bedside with a cup of Turkish coffee, as she must have come to her sleeping son many times to awaken him. In Genet's mind the mother and son become reworked as emblems of the pietà in which sometimes Genet himself figures as the son (he recalls certain sculptures in which Mary is represented as younger than her crucified son). The images of the pietà become stronger over the years when Genet hears rumours that Hamza has been tortured and killed. At last Genet, fourteen years later and towards the end of the book (and his own life), revisits the mother and learns that Hamza is living safely in Germany, but this information in no way weakens Genet's conception of the holiness of this couple.

Psychologically Genet's reverence for Hamza's mother resolves his own feelings of rage at his real mother for having abandoned him. Even when Genet was in his sixties he told someone that if he knew where his mother was buried he'd spit on the grave — a remarkable fury against an unmarried servant girl who'd kept her child with her for seven months until poverty had forced her to hand him over to Public Welfare. She died during the influenza epidemic of 1919 when she was thirty and Genet nine (Genet may never have known when and how she died).

Philosophically Genet recognizes that Hamza and his mother are simply two more people in an overpopulated planet. She may possess a rare natural courtesy and may speak the purest Arabic, but Genet doesn't prize her for these qualities. Rather, like a lover, he lists the beloved's virtues after the fact to justify (or elaborate) his love, which is as strong as it is inexplicable. Love is the form of captivity that permits us at one and the same time to see the universality *and* the particularity of a person. Love reconciles Genet's feelings that everyone is of equal value and that each person is priceless. As Genet puts it, emotions live on and only the people who entertain them die: "The happiness of my hand in the hair of a boy another hand will know, already knows, and if I die this happiness will go on."

Such is the wisdom of a book that a philosopher compared recently in a seminar to the Bible. Like the Bible, *Prisoner of Love* is about chosen people (Panthers, Palestinians) without a homeland. Like the Bible, Genet's book is polyvalent, inconsistent, an invitation to exegesis. Like the Bible it is a book of memory, of names. It alternates serenity and bellicose hate, history and poetry, epic and lyricism. Like the Bible it is the Only Book, one meant to be read again and again and that is constructed canonically, as though the first-time reader has already read it. Indeed Genet has invented a new sort of book altogether — a new kind of prose and a new genre. The prose is sometimes ruminative, almost grumbling, like that of the late Céline, the man most French critics believe is Genet's only rival as a stylist in the twentieth century after Proust. Like the Céline of *Castle to Castle* or *Rigadoon*, Genet backs into his subjects, starts talking around something long before he identifies it. Like Céline, Genet appears to be casual and conversational, but through recurrence he heightens each subject until it turns mythical.

Genet always constructed his fiction like cinematic montage, alternating one story with one or two others. In *Prisoner of Love* the intercutting becomes rapid, constant, vertiginous — a formal device for showing the correspondences between elements where no connection had been previously suspected. In two pages Genet can make unexpected links between Mozart's scatology, a desire for a house, the prudish way the early Church Fathers referred to the Virgin's breast, the invisible cell that glided about around Saint Elizabeth, Queen of Hungary, the words of a Sufi poet, and so on.

In Genet's novels the poet's urge to uncover correspondences is encoded in brilliant metaphors. In *Prisoner of Love* metaphors have been replaced by a different method — radical juxtaposition without copula, that is, the tight sequencing of different subjects without transition. This method emphasizes the sovereignty of the observer — makes him into a god.

The genre established by Genet is a curious mixture of memoir, tract, stylized Platonic dialogue based on actual conversation, allegorical quest, epic. Written when Genet knew he was already afflicted with terminal throat cancer, the book necessarily makes us think of Chateaubriand's *Memoirs from Beyond the Grave*. Like Chateaubriand, who wrote about his years of poverty in London when he was the overfed ambassador to Britain, Genet is careful to establish the conditions under which he is composing his book and to distinguish them from the circumstances he is narrating. Like Chateaubriand, who lived through many different regimes and who rose and fell in favour more than once, Genet is a non-aligned observer of political events. And like Chateaubriand, who could separate Napoleon's true genius from the idol people made of him after he was deposed, Genet is never taken in by legends.

But again even the persona of the narrator in *Prisoner of Love* is torn with contradictions. He may be a seer but he is also a sham, a naïve outsider, a burden, a big pink baby in the strong arms of Black or tan fathers. He is also Homer, and the soldiers are his Hectors and Achilles. Chateaubriand quotes, in speaking of Napoleon, an imaginary epitaph from the Greek Anthology: "Don't judge Hector by his small tomb. The *Iliad*, Homer, the Greeks in flight, there's my sepulchre: I am buried under all these great actions." Homer may be a blind, weak, ancient poet, but the glory of even the wiliest warrior depends on his frail voice. Genet often makes explicit reference to his Homeric powers; in a thousand years people will know of the Palestinian exodus only in his version.

ROBERT STONE

The Red Universe

Stephen Crane and *The Red Badge of Courage*

oth Stephen Crane and *The Red Badge of Courage* have a quality of mystery. The process of composition is always mysterious, but here the term applies particularly.

In the winter of 1893, a twenty-two-year-old from New Jersey, a youth of literary and bohemian pretensions living at the Art Students League, announced to his friends that he proposed to write an "historical romance, a pot-boiler" about the American Civil War. Young Stephen Crane had a painter friend named Linson with whom he sometimes attempted collaboration on humour pieces that left most editors unamused. Linson owned a set of *Century Magazine's* series "Battles and Leaders of the Civil War," which he had stacked on a divan in one corner of his studio. Over the freezing winter months, Crane, whose impoverished style of living quite threatened his health, browsed the magazines and began writing a novel while Linson painted. Sometimes, stationery being unaffordable, he wrote on butcher paper. Later Linson remembered Crane squatting among the stacked magazines and complaining about the war memoirs: "I wonder that *some* of these fellows don't tell how they *felt* in those scraps! They spout eternally of what they *did* but they are emotionless as rocks!"

It turned out that Crane was not good at "pot-boilers," lacking the appropriate patience, discipline, and sensibility. Perhaps for the same reasons, he was already showing very little promise as a newspaperman. In fact, by 1893 Crane had already written one highly unsuitable novel, called *Maggie: A Girl of the Streets.* Rather than make his fortune, Crane had spent every penny of his schoolboy savings to have it privately printed. Dealing with slum life in and around the Bowery, *Maggie* was not considered a respectable publication, and only its obscurity spared the young author involvement in a scandal.

With the publication of this unlikely youth's second book, *The Red Badge of Courage*, American literature entered the modernist age. Like all great works, *The Red Badge of Courage* can claim the whole of literature as antecedent and remain unique. Perhaps there are earlier novels that have so combined psychological intimacy with dense external detail. Few since have done it so simply and surely and eloquently. The effect is of light, the clear light of nature illuminating an utterly realized landscape. Clarity is the essence, clarity of thought and of description.

William Dean Howells, who was one of Crane's earliest and strongest supporters, liked to say that Crane's genius had "sprung to life fully armed," like Athena. But Athena sprang from the head of a god. *The Red Badge of Courage* and its author seem to have appeared out of the seamless American ether. Stendhal had seen Marengo and Moscow in flames. Tolstoy had commanded troops in the Caucasus. Crane's most strenuous experience before the composition of *The Red Badge of Courage* seems to have been a semester catching for the Syracuse University baseball team.

Today *The Red Badge of Courage* is in the canon, as it should be, an educational rite of passage. High-school students continue to receive it as an assignment, and many of its young readers discover what the rest of us may have forgotten: that its power is shattering and undiminished by time. To reread it after many years is a rich and disturbing experience.

There is a tragic irony in the fact that so many of the young have had *The Red Badge of Courage* thrust on them. As everyone remembers, it is a novel about youth's experience of war by a young writer who himself had no such experience. Most of its first-time readers are approaching the end of their adolescence. If they are open to books, they can hardly resist identifying with its young soldier-protagonist, Henry Fleming. He stands on the brink of adulthood at its most terrifying and dangerous, facing the most dreaded and celebrated of all human endeavours. So accomplished is the realism that it persuades completely. How many who have read *The Red Badge of Courage* in high school over the years — it's impossible not to wonder

— from Belleau Wood to Bastogne to Phu Bai, have approached their first battle thinking of Henry and hoping to share his pilgrimage and survival? Yet down the generations comes this surly objection, this adolescent murmur, "He wasn't there." It's a muted objection because of the book's uncanny power, but it's always present.

Modern readers, the sort of readers that Crane was in a sense creating, highly value authenticity. We've been trained to it. Crane's heir and disciple Hemingway, with his anti-intellectualism and his vanity, claimed to set great store by authenticity. But if the existence of *The Red Badge of Courage* proves anything, it's that fiction justifies itself entirely on its own terms. For reasons we imperfectly understand, Crane in Linson's studio was seized by inward visions of hallucinatory intensity which, through the strength and simplicity of his language, he was able to transmit intact to his readers. It is as good an example of the primary process of fiction as literature affords. Mysterious though it is, it represents a unitary personal vision about which we may make certain observations.

One consistently fascinating quality of the narrative is its psychological sureness. Of young Henry Fleming we read:

He had, of course, dreamed of battles all his life — of vague and bloody conflicts that had thrilled him with their sweep and fire. In visions he had seen himself in many struggles. He had imagined peoples secure in the shadow of his eagle-eyed prowess. But awake he had regarded battles as crimson blotches on the pages of the past. He had put them as things of the bygone with his thought-images of heavy crowns and high castles. There was a portion of the world's literary history which he had regarded as the time of wars, but it, he thought, had been long gone over the horizon and had disappeared forever.

From his home his youthful eyes had looked upon the war in his country with distrust. It must be some sort of a play affair. He had long despaired of witnessing a Greeklike struggle. Such would be no more, he had said. Men were better, or more timid. Secular and religious education had effaced the throat-grappling instinct, or else firm finance held in check the passions.

This passage is really much more complicated than Crane makes it seem, and it does a number of things at once. While involving the reader's imagination in the character's situation, it simultaneously defines the character, telling much that we need to know about young Henry's education, inner life, and cast of mind. As the narrative proceeds, the intensity and vividness increase. Things take on a coloration that the reader only gradually recognizes as fear. The key word is "recognizes." Little by little, the reader is displaced by Henry Fleming. Before it is declared, Henry's growing fear surprises and overtakes us. Then:

A little panic-fear grew in his mind. As his imagination went forward to a fight, he saw hideous possibilities. He contemplated the lurking menaces of the future, and failed in an effort to see himself standing stoutly in the midst of them. He recalled his visions of broken-bladed glory, but in the shadow of the impending tumult he suspected them to be impossible pictures.

In the darkness of the night before his first flight:

He wished, without reserve, that he was at home again making the endless rounds from the house to the barn, from the barn to the fields, from the fields to the barn, from the barn to the house. He remembered that he had often cursed the brindle cow and her mates, and had sometimes flung milking stools. But, from his present point of view, there was a halo of happiness about each of their heads, and he would have sacrificed all the brass buttons on the continent to have been enabled to return to them. He told himself that he was not formed for a soldier. And he mused seriously upon the radical differences between himself and those men who were dodging implike around the fires.

From this point on the reader's fortunes are Henry's, not only for the rest of the book but, as it were, for life. That is why so many young soldiers — perhaps astonished to find themselves soldiers, having thought, incorrectly, that men had become better, or more timid — have so closely pondered *The Red Badge of Courage*. But even if war stopped coming back for more unlucky generations, its power would hold.

How did Crane do it? How does genius do what it does, know what it knows? One thing is certain: young Stephen Crane there in Linson's studio had a number of the elements required for a great novel. For one thing he was prodigiously gifted. For another he had a vision of life and the world, complete and thoroughgoing. At the mere age of twenty-two he may not have had the right to one, but he had it all right: *The Red Badge of Courage* is its artistic rendering.

Part of genius is timing. The disaster of Crane's premature death obscures his placement in literary history. If all had gone differently he might have sat with Robert Frost as an ancient of the arts at President Kennedy's inauguration. He was roughly contemporary with Frost, and with Joyce and Pound. He belonged to the century he never lived to see. He was that Anglo-Saxon phenomenon, the minister's child, the preacher's kid or "PK," as they said at Syracuse University when Crane attended. The language of overcoming, of elevated striving and moral improvement, was in his childhood's ear. His talent, together

with his vision, turned that language into something wonderful.

The Reverend Jonathan Townley Crane, D.D., Stephen's father, did not possess his son's gifts but was also an author. *Popular Amusements* (1869) was one of his books. *Arts of Intoxication* (1870) was another. (He was against them.) Dr. Crane followed these up with *Holiness, The Birthright of All God's Children* (1874). (He was in favour.) When Stephen was not yet nine, Jonathan died prematurely, and this may have had quite a lot to do with the vision that informs *The Red Badge of Courage*.

The vision is of what Stephen Crane elsewhere called the Red Universe. It is a spectre of the world as never-ending struggle, a struggle that must be endured and even embraced. In it, life is hard and unforgiving, without security, without peace. Yet in the very inferno is a great beauty that can belong to the strong. That is what *The Red Badge of Courage* is about: the earth as battleground and field of blood, terrible, infinitely desirable. At the close of the book Henry Fleming is rewarded with a vision for the courage he ultimately displays after running away. He sees things as they are in their dreadful majesty. He believes he has the courage now to accept them:

> With this conviction came a store of assurance. He felt a quiet manhood, nonassertive but of sturdy and strong blood. He knew that he would no more quail before his guides wherever they should point. He had been to touch the great death, and found that, after all, it was but the great death. He was a man.

Thus life as pilgrim's progress, as a moral journey. Reading it we are reminded that Stephen Crane was also a contemporary of Neitzsche and Theodore Roosevelt. Perhaps we have learned a few things over the past hundred years. We too hope that men will become better, or more timid.

Of course it is not possible to say what formed Stephen Crane's vision of the world as war. We can speculate about the loss of his father or premonition of his own early death or prophecy of the next century itself. In his day Americans were forgetting what they had learned about war at Chancellorsville and Gettysburg. They were reaching out, growing adventurous again. They sang about the fateful lightning, but they had forgotten what it was like.

"War when you are at it is horrible and dull," Oliver Wendell Holmes, late of the 20th Massachusetts Volunteers, told a Harvard graduating class in 1895. "It is only when time has passed that you see that its message was divine." A war with Spain was only a couple of years away, and some in his audience would be in it. For the neo-Roman republic, an imperial age was beginning. Crane himself had only a short time to live. He had inherited his father's constitution and undermined it, partly by his never-ending journeys to every available war in quest of authenticity. As combat correspondent in the Balkans and Cuba, he bent his descriptive powers to the service of Hearst and Pulitzer. He always felt he had to justify writing *The Red Badge of Courage* without having been there.

When Stephen Crane died young in 1900, the United States saw itself as young also, setting out on a great journey. If our young friend Henry Fleming survived the war, he would no doubt have learned in time that life resists the unitary vision. Fiction will probably always pursue it nevertheless, doubtless in vain but as gloriously as possible. And in it we can be sure that courage — peremptory, embarrassing word — will always be required.

HILLMAN DICKINSON

T. E. Lawrence and Guerrilla Warfare

Lieutenant Colonel Dickinson was a student at the U.S. Army War College, Carlisle Barracks, Pennsylvania, in 1967 when he wrote this essay.

"I deem him one of the greatest beings alive in our time. I do not see his like elsewhere. I fear whatever our need we shall never see his like again." – *Winston Churchill*

"Do use me as a text to preach for more study of books and history, a greater seriousness in military art.... With 2,000 years of examples behind us we have no excuse when fighting, for not fighting well." – *T.E. Lawrence*

"How few nevertheless profit by that experience. Because he did, T.E. Lawrence not only earns a place among the masters of war, but stands out among them by the clearness of his understanding of his art." – *B.H. Liddell Hart*

n the world of today an understanding of the art of guerrilla warfare is vital to the soldier, essential to the statesman, necessary to a wide range of government officials, and useful to the well-educated man. Among guerrilla leaders T.E. Lawrence ranks as one of the most successful and as first in the quality of his writing. There is little excuse for ignoring Lawrence's experience or his lucid explanations of guerrilla strategy and tactics.

Although Lawrence was a great proponent of airpower and modern weapons, he believed that guerrilla warfare was relatively invulnerable to counteraction based principally on the use of airpower. He visualized the properly organized guerrilla force as "an intangible vapour" which presents few if any worthwhile targets to sophisticated weapons systems. Both the U.S.S.R. and Communist China have incorporated guerrilla war as a cornerstone of national strategy. The Chinese description of the United States as a "paper tiger" is probably based in part on the belief that sophisticated weapons are ineffective against guerrilla and subversive force. Throughout the world guerrilla warfare has already proven to be well suited to this age of limited warfare.

What causes then have led to so great a contrast between the worth of Lawrence's deeds, theories, and writings and the small awareness of them in this country? He devised and inspired the strategy and tactics of the World War I Arab revolt against the Turks. He "led" that revolt through advice and example. He made the struggle for Arab independence an integral, valued part of the Allied World War I campaign to defeat Turkey. His methods produced for the Arabs a favourable casualty ratio of more than one hundred to one. During the last weeks of the war, the Arabs held immobile and surrounded twelve thousand Turks in Medina while defeating in the north the 4th Turkish Army numbering forty thousand. Not a single British "advisor," flyer, or soldier was killed.

During the early stages of the war between twenty-five thousand and one hundred thousand Turks were killed, wounded, and captured or tied down. Lawrence and his Arabs destroyed fifty-seven bridges and over twenty-five trains in 1917 alone. Later, twenty-five bridges were destroyed in one fourteen-day period in 1918. Huge lengths of rail and telegraph line, much rolling stock, and numerous stations were destroyed.

Arab forces were approximately ten thousand but seldom more than six hundred men were committed at one time. During the last few days they were joined by as many as three thousand local residents. A few hundred additional British and French soldiers were involved in supporting roles or as associated regular troops during certain missions. British naval support was used when possible. One source reports the total Arabs killed in action during the entire war as less than four hundred but records may be unreliable. British advisors seldom exceeded one per thousand Arabs.

Such successful results deserved emulation. Since World War I Lawrence's strategy and tactics have been followed by his relative, Orde Wingate, by Field Marshall Wavell, by Albanian guerrilla leader Julian Amery (who wrote, "Our masters were Lawrence and Wingate"), and by many other guerrilla leaders. Most significantly B.H. Liddell Hart has noted in an article in *The Marine Corps Gazette*:

> The widespread use of guerrilla warfare in World War II can be attributed principally to the deep impression that Lawrence made on Churchill and which led him soon after the withdrawal from France to make it Britain's policy to utilize guerrilla warfare as an immediate counter to the German advances.

Lawrence continued his work after the end of World War I to secure a reasonable settlement for the Arab cause. Sir Henry McMahon remembered him at the 1919 peace conference in Paris as the only person who appeared to know everyone and everything and who had access to the "Big Three," Clemenceau, Lloyd George and Woodrow Wilson. He assisted in devising methods for pacifying areas of continuing unrest. He personally directed certain of these actions. Churchill said of his efforts at the 1921 Cairo conference, "His purpose prevailed."

How then can the strategic worth of his writings be so erratically known? For example, his works are virtually unknown among many career military officers in this country. His works are infrequently listed in the multitude of guerrilla warfare bibliographic lists. He is not mentioned in encyclopaedias published in the United States. In contrast, the *Encyclopaedia Britannica* still carries Lawrence's own description of guerrilla warfare, and Sargent Schriver quotes him in explaining the fundamental concepts of the Peace Corps.

Undoubtedly, the reasons for such contrasts are diverse. Apparently it is difficult for many persons to realize that *Seven Pillars of Wisdom*, a major classic of English literature, can also be a classic of military strategy in an area of current interest. It is certainly true that Lawrence was the object of numerous smears and disparaging articles written, for the most part, by persons who had no first-hand knowledge of his accomplishments and who were proponents of groups whose aims he opposed. Among such groups are the French whose aims in the Mid-East he opposed, the Indians whose aims he opposed in the same area, the supporters of Ibn Saud, certain Zionist groups who opposed any supporter of the Arab cause (in spite of Lawrence's admiration for and support of Dr. Weizmann and many Zionist aims), and certain groups in Britain who supported extreme forms of British colonialism. It is moreover true that Lawrence lived an unconventional, masochistic, aesthetic life. He worked before, during, and immediately after the war on projects for British Intelligence and for the British Foreign Office. Because of these connections certain actions were not clearly explained for many years and some pertinent facts may still not have been released. Combined with adventures that were in truth ultra-romantic, these facts have led to the creations (particularly in the illustrated lecture and the motion-picture media) of an image which is seldom penetrated by the serious student of guerrilla warfare.

Lawrence organized his thoughts by separating consideration of the strategical view (or overall view of each factor relative to the whole effort) from the tactical view (of arrangements designed as a means to the end). From these two classical viewpoints he then examined the three elemental categories to which he assigned major importance: the algebraical, the biological, and the psychological. The general usefulness of these three categories in military thought is only gradually being realized today. His emphasis on the importance of psychological factors was a major innovation in modern military practice.

Algebraical factors are those which can be quantitatively expressed. They include factors of terrain, mobility of units, weapon firepower, logistics and average effectiveness of military units. In short, under this title Lawrence included all those items which today are considered proper for inclusion in a quantitative war game or system study.

He clearly differentiated between these algebraical factors and the biological factors in war. By biological he meant the uncertain factors which cannot be quantitatively expressed. As the term biological implied, these factors are typical of the affairs of man but he also applied the term generally to other factors which cannot be quantitatively expressed. Under this heading fell the various factors which make handling man in battle an art — the incalculable variabilities, illogics, brilliance, heroism, or failings which make all estimates uncertain. These then are the factors which the systems analyst can handle, if at all, only in an inadequate way — inadequate because the genius of leadership can dramatically warp the average in any single real-life situation. The commander's reserve is the traditional hedge against the vagaries which may result from the biological factors. Lawrence believed that nine-tenths of leadership and tactics were algebraically certain and could be learned but that the biological, the incalculable one-tenth, was the test of a commander's instinct and could be developed only through continued practice of the mind.

Psychological factors formed his third category. Both mass psychology and individual psychology were elevated to major importance in his thought and practice. The importance of arranging men's minds in order of battle was elevated to equal importance with the physical arrangement of an order of battle. Next

After the triumph :— which was not so much a triumph as homage by Allenby to the mastering spirit of the place —— we drove back to Shea's headquarters. The A.D.C.'s pushed about, and from great baskets drew a lunch varied and elaborate and succulent. On us fell a short space of quiet, to be suddenly shattered by Monsieur Picot, the French political officer (permitted by Allenby to march beside Clayton in the entry) who said in his fluting voice "And tomorrow, my dear General, I will take the necessary steps to set up civil government in this town."

It was the bravest word on record, and a silence fell on us, as when they opened the seventh seal in heaven. Salad and chicken mayonnaise and foie gras sandwiches hung in our mouths unmunched, while we turned our round eyes on Allenby and waited. Even he seemed for the moment at a loss; we began to fear that the idol might betray a frailty...... but then he grew red and swallowed: his chin coming forward in the way we loved, and he said firmly "In the military zone the only authority is that of the commander in chief, MYSELF." "But Sir Edward Grey—" began M. Picot feebly. He was cut short. "Sir Edward Grey referred to the civil government which will be established when I judge that the military situation permits": and then we got into our cars again and in the sunshine of a great thankfulness sped down the mountain side into our saluting camp.

Manuscript page from *Seven Pillars of Wisdom*

was the important effort to arrange the mind of the enemy soldier and beyond that to arrange the minds of the citizens of the friendly nations, citizens of the hostile nation, and neutral onlookers as well. Current psychological warfare doctrine has closely followed this pattern.

Lawrence established a logical pattern of thought which is classic in simplicity and generality. His thinking reflects a most exceptional familiarity with original military writings — the classics of military history. At Oxford he had branched from his interest in medieval fortifications to readings such as Creasey's *Fifteen Decisive Battles of the World*, Henderson's *Stonewall Jackson*, Mahan's *Influence of Sea-Power on History*, Napier's *History of War in the Peninsula*, and Cox's *Marlborough*. He studied the classic strategists to include Procopius (Belisarius's military secretary who advocated indirect means for avoiding pitched battles and describes the hit-and-run tactics which broke the morale of Gothic lancers and archers), Demetrius, Poliorcetes, Vegetius, Napoleon, Clausewitz, Saxe (his favourite and the source of the idea that war can be won without fighting battles), Guibert, Caemerrer, Moltke, Van der Goltz, Jomini, Willisen, and Bourcet (the proponent of flexible alternatives in every plan, Bourcet apparently existed in only one copy in England, and that was in the War Office). It is surprising to note that in spite of many similarities between Sun Tzu's strategy and that of Lawrence, he apparently had not read the translation of Sun Tzu which was made in 1910 at the British Museum, probably because from this time until 1914 he was fully engaged in archaeological work in the Mid-East.

In addition to his reading, Lawrence had, during holidays, visited a number of battlefields in England and France. He had followed in detail the actions of the Crusades. These readings and experiences were added to more than three years experience as a field archaeologist in Syria and Egypt during which time he directed more than two hundred Arab helpers and developed close ties with many important Arabs and Kurds. He performed tasks for the British government ranging from assisting in protective preparations for the consulate in Aleppo, when a Kurdish revolt threatened in Syria, to assisting in the preparation of a map of the Sinai for British Intelligence.

Such was the background of information from which emerged his military strategy and tactics. It was a background of detailed area knowledge coupled with a lack of prejudice for specific military practice and fashions. Lawrence was uniquely equipped with background fact and experience and uniquely free from conservative pressures — free from a preference for the familiar which might inhibit innovation.

Lawrence's methods did not constitute a reversal of principles but were a dramatic reversal of military practice. Indeed for this very reason his practice illuminates the most basic aspects of "the principles." Perhaps most remarkable was his clarity of thought in the selection of his ultimate objective — "unmistakably geographic, to occupy all Arabic-speaking lands in Asia," as he wrote in his article, "The Science of Guerrilla Warfare," which appeared in the 1930 edition of the *Encyclopaedia Britannica.* All events and elements of the irregular war were analyzed with this aim always in view. Carried to their logical limit the conclusions were often startling. For he reasoned (in the classic method of indirect proof) if the enemy left Arabia quietly, then the war would end. Therefore, it was impossible that the killing of the enemy or the destruction of his military units could be the ultimate objective. Rather such actions could only be courses of action or means to the end, to the fundamental objective — control of the land.

Lawrence's strategic genius is rooted in his ability to make fundamental re-evaluations of the utility of possible actions in the light of his objective. In particular, Lawrence realized that, to the Turks, equipment was more precious than men. Further, he saw that a dearth of transport equipment could immobilize and demoralize the Turkish Army by accentuating the shortage of materiel. He then applied the maxim (applied usually to manpower and firepower): "Be superior at the critical point and moment of attack." However, he chose to apply it to one type of materiel — to empty stretches of railroad, to vulnerable rolling stock, and to rail stations. In a classic but intentionally over-simple calculation Lawrence computed that a Turkish post of twenty men was need to control each of the Arabs' one hundred and twenty thousand square miles. The requisite six hundred thousand-man Turkish strength was far above the available one hundred thousand. Hence, he concluded, success was obtainable.

Lawrence was wary of conclusions reached by analogy yet was a master in the use of analogy to illustrate his concepts stimulatingly and simply. From Mahan he learned that, as he wrote in 1930 in "The Evolution of Revolt" in the first issue of *The Army Quarterly,* "he who commands the sea is at great liberty, and may take as much or as little of the war as he will." By analogy he substituted the word desert for sea. Guerrilla practice since Lawrence has added validity to the analogy and generalized to include the words jungle and difficult terrain as well as desert. (Recent Chinese writing has taken up this cry — use the countryside to encircle and finally capture the cities.)

Reasoning from his premises to the extreme conclusion, Lawrence became convinced that the ultimate economy of force could be achieved in fact by being everywhere, except at the critical point, and in everything, except key equipment, weaker than the enemy. Thus he determined to reverse the practice of maintaining enemy contact and instead fight a war of detachment containing the enemy by the silent threat of a vast unknown desert. To be sure, the detachment was one-sided since the Arabs continued to obtain detailed information about the Turk. As a result of such strategy, the ultimate in security, simplicity, and mobility was achieved for the Arab force. Since the Arab Army had too few of both men and materials the strategy was a masterful turning of weakness into strength. Moreover, the war of detachment prevented casualties and the resultant "widening ripples of sorrow" which were destructive of force and home morale. It is impressive tribute to the success of the strategy that many Turks on the Arab front never had a chance to fire a shot while, paradoxically, the Arabs were never on the defensive.

A clearly implied requirement of the strategy of detachment is a major effort to reduce the biological — the uncertain — element in war. Faultless intelligence allows planning with certain knowledge of enemy capability. Lawrence's personal efforts to obtain intelligence were coupled to his efficient development and organization of intelligence and counterintelligence sources. His genius of leadership was nurtured by a remarkable ability to reduce the unknown of enemy, terrain, men, and equipment. As the corollary to reducing his own uncertainty he emphasized every effort which magnified the uncertainty facing the enemy.

The strategy of detachment was tied to an effective counterintelligence effort and to development plans which allowed flexibility in execution. As he wrote in 1923 to Colonel E.P. Wavell (later Field Marshal):

There is one thing of which every rebellion is mortally afraid — treachery. If instead of counter-propaganda (never effective on the conservative side) the [Turkish] money had been put into buying the few venal men always to be found in a big movement, then they would have crippled us. We could only dare these intricate raids because we felt sure and safe. One well-informed traitor will spoil a national uprising.

In the same letter and for the same reason he emphasized the value of mobility:

As you say it's greater mobility than the attack (speed and time over hitting power).... If the Turks had put machine guns on three or four of their touring cars, and driven them on weekly patrol over the admirable going of the desert east of Amman and Mann, they would have put an absolute stop to our camel-parties and so to our rebellion. It wouldn't have cost them twenty men or £20,000 *rightly applied.*

Again Lawrence used oversimplification for the purposes of illustration. Both in the Wavell letter and elsewhere he made the point that detachment can be maintained even in the face of airpower. (This view was in sharp contrast to the effective future he predicted for airpower when used against sophisticated armies.) Lawrence believed that guerrilla tactics could nearly muffle the physical effect of airpower, leaving only the morale value.

Bourcet has emphasized that every plan should have several feasible branches. Lawrence described his concept of a plan as hand-like with the fingers representing feasible courses of action — each available for use if needed. He supervised the execution of plans with exceptional human skill and unsurpassed coolness in action.

As a summary of his methods for determining the algebraical factors and reducing the uncertain factors he wrote to B.H. Liddell Hart in 1933:

Will you strike a blow for hard work and thinking? I was not an instinctive soldier, automatic with intuitions and happy ideas. When I took a decision or adopted an alternative it was after studying every relevant — and many an irrelevant — factor. Geography, tribal structure, religion, social customs, language, appetites, standards — all were at my finger-ends. The enemy I knew almost like my own side. I risked myself among them a hundred times, to *learn.*

Lawrence expended much effort to exploit the third factor of his strategy, the psychological. Xenophon has used a term which he adopted, "the diathetic," the predisposition of friendly and enemy forces to achieve desired ends. Lawrence said that the Arab cause "had won a province when the civilians in it had been taught to die for the ideal of freedom: the presence or absence of the enemy was a secondary matter."

Lawrence also developed ingenious and psychologically sound methods of teaching the civilians to fight. One recruiting trick was to assemble a tribe of prospective recruits within sight and hearing of a Turkish railroad bridge (in a manner reminiscent of a service school demolition class) and then destroy the bridge after emplacing a substantial overcharge of dynamite in order to make a proper impression on his audience. He exploited Arab victories psychologically by sending the best Arab leaders to spread the word, recruit intelligence agents, and arouse the countryside in preparation for future advances. During the first years of the effort no publicity was given in Allied countries to the guerrilla war. As the Arab effort became more successful, discreet publicity proved valuable in assuring a continual flow of material support.

All possible methods were used to predispose the Turkish Army to defeat. One cardinal rule was the good treatment of prisoners and deserters. Extensive publication was given to this rule. The Arab practice in this regard was generally good even by western standards. This is true notwithstanding a few instances where prisoners were killed after the Arab forces involved had been incensed by Turkish atrocities. Backed by the threat of the "tip and run" strike from the desert, his policy of good treatment was exceptionally successful. Allenby (Theatre Commander-in-Chief) notes that photographs of the Sherif of Mecca and his proclamation of independence from Turkey along with cigarettes were dropped over Turkish lines and resulted in many desertions by Arab troops in the Turkish Army. One source indicates several hundred thousand desertions from the Turkish Army occurred in the theatre of operations during the war.

Lawrence's guerrilla tactics were based on the use of tribal principles of war whenever possible. He adjusted the military effort and methods to the tribal manners and customs. He seldom used units larger

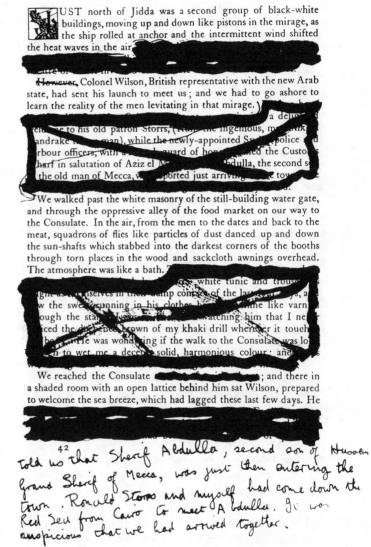

A page of the Subscribers' Text, abridged by Lawrence, for *Revolt in the Desert*.

than two hundred men — tribal raiding party size. Since men of one tribe could not be used in the territory of another he turned a handicap into a tactical, and often strategical, strength by using one tribe one day and another the next — but in a distant area. Thereby he avoided what might have been a tactical handicap and created from it both tactical and strategic mobility while simultaneously maintaining the morale of his force.

To the speed of the tribal raid he added a key factor — the firepower of air-cooled machine guns which were carried by every other man and used as automatic rifles. The lack of Arab mechanical repair ability he turned to advantage by requiring that automatic weapons which jammed in battle be discarded immediately in favour of the back-up rifle. In demolitions he excelled. To appreciate the detailed attention he gave this subject it is only necessary to read his article in the *Journal of the Royal Engineers* of January 1919. Speed in demolitions was emphasized until bridge pier demolitions took one man thirty to forty seconds often under fire. These demolition men were transported, when possible in the later days of the war, by armoured car. Speed, concealment, and accurate fire were key tactical principles.

Lawrence emphasized the importance of intellect and simple individual action in guerrilla warfare. The value of man in such a war depended almost entirely on quality not quantity. Gazelle hunters were prized for their marksmanship. In no sense was discipline used to submerge this individuality. His ideal was to make action a series of single combats and his ranks an alliance of independent initiative. As a subsidiary advantage the very diversity of the force contributed to frustrating enemy intelligence. His own tactical intelligence was based on the local knowledge and information sources of the Arab fighters, whom he used in their own home regions, and supplemented when practical by air reconnaissance.

The psychological factor of leadership was always a key element. Lawrence's "27 Articles" (originally published for new advisors in commandment form as an issue of the army's classified "Arab Bulletin" of August 20, 1918) give a clear insight into the depth of his thought on the psychology of leading through advice and on the importance of detailed knowledge of the customs and language of the area. They are well worth study even today and far excel in general usefulness and detail Mao's later but more widely known "Eight Points." The success of Lawrence's efforts to maintain morale among the Arabs is indicated by one report of an Arab victory which he received: "I sallied forth with my people, drinkers of the milk of war. The enemy advanced to meet us, but Allah was not with them." As a leader of British troops Lawrence is remembered for "a rousing talk" (to new troops, on their role and conduct in Arabia) which he delivered shortly before the war ended, standing in front of a campfire, dressed in the white robes of a sherif.

Lawrence generalized his guerrilla strategy and tactical experience to future world problems with a remarkable prescience. The accuracy of past predictions is important today because it is indicative of a fundamental value in his concepts and in his method of logical analysis. In 1916 as his efforts with the Arabs began he said in the "Arab Bulletin":

They are weak in material resources and always will be, for their world is agricultural and pastoral and can never be very rich or strong. If it were otherwise we would have to weigh more deeply the advisability of creating in the Near East a new power with such exuberant national sentiment.

In the same year he wrote:

It is curious how with each modification of the condition of Russia her potential influence has steadily increased ... and the Bolshevist success has been potent example to the East of the overthrow of an ancient government.... It has changed the Russian area ... to an area of influence, a base of preaching or action.... Further, it will provide a frontier permanently open, and an unlimited source of armament.

Also in 1920 he emphasized that Zionism and the consequent importation of European knowledge and technique was of the highest importance for the development of the area although several generations of evolution would be required before the full results were achieved. Most interestingly, he predicted that the presence of Jewish people would inevitably raise the material level of the whole Arab world. His advice (as early as 1915) on British involvement in the Palestine arrangements was succinct: "Don't touch it with a barge pole." He persuasively recommended, in 1920, a new British policy of actively imposing self-responsibility on the developing areas:

> We have to be prepared to see them doing things by methods quite unlike our own, and less well: but on principle it is better that they half-do it than that we do it perfectly for them.... We will find our best helpers not in our former most obedient subjects, but among those now active in agitating against us, for it will be the intellectual leaders of the people who will serve ... not the philosophers nor the rich, but the demagogues and the politicians.... We have to demand from them provisions for their own defence. This is the first stage towards self-respect in peoples.

It may be presumptuous to ask how Lawrence's thoughts and methods apply today. Yet not to comment on the current applicability of his theory and technique is to admit the sterility of all historical example and method.

His method of logic and analysis is a valuable, general example to follow. It emphasized the importance of considering the algebraical, the biological or incalculable, and the psychological factors in relation to the fundamental objective in order to maximize the friendly and minimize the enemy advantages. For example, the objectives of the Communist guerrilla in Asia today is both different and more difficult than was the Arab objective. The Viet Cong aim cannot be simply geographic, as was the Arab aim when faced by a foreign invader. Rather the Viet Cong must destroy an existing native government and in addition control the geographic area. Thanks to U.S. assistance, the Viet Cong must simultaneously face both a sophisticated military force and a native military force which is much less dependent on a sophisticated logistical base. A careful determination of the fundamental Viet Cong objective is essential in order to understand their actions, to establish proper indicators of success in opposing their actions, and to establish the relevance and effectiveness of possible actions.

Other lessons undoubtedly await experienced readers. Lawrence's recommendations for a careful reading of history, for enthusiasm in the application of new technology, for the introduction of enhanced mobility, for an understanding of the proper and improper role of air-power, for psychological methods, for the importance of language training, for the importance of detailed area knowledge of all types, for the role of intelligence, for the proper role of advisors, for the judicious use of gold, and for hard intellectual effort by leaders all may be fruitful subjects for examination in today's context. There is no excuse when fighting for not fighting well with such experience so readily available for examination.

Books and pamphlets are among the hardest things to disinfect, and in many cases it is best to burn them. Books owned by a school and used first by one and then by another pupil need frequent disinfection. One good way to do this is to suspend the books by their covers with their leaves all widely spread apart. A formaldehyde candle burned underneath them in such a way that the gas will reach every part of the books will disinfect them very well.

Disinfecting books

Some men in Germany recently tried an experiment. They removed the most soiled portions from free textbooks that had been used for a time in a common school. Then they soaked these parts in salt and water. When the water was given to some guinea pigs, more than one-third of them became

BEFORE USING SECOND-HAND BOOKS, ONE SHOULD BE SURE THAT THEY DO NOT CONTAIN DEADLY GERMS.

sick with tuberculosis. Such an experiment makes the danger from old second-hand books very plain. Remembering the things you have already learned, do you not think this danger would be much less if every pupil had clean hands and took care never to wet the fingers with saliva in turning the leaves of a book?

VICTORIA GLENDINNING

The Truth About Biography

This is the text of a talk Victoria Glendinning gave at Harbourfront in Toronto.

 iographers have only recently become self-conscious. Only in the last fifteen years or so have methods and intentions, techniques and choices, come under scrutiny. The biographer can no longer conceal herself completely behind or inside her subject, like a child dressing up in an adult's finery. We have had to ask ourselves what the hell we think we are doing, because other people have been asking that question. The Berlin Wall between fiction and biography, between autobiography and biography, between politics and biography, has huge breaches in it.

If we knew where truth was — if we could see it coming, and recognize it — then everything would be easier. But the truth about writing, and love, and gardening, and anything worthwhile, is more like mercury, it spills out into little balls and runs into corners. It's true, however, that most writers find some area in which their particular set of tools seems to work best. Publishers and readers also prefer this. Novelists become associated with a genre, poets with a group. But it's also true that most writers find it a lot more fun to break out and do different things. I suppose I've been doing that in a very small way.

I am in the middle of writing about Anthony Trollope, waist-deep in it, and I have never enjoyed anything so much in my life. I don't want it ever to end, though before I would have said that such a situation would be impossible. I have written biographies of women who wrote, and who had their main careers in the first half of this century — Elizabeth Bowen, Edith Sitwell, Vita Sackville-West, Rebecca West. I've always subscribed to what you could call the drift-net view of life — that things happen to you by chance, and you pick up what turns up. This, like writing biography, is a form of self-concealment; it works for a while but by the time you reach middle age the strategy begins to look pretty thin. There is a pattern — the kind of pattern that biographers search for in their subject's lives, in order to give it coherence and artistic unity; the kind of pattern that novels make of life — anything to avoid the abyss of the random and the meaningless. I find the random and the meaningless dangerously compelling. To counteract this attraction I spend my time arranging and ordering anything within reach.

Biography seems at first view the ideal medium for an arranger and orderer, and for a self-concealer. Diffidence and uncertainty come into it too. If you cannot be sure that you yourself are authentic or even interesting, you can write about and re-create someone who is.

What you forget is that a diamond ring can be boring, and a piece of glass can be a work of art, everything depends on what you do with it. Trollope's plots, for example, are banal and repetitive — what makes for tension is the particular people with their particular intractable characteristics who find themselves in these situations. In *He Knew He Was Right,* for example, Trollope sets up a very simple scenario of a loving husband objecting to his loving wife receiving visits from another man, though he does not for one moment suspect his wife of infidelity. As a plot for a three-volume novel, this is tepid. But because the husband is stubborn, bent on domination, and capable of sustaining a quarrel, and because the wife too is stubborn, and possessed of the kind of integrity which will not allow her to submit to a ruling she believes to be unreasonable, the novel builds up into a major and stomach-churning tragedy of psychopathology, madness and loss. As in fiction, so in biography: it's not so much the story of the life, but what you do with it, and beneath that, the empowering but not always acknowledged reasons why you chose that particular subject, or why it chose you.

The diffidence I spoke of comes in here. I guess I wrote about women because at least I know what women are like. I could "enact" another woman without fear of going too horribly wrong. I have never been sure whether men were just like women, only had different bits on their bodies, or whether they were altogether different. (I have this difficulty with Trollope in another form: were people living one hundred and fifty years ago just like us, only with different clothes — the dressing-up image remains central — or did they have different bits, in their minds?) Admittedly I chose difficult, odd and displaced women, who used and transcended their oddness in their writing. Elizabeth Bowen was Anglo-Irish, like a spy, as she said, in both cultures; Edith Sitwell was unhappy, unloved, and very peculiar to look at; Vita had a double life; and so on. I cannot tell you whether I chose these women because I felt a little monstrous myself, and was reassured by the way they mediated monstrousness and made something valuable of it; or whether I felt myself to be horribly ordinary, and was

drawn to them by their extraordinariness. I don't know which way it was; my self-concealment extends to concealing myself from myself. Perhaps it's the same for everyone. But I no longer believe that there wasn't a pattern, a submerged choice in all this.

When I was near the end of the Rebecca West book I found I was writing another book — a novel — round the edges of my life, not really believing that it was going to be one, or get finished. But it did. Though one might say that, had I faced up to what I was doing, instead of treating it like an illegitimate child in a Trollope novel, unacknowledged by the family and unfit for marriage with the gentry, it would have been a better novel. One of the themes of the novel *The Grown-Ups* is that there aren't any grown-ups, just children — running the world, God help us — in grown-up clothes and bodies, with thinning hair and beer bellies. (Back to enacting and dressing up.) The other thing I found myself doing in the novel was creating a man — a monstrous man. I felt able to write about a man in fiction as I had not presumed to do in biography. I had lived with men, beloved men, all my adult life — two husbands, four sons — and it was disturbing but also fun to unload onto poor Leo Ulm, in the story, the male characteristics that I found infantile, untenable, selfish, brutal, intolerable.

But even this is not simple, the balls of mercury roll off into another corner, since I also think that most of the characteristics traditionally attributed to men — toughness, courage, firmness, practicality, the ability to face unpleasant facts and to take action — actually belong to women, at least to the women I know; while the traditional attributes of women — timidity, a dislike for the unpleasant, the need for support — often belong to men. Trollope is very good on this. He wrote explicitly — this is not a matter of my interpretation — about women who were more like men than men are meant to be, and vice versa, and what he

called man-womanliness and woman-manliness, the things that Virginia Woolf was to write about, before Virginia Woolf was born. His heroes cry; his stern prime minister shyly strokes his adult son's hair. This is not a side of Anthony that is often discussed, even though everyone remembers Mrs. Proudie and her downtrodden bishop husband.

I could not have attended properly to Anthony Trollope if I had not invented Leo Ulm in the novel. Leo Ulm carried off all the animus against the opposite sex that I did not know I had. If it were not for Ulm, it might all have got transferred on to poor Anthony. As it is, I spend my days with him with uncluttered love. Not that I chose Anthony. Richard Cohen of Century Hutchinson came to me with the idea. I turned it down flat. What a ridiculous idea. I've never written the biography of a man, I've never written about the nineteenth century. This last was a lie: the first book I ever wrote, which no one in the world has read, was about my Victorian great-aunt who was one of the first women to go to Cambridge and who died aged twenty-two, stifled by asthma and family pressures. Anthony had asthma too, by the way, not to mention family pressures, and he never even got to the university. So it goes. And in any case, a day or two later I knew that Anthony Trollope was the person I wanted to write about more than anything else in the world, and by the time I got stuck into the research I would have killed anyone who took the project away from me.

I've been pretty near killing, as it happens. When I took the book on, it seemed an original idea; the last full biography of Anthony Trollope, by James Pope-Hennessy, was in 1971. But as the months passed I learned that not one, not two, but three academics — two Americans, one English — were working on massive biographies of my man, and had been at it for years. This is the biographer's nightmare. You have to live with it, and believe that your own will be different. Sex, or at least gender, comes into this, as it does into everything. Women critics have written good studies of aspects of Trollope's work, but no woman has yet written his life.

There is one big difference about writing the biography of a man and that of a woman, and it is to do with inner and outer, private and public. The story of a woman writer, up until recently, as maybe even now, is the story of a private life. Historically, it is the only life she has had, and private life has been, overwhelmingly, the subject of women's fiction. When a woman writes about a woman, it is the inner life which she is investigating, even if in parallel with the trajectory of a career. The landmarks in her biography tend to be her emotional attachments. What woman novelist has taken on, as Anthony Trollope did, a whole society, church and state, the law and justice, public morality, the choices a public man must make between men and measures, political expediency and personal conviction; ambition, public dishonesty, corruption — and money, and again money?

It was not politics itself that fascinated him so much as the politics of politics. The personal is political, for Anthony Trollope. It is idle to divide his novels into the political novels and the others. What can be more political than the beginning of *Barchester Towers:* "Who was to be the new Bishop?" This is fiction in the public arena. And yet no one has written with more sensitivity about private life — the negotiations between married couples, the lies and intricacies of love affairs, the ambivalence even the most committed lover feels, and the way couples talk, desultorily, in bed. Brothers and sisters, mothers and daughters, fathers and sons. His findings are often bleak. His novels may read like drawing-room comedies, but when you strip them down there is an armature of blackness in the centre: *The Last Chronicle of Barset* is a prime example. His women, in dialogue as elliptic and cruel and needling as Ivy Compton-Burnett's, voice opinions which still need voicing today. Because of his truly disastrous childhood and youth, which is part of the story to tell, Anthony could not follow the professions thought suitable for a young man of his kind — the law, the church or Parliament. But he does it all in his fiction. His own views spill out of his narrative, like the sermons that in real life he abhorred. Like an advocate, he enacts each of his characters, putting their case in that person's own person, and acting for the prosecution as well. This is why he is like the Bible or Shakespeare, you can extract from his work what will reinforce your own opinions, and what has traditionally been extracted from Trollope is a masculine, bluff, clubbish, roast-beef kind of traditional Englishness. But it is only half the story. He can enact a subversive, or a skeptic, or a tormented woman, with equal verve and precision. He knows how women talk when men are not present. He knows, without mockery, why women become frustrated and unhappy. Over and over he writes about a woman alone in her room, stealing a moment to herself before going downstairs to meet some crisis. Sometimes she just stands there, or absently tidies her hair, or once, in *Miss Mackenzie,* kisses her own reflection in the mirror in an upsurge of sexual life — and Miss Mackenzie is not pretty or young. It is a nothing moment; but nothing could be more private.

The intersecting, and sometimes clashing, of public and private is a challenge for his biographer, and it is a topic of Trollope's own. His wayward and irresistible Lady Glencora, who actually says she knows she would make a better prime minister than her sober, thin-skinned, honourable husband Plantagenet Palliser, makes the essentially female mistake — if mistake it be — of making no distinction between public and private, and employs private strategies for public purposes, and vice versa. A man cannot be both private and public at the same time, Anthony wrote. Palliser himself, as the Duke of Omnium, lectures his son about this over dinner at the Beargarden Club: In private life, he said, you choose your own associates and are responsible for your choice. In public life you are concerned with others for the good of the state, or for something else outside yourself. You are accountable.

It's my feeling that previous biographies have concentrated principally on Anthony Trollope's accountable, public and outer self — the facts of his life, how he was with his friends and associates, how and when he wrote, all the details of his career, firmly set in that outer world of Victorian England. This is because his biographers have been decent chaps, with a decent chappish respect for the private affairs of another decent chap. Anthony himself encouraged this approach. If you have read his autobiography, you will remember that it is cunningly tailored as a self-help story, a how-I-did-it-story, with lots of concrete information about how much money he made from each book. Of his marriage, for example, he has just this to say: "My marriage was like the marriage of other people, and of no special interest to any one except my wife and me."

Well, it's of interest to me, Anthony.

And if his marriage was like the marriage of other people — what is marriage like, or what did Anthony think it was like? Study his family history — I want his resourceful, brilliant, resilient mother to be as real in the story as he is — she may be reckoned a heroine of the feminist revolution but she was not a comfortable mother for Anthony. There is his father — morose, sick, difficult, despairing, a bully and a failure, addicted to calomel, which is a preparation of mercury, and toxic. Elder brother Tom, also something of a bully, and mother's favourite and her husband-substitute; two more brothers, who died; and the tubercular sisters, Emily and Cecilia. Listen to what he has to say in

the novels — about intimacy, need, desire, insecurity, family violence, betrayal, ambivalence, devotion, the way women love, the way men love. About home, women's clothes, bedrooms, women's bodies. Above all, about honesty and dishonesty.

Biographers know the dangers of extrapolating the life from the work. Biographers who have written novels know at first hand the ridiculous assumptions people make about the real-life sources of their plots and characters. Novelists can write in a what-if mode, about something that might have happened but never did; they reverse genders, take revenges or, as more often with Anthony, make compensations or award themselves triumphant adventures, in fantasy. He daydreamed his unhappy boyhood away in long serial imaginings of which he himself was the hero; the daydream technique got transferred to novel-writing. He wrote about himself, in that he was enacting all his characters, and the preoccupations that fuel his stories are his own. When he wrote his life of Cicero he said: "The man of letters is, in truth, ever writing his own biography. What there is in his mind, is being declared to the world at large by himself." What is on his mind, as well as what is in his mind. Correlating the preoccupations of specific novels with what was happening in his own life, I have sometimes felt that he was sending messages — to his wife Rose, to his own children, to the spirits of his parents, to himself.

The bit I quoted from his Cicero book gives one the green light to look at the books in this way. And against any residual feeling of prurience, in the face of the prevailing chappish decency that surrounds biographical writing about Trollope, I would set something he wrote in his life of Thackeray: "The desire is common to all readers to know not only what a great writer has written, but also of what nature has been the man who produced such great work."

So I listen — to letters and the other usual sources,

as well as his novels and travel books — and I learn what he felt about an enormous number of things, not just emotional questions. The authorial voice booms out of the pages — sometimes impersonally, in mini-editorials, sometimes in the first person, with "I" breaking through, and it is not the ironic unreliable author of the self-conscious modern novel, it is Anthony. He is not thought of as a literary theorist, but there is a complete theory of novel-writing to be extracted from his comments, within the narratives, on what he is doing and why. I know what and how he thinks about democracy, picnics, boots, age and ageing, art and architecture, crinolines, hairstyles, Catholicism, dancing, wine, flirting, gardens, bad smells, illness and insanity, cigars, male friendships, spiritualism, swimming, food, and the way dinner should be served. I learn what attracts and what repels him — in dinners, in sex, in drawing-rooms, in landscape.

In the course of learning what he thinks, I have learned not only what is in his mind but more about his outer world. Small, but interesting things. One of them is about curry powder, another about teeth. But he writes in his autobiography, for example, that when he was tested for entry to the civil service — it was only a humble junior clerkship in the post office — he was given an old quill pen to write with, and disgraced himself with blots and mistakes.

The point for him, I discover in my wide if random reading of social history, is not that it was a quill pen, which was standard in 1834, but that it was an old quill pen. Flocks of geese were bred for the purpose of converting their plumage into writing instruments; goose quills were bought in large bundles, and sharpened to be used as pens as needed, and each had a very short life; a quill pen was far more expendable than, say, a ball-point today. So to try the boy out with an old one was a mean trick.

There are no photographs of Anthony Trollope, born in 1815, before he was bulky, balding, bearded and bespectacled. Ironically, as a young surveyor's clerk for the post office in Ireland, he was living ten miles away from a pioneer photographer, the third Countess of Rosse, at Birr Castle.

But even if, in one of her early street scenes, she had caught, in the background, the young Trollope going about his business, we would not recognize him. The past is irretrievable, and the weird connections with "now" that you come across are like chains linking you with a reality you can sense but not see.

Sometimes you get close. My visit, for example, to an old lady in an Essex village, her memory nearly gone. All she says is, "These were good people, they were fond of one another." She is the granddaughter of Anthony's brother-in-law John Tilley — one of his oldest friends, Cecilia's husband, and the man with whom Anthony was dining the night he had the stroke from which he did not recover.

Miss Tilley has in her cottage the crumpled piece of paper which was Anthony's certificate of employment in the post office as a hobbledehoy nineteen-year-old in 1834 — he was to be in the room of Mr. Diggle, and against Mr. Diggle's name someone at the time scribbled "dismissed" in pencil.

The old lady also had a long, long, breathless, unpunctuated letter from Anthony's sister Cecilia, written when she had been three months married to John Tilley; it is written to her mother, and she is trying to tell her mother she is pregnant, and happy about it. She tried to tell intimate everythings to her mother in that letter without actually using the words. "Words are things," wrote Anthony, in a very modern formulation, by the way. And as for Cecilia's real-life delicacy, it was shared by some of Anthony's sweeter fictional heroines, but not all. Kate in *Can You Forgive Her?* says: "Oh, indelicate! How I do hate that word. If any word reminds me of a whited sepulchre, it is that: —

all clean and polished outside with filth and rottenness within.... Delicacy with many women is like their cleanliness. Nothing can be nicer than the whole outside get-up, but you wouldn't wish to answer for anything beneath."

Anthony had a horror of women's dirty underwear. It becomes the metaphor for all kinds of hypocrisy. It must have been the fault of some poor girl with whom he becomes entangled in his years in cheap London lodging houses. (I have become very fastidious, I may say, since I realized how important what he called "niceness" was to him.)

But he was no prude in his sense of humour. Like Thackeray, he made rude jokes in private, about tits and worse. But he was compelled to be delicate in his fiction so that the circulating library would stock his books; and they had to be suitable reading for young girls in rectories. He got round this, so that often what he writes can be read on two levels, sexually. Healthy indelicacy is always on the brink of breaking out.

I was describing ways in which the past touches the present. Anthony spent years of his young manhood in Ireland working for the post office, and wrote his first novels there.

The very first is *The Macdermots of Ballycloran,* about a family in dissolution, sexual betrayal, and murder. On the first page he described what inspired him to write it. He was in a small town called Drumsna, in County Leitrim, and with a friend from England he went for a walk, away from the river, and after about a mile they came to a ruined bridge over a bog-stream and, on the right, a broken-down entrance, two brick pillars with no gates. A tall fir lay fallen across the avenue, which led to a ruinous house. The roof was off, there were docks and sorrel all over what had been the garden, and local people were using it to keep their animals and timber in.

"We wandered about the place," Anthony elaborated in his autobiography, "suggesting to each other causes for the misery we saw there, and while I was still among the ruined walls and decayed beams I fabricated the plot of the Macdermots of Ballycloran."

I myself was in Drumsna just a few weeks ago, on the very same date in September that he found the ruined house, by the sort of pure chance that cannot be chance, and we followed the route described in the novel — and we came upon the ruin, still there just as he had seen it in 1843. Maybe the ivy has a stronger grip, maybe more walls have fallen, but there are still docks and sorrel in what had been the garden, and local farmers are still using the place as a store.

There is a triple suggestiveness here — was it the ghosts of the original dispossessed owners that we dreamed we saw, as Anthony did when he conceived his story: or was it his fictional inhabitants of the house, the unfortunate Feemy Macdermot (she had dirty underwear too by the way) and her brother, and her despairing father, senile at fifty (an echo of Anthony's own father); or was it Anthony himself and his old schoolfriend John Merivale, wandering round with their hands in their pockets, and wondering?

Nowhere but in Ireland, I feel, could the past lie so undisturbed that it is the present. In Anthony's second novel, also set in Ireland, he complained how the sons of squireens were as offended by the idea of doing any work as if one had suggested that they should sit stitching like a tailor cross-legged in a shop-window in Carrick-on-Shannon. A contemporary reference, one might think, of little application in the modern world.

But on the same trip last month, in a little town called Granard not far from Carrick-on-Shannon, what did I see but a tailor sitting stitching cross-legged in his shop-window. History leaks backwards and forwards.

The language of Anthony's *The Way We Live Now,* about the financial world and its corruptions — consisting of insider dealing and junk bonds, no less — is

startlingly modern — phrases such as a man being "something in the City," phrases like "the new dispensation," the proliferation of young men who don't do any actual work but call themselves "company directors" — all this is about now.

I shan't be present in the book I am writing, not in the way that Peter Ackroyd is in his *Dickens*. Nevertheless Trollope will be my Trollope. It will be my truth, or my rolling-away collections of truths, about him. It's not just going to be a book about Trollope and women, though it may seem like it from what I've said today. One cannot but write, or talk, about what is in one's mind at a given moment. Like his deleterious Lady Glencora, I want to infiltrate both the public and private where he is concerned — to bridge the gap not only between the world of affairs and the domestic interior, but between bourgeois decorum and white

muslin dresses and the filth, shit, drunkenness, licence, and subhuman ragged poverty of the streets; between the modesty of young wives and the sudden uncompromising realities of marriage. (The chamber pot under the bed.) What actually infiltrated every corner were what the Victorians called "blacks" — the specks of soot from a thousand thousand chimneys, blown through the cracks of window frames and settling on antimacassars, table covers, collars and cuffs, bedlinen and, as Trollope put it in a phrase of darting intimacy, even penetrating women's "daintiest recesses."

Unlike the inexorable smuts, I may fail, in which case it'll be just another biography. Every writer here, and every architect, painter, carpenter and cook, must know how, before a work is finished, the idea of what it still could be shines.

DIANA HARTOG

Circumstantial Evidence

Janet Lewis's *The Wife of Martin Guerre*

t is a warm February afternoon in 1982. The train slows, lurches to a stop beside a long, marigold-yellow station house, with the sign PALO ALTO propped on its roof. Tall eucalyptus trees border the parking lot — crowded with Volvos and Audis and the odd Mercedes-Benz. From this point the campus of Stanford University stretches languidly west; its outer limits rise into rolling green hills, which are cut diagonally by the white, determinedly-straight line of the Linear Accelerator, two miles long, where atoms travel in style. It was here in Palo Alto in the fifties that Ken Kesey — devotee of the curved ball — swallowed his first, supervised doses of LSD. In the forties, of course, women were being urged into the factories and one's Japanese gardener hustled off to an internment camp as an enemy alien. But in the late thirties, before the upheaval of the War, Janet Lewis, with time to herself — her children off to school, her husband teaching at the University — sat down every morning at her typewriter. And produced a classic, an historical novel of a mere one hundred and nine pages, *The Wife of Martin Guerre*; a book that, since its publication in 1941, has been kept continuously in print, inspired several plays and an opera, and been praised by the *Atlantic Monthly* as "one of the most significant short novels in English."

Janet Lewis began as a poet, her first published work appearing in *Poetry* magazine when she was twenty-one. Born in Chicago in 1899, she attended the University of Chicago, majoring in French. But she always wrote. Her father a novelist and poet and teacher, her mother loving literature and music, the young Janet Lewis was taken to the opera in her teens. Now, in her eighties, she combines these interests to write libretti. But her first efforts were under the discipline of poetry. At the University of Chicago she met Ivor Winters, a leading member of the Poetry Club who was to become her husband as well as a noted critic and poet. In 1927 they moved to California, Winters to teach at Stanford, Lewis to keep their home and raise two children.

But she kept writing — at one point typing a

manuscript while holding her small daughter on her lap. She tackled short stories, and developed a clean, rather formal prose style, a style transparent as she could make it. Then, in 1937, when she was becalmed between writing projects, her husband handed her a fat anthology, dated 1873 and entitled *Famous Cases of Circumstantial Evidence*: "Here, why don't you write a story based on one of these?"

The case Janet Lewis found herself drawn to was that of Martin Guerre, a peasant of the village of Artiques in sixteenth-century France. Married at a young age to Bertrande de Rols, Martin chafes under the feudal authority of his father, who, by tradition, will remain the head of the family until his death. Martin is remote and troubled. He grows more and more removed, and when his father accuses him of stealing the family grain, Martin at nineteen announces to Bertrande that he must leave — just for a week or so, until it's safe to return. He is gone for eight years.

During his absence, Bertrande remains faithful, raising their son Sanxi and taking charge of Martin's household upon the death of Martin's father. And from expecting her husband's return any week now, or perhaps in the fall, and surely by spring, Bertrande finally arrives at a calm acceptance: he will never come back. It is of course at this moment that Martin Guerre returns — filled out, bearded, matured in the wars. He is welcomed back into the family as its feudal head, its "de capo." The estate thrives, and Martin endears himself to servants and family alike. And Bertrande thrives under the love and protection of her returned husband, who seems to be of a far more kind and generous nature than the man she remembers. Two years pass, Bertrande bears another child. But even before the child is born, a suspicion grows in Bertrande, in fact, it's been there from the first night of homecoming: is this man who calls himself Martin Guerre truly her husband returned, and the rightful claimant to the family estate, and to her love? The story pivots on this single sliver of doubt, sharp as glass, that lodges in the heart of the wife of Martin Guerre.

This is Janet Lewis's distinctive rendering of the case recorded at the 1559 trial of Martin Guerre. She was the perfect person to write what has been called a "perfect" book. At the time Janet Lewis came upon *Famous Cases*, she was forty; as well as her familiarity with the French culture and language, she brought experience, intelligence, and, above all, wisdom, to the story of Bertrande de Rols. And she created that rare creature in literature: a female protagonist whose struggle with the deepest questions of truth constitutes a tragedy. Bertrande knowingly destroys her own life in order to preserve intact her soul.

"I built my case — that is to say, the character of Bertrande — upon her own words to the court.... She is, then, in my story, what at that dreadful moment she had wanted to be." So Janet Lewis remarks in a 1982 article tracing the sources of *The Wife of Martin Guerre*.

We are standing in the small, cool kitchen of her cottage, waiting for the water to boil for tea: Janet Lewis, myself, and the well-dressed matron so kind as to meet the arriving train. On the way here, as her blue station wagon curved smoothly through the shaggy green landscape of the university endowment lands, this friend and devotee of the author had screened me thoroughly. It seems there have been other pilgrims before me, coming to pay their respects. And as the car drew near to the cottage where Janet Lewis, now a widow, lives alone, I was treated to that tense, polite regard reserved for the stranger, the visitor who casually leans too close to a cherished and irreplaceable vase.

The small, lean woman who greeted us at the door appeared no delicate object. Her voice was clear and firm, quite young; her carriage erect. At eighty-three,

Janet Lewis had reached that plateau where the body, wrung of extra flesh, settles into its bones and appears to coast, indefinitely. But as she turned and led us through the living room — its walls lined with books, its wood floor gleaming — a slight limp betrayed her gait: she was due to undergo an operation on her hip the following week.

Now, as the two friends speak of the necessary arrangements, there is time to look around. The windows of the kitchen are shaded from outside by trees and bushes benignly allowed their head. Inside, little distinguishes this from one's grandmother's house: the graduated cannisters along the counter, the row of cups hung from hooks; all is clean, orderly, ordinary. The kitchen of a woman who has written a body of work that, as the *Christian Science Monitor* noted in May of this year, "seems certain to outlive us all," the reviewer deeming Janet Lewis "one of America's prose stylists."

Being more interested in the wife than in Martin Guerre himself, Janet Lewis wrote a first and rather short version of the story. "I had no information about the case other than that in *Famous Cases,* and I had no idea what a famous case it was, and is." The question of Bertrande's reasons for accusing the man she loves of being an imposter, the question of when she changed her mind, and why, is what caught her imagination.

... one day, seeing Martin returning from a ride with Sanxi, and seeing the easy comradeship between the two, [Bertrande] said aloud:

"It is not possible that this man should be Martin Guerre. For Martin Guerre, the son of the old master, proud and abrupt, like the old master, could never in this world speak so gaily to his own son. Ah! unhappy woman that I am, so to distrust the Good God who has sent me this happiness!"

... she could not refrain, the moment that they were left alone that evening, from accusing her husband of being other than the man he represented, and of asking for proof of his identity.

"Proof? But why proof? You have seen me. You have felt the touch of my lips. Behold my hands. Are they not scarred even as you remember them? Do you remember the time my father struck me and broke my teeth? They are still broken. You have spoken with me; we have spoken together of things past. Is not my speech the same? Why should I be other than myself? What has happened to give you this strange notion?"

Bertrande replied in a barely audible voice:

"If you had been Martin Guerre you would perhaps have struck me just now."

He answered with gentle surprise:

"But because I struck you on the day we were married, is that a reason I should strike you now? Listen to me, my dearest .... If I return to you with a greater wisdom than that which I knew when I departed, would you have me dismiss it, in order again to resemble my father? God knows, my child, and the priest will so instruct you, that a man of evil ways may by an act of will so alter all his actions and his habits that he becomes a man of good. Are you satisfied?"

"And then," said Bertrande, in a still smaller voice, marshalling her last argument, "Martin Guerre at twenty had not the gift of the tongue. His father, also, was a silent man." At this her husband, hitherto so grave, burst into a laugh which made the Chamber echo, and still laughing, with his broad hand he wiped the tears from his wet face.

For a time Bertrande is placated. But with the birth of her child, her suspicions do not pass away, as Martin said they would, but rather strengthen daily, and "her happiness ... shone the more brightly, was the more greatly to be treasured because of the shadow of sin and danger which accompanied it." As Janet Lewis remarks, "France at that time was Catholic. Bertrande lived in a world where there were moral standards.... The contemporary reactions are very amusing. Most of them are impatient with her. They say, Why didn't she take what she had? and so forth."

But as time went on Bertrande found herself more and more surely faced with the obligation of admitting herself to be hopelessly insane or of confessing that she was consciously accepting as her husband a man whom she believed to be an imposter.... For days and weeks she turned aside, as in a fever, from what she felt to be the truth, declaring to her distracted soul that she was defending the safety of her children, of her household, from Uncle Pierre down to the smallest shepherd, and then at last, one morning as she was seated alone, spinning, the truth presented itself finally, coldly, inescapably.

"I am no more mad than is this man. I am imposed upon, deceived, betrayed into adultery, but not mad."

The spindle dropped to the floor, the distaff fell across her knees, and though she sat like a woman turned to stone and felt her heart freezing slowly in her bosom, the air which entered her nostrils seemed to her more pure than any she had breathed in years, and the fever seemed to have left her body. She began then quietly to array before in this clear passionless light the facts of her situation as she must now consider it, no longer distorted through fear or shame or through the desire of the flesh.

We take our tea into the living room. Janet Lewis speaks with mild surprise of the continuing interest in the book she wrote more than forty years ago. A man at MGM holds an option; readers respond by sending her dramatic versions, poems; an opera — for which she wrote the libretto — was performed in New York in 1956. "And now I hear the French are making a film called *The Return of Martin Guerre* — the screenplay written by Robert Laffont — but they've gone back to the original source, the court record of Jean de Coras." [A French translation of Lewis's book, *The Wife of Martin Guerre*, was published in 1947.] The original court record, written down when it was still fresh in the mind of Coras, one of the judges at Martin Guerre's trial, did not come to Lewis's attention until 1964 — too late to amend mistakes handed down through various translations, and which could have changed the implications of the story to some extent. Janet Lewis was engaged in translating the court records from the legal, sixteenth-century French, and was uncovering new facts, particularly as to the character of Bertrande's Uncle Pierre. Written now, she says, *The Wife of Martin Guerre* would be a different story: 'I think, perhaps, I was lucky I didn't know too much."

For though her "wrong guesses" were psychologically right in terms of building the strong character of Bertrande, Lewis prefers to stay as close to the facts as possible when writing historical fiction. The essential shape is provided: "Your characters can't run away with you when you know what they are going to do. I mean, they are fated to do, you see, what they have done. They have to move toward their own destiny."

A final incident occurs which confirms for Bertrande her suspicions as to Martin's identity: an old comrade-at-arms of Martin's, travelling through, is rebuffed by her husband. The man then claims that he is a fraud: the real Martin Guerre lost a leg in the wars. And though Bertrande confides to the priest, and to Martin's sisters, to no avail, it is only after a prolonged illness that Bertrande is finally believed by Pierre Guerre, Martin's uncle.

Less than a week later armed men from Rieux arrived at the farm and arrested the master of the house. They brought him in irons from the field to the kitchen for a final identification by Bertrande.... Sanxi, seeing his father in chains, burst into a passion of weeping, flung himself, first upon his father, and then, kicking and scratching, upon the two guardsmen.

"Madame," said his father quietly, above the turmoil thus raised, "is it indeed you who do this to me?"

A trial is held at Rieux. From the conflicting testimony of a hundred and fifty people, a witness steps forward to claim that he has known the accused "since the cradle," and that he is none other than a certain Arnaud du Tilh — a rogue who had talked to him only recently of playing the part of Martin Guerre. The prisoner is condemned to suffer death by decapitation before the house of Martin Guerre.

"Not death! Not death! No, no, I have not demanded his death!"

Bertrande stood, growing very pale, confronting the judges with surprise and horror in her features....

The prisoner had started also at Bertrande's cry. In spite of the sentence just passed upon him, his eyes were clear, and his face bright, one would have said, with joy.

The verdict is appealed at once by Martin's sisters. The parliament of Toulouse finds the evidence inconclusive and calls the witnesses for a second trial — scheduled for the fall. It is a long wait for Bertrande. Yet she allows no one to dissuade her in her determination to rid herself of the imposter.

... Bertrande, returning from church the evening before her departure [to the trial in Toulouse] crossed the courtyard toward her house, wearily. She saw the housekeeper sitting near the doorway killing doves, and sat down beside the old woman.

"You have made your prayers, Madame," said the old woman.

"Yes."

"I wish that had made them for a better cause."

"How can you know what prayers I made?"

"I cannot know, Madame. I only know that since you have had this strange idea of yours, nothing goes well for us. And all was well before. So well."

She sighed, leaning forward, holding the dove head down between her hands, the smooth wings folded close to the smooth soft body, while the dark blood dripped slowly from a cut in the throat into an earthen dish....

"What would you have me do?" Bertrande asked at length. "The truth is only the truth. I cannot change it, if I would."

The old woman turned her head without lifting her shoulders, still leaning forward heavily above her square, heavy lap....

"I, Madame?" she said.

Bertrande looked into the tired affectionate brown eyes and nodded.

"Ah," said the housekeeper, turning once more to the dove which now lay still in her hands, "Madame, I would have you still be deceived. We were all happy then." She laid the dead dove with the others, and stooped to pick up the dish of blood.

In researching *The Wife*, Janet Lewis had her travels in France in the early twenties to draw on; beyond that, "I began by reading a book on the Ancien Régime by Frantz Funck-Brentano that had a lot of stories in it and lots of quotes from contemporary writers that gave a feeling of life then. I read guide books. I talked to a skier from Luchon to find out how the snow was in the Pyrenees. And I had an old French woman as a neighbour here with whom I used to visit. She gave me the whole episode of the housekeeper's killing of the doves."

But for the complex delineation of Bertrande, Janet Lewis obviously drew on her own depth of character, her own knowledge of the workings of the human soul. Courage and folly look remarkably alike. The values we suffer to obey offer our only means towards transcendence. Grace, if you will. As Lewis notes elsewhere, in the preface to another of her historical novels, there is that "great company of men and women who have preferred to lose their lives rather than accept a universe without plan or without meaning."

"And might I be wrong?" [Bertrande] asked herself again as she mounted the stone steps and stood waiting before the great closed door.... A hum of voices which had filled the [courtroom] ceased suddenly as she appeared. In the abrupt silence she heard the admonition of the judge and, lifting her eyes, saw before her at the distance of only a few feet, the man for who she had felt for one extraordinary year a great and joyous passion. He was regarding her with a look at once patient, tender and ironic. In her distress she saw no other face, and could not bear the contemplation of that tender gaze. She looked down, dropping her head forward, while the blood beat upward into her face and then receded. Who was this Arnaud du Tilh? What manner of man was he that he did not return her hatred with hatred...?

At the tribunal in Toulouse, one hundred and fifty witnesses have been called from the hearing at Rieux, plus thirty new ones. Throughout the day, the balance of evidence shifts back and forth. Both the accused and Martin Guerre share an extraordinary number of characteristics: two broken teeth in the left jaw; a scar on the right eyebrow; the trace of an ulcer on one cheek; a missing nail on the left forefinger; three warts on the left hand, two of which are on the little finger. The judges decide that, "it was beyond human ingenuity for any man to impersonate so well, to know so many intimate details of the life of another man, and to exhibit so close a physical resemblance to another man...."

The court clerk picks up his pen to put the verdict of innocent down in writing, when a commotion is heard at the outer door. A soldier enters, the stone floor echoing with the tap of a wooden leg. "The judges surveyed the newcomer. He was sunburned, and bearded, but through the beard the shape of the cleft chin was easily discernible. His left eyebrow was scarred; there was a trace of an old ulcer on one cheek. He returned the scrutiny of the judges of Toulouse with eyes which were arrogant, grey and cold. "Body of God," said one of the justices, sinking back in his seat in something not unlike despair, "this is either Martin Guerre or the devil..."

Bertrande is recalled to the courtroom.

She made her way through the crowd toward the space before the judges.... In the silence of the room the insatiable interest of the crowd beat upon her like a sultry wave. She reached the open space, and stopped. There she lifted her eyes at last and saw, standing beside Arnaud du Tilh, the man whom she had loved and mourned as dead. She uttered a great cry and turned very pale.... Then, reaching out her hands to Martin Guerre, she sank slowly to her knees before him. He did not make any motion toward her, so that, after a little time, she clasped her hands together and drew them toward her breast, and, recovering herself somewhat, said in a low voice:

"My dear lord and husband, at last you are returned. Pity me and forgive me, for my sin was occasioned only by my great desire for your presence, and surely, from the hour wherein I knew I was deceived, I have laboured with all the strength of my soul to rid myself of the destroyer of my honour and my peace."

The tears began to run quietly down her face....

But Martin Guerre ... said to his wife with perfect coldness:

"Dry your tears, Madame. They cannot, and they ought not, move my pity ... the error into which you plunged could only have been caused by willful blindness. You, and only you, Madame, are answerable for the dishonour which has befallen me."

Bertrande did not protest. Rising to her feet ... she recoiled from him a step or two in unconscious self-defence, and the movement brought her near to the author of her misfortunes, the actual Arnaud du Tilh.

In the silence which filled the courtroom at Martin's unexpected severity, a familiar voice close to her elbow pronounced gently:

"Madame, you wondered at the change which time

and experience had worked in Martin Guerre, who from such sternness as this became the most indulgent of husbands. Can you not marvel now that the rogue, Arnaud du Tilh, for your beauty and grace, became for three long years an honest man?"

"Sirrah," answered Bertrande, "I marvel that you should speak to me, whose devotion has deprived me even of the pity of my husband. I once seemed to love you, it is true. I cannot now hate you sufficiently."

"I had thought to ask you to intercede for mercy for me," said Arnaud du Tilh.

"You had no mercy upon me, either upon body or upon soul," replied Bertrande.

"Then Madame," said du Tilh, there was at last neither arrogance nor levity in his voice, "I can but die by way of atonement."

The court record, by Jean de Coras, printed in 1570, ends thusly:

Again the said du Tilh, having been heard, persisted in the confession, even to three and four times; and even again on the ladder to the gallows in front of the house of the said Martin Guerre, where the execution was carried out, he confessed frankly to having constructed and carried out the said imposture in the manner heretofore described, asking pardon of the said Martin Guerre and Bertrande de Rols, espoused, and of the said Pierre Guerre, uncle of the said Martin, with great manifestations of repentance, and detestation of his deed, all the while crying upon God for mercy, through His Son Jesus Christ.

And thus he was executed, his body hanged, and afterwards burned.

You will notice I have said nothing in this paean to Janet Lewis of the tyranny of Language. Why? It's very simple. *The Wife of Martin Guerre* is a perfect creation. Language and Janet Lewis are not on fighting terms. Moreover, by virtue of the clarity of her style and the clarity of her soul, Language, in certain wonderful passages, is enabled to disappear — the very best of transcendental states. For this chance, in the guise of *The Wife of Martin Guerre*, Language should be eternally grateful.

(Opposite page) Sergio Trezzi, Lake Como, Italy. Brick reader since 1989.

ROHINTON MISTRY

Journey to Dharmsala

t was still raining when we stopped outside Hotel Bhagsu. I took my socks off the taxi's corroded chrome door-handles where they had hung to dry for almost four hours, and pulled them over my clammy feet. The socks were still soggy. Little rivulets ran out of my shoulder bag as I squelched into the lobby. The desk clerk watched with interest while I fastidiously avoided a trail of water that ran from the leaky umbrella stand to the door. Why, with the shoes already sopping wet? he must have wondered. I was not sure myself — perhaps to emphasize that I did not generally go about dripping water.

As I signed the register, shaking raindrops from my hands, the desk clerk said that candles would be sent to my room before dark. Candles, I asked?

He had assumed I would know: "There is a small problem. Electricity workers are on strike." Worse, the strikers were sabotaging the power lines. No electricity anywhere, he emphasized, in case I was considering another hotel: not in Upper Dharmsala, not in Lower Dharmsala, nowhere in Kangra District.

I nodded, putting out my hand for the room key. But he held on to it. With that circular motion of the head which can mean almost anything, he said, "There is one more problem." He continued after a suitable pause: "There is also no water. Because of heavy rains. Rocks fell from the mountains and broke all of the water pipes."

He seemed surprised by the lack of emotion with which I greeted his news. But I had already glimpsed the handiwork of the pipe-breaking avalanches during my four-hour taxi ride. The car had laboured hard to reach McLeod Gunj, up the winding, rock-strewn mountain roads, grinding gears painfully, screeching and wheezing, negotiating segments that had become all but impassable.

Perhaps a bit disappointed by my stolidity, once again the desk clerk assured me it was the same in Upper and Lower Dharmsala, and in all of Kangra District; but management would supply two buckets of water a day.

So there was no choice, the hotel would have to do. I requested the day's quota hot, as soon as possible, for a bath. He relinquished my room key at last. Its brass tag had Hotel Bhagsu engraved on one side. "What is Bhagsu?" I asked him, picking up my bag.

"In local language, means Running Water," he said.

The room had an enormous picture window. The curtains, when thrown open, revealed a spectacular view of Kangra Valley. But I could not linger long over it, urgent matters were at hand. I unzipped the bag and wrung out my clothes, spreading them everywhere: over the bed, the chair, the desk, the door knob. Wet and wretched, I sat shivering on the edge of the bed, waiting for the hot water and remembering the warnings to stay away from Dharmsala while it was in the clutches of the dreaded monsoon.

When the Dalai Lama fled Tibet in 1959, just hours before the Chinese conducted a murderous raid on his Palace in Lhasa and occupied the country, he found refuge in India. For months afterwards other Tibetans followed him, anxious to be with their beloved spiritual leader. The pathetic bands of refugees arrived, starving and frostbitten — the ones lucky enough to survive the gauntlet of treacherous mountain passes, the killing cold, and, of course Chou En-lai's soldiers. Each arriving group narrated events more horrific than the previous one: how the Chinese had pillaged the monasteries, crucified the Buddhist monks, forced nuns to publicly copulate with monks before executing them, and were now systematically engaged in wiping out all traces of Tibetan culture.

The Dalai Lama (whose many wonderfully lyrical, euphonious names include Precious Protector, Gentle Glory, and Ocean of Wisdom) spent his first months of exile in anguish and uncertainty. Faced with unabating news of the endless atrocities upon the body and soul of Tibet, he eventually decided that Dharmsala was where he would establish a government-in-exile. Perhaps this quiet mountain hamlet in the Himalayas reminded him of his own land of ice and snow. Soon, a Tibetan colony evolved in Dharmsala, a virtual country-within-a-country. Visitors began arriving from all over the world to see Namgyal Monastery, Tibetan Children's Village, the Dalai Lama's new temple, or to study at the Library of Tibetan Works and Archives.

As a child, it always struck me with wonderment and incredulity that I should have an uncle who lived in Dharmsala. In this remote mountain hamlet he ran the business which has been in the Nowrojee family for five generations. To me, a thousand miles away in Bombay, this land of mountains and snow had seemed miraculously foreign. Photographs would arrive from time to time, of uncle and aunt and cousins wrapped in heavy woollens, standing beside three-foot-deep snow drifts outside their homes, the snow on the roof like thick icing on a cake, and the tree branches delicately lined with more of the glorious white substance. And in my hot and sticky coastal city, gazing with longing and fascination at the photographs, I would find it difficult to believe that such a magical place could exist in this torrid country. Now there, somewhere in the mountains, was a place of escape from heat and dust and grime. So, to visit Dharmsala became the dream.

But for one reason or another, the trip was never taken. Those old photographs: snow-covered mountains and mountain trails; my cousins playing with their huge black Labrador; uncle and aunt posing in the *gaddi* dress of native hill people, a large hookah between them: those old black-and-white photographs curled and faded to brown and yellow. Years passed, the dog died, my cousins got married and settled elsewhere, and my uncle and aunt grew old. Somehow, the thousand miles between Bombay and Dharmsala were never covered. There was always some logistical or financial problem, and travelling third class on Indian trains was only for the foolish or the desperate.

Then, by a quirk of fate, I undertook a different journey, a journey ten thousand miles long, to Canada, and I often thought about the irony of it. So this time, back in Bombay to visit family and friends, not monsoon rain nor ticket queues nor diarrhoea nor avalanches could keep me away from Dharmsala.

Thus twenty-eight hours by train (first class) brought me to Chakki Bank, in Punjab. It was pouring relentlessly as the first leg of the long journey ended. "Rickshaw, *seth*, rickshaw?" said a voice as I stepped off the train. I quickly calculated: there could be a big demand for transportation in this weather, it might be prudent to say yes. "Yes," I said, and settled the price to Pathankot bus station.

Outside, auto rickshaws — three wheelers — were parked along the station building in a long line. Enough for everyone, I thought. They had black vinyl tops, and plastic flaps at the side which could be fastened shut, I noted approvingly. I followed my van.

And we came to the end of the line. There, he placed my bag in a pitiful cycle rickshaw, the only one amidst that reassuringly formidable squadron of auto rickshaws. The cycle rickshaw had open sides; and old gunny sacks tied to the top of the frame formed a feeble canopy. I watched in disbelief, appalled by my bad luck. No, stupidity, I corrected myself, for it was clear now why he had come inside the station to solicit a fare. That should have made me suspicious. Once upon a time it would have.

The cycle rickshawalla saw my reaction. He pointed pleadingly at the seat, and I looked him in the face, something I never should have done. I am trusting you, his eyes said, not to break our contract. The auto rickshaws taunted me with their waterproof interiors as I stared longingly after them. Their owners were watching, amused, certain I would cave in. And that settled it for me.

Within seconds of setting off, I was rueing my pride. The gunny sacks were as effective as a broken sieve in keeping out the rain, and despite my raincoat I was soon drenched. The downpour saturated my bag

and its contents — I could almost feel its weight increasing, minute by minute. The cycle rickshawalla struggled to pedal as fast as he could through streets ankle-deep in water. His calf muscles contracted and rippled, knotting with the strain, and a mixture of pity and anger confused me. I wished the ride would end quickly.

In Pathankot, he convinced me a taxi was better than a bus in this weather. Afterwards, I was glad I took his advice: on the mountains, buses had pulled over because the avalanches, the pipe-breaking avalanches, had made the roads far too narrow. Meanwhile, I waited as the rickshawalla and the taxi driver haggled over the former's commission.

And four hours later I was draping my underwear, socks, shirts and pants over the door knob, armchair, lampshade and window. There was a knock. The houseboy (who doubled as waiter, I discovered later in the restaurant) staggered in with two steaming plastic buckets, one red and the other blue. He looked around disbelievingly at my impromptu haberdashery. "All wet," I explained. He smiled and nodded to humour the eccentric occupant.

I wondered briefly where the water in the buckets came from if the pipes were broken. My guess was a well. In the bathroom, I splashed the hot water over me with a mug.

Dharmsala is a collection of settlements perched across the lower ridges of the Dhauladur range. The Dhauladur range itself is a southern spur of the Himalayas, and surrounds the Kangra Valley like a snow-capped fence. McLeod Gunj, at seven thousand feet, is one of the highest settlements. I had passed others on my way up by taxi: Lower Dharmsala and Kotwali Bazaar, the main commercial centre crowded with hotels, shops, and restaurants; Forsyth Gunj, a one-street village; and, of course, the huge military cantonment, which was the beginning of everything, back in the British days.

Early in this century, the British were considering making Dharmsala their summer capital; they found the plains unbearable in the hot season. But an earthquake badly damaged the place in 1905, and they chose another hill station, Simla, a bit further south. (Later, my uncle would describe it differently: the official in charge of selecting the capital was travelling from Dalhousie to Dharmsala when he caught dysentery on the way, reached Dharmsala and died. The idea of Dharmsala as summer capital was promptly abandoned.)

I wanted to see more of McLeod Gunj and Upper Dharmsala. But first I was anxious to meet my aunt and uncle. Next morning, I telephoned them at their general store, and they were delighted to hear my voice. The line was so bad, they thought I was calling from Bombay. No, I said, Hotel Bhagsu, and they insisted I come immediately, their place was only a five-minute walk away.

It was still drizzling. Along the side of the hotel, under every rain spout, was a plastic bucket. My red and blue were there as well. The houseboy was standing guard over them, watching them fill with the run-off from the roof. He looked away guiltily at first when he saw me. Then he must have decided to put the best face on things, for he acknowledged me by smiling and waving. He seemed like a child caught red-handed at mischief.

My uncle and aunt were sorry for the way my visit had begun. "But didn't anyone tell you? This is not a good season for Dharmsala," they said. I had been warned, I admitted, but had decided to come anyway. They found this touching, and also confusing. Never mind, uncle said, perhaps half our troubles would soon be over: the military cantonment had dispatched its men to find and repair the sabotaged power lines. The only snag was, as soon as they mended one, the

strikers snipped through some more.

As for water, said my aunt, not to worry, their supply had not been affected, I could shower here.

Not affected? How? Just then, customers arrived, asking for candles. My aunt went to serve them and my uncle told the story.

During the devastation of the 1905 earthquake, the Nowrojee Store was practically the only structure that survived. Uncle's grandfather had handed out food and clothing and blankets from store supplies till proper relief was organized by the British District Commissioner. When McLeod Gunj was back on its feet, the District Commissioner wanted to show his gratitude to the family. He gifted a mountain spring to them, and arranged for direct water supply from the spring to their house. That private pipeline was still operating after eighty-odd years, and had survived the present avalanches.

I promised I would use their shower in the evening. Then more customers entered, and he had to assist my

133

aunt. Local people were inquiring if the newspaper delivery was expected to get through to Dharmsala. Foreign tourists in designer raincoats were seeking out the sturdy black umbrella which, locally, was the staple defence against the rains. The tourists were also laying in a stock of Bisleri mineral water.

There was a lull in business after this surge. My aunt suggested that uncle take me around Dharmsala for a bit, she could hold the fort alone. So we set off for a walk.

At first the going was slow. Almost every person we passed stopped to exchange a few words, mainly about the weather, and which roads were closed and which were still passable. But it was heartening to see the Tibetan monks, in their crimson robes, always smiling joyfully. For a people who had suffered such hardships and upheavals, struggling to start life over again in a strange land, they were remarkably cheerful

and happy. Perhaps this, and their Buddhist faith, is what sustained them. They had the most wonderful beaming, smiling faces. Just like their spiritual leader, whom I had watched some time ago on "Sixty Minutes," whose countenance seems to radiate an inner well-being.

Exchanging *namaskaars* with everyone we met (the folded-hands greeting, which translates into: I greet the God in you, common to Hindus and Buddhists), we arrived at a tall gold-crowned structure at the centre of a group of buildings. It was a *chorten,* a religious monument, dedicated to the memory of all those suffering under Chinese occupation in Tibet. The faithful were circling round it, spinning two rows of prayer wheels and reciting mantras.

We left the little square and the buildings which housed Tibetan handicraft shops, restaurants and hotels. Further down were the Tibetan homes: shacks and shanties of tin and stone, and every window was adorned with flowers in rusty tin cans. Faded prayer flags fluttered in the trees overhead.

The road climbed steeply. Before I knew it, the buildings and the *chorten* were below us. My uncle turned and pointed. There used to be a beautiful park there, he said, at the centre of McLeod Gunj, but it had to go when the refugees came.

During our walk I had gathered he loved the Tibetan people, and had done much to aid them. I could hear the respect and admiration in his voice when he talked about the Dalai Lama, whom he had helped, back in 1959, to acquire suitable houses and properties where the Tibetans could start rebuilding their lives. But now as my uncle told the story of Dharmsala and the arrival of refugees, I could not help feeling that there was also some resentment towards these people who had so radically changed and remade in their own image the place where he was born, the place he loved so dearly. My aunt, who likes the hustle and bustle of big cities and gets her share of it by visiting relatives periodically, said he would pine away if she ever insisted they leave Dharmsala.

We continued to climb, and on the mountain spur that dominates the valley rose the golden pinnacles of Thekchen Choeling, the Island of Mahayan Teaching, the complex which was the new residence of the Dalai Lama. His cottage had a green corrugated roof, and the temple was a three-storey lemon-yellow hall topped by gold spires. On a low verandah surrounding the temple, a woman was performing repeated prostrations. She was making a circuit of the temple, measuring her progress with her height.

We removed our shoes and went inside. The main hall had a high throne at one end: the Dalai Lama's throne, on which he sat when he gave audiences and preached. There would be no audiences for the next few days, though, because he was away in Ladakh to deliver the Kalachakra — Wheel of Time — Initiation. Behind the throne was a larger-than-life statue of the Buddha in the lotus position. The Buddha was locked in a huge glass case. Myriads of precious and semi-precious stones formed a halo around the Buddha's solid gold head, and hence the locked glass: things had changed in Dharmsala; the increase in population and the tourist traffic forced the monks to take precautions.

The changes were having other effects, too. The mountain slopes were being rapidly deforested by the poverty-stricken population's hunger for firewood. And, as elsewhere in the world, the disappearance of trees was followed by soil erosion. My uncle had pointed out the gashed and scarred hulls on our climb. He said that so many mudslides and rockfalls were unheard of in the old days; and there was less and less snow each year.

I thought of those photographs from my childhood. Their memory suddenly seemed more precious than

ever. The pristine place they had once captured was disappearing.

Inside the temple, at the throne's right, more statues were displayed. One of them had multiple heads and arms: Chenrezi, the awareness-being who symbolizes compassion in the Tibetan pantheon. The legend went that Chenrezi was contemplating how best to work for the happiness of all living things, when his head burst into a thousand pieces as he realized the awesome nature of the task. The Buddha of Limitless Light restored him to life, giving him a thousand heads to represent the all-seeing nature of his compassion, and a thousand arms to symbolize the omnipresence of his help. But now Chenrezi, along with other statues bedecked with gold and jewels, was locked behind a floor-to-ceiling collapsible steel gate.

The rain finally ceased. My uncle wished the mist would clear so he could show me Pong Lake in the distance. When the moon shone upon the water, he said, it took one's breath away. But the mist sat over the valley, unmoving.

Descending the temple road, we saw several monks, prayer beads in hand, walking a circular path around the complex. They were simulating the Lingkhor, the Holy Walk circumscribing the Potala, the Dalai Lama's palace in Tibet. Round and round they walked, praying, perhaps, for a time when he would be back in his palace, and they treading the original Lingkhor.

Inside: the woman, making a mandala of her prostrations around the temple. Outside: the monks, creating circles of prayer around their beloved leader's residence. Circles within circles. The Wheel of Time.

Back at the general store, bad news awaited: the taps were dry. The Tibetan refugees (everyone, Tibetans included, used that word, despite their having lived here thirty years; perhaps clinging to this word kept alive the hope of returning to their Land of

Snows) had discovered that the Nowrojee pipeline still held water. They had cut it open to fill their buckets. Strangely, my uncle and aunt were not too upset. It had happened before. They just wished the people would come to the house and fill their buckets from the taps instead of cutting the pipe.

Later that night, I found my way back to Hotel Bhagsu with a borrowed flashlight. My uncle accompanied me part of the way. Near the incline that led to the hotel, where the road forked, there was a little lamp in an earthen pot, sitting at the very point of divergence. How quaint, I thought. A friendly light to guide the traveller through the pitch-black night. But my uncle grabbed my arm and pulled me away. He said to tread carefully to the right of the lamp, by no means to step over it.

What was it? Something to do with Tibetan exorcism rites, he answered. Did he believe in such things? He had lived here too long, he said, and seen too much, to be able to disbelieve it completely. Despite my skepticism, he succeeded in sending a shiver down my spine. It was only the setting, I explained to myself: a pitch-dark mountain road, the rustling of leaves, swirling mists.

Back at the hotel, the desk clerk apologetically handed me the stubs of two candles. Dharmsala was out of candles, what remained had to be strictly rationed. I asked for water.

One more day, I decided, then I would leave. There was not much to do. The avalanches had closed the roads further north, and the side trips I had planned to Dalhousie, Kulu, and Manali were not feasible. The houseboy knocked.

He was carrying the red bucket. "Where is the blue?" He shook his head: "Sorry, not enough rain. Today only one bucket."

The electricity was back next morning, I discovered thankfully. Around nine, I went to the empty restaurant and ordered tea and toast. Afflicted with a bad stomach, I had been virtually living on toast for the past three days. The houseboy in the persona of waiter took my order cheerfully and left.

Thirty minutes later I was still waiting. The door marked Employees Only was ajar, and I peered into the kitchen. It was empty. The backyard beyond the kitchen window was deserted too. I went to the front desk. No one. Finally, I ran into the night watchman who had just woken. "What is going on?" I asked him with manufactured testiness, remembering long-forgotten roles and poses. "Waiter has disappeared, no one in the kitchen, no one on duty. What has happened? Is this a hotel or a joke?"

He studied his watch and thought for a moment: "Sunday today? Oh yes. Everyone is watching *Ramayan*. But they will come back. Only five minutes left."

The Ramayana is one of the two great Sanskrit epics of ancient India. The other is the Mahabharata, which recently found its way in translation onto western stages in Peter Brook's production. But when the Ramayana, the story of the god Rama, was made into a Hindi TV serial, sixty million homes began tuning in every Sunday morning, and those who did not own TVs went to friends who did. In the countryside, entire villages gathered around the community set. Before the program started, people would garland the TV with fresh flowers and burn incense beside it. Classified ads in newspapers would read: Car For Sale — But Call After *Ramayan*. Interstate buses would make unscheduled stops when the auspicious time neared, and woe betide the bus driver who refused. Ministerial swearing-in ceremonies were also known to be postponed.

The series ended after seventy-eight episodes which, however, were not sufficient to cover the entire epic. In protest, street sweepers went on strike and there were demonstrations in several cities. The Ministry of Information and Broadcasting then sanctioned a further twenty-six episodes in order to bring *Ramayan* and the strike to their proper conclusions.

But the story does not end there. Not satisfied with burning incense and garlanding their television sets on Sunday mornings, people began mobbing the actor who played the role of Rama, genuflecting wherever he appeared in public, touching his feet, asking for his blessing. To capitalize on the phenomenon, Rajiv Ghandi's Congress Party enlisted the actor-god to campaign for their candidate in an upcoming election. The actor-god went around telling people that Rama would give them blessings if they voted for the Congress Party, and how it was the one sure way to usher in the golden age of Rama's mythical kingdom of Ayodhya.

At this point, the intellectuals and political pundits sadly shook their sage heads, lamenting the ill-prepared state of the masses for democracy. Suspension of disbelief was all very well when watching television. But to extend it to real life? It showed, they said, the need for education as a prerequisite if democracy was to work successfully.

When it was time to vote, however, the masses, despite the actor-god and the shaking heads of the intellectuals, knew exactly what to do. The Congress candidate went down in a resounding defeat, and the actor-god became sadly human again.

My waiter returned, promising immediate delivery of my tea and toast. I threw my hands in the air and pretended to be upset: How long was a person supposed to wait? In response to my spurious annoyance, he affected a contrite look. But, like me, his heart was not in it. Like the voters and the actor-god, we played out our roles, and we both knew what was what.

In Bombay, at the beginning of the trip, I had listened amusedly when told about the power of the serial. Intriguing me was the fact that what was, by all

accounts, a barely passable production lacking any kind of depth, with embarrassingly wooden acting, could, for seventy-eight weeks, hold a captive audience made up not only of Hindus but also Muslims, Sikhs, Parsis, Christians — cutting right across the religious spectrum. Could it be that under the pernicious currents of communalism and prejudice there were traces of something more significant, a yearning, perhaps, which transcended these nasty things, so that the great Sanskrit epic of ancient India, a national heritage, could belong to all Indians?

I had not expected to receive a personal demonstration of the Sunday morning power that *Ramayan* wielded. Least of all in this faraway mountain hamlet. In a way, though, it was fitting. Everywhere, *Ramayan* brought diverse communities together for a short while, to share an experience. But in Dharmsala, the native population and the refugees have been sharing and living together for many years. Even the electricity saboteurs co-operated with the show. Of course, shortly after *Ramayan* the region was once again powerless.

Halfway between McLeod Gunj and Forsyth Gunj was an old English church my uncle had told me about. The pure scent of pine was in the air as I walked to it. The rock face of the mountain appeared to have burst into fresh green overnight. The rains had given birth to countless little streams and rivulets that gurgled their descent. Sometimes, at a bend in the road, the noise of water was so loud, it seemed that a huge waterfall was waiting round the corner. But it was only the wind and the mountains playing tricks, orchestrating, weaving and blending the music of the newborn runnels and brooks into one mighty symphony of a cataract.

The church of the beautiful name came into view: the Church of Saint John in the Wilderness, a lonely reminder of the British Raj. It looked very much like any English parish church. The grounds were in grave neglect. A tall pine had fallen across the walkway, brought down by the rains, no doubt. Sunday morning service was in progress. Tourists and local residents made up the scanty congregation.

I walked around to the back and found myself in the churchyard. A ten- or twelve-foot monument dominated the cemetery. Intrigued, I went closer. James Bruce, Eighth Earl of Elgin and Twelfth Earl of Kincardine (1811-1863), read the inscription, barely legible. And then, the positions he had held in the far-flung corners of the Empire: Governor of Jamaica, Governor General of Canada, Viceroy and Governor General of India.

I examined other gravestones. But weather and time had successfully effaced most of the words. A date here, a first name there — Dear Wife ..., or: Faithful Husband ..., and then, Final rest ..., and: Heavenly Peace — these fragments were all I could read.

I went back to Lord Elgin's grave and sat before it on a stone ledge. The churchyard was deserted. I read again the words carved in stone, thinking about this Viceroy who had died in Dharmsala, so far from his own country. I imagined the long journeys he had undertaken for Queen and Country: what had he thought about this ancient country? Had he enjoyed his stay here? How might he have felt at having to live out his life in distant lands, none of them his home? Sitting on the moss-grown ledge, I thought about this man buried here, who, one hundred and twenty-five years ago and more, had governed them both, my old country and my new; I thought about the final things.

The weather-beaten gravestones, the vanished epitaphs, the disappearing inscriptions, somehow brought back to me the fading, indistinct photographs of uncle and aunt, cousins and dog, snow on the rooftops and trees. How far away was it — that Dharmsala of my imagination and of my uncle's youth — how far from what I had seen? As far away, perhaps, as the world of empire in whose cause Lord Elgin had undertaken his travels.

I thought about my own journey: from the Dharmsala of childhood fantasies to the peaceful churchyard of Saint John in the Wilderness; and then, amidst the gentle ruins of weatherworn, crumbling gravestones. back to the fading, curling photographs. To have made this journey, I felt, was to have described a circle of my own. And this understanding increased the serenity of the moment.

It started to drizzle. I put on my raincoat and opened my umbrella. As it gathered strength, the rain streamed down the sides of Lord Elgin's monument and blurred the words I had been reading. Thoughts of departure, of descending from the tranquillity of the mountains into the dusty, frenetic plains, began gnawing at the edges of the moment. But I pushed them away. I sat there a little longer, listening to the soothing patter as the rain fell upon the leaves and on the gravestones all around.

JOHN BERGER

Intellectuals

s I write, Beirut is yet again under siege. In Istanbul five intellectuals, all over the age of seventy, have begun a hunger strike in protest against the conditions of political prisoners, two of whom have just been killed in prison. Every economically underdeveloped country has become poorer in the last month. For several years now, millions of working families in the north of my own country have been abandoned and written off in their misery of unending unemployment.

It is necessary, I think, to recall such facts before a discussion concerning the Intellectual, a discussion which inevitably has to consider the tenuous relationship between theory and practice.

Then, I want to admit a personal conflict within myself. The artist within me — the storyteller, the poet — tolerates badly what he understands by Intellectuals. For him their use of words is (usually) so facile that it resembles lying. At the same time the intellectual within me — the polemicist, the art theoretician, the social analyst — considers that all artists run the risk of pathological egocentricity.

The subject is not an easy one, for it is full of contradictions. Nevertheless I would like to try — even at the risk of great simplification — to talk about a change that may be taking place.

The word *intellectual* — referring to a person — was first used during the nineteenth century. The term referred essentially to a new type of publicist, not to be confused with the earlier categories of scholar, historian, philosopher, humanist, teacher, scientist. What exactly was his function? Can any generalization cover the full range of examples available? From Ruskin to George Orwell, from d'Annunzio to Ego Kisch? It may help to ask: why did the nineteenth century offer or demand a new kind of life's work?

A new intellectual space had been created in Europe — and the phenomenon was essentially European — by literacy and therefore by the growing presence of newspapers, pamphlets and popular books; and, equally, by the newly won principle of democracy, whereby government and government decisions were meant to be subject to public opinion, publicly (as distinct from secretly) mobilized either *en masse,* or in pressure groups.

The intellectual and the journalist were born at

about the same time, to work in the same field. Their roles could overlap, but they were different. The intellectual offered opinions; the journalist offered events. It seems to me that these opinions were all charged, in the way that they were written and in the way that they were read, by an unanswered, unresolved question which hung over the European century of 1840 to 1940.

This persistent question was: *Who is governing who and by what right?* It led to a myriad other questions because, so long as it remained unanswered, nothing could be taken for granted concerning the justice of the status quo in any domain. It is interesting to note here the proverbial enmity between lawyers and intellectuals. Both pleaded: the first before judges, the second before readers: the first according to a legal code, the second before open horizons.

This new, urgent, unanswered question constituted a kind of no-man's land between rulers and ruled. And it was on this terrain that intellectuals spoke, each one with her or his individual voice. Both rulers and ruled, the voted and the voters, needed these voices. The rulers needed them (or some of them) so that they, the rulers, might be legitimatized. Rule in itself no longer carried its own justification. The ruled needed the voices (or some of them) so that their own aspirations might be articulated and claimed within a framework of modern thought and action.

My use of the word *voices* is perhaps misleading. I do not want to suggest that intellectuals served simply as a chorus. They reasoned, they thought, they looked backwards and forwards in history, they sometimes displayed great independence and courage. They were listened to, however, because their voices, filling the no man's land of an unanswered fundamental political question, were doubly needed. However sombre or affirmative their arguments, the intellectuals of this European century spoke in a tone of supreme confidence. This confidence came, not usually from their conclusions, but from their awareness of being doubly needed.

Some belonged to the Left and represented the new aspirations, others belonged to the Right and offered legitimacy. Yet, however opposed their positions, most intellectuals in their heyday formed a single cultural group. Members of opposing factions might even go to the same café. They constituted a modern confraternity, and in their texts and explanations continually referred to one another.

Their century is now finished. It is over because the unanswered question has been — not answered! — but superseded. *Who is governing who?* has been replaced by Consumerism, with its dreams of acquisition and, even more powerful, its fears of deprivation. A fatal feature of our present societies is that Consumerism and unemployment go hand in hand. Little of course, or nothing, passing between the hands.

On the no man's land has been built a supermarket. Most social and political issues are now treated with public-relations and marketing techniques. These include media publicity, instant public-opinion polls and a new art of political address adapted for television. The essential aim of such an art is to simulate a "sincerity," whereby the ruler appears to speak to the ruled as if their relationship were an intimate one, as if there were no distance or disputed ground between them. To some degree the professional interviewer who provokes this "intimacy" has replaced both the intellectual and the journalist.

Thus neither rulers nor ruled have much need of intellectuals in the old traditional sense. Those who rule are today legitimatized by manufactured "popularity," while the aspirations of the majority of the ruled are temporarily smothered by manipulated consumerist fears and promises. It is here that advertising achieves its political, as distinct from economic, purpose:

politics have become management.

When it is noted that no new intellectual "stars" have replaced those of the last generation (of, say, Sartre or Bertrand Russell) there is no reason to deduce a generational insufficiency. They would be there today if the space for them was open. It has been closed — along with the question which animated their first appearance.

The telephone has just interrupted me. A call from New York from a man I don't know. Ron Carver, a union organizer. He is collecting money to buy paintings by Ralph Fasanella, who, now in his seventies, is probably the only true proletarian painter of Manhattan — most of his life he earned his living as a worker. Private collectors have begun to acquire his canvasses to decorate their home. Ron Carver is buying them to give to museums so that those whose lives the paintings are about will be able to see them for themselves. A boost to their confidence.

Those who yesterday might have been traditional intellectuals may tomorrow perform another role, for which as yet there is no clear name. Gramsci foresaw this development when he spoke of a future need for "organic intellectuals," by which he meant thinkers and spokesmen who belonged "organically" to the ruled.

Fifty years after Gramsci we can perhaps more easily understand what this means. The nominal question about government has been replaced by a more fundamental and organic one: *How to survive?*

This question may seem minimalist, but in fact it is total. Ultimately the future of the world depends upon it. It begins with the entire planet and the threat of nuclear war. It concerns the life of cities, communities, national minorities, poor nations. How to survive in Rio de Janeiro, in Nicaragua, or in Rochdale?

It would be a mistake to believe that the question can be reduced to a purely ecological one — important as this is. It is not only the survival of nature which is threatened, but also the survival of politics and culture — which is to say the survival of human self-respect.

For self-respect to survive, it is necessary that the long historical experience of the ruled be at last articulated in such a way that it offers a sense to life, an explanation of the world, which can challenge the opportunism, ruthlessness and anonymity of corporate power — in both its economic and military practices. Every day these practices ignore, violate, trivialize and insult such experience.

A striking feature of our time is that its sense of history is now most intense, not in universities, but in popular movements of survival and struggle. Faced with the infantilism (barbarism) of ruling élites, the initiative of maturity has passed to the underprivileged and displaced. One is reminded of the New Testament.

Collective nostalgia is always a form of privileged decay. Primitivism is usually a mask for cruelty. Modern technology is essential to the modern world. The danger is that the instantaneity of its techniques defines its aims. Instant profit. Instant greed. Instant prestige. The instant future. This is why a sense of history has become a condition for our survival.

The most urgent task today for those who might once have been traditional intellectuals is to invoke the historical experience of the ruled, to underwrite their self-respect, and to proffer — not to display — intellectual confidence.

LINDA HUTCHEON

Christa Wolf as Cassandra

he accountability of the artist and the intellectual in both the public and the private spheres has become one of the obsessions of the nineties, but it has been the constant concern of Christa Wolf, arguably the best-known German woman writer of this century. There are personal reasons for the predominance of this theme in her work, as Wolf has always been the first to point out.

Born in Landsberg an der Warthe (now Gorzow Wielkopolski in Poland) in 1929, she grew up in (and was part of) Hitler's Germany, and it was through her searing self-investigation in *Kindheitsmuster (Patterns of Childhood)* that she sought to come to terms with what this meant to both her and her country — what we used to call East Germany — where her family fled in advance of the Soviet army in 1945. At twenty, Wolf discovered Marxism and, as she put it, what had once been "real" gradually became "unreal." (Thirty years later feminism would have precisely the same enormous impact on her thinking and writing.)

Because of this reading of Marx (while studying German literature and philosophy at Jena and Leipzig), Wolf became a member of the SED, the Socialist Unity Party, and for the next twenty years she was active in the Central Committee of the SED and in the Writers' Union. A committed socialist, she has always believed that self-criticism is the only way to match ideals and reality, and so, for Wolf, this has meant being willing to raise a consistently oppositional voice, even (and especially) within socialism. In her eyes, the GDR potentially represented liberation from life in an antagonistic class society in which the only position the writer could hold with integrity was that of alienation; among East German political and historical advantages, she once listed the possibility of a "profoundly committed life" wherein literature could engage actively in social processes, rather than simply chronicling them. In practice, however, she found that German socialism often meant conformity and repression, and this sort of contradiction is what she has spent her life confronting and exposing, often finding herself cast in the unwilling role of Cassandra.

In her work in the early sixties, as both critic and novelist, Wolf willingly adopted the then dominant Lukacsian and Socialist Realist view of the broader social function of the writer and of literature. The

publication of *Nachdenken über Christa T. (Quest for Christa T.)* in 1968, however, marked her first departure from these strictures and her first defence of what she would come to call "subjectivity authenticity" — the author's self-reflexive concern for the social and moral dimensions of her own subjectivity within the collective ideals of socialist society. Condemned as pessimistic, antisocial, self-indulgent, decadent, bourgeois individualism, this book was officially blocked and its publication in the GDR delayed; it also cost her the candidacy of the SED Central Committee in 1968.

Increasingly openly critical of such cultural censorship, Wolf nevertheless remained a committed socialist, even after her 1977 public protest against the expulsion of GDR political writer Wolf Biermann, a protest that caused her to lose her executive position on the Writers' Union after a formal reprimand for disloyalty to the state. While many of her writer friends chose this moment to move to the Federal Republic,

Wolf and her husband stayed on — as they do today under even more difficult political conditions, perhaps — urging writers not to abandon the ideals of socialism. At the time of the fall of the Berlin Wall, Wolf became a public opponent of unification. But she also published *Was bleibt? (What Remains?),* a brief account of the years of isolation after the Biermann protest when the Stasi, the secret communist state police, kept her under unnerving surveillance.

Ever critical of abuses but ever faithful to ideals, Wolf has remained loyal to her belief in the possibility of a humane and just socialism. Nevertheless she has recently come under vehement attack for waiting until it was safe — and perhaps opportune — to publish this account. Even more damning has been the accusation that she had been a privileged state writer, thus calling into question her integrity while also associating her with a now-discredited regime. According to her supporters, such as writer Günter Grass, this distortion of her constantly oppositional position within the GDR can be seen as a political ploy, one that reveals the hidden conservative agenda behind German unification: that is, the desire to erase the history of the GDR and, with it, that of the conveniently named National Socialism. Certainly, thanks to verbal excesses, that connection has been made frequently enough in the last year. As one of her defenders has argued (in the *Nation*): "Wolf is a sacrificial lamb in a larger project: the ideological shaping of united Germany."

Wolf's case is, indeed, a complex one: for the last fifteen years she has been neither a state writer nor a dissident, but an oppositional voice speaking from within who has persisted in believing in that Utopian possibility of justice and tolerance within socialism — even in the face of the manifest contradictions of lived social reality in the GDR.

Interestingly, these recent attacks have come from precisely the same quarters as had the praise that made her the important cultural figure she is today. Her international reputation grew rapidly in the eighties and nineties, with the publication of *Kein Ort. Niergends (No Place on Earth)* in 1979, *Kassandra. Erzählung* and *Voraussetzungen einer Erzählung* (published together in English as *Cassandra: A Novel and Four Essays)* in 1983, and *Störfall (Accident)* in 1986. In the last decade she has been awarded all the major German-language prizes for literature and become almost a cult figure in Europe. The reason for this was not solely her socialist ideals or the sense one might have of her personal integrity — both under attack today — but the fusion of these with other politicized global concerns of our times: feminism, pacifism, environmentalism. It is this range that may well enable her to weather the storm of temporary and parochial German anti-leftist politics today. Her concern for the dialectic relationship between the social and the subjective — the cause of her break with the official GDR

policies of Socialist Realism — has been extended from its original focus on the issue of class to include that of gender.

In her 1981 address to the *Berliner Begegnung zur Friedensforderung* at the Academy of Arts in East Berlin, Wolf linked women's exclusion from the creation of cultural, moral and aesthetic values in European culture with the increasing destructiveness of society, as witnessed by the threat of both nuclear and ecological disaster today. The history of this exclusion is explored more fully in *Kassandra,* where the protagonist articulates her awareness of the complex power of patriarchy in these moving terms:

> I remember that suddenly I paused, sat for a long time without moving, struck by the lightning realization: This is pain.
>
> It was pain, which I had thought I knew. Now I saw that until then it had barely grazed me. You do not distinguish the boulder that buries you beneath it, but only the force of the impact; so my pain at the loss of everything I had called "father" was threatening to crush me with its weight.

As a consistently oppositional thinker, though, Wolf refuses any simplistic blaming of patriarchy or any retreat into radical feminist separatism or sectarianism. She sees women both as victims of a male order and as the hope for the future, for they are "less disfigured" by the modern world they have not had a hand in creating. Rejecting any biological essentialism or even idealization, Wolf is always careful to historicize. Her interest, as she explained in an interview a few years ago, is in "those women who recognize and seize the historical moment presented to them, no matter how difficult that may be. They are able earlier than most men to articulate how a new way of life and a new era might feel." The Utopian impulse of Marxism meets the similar impulse in feminism and pacifism, as *Kassandra* illustrates so well.

That this particular configuration of concerns left some non-socialist and non-German readers puzzled and even irritated is clear from the North American reviews of that book. Wolf's Cassandra was castigated by the *New Republic* for being "not the daughter of Hecuba, but of Rosa Luxemburg"; the *New York Times Book Review* made her story into that of her creator and unkindly described it as a tale of "the mental anguish of a woman trying to understand the world around her but lacking the knowledge and mental discipline to offer persuasive and practical solutions." From the perspective of Reaganite America, perhaps anyone trying to rewrite the canonical accounts of the heroic male past from the point of view of a non-heroic woman — from the losing side — might be suspect.

The Greek version of the tale — that of Homer, Aeschylus, Euripides — is well known: Cassandra, the most beautiful of the daughters of the Trojan king, Priam, was offered by Apollo whatever she wanted in return for her sexual favours. Requesting and being granted the gift of prophecy, Cassandra then refused the sexual part of the god's bargain and, as a punishment, was condemned forever to tell the truth but never to be believed. To no avail, then, she prophesied the fall of Troy, should war with the Greeks be waged, and subsequently the bloody fall of the House of Atreus.

In Wolf's version, Cassandra is a seer, yes, but what she sees is ... the obvious: greed, pride, mendacity, aggression, repression, crimes committed in the name of honour. She possesses what Wolf once called the "hard-headed vision" of women who take their share in responsibility and thus avoid having their vision "clouded" by "deluded political thinking." Not really a tragic or heroic figure, this Cassandra is often a rather ordinary daughter, sister, lover, professional woman — demystified but also granted new dignity as a self-possessed individual with integrity and autonomy. Her prophetic powers become less significant than her ability to bear witness and to offer a Utopian collective alternative vision based on the unheroic dailiness of social experience within a community. This is her description of the communal world of peace outside Troy and its war:

Aeneas came, he sat beside me, he stroked the air above my head. I loved him more than my life. He did not live with us like many young men whom the war had damaged in body and soul. They arrived like shadows; our blazing life restored their colour, blood, zest. When I close my eyes I see the picture. Mount Ida in the shifting light. The slopes with their caves. The Scamander, its banks. That was our world, no landscape could be more beautiful. The seasons. The scent of the trees. And our free existence, a new joy for each new day. The citadel did not reach as far as here. They could not fight the enemy and us at the same time. They left us alone, took from us the fruits we harvested, the cloth we wove. We ourselves lived in poverty. I remember that we sang a lot. Talked a lot, evenings by the fire in Arisbe's cave, where the figure of the goddess on the wall seemed to be alive. Killa and other women used to pray to her and place offerings. No one tried to stop them. We knew we were lost, but we did not force that knowledge on those who needed a firm hope. Our good cheer was not forced, though it never lost its dark undercoat. We did not stop learning. Each shared his own special knowledge with the other. I learned to make pots, clay vessels. I invented a pattern to paint on them, black and red. We used to tell each other our dreams; many of us were amazed at how much they revealed about us. But more than anything else we talked about those who would come after us. What they would be like.

Whether they would still know who we were. Whether they would repair our omissions, rectify our mistakes. We racked our brains trying to think of a way we could leave them a message, but did not know any script to write in.

Wolf's Cassandra is even more of an oppositional figure than was Schiller's because she is historicized in the context of what the novella calls "property, hierarchy, and patriarchy." And what is equally important is that she is never only a critic of the existing order; she also offers an alternative vision.

So too does Wolf. Rejecting the "blood red thread" of linear plot structure so dear to what she sees as a male narrative drive, Wolf structures *Kassandra* as a densely and intricately woven — and unfinished — fabric: "There are wefts which stand out like foreign bodies, repetitions, material that has not been worked out to its conclusion." This description is taken from the start of the four essays that are published with the novel in the current English and German editions. Similarly rich fabrics, these generically diverse essays began as lectures in Frankfurt in 1982, never intended for publication in the East (when they were, considerable cuts were made by the censors, especially where Wolf's position on unilateral nuclear disarmament contradicted official policy). They take the forms of a travel journal, a work diary, a letter — all forms which stress living process over finished product. This is another constant in Wolf's writing: from her earliest interviews on, she has been stressing that writing is a "process that continually runs alongside life, helping to

shape and interpret it: writing can be seen as a way of being more intensely involved in the world, as the concentration and focusing of thought, word and deed." She has always argued that to present a writer's "subjective authenticity" as the basis of art is not a retreat from the burning issues of the day, but is instead "interventionist" in the strongest sense of the word. Today she is living out the consequences of this belief.

She once, Cassandra-like, said that only the subject who is prepared to undergo unrelenting exposure should take on such a task, for only through such self-examination can the productive tensions and mergings of author and material, of personal and public, come about.

That this dialectic process occurs in a specifically narrative form is another constant in Wolf's writing: her earliest essays and lectures are already in the form of stories. She has always called all her writing simply "prose," but it is also narrative, for it gives more than information (the task of media prose) and facts (the task of scientific prose). It is also the product of other narratives, other stories. One of the reasons why Wolf is such a "difficult" writer is that she is a complex reader, and rereader. *Kassandra* is a rereading of not only Homer, Aeschylus, Euripides, Herodotus, Aristotle, Schiller and Kleist, but of Thomas Mann, Goethe, and a host of women writers from Sappho to Ingeborg Bachmann. It is as much Cassandra, then, as Wolf herself who could say: "Without books I am not I" — one of the oft-cited Wolf's most oft-cited comments.

A few years ago — before unification — an article in *Die Presse* called Wolf *"eine grosse Moralistin,"* and it is true that the terms "moralist" and "moral" appear as often as does the label "political" in the vast amount of writing about her in the last decade, both in the academy and in the media. She has admitted to being able to write only about things that disturb her, especially about the contradictions within herself and her culture. Just as she had openly rejected both crude historical determinism and "soulless pragmatism" that she had seen in the GDR, she also rejects what she calls both the "moral voyeurism" and the contempt for the very idea of morality in some Marxist theorizing. Her ethical interest is a practical one in how our world must be adapted to a morality of human dignity. Arguing that socialist (and feminist and pacifist) writers can be moralists too, Wolf refuses any separation of the moral and the political. In the wake of postmodern challenges to humanist moral universals, the concerns for the moral and the general have of late been "transcoded" into concerns for the political and the particular.

For Wolf, this would be a false separation. In *Kindheitsmuster,* she chose to come to terms with her own and her nation's Nazi history, not in order to exorcise the past, but in order to understand the present. The ethical question she asks of all Germans is: "How did we become the people that we are?" Perhaps not everyone wants an answer.

Her "subjective" interest in social issues has specifically been in the conditions that produce, to use her own list, "obsequiousness, conformism, mistrust, the compulsion to succeed and the inability to feel love and grief" — in any nation. Only after an analysis of such conditions can one begin to posit alternative visions, visions which are always, for her, part of the now-historical legacy of the GDR's ideal (if not real)

Utopian socialism. In an interview almost twenty years ago, Wolf said that literature under socialism should both create and analyze "the conditions under which human beings can realize their own potential as moral beings." But this expression of a Utopian moral impulse is immediately followed by a warning that these conditions are also those that are "necessary to ensure that the human race neither blows itself up nor otherwise destroys itself."

In 1986, in *Störfall,* her meditation on the Chernobyl nuclear disaster and on the promises and failures of technological advancement, Wolf repeated this hope, but with more of an edge, more of a worry that time may be running out for the human race and the planet earth, that she may indeed be living the role of Cassandra in more ways than one. She has not fallen prey, as so many might have, to cynicism or irony in the face of either the recent personal attacks or the challenges to her pacifist, environmentalist, feminist, and (especially) socialist beliefs; she continues to probe both those challenges and her own beliefs, willingly opening old wounds and new, arguing that this is the responsibility of the writer who is determined to be held accountable — and to be heard. In an early essay she wrote that writing was one operation in that "complex process to which we give the splendid and simple name 'living.'" This combination of accountability, Utopian hope, and a very real "faith in the terrestrial" and the everyday is what has helped make Christa Wolf into one of the most timely of today's writers, one whose prophecies we dare not leave unheeded, however temporarily out of favour she may be in the micro-political context of a unified Germany (and Europe) today.

An Interview With Russell Banks

ussell Banks is among a handful of American fiction writers who, over the last decade, have reinvented American realistic fiction in the short story and in the novel. Like some of his peers (he mentions Toby Wolff, Don DeLillo, Bobbie Ann Mason, and Lynn Sharon Schwartz, among others) Banks has been something of a late bloomer, not publishing his first book (a collection of short stories) until he was thirty-five. Previously, Banks was perhaps best known for his activities in the American small press, most notably with the magazine *Lillabulero*, which he founded with his longtime friend, poet William Matthews. From the mid-sixties until the early seventies, *Lillabulero* published early work by many prominent contemporary American authors, including Joyce Carol Oates, Robert Creeley, Tom Clark, Leon Rooke, and James Tate. The *American Dictionary of Literary Biography* credits *Lillabulero* with being "instrumental in elevating small press publications to respectability in the literary community."

Continental Drift, in the wake of earlier efforts like *Trailer Park,* firmly established Banks as a master of the blue-collar tragedy. In parallel chapters the novel relates the grim stories of Bob Dubois, a New Hampshire furnace repairman who abandons an empty, predictable life in the north for an even emptier promise of a new beginning in Florida, and Vanise Dorsinville, who flees Haiti for the "promised land" of America. The stories converge in a rainstorm off the coast of Florida, where Dubois finds himself party to the drowning of a boatload of smuggled Haitian refugees, forced from the boat at gunpoint in an effort to elude the Coast Guard.

Like Dubois, Wade Whitehouse, the "hero" of *Affliction,* Banks's seventh novel, is shortsighted and his dreams are generated and then destroyed by the socio-economic realities of contemporary America. Banks lays out the constrained passage of his characters' lives in heart-breaking detail — from the squalid reality of life in a south Florida trailer park to the dark cycle of abuse and domestic violence which afflicts, and ultimately consumes, Whitehouse. Banks's America is populated with abused wives and abandoned children, men of limited abilities and imagination who buckle and ultimately collapse under the pressure of lives over which they have only fleeting control.

Though he works primarily in a realistic tradition, Banks has formidable stylistic range. His short novel *The Relation of My Imprisonment* (1983) reads like a Kafka parable while *Hamilton Stark* (1979) employs a dizzying array of narrative strategies in dissecting the anomalous life of a New England pipefitter. The story does not so much proceed as accumulate, in second- and third-hand anecdotes, in quotations and details from the man's life, and, most importantly, in the widely differing accounts of his character in selections from "novels-in-progress" written by his friend (whose name we are never told) and Stark's estranged daughter Rochelle.

Banks appears to thrive on these kinds of risky literary ventures. *The Book of Jamaica* (1980) deals with life among the island's maroons; *Continental Drift* spends a great deal of time focussed on the spiritual life of Black Haitians, in particular the rite and ritual of the *voudon* religion. *Affliction* is overtly concerned with the psychological mechanics of domestic violence, and includes painful material from the author's personal history.

"I can really see my life as an obsessive return to the 'wound'," says Banks in a recent article by Wesley Brown in the *New York Times Magazine*. Like Wade Whitehouse, Banks fell victim to an abusive father at an early age, and found himself repeating the cycle of violence and abandonment in early adulthood. Like Wade Whitehouse and Hamilton Stark, Banks is from a difficult, working-class New England background, and toiled as a pipefitter himself before finally deciding to complete his education at Chapel Hill, North Carolina.

In recent years, Banks has taught at the undergraduate creative writing program at Princeton University. He spoke with *Brick* from his home in the hills near Lake Placid, New York, and again during a visit to Toronto for a reading at Harbourfront to launch *Affliction.*

Connolly: One of the first things which struck me about your novels was how literate they were. You seem very conscious of what has already been written, where similar questions have come up in literature before. Do you see yourself and your work as part of a literary continuum or tradition?

Banks: I don't think I'm any more or less conscious of tradition than most fiction writers are. It may be that I'm less intent on hiding that side of it, affecting ignorance of precedent. It's the ground that it stands on. It's a legitimate subject for any work of art. In my work precedent and tradition are part of the subject matter sometimes. The work is commenting on and arguing with, sometimes simply honouring its ancestors.

Connolly: Do you do a lot of research into past literature?

Banks: Not in those terms. I think like most writers, most readers too, I've internalized the sources to a large degree. It runs along as a melody in the middle of what I'm hearing while I'm writing. Very much like a jazz musician can hear all the music he's ever heard while he's playing. Not all of it, maybe, but huge chunks of it while he's playing. So you don't have to consciously sit and look it up or go through the ten-foot shelf of Harvard Classics. You have most of that already in your ears.

Connolly: But you seem conscious of it when it does arrive on the page.

Banks: I delight in it and I invite it in. I don't have any desire or need to be a "great original." Or seem to be a great original. I don't think any of us really are. Some writers would rather seem to be than others. I have no particular interest in seeming to be.

Obviously there are some traditions I have more affinity for than others. In fiction I'm responsive to work that has been willing to consciously play with, and honour, and argue with, other works of art. That means that I'm probably a lot more inclined to work out of a tradition in English literature coming out of Laurence Sterne all the way through to Joyce and more contemporary work — Flann O'Brien and so forth.

Connolly: You also seem to include rather a lot of philosophy. That quote from Kierkegaard that opens *Hamilton Stark* for instance.

Banks: Ideas are important to me. But I'm not as interested in ideas as I am in characters who have ideas, to their detriment or to their greater dignity. Sometimes it's both, as I think is the case in *The Relation of My Imprisonment,* or the narrator in *Hamilton Stark.*

Connolly: One of the most original aspects of your novels is the narrative structure. I was thinking that *Continental Drift* for example must have taken an awful lot of mapping out in advance.

Banks: Well, the structure of *Continental Drift* happened to come to me pretty clearly with the initial conception of the book. I didn't have to do much mapping in that regard. I knew from the beginning that I wanted to bring together this Haitian refugee and American boatman or smuggler or whatever you want to call him, and that he would come from northern New England or French Canada in some way and that she would come from the heart of the Caribbean and they would meet naturally in Florida. Once I knew that then it seemed to me perfectly obvious what I had to do — I just had to cross-cut — go back and forth and keep both their stories operating. The logic of the image created the form and the image was there before I began to write. It came in a flash, grew in fact out of a newspaper clipping I had seen of an event not unlike the one in *Continental Drift,* where Haitian refugees were forced off a boat by its captain when the Coast Guard had come upon them, and the Haitians were drowned. It was one of those articles that were quite common in newspapers in the early eighties. But this one particularly struck me because the captain had forced them off the boat while they were in sight of land. And they had drowned. Right there that afternoon, while reading it, I knew how the book should be built. *Hamilton Stark,* which is a lot more intricate in a way, and digressive in its structure, needed more conscious planning and rewriting and reworking as I went. I really didn't know where I was going for the longest time on that.

Connolly: When you do a lot of conscious work in a text do you find it hard sometimes to keep it fresh?

Banks: Well, it's always the risk you run. You're not exactly peeling off the skin of an onion, you're just sort of smoothing it out and losing any connection, any adhesion. I've had that happen to a work because I had rewritten it too many times and lost any emotional connection that I might have had to it.

There's a kind of revision though that allows you to re-ignite what you're doing — which is a more radical form of revision. At some point you stop and go away from it for a while, so that when you come back you're able to radically revise. Change the whole point of view, or re-engage the book in such a significantly different way that it becomes adhesive again.

I see it in student work a lot, where a piece is revised so steadily and so assiduously that it's gone. It's like sanding a piece of wood until there's no wood left and they have to look around for another block of wood to work on. As you get older that's less likely to happen. You're more aware of how to revise. You know that changing the punctuation and cleaning up the grammar and maybe moving some of the characters around ultimately doesn't solve the problem. If it doesn't solve the problem then you're going to have to make a more radical reinvention of the story, and go into it more aggressively. That's the hardest thing in a way to teach students. How to revise aggressively. You say revise and they think that what you're talking about is sanding and shining and cleaning up — things like that instead of "re-vise," which means to re-envision the entire thing.

Thomas Berger said somewhere that all the problems of writing come down to the approach to the thing written about. Your approach to the event or character written about is where all the technical and moral and linguistic and formal problems of writing occur.

Connolly: Those two bracketing pieces in *Continental Drift* which serve as epilogue and prologue. I was wondering how many people told you: "Take them out, Russell. They don't fit."

Banks: [*laughs*] Most people in the end, I think, understood and appreciated their presence in the book formally and imaginatively, and probably in some ways morally. But there were a lot of people — book reviewers and in particular British book reviewers — who were offended by the directness of the Invocation and the Envoi. People who were offended by the directness of it didn't bother me in the slightest. The intent of any writer is to be as direct as possible. You're only indirect when you can't be direct for some reason. And I found a way for myself to be as direct as possible. You're only indirect when you can't be direct for some reason. And I found a way for myself to be direct in that book with the Invocation and the Envoi. To say this is what I'm doing and this is how I'm going to do it at the beginning and to say this is what I think I've done and this is what I hope will happen as a result at the end.

Connolly: The Envoi is extremely important. It's such a different book without it. It ends on such a note of despair otherwise that it would almost be too much to accept.

Banks: That's right. It would have been for me, would have been bleaker than I really feel. You'd say, "What an exercise in futility this is to write a book like this."

Connolly: When you have the spiritual sense that your books seem to convey it's hard to get a sense of the positive out of them. There really isn't an awful lot of dignity in the way Bob Dubois goes out, even though he's made what turns out to be a very foolish effort to make amends for what he's done.

Banks: Well, I can't argue with you there. His death wasn't meant to be uplifting or ennobling. What I was trying to do was describe a life that was, despite its failures and inadequacies — and its end — a noble life. And not to do it in a Shakespearean way.

Connolly: I wanted to ask you about *Hamilton Stark*. Really, the book is an evasion of itself, of its own telling. It's an evasion of identity. It's almost a book about not writing a book.

Banks: That's an interesting response. I think it's true what you're saying.

Connolly: Do you think there's something a bit entropic about the accumulation of conflicting information about the lead character that is set up in that book? As if the more information you acquire about a subject the more shrouded it becomes.

Banks: Yes, that was one of the things that book was about. That and parody. I think I was parodying the fictional conventions that ride on information. I'm interested in the idea you've raised there that it's a book about evasion. Because in a sense it's meant to be its own untelling. The truth of the matter lies in what it finally can't say and doesn't say.

It isn't so much about not writing a book as it's about not revealing the truth. Telling the truth but not revealing the truth. Especially as regards a certain kind of male presence in the world. Hamilton Stark is the archetype for that kind of male presence.

Connolly: I read it after I read the new book and *Continental Drift* and it seemed to reveal a lot about your obsession with this particular kind of character. You really can't read *Affliction* and *Continental Drift* without seeing the similarity in the two characters.

They're different people but they're the same type, as Hamilton Stark is to an extent. That's obviously an obsession for you.

Banks: They share a sociology with each other. Wade Whitehouse and Bob Dubois besides coming from the same part of the continent also came from the same class and very similar backgrounds. And I share that with them. They're very different from, in Wade Whitehouse's case, brother Rolfe the narrator, and in Hamilton Stark's case, the narrator of his story. In some ways the process of writing *Affliction* was a re-gathering and a rewriting of *Hamilton Stark*. A return, in a more conscious and maybe a more emotionally mature and knowledgeable way, to the central themes and concerns of that book. I have technical means that I really didn't have then. I was aware of the sociological connections and even the thematic connections but not that it really was in a lot of ways a rewriting. It was only possible for me after having written the other books over the intervening years, so that I could approach the subject matter as pointedly and directly as I did in *Affliction*.

Connolly: In *Hamilton Stark* there are a lot of interesting questions raised about identity — the distinction between what a person actually is and how other people see him. That seems to be connected also to questions about writing, about creating a person. Do you think people can see others the way they actually are, or do they see an imaginative creation, or a conglomerate of other people's perceptions about that person?

Banks: I think our characters are a direct expression of our own needs, just as the figures in our dreams are. Who they are is what they need of the world and how those needs get revealed. That comes close to my understanding of personal identity as well. Who we are is very much how our needs are expressed.

Connolly: At one point in that book a character says that you have to be careful of certain kinds of anomalous people. They tend to swallow up the whole world.

Banks: [*laughs*] Well, "Madame Bovary, c'est moi," you know. Hamilton Stark is me and so is Wade Whitehouse and Bob Dubois. I think that's true for any novelist. Finally, you are your characters. The whole process of writing is one of self-discovery, externalizing these fantasies and phantasms and images, and using observable behaviour as a way of making known to yourself the nature of your own *character*.

Connolly: Do you think that's why it's easier to invent a character than evoke one based on a real person?

Banks: Yes, and what's a "real person" anyhow? [*laughs*] I don't even know any real people. If you get to that point you might as well enjoy yourself and invent a character. You're not going to get blamed for making portraits anyhow so why not have fun with it?

There's also the more mundane concern that you don't really know yourself that well. If you think you really are adhering to a real person or yourself as you know it, chances are that self-servingness and lying and self-interestedness are going to determine your choices. Autobiography is always self-advertisement. It is inevitably and necessarily self-invention.

Connolly: This seems to be a real concern in all your work. The idea that the invented has more power than what's commonly held to be real, or objective.

Banks: And I suppose in some final sense I'm trying to dramatize the value, the creative power that language has to determine reality. I mean if it weren't true politicians wouldn't be so nervous about language. Or theologians, or any of the other people who are supposed to be dealing with reality. It's clear that language is what creates reality for us.

So that's what I mean by the imagination having the

power to create reality — the artist's imagination, and the imagination of the advertisers, and of corporate interests, and of governmental and clerical interests. I mean look at what happened to Salman Rushdie. It's his reality versus the Imam's reality. Which one is going to be the operative one, is what the argument's about. For the Imam, and now for Salman, it's a matter of life and death.

Connolly: At its basis it's a very primitive thing.

Banks: Oh, I think it is, absolutely. It's at the centre of the species' experience.

Connolly: The Haitian story in *Continental Drift* for instance. It's interesting that the one overt religious experience is so closely related to that kind of primitivism. That moment when Vanise squats in the sand and draws her symbols and the dog arrives is a perfect example of that. She needs a *loa* and the dog is created out of that need.

Banks: And it's real. It's a talking dog. I wanted it to be as real as they were and as real as Bob Dubois — from the same level of reality.

Connolly: That depiction of Haiti and that part of the world — almost as an imagined place — have you had much reaction, positive or negative, to your approach in that sense?

Banks: I haven't had any negative responses. I haven't had anyone write letters saying that was a comic-book portrait of life in Haiti or the Third World or anything like that. In fact, quite to the contrary. To my gratification — because I was anxious about it. Any time you start to portray lives that are radically unlike your own you run the risk of misrepresenting those lives. And I was extremely relieved when a number of very knowledgeable people, Haitians and others, wrote or spoke to me and told me that I had gotten it right. Especially the *voudon* and the central role it plays in the life of Haitians. Because I had great respect for that and what I know about it is enough to lead me to deal with it with great modesty — well, not modesty, maybe humility. Because I think I'm very immodest in my use of it in that book. But I approached it with an awareness of its complexity and the difficulty of getting it right. And so I was very gratified not to have blown it in that regard.

I was also gratified to hear from Black writers and from women especially who had thought that I had gotten it right. That kind of relieved me. The same thing with *The Book of Jamaica* which deals with life among the maroons in the back country of Jamaica. That's extremely specialized stuff. And it's obvious to any reader that I'm white and I'm North American and male, and so any entry I have to that world is going to be tentative and restricted.

Connolly: You've spent some time in the Caribbean.

Banks: Yes, I lived in Jamaica and I travelled pretty widely all over the Caribbean. But spending some time there doesn't give you access to a culture beyond the most superficial detail. So I had to make a lot of intuitive jumps and I had to do a fair amount of research, too. Library rat kind of research — hanging out late at night and going through the materials.

Connolly: Perhaps even your consciousness of that guaranteed that it wouldn't become a problem.

Banks: And also certain technical moves. For instance, I tried really hard to stay out of Vanise's head and only trusted myself to go into the heads of characters where I could be reasonably sure of what was going on. I could describe the world, not as a Black Jamaican perceives it, but a world in which a Black Jamaican is present. Because I've been to that world and I know what it looks like. But I had to be very careful regarding point-of-view when dealing with that part of the book's consciousness.

Connolly: It creates a nice counterpoint in *Continental Drift*. The world completely defined by the limits of the mind, as in the case of Bob Dubois's sections, and then the opposite in Vanise's sections where her world is completely limited physically.

Banks: She wasn't, but the narrator's point of view limited itself in that way. Of course, she herself has as much an interiorized view of the world as Bob Dubois. I just didn't choose to try and present that.

Connolly: There was enough claustrophobia just in her attempt to cover twenty miles to the coast of Florida.

Banks: Just the physical circumstances. Yes, absolutely.

Connolly: Are you at all worried about the reception of *Affliction* on the subject of male violence?

Banks: I am a little. On the first level you have all that dread and anxiety whenever a book is about to be published. The kind of thing that made John Cheever, whenever he had a book come out, leave the country. He didn't come back until all the reviews were in and its fate was decided. That's a little extreme, but I do have some anxiety about it, as I have with every book I've published. You work a couple of years on something and it's all delayed gratification and delayed response. You don't know whether you're slightly schizophrenic and people are just conning you — your spouse, your editor or whatever. [*laughs*] I have the nervousness that one has when one approaches a really big reality check.

That's there. And then I'm aware that I'm dealing with decidedly unpleasant subject matter, and yet a subject that I think is very important in our society and needs to be talked about and, I think, needs to be dramatized in fiction. And rarely gets dramatized in fiction. When I sat down to write this book I started looking for models and was thinking that there was damn little of it that wasn't strictly limited to domestic violence as experienced by a child or a woman. There was almost nothing written about it as it was experienced by the perpetrator, the adult male. And anyone who has studied domestic violence knows that the perpetrator has almost been a victim of it. I felt that the only way to tell the story was to tell it from the point of view of the perpetrator. That was the real puzzle.

Connolly: It would be easy for someone to label you — stupidly I think — as an apologist for Wade Whitehouse.

Banks: Oh yes, that's going to happen. Readers, reviewers here and there will read the book and slam it down and say that's what it is. I certainly don't take that kind of criticism seriously.

Also I've gotten some pretty affirmative readings from women who think really hard and seriously about these subjects and who are extremely sensitive to the way men are inclined to be self-servingly unconscious in this area. I'm thinking of people like Lynn Sharon Schwartz and Joyce Carol Oates and a few others who've reassured me that this is not the case here. That this is not self-serving or an apology in any way. It's rather an unpleasant truth.

Connolly: There's a nice emancipatory facet to the victims' roles in that book as well. Because a lot of people don't understand why a woman would stay with someone who is violent or abusive in that way. Why a woman puts up with it.

Banks: That's right. That's key to the whole story as well. How can you love somebody who's violent? If you get close enough to someone who's violent, as from the child or the spouse's perspective, you see why they're loved. Because they're human beings, they are lovable. They are violent human beings but you can love them. And almost everyone who flees a violent spouse does it against her will. It's a terrifying and heart-rending conflict.

Connolly: Wade's wife, Lillian. Her character is one of the strongest in the book as a result of that, I think.

Banks: And I hope, too, you can see how Margie, the new woman, is moving into that position by falling in love with him, and is taking a risk and rationalizing in order to do it. I also hope that you end up in some ways seeing Wade's father as a character who is redeemable as well. He may be a set character to turn into a villain but what I hoped to do was make him also into a victim, himself.

Connolly: The double perspective that's created with the narrator being Wade's brother is interesting in that respect. There's that scene in which Wade is completely focussed on the monstrous image of his father while Rolfe sees them as rather absurd actors. The father does look like a small man from his perspective.

Banks: Yes. Pathetic and weak. But in Wade's fevered imagination, his father is enormous, a mythical giant.

Connolly: The role of the brother as the teller of the tale is interesting in other ways as well. Especially at the point in the novel when he is having nightly conversations with Wade about his conspiracy theory. There's the moment when the narrator becomes extremely sinister, almost responsible for pushing Wade down the wrong path.

Banks: That's right. You're picking up on a shift in the book which is important to understanding it; where the narrator becomes complicit and where Wade becomes a kind of stand-in for him, acting out in Wade's life the rage and hurt the narrator has essentially denied in his own life. They share childhoods. They share an orientation towards the world at least in terms of male violence that's very similar. One is a denier. He protects himself from it by organizing his life so rigidly and narrowly as to exclude all other human beings. Wade doesn't deny, but he's trapped by it. Because he doesn't deny it he has to grapple with the violence directly. His life leaves all sorts of openings for it. Every time he's under stress it enters his life.

So the narrator at that point does start to manipulate and manoeuvre Wade because he's working out his own relation to the past. It's that denier that I'm really interested in. The male who denies that he participates in this culture of violence. So that in the end when he says "I'm still here," I want that to have a kind of dark thud. [*laughs*]

Connolly: It did for me. That concept of somebody who has knowledge but doesn't understand is quite important. He has a very real understanding of what makes his brother work, but seems to be a cold fish about it.

Banks: Yes, and he doesn't understand himself at

all. He's an unreliable narrator in that regard. And that point you mentioned in the book where you start to say, "Wait a minute. He's manipulating Wade in certain ways." It should be perfectly clear then that this man is in some important way not to be trusted.

Connolly: I'm wondering if there's a little bit of writerly guilt coming out in that character as well.

Banks: How do you mean?

Connolly: The idea of grappling with life through art as opposed to doing it in that kind of head-on, futile, but in some ways admirable way Wade goes about it.

Banks: I don't really think so. He is telling the story and putting it down. It's his obsession that lets him finally tell the truth even if he himself doesn't recognize it.

Connolly: So you're comfortable with the structural voyeurism that goes along with being a writer.

Banks: Well, I'm comfortable with the abilities of art to transcend the limits of what the writer already knows. If the book says more than Rolfe knows, and I think it does, then I don't see anything in it but an affirmation of the act of writing. Because you do, if you stay honest enough and alert enough in the writing, you do end up saying more than you know. And, if for no other reason, that makes it worth doing. Language is behaviour, finally, and the degree to which it is out there and you can see it is the degree to which you can learn about who you are, about your own character, as we were saying earlier.

Connolly: As you say, it seems to take more than just "knowledge." In *Hamilton Stark* there's a scene in which the intellectual is lampooned. Wade's brother is an intellectual of sorts. He's an academic and he lives in the world of reason.

Banks: Yes, compared to Wade he's certainly meant to be. He stays up late and reads the history of the world.

Connolly: He's silly in the same way that the characters in *Hamilton Stark* seem silly in their posturing. At one point in *Hamilton Stark* one of the characters says that American intellectuals, because they don't have an intellectual style which is old enough, mimic European style. But at the same time they're so divorced from an awareness of Europe they have to invent what they're mimicking.

Banks: [*laughs*] Did I say that? I don't wildly disagree with the statement, even though I must have made it about fifteen or twenty years ago. I think that's one strong and unfortunate tendency among American intellectuals, that they mimic, and essentially mimic what they invent. Which is a way of saying I guess that they don't have an authentic intellectual culture. I think that's increasingly less true about American intellectual life, though, as we become less dependent on the European tradition and more secure in our own difference.

And as we become more consciously pluralistic. We are a pluralistic society and that is the degree to which we are authentic in an intellectual sense. The presence — well, the *acceptance* let's say, the presence has been there from the start — the acceptance in American intellectual life of Black experience, as it's presented and understood by Black writers and thinkers, and of Native American, and Meso-American and Asian-American. All of these hyphenated American experiences have become legitimatized to Americans, Anglo and non-Anglo. When this is true I think we are free of that trap of mimicking something that we are making up. To me that's been the most exciting thing about writing in America in the latter part of the twentieth century. This wonderful sense of freedom from the parochialism of Anglo-American intellectual life. It's a terrifically exciting time to be thinking things through.

Connolly: That's why I've been enjoying myself in American writing — and what I sometimes lament is lacking in Canadian writing, to a large extent.

Banks: Is it?

Connolly: It is and it isn't. I think we are very self-conscious about being multi-cultural in this country and a lot of falseness and lip-service comes out of that. It probably just takes a long time saying "this is important" before it actually becomes a reality.

Banks: There's also an ongoing, deep argument between Anglophones and Francophones which, instead of a mutual acceptance, is part of the same culture. It's disappointing because I had hoped that in some ways Canada might turn out to be a model for pluralistic culture, just as I guess Pierre Trudeau hoped that it could be, too. But the tension is too great and they tend instead to polarize and break apart from one another.

Connolly: I'll shift gears here because I want to get back to the whole idea of tragedy in the novel, and the idea of transcendence, which I think is unusually depicted in your novels. At the end of *Continental Drift* there's the statement you make that "good cheer and mournfulness over lives other than our own, even wholly invented lives, deprive the world of some of the greed it needs to continue to be itself. Sabotage and subversion, then, are this book's objectives."

That's a pretty anarchistic approach to transcendence.

Banks: Well ... ambitious, I guess. One wants to transcend the mundane, transcend the mortal limits of one's everyday life. It's not provided by the day-to-day dreams of the people in the book and it's not provided by conventional religious programs, and it's not provided by family or through identification with class or any kind of group. Yet I think transcendence is possible and I've experienced something like it on occasion through art, and by means of rite and ritual. Certain transcendental flashes. And by the presence of some extraordinary, inescapable, all-encompassing truth. But they're very very rare and difficult of access. What

you hope you could do with your book is provide that kind of experience both for the reader and for the character with whom the reader might have identified.

Connolly: Traditionally that form has been the tragedy.

Banks: Yes, but not because it's tragic in the conventional sense. That's one of the means by which it is possible, but there are others. Recognition, I think, is crucial. Recognition of the large view. If a character whose life has been consumed by the mundane is brought to a point where he can actually recognize or take the large view, then that should provide a means by which transcendence is possible, for the reader and for the character. Getting a character to that point is not an easy matter. Tragedy is one way to do it. I would find that hard to do the conventional way simply because I don't really believe in heroes. I don't believe in human beings that are larger than other human beings. So conventional tragedy doesn't work for me. It violates my basic sense of belief.

Connolly: You said earlier that your sense of tragedy wasn't Shakespearean. I thought that was an important point. We're not dealing with "great men" here.

Banks: No. I think that's a mischievous idea, the idea of the great man. It's a destructive and dark notion in our society. It's a great delusion that there are such things.

Connolly: There's a certain arrogance associated with Shakespearean tragic heroes. The idea that they are somehow responsible for such massive amounts of punishment. Bob Dubois's sins seem to be sins of omission rather than sins of commission. In the same sense you get terribly sorry for Wade, who's got this damn toothache and his life falling apart, and no help, especially from people like his brother, who he assumes to be sensible.

Banks: They have flaws, I suppose, but they are

the normal human type of flaws. They didn't sleep with their mothers and kill their fathers. At least not right away.

Connolly: That's reflected in the endings in those three novels. *Hamilton Stark* has that very strange image of walking into nothing. In *Continental Drift* one does get a sense that he had achieved something before he died but it's a not-at-all-usual depiction of transcendence or catharsis. And transcendence at the end of *Affliction* seems to be just a matter of Wade being able to escape.

Banks: Well, they all end with altar tables, in a sense. A mountain top with white snow in *Hamilton Stark*, and *Continental Drift* with the loading dock of a pier where a *voudon* ceremony has just been held. The sacrifice there is very literal. And in *Affliction* the work bench in the barn, and the funeral pyre. At that moment if Wade knows anything he knows everything, if he doesn't know everything he doesn't know anything. And so there's a very ritualized moment that ends each of them. I just thought of it this minute, actually. They're oddly similar.

Connolly: There's a cosmology set up in *The Relation of My Imprisonment* that's interesting in relation to tragedy as well. There's a transcendent realm in the mind of the protagonist, but it's really a rumour more than anything else.

Banks: A rumour he chooses to believe. There was an interesting piece in the *Village Voice Literary Supplement* last week. It was a review of *Affliction*. One of the things the writer picked up on was, yes, this is a tragedy, and so was *Continental Drift*, but it's a different sense of tragedy that you get, I think he said, in Philosophy 101. It's a more Brechtian sense of tragedy, in that social and historical forces have replaced the gods, and everyman and everywoman have replaced princes and kings. And I felt very comfortable, even happy with that distinction.

Intellectually, I think it's an interesting shift. Perhaps the only way you can have tragic heroes and heroines in our time is if you displace the notion of the gods, in the equation that leads to destiny, with history, economics, social forces. I have no trouble thinking of Wade Whitehouse or Bob Dubois as tragic figures in that context. Because those are the gods they are working with, and it's their dicta that they are trying to work their own destiny against. And ultimately failing to do it. If we respond to his failure with pity and fear then it's because we are able to see the power of history and society in the same way as the ancients perhaps saw the power of the gods.

Connolly: You have to have some sense of a cosmology in dealing with the tragic in any sense. I was wondering if your idea in *The Relation of My Imprisonment* was related in any way to Kafka's kind of tragedy. The idea that there is a transcendent realm, but you have no access to it. It appears as essentially a rumour.

Banks: Not literally. It's not too hard to translate, though, in my own terms. You can't get free of history. In that sense you can never get there. And there is some realm no doubt that is outside the realm of history. But it's outside the realm of ordinary human beings' possibilities. To be free of history you have to be dead. It's there, but it's not accessible.

Connolly: In *The Relation of My Imprisonment* there's also that sense of the dead speaking back, and being a tangible force in some peoples' lives. It interested me that the ideas were self-generated, and the self-generation seems to guarantee its power.

Banks: Yes, it's self-invoked. I don't know whether I'd want to say it guarantees its power. But it's the only accessible route, via the individual's imagination.

Connolly: I get a sense that subjective and objective reality aren't really that much of an opposition for you. Whether it exists outside the human perception or not doesn't seem, finally, to be a big problem.

Banks: Yes, I don't like to slide into an easy dichotomy between idealism and materialism, one way or another. Obviously our ability to act depends upon the degree to which we can make contact with the outside world and our behaviour reflects and expresses the nature of that contact. What's ultimately outside us is probably irrelevant. That doesn't mean it doesn't exist. But if I'm primarily a moralist, and I think I am, not a metaphysician and certainly not a material scientist, I'm most concerned with what determines our behaviour and how much control we have over our behaviour. The dichotomy or split between idealism and materialism only interests me insofar as it's a description of the two poles of human experience. Our attempts to bridge those gaps and what happens when we do is what most interests me. I think that's true, for most artists.

Connolly: You deal so often with certain kinds of faith. Vanise's loss. The question of their objective existence is irrelevant, really.

Banks: But I don't want to come down with some easy, relativistic view — you know, if it works for you it must be good. It's the power of Vanise's imagination and her access to those levels of imagination that in some ways makes her stronger than Bob Dubois. Because she has no access to that level of reality. Only at the end of the book, where he finally acquires some sort of historical perspective on his own life, does he really have any access to anything larger than his immediate life. It's in that recognition scene near the end of the book, coming across on the boat, where he looks at the Haitians and he sees that they're like him and he's like them and he suddenly sees himself in the large view. It's the first time in the whole book that he's had a larger view than "I want to get to Florida," or "I want to make it," "I want to get a boat and be in control." This immediate gratification, this immediate

sense of purpose is finally cut with the larger view at that point. By then it's a little too late, but at least it's there.

For Vanise, her access to her *loas,* to that level of reality, comes out of a cultural continuum. From the personal to the tribe, through the language and the physical reality, it's a continuum. For Bob, that continuum has been broken. He's a product of western materialism and secularism. So he can't get to that perspective. But he can get to an historical point of view, which is what the book struggles to do. That's really hard for Bob Dubois. It's hard for anyone; it's hard for a middle-class intellectual. That's perhaps the only way that his behaviour can take on more meaning than simply that of immediate gratification.

Connolly: It's interesting, again as it relates to your sense of the tragic, that Bob and Wade are capable of that whereas the people around them don't seem to be. It's a double-edged sense of a tragic hero — they have tragic flaws, but they also have tragic capacities.

Banks: Gifts, yes.

Connolly: There are bleak implications there as well. The fact that someone with imagination gets lead into all sorts of dangerous and frightening areas that people who lack imagination may not. Do you feel that's true?

Banks: Yes. At least he has some awareness of his depth at the end. In those last seventy-five pages Bob Dubois knows what he's up to, and in the end Wade Whitehouse does too. Even though he adopts a kind of "scorched earth policy" towards Lawford, New Hampshire, and his own family life. Nevertheless I didn't want him to be perceived as a madman, someone who has lost it. I wanted him to be marching through this awful, dark landscape doing what he must. There is a terrible irony to it. I mean Oedipus could have stayed at home and loved his mother and all the rest of it. But then we wouldn't be interested in them anymore — if they just minded the store and couldn't make that leap.

Connolly: Wade's escape is interesting and problematic.

Banks: Yes. There isn't that kind of ultimate punishment. What Wade has done is destroy the man that is most like him in the town — Jack — and he's destroyed his own father. And he has moved out from that bearing this tremendous burden. Obviously, as he moves on now, he's afflicted in different ways. Now he's afflicted with guilt and in some very primeval way slain the father and slain the youth in himself.

Connolly: He's almost marooned himself, historically.

Banks: I'm hoping to write a sequel. In fact, I've got a vague idea of three books involving Wade Whitehouse if he maintains my interest, and I think he will. I am fascinated with him in a lot of ways; fascinated by the difficulties of a character like Wade. And I've grown awfully fond of him, despite his terrible behaviour.

Connolly: Is there a political level to your fascination with people like Wade and Bob Dubois? Do you think of it as something important in your own culture, especially in conservative times, to bring out and describe the lives of these kinds of people?

Banks: That isn't why one goes about doing it. You imaginatively enter the life of a character like Wade Whitehouse because you *can* enter that life. Because you can enter that life with greater force and clarity that I, for example, could enter a character like Toni Morrison or John Irving or John Updike might. I can't enter those characters with the same clarity that they can enter them. But I can enter the life of Wade Whitehouse, for reasons that are obvious and for other reasons that are not known to me. Having done that, I'd be falsely naïve in saying that there are no political values being expressed in that choice. I do feel a sense

of urgency that people like Wade Whitehouse be permitted to be central in fiction. It's important to me. I wish they were central in every other respect in society. They're only marginal in every other respect at the moment.

Connolly: Some people up here tend to wrongly equate American culture and American economics. Perhaps because politics and culture have a different relationship here.

Banks: Certainly in the States it seems to be more antagonistic.

Connolly: You seem to be working within a long and I think distinguished liberal tradition in the American novel.

Banks: I feel very comfortable in that tradition. A writer who's very important to me in that sense is Nelson Algren, a Chicago novelist who wrote *Walk on the Wild Side* and *Man with the Golden Arm*. He regarded himself as heir to Dreiser and Sherwood Anderson and Stephen Crane, and so on. A very powerful and important tradition in American fiction. I think that it's being rediscovered by fiction writers of my generation, who feel much closer to writers of that ilk than they do to writers who have been more celebrated in the last couple of decades — who are more concerned with metafiction, *nouveau romans* and American literature as an extension of European literature. I think of John Edgar Wideman, and even Don DeLillo. Rose-Ellen Brown, Lynn Sharon Schwartz, Joyce Carol Oates, Bobby Ann Mason, Anne Tyler. All writers of various interests and stature, but with a definite involvement with the historical realities of their characters. The social reality they are dealing with is that of the lower middle class and the lower class and of ethnic minorities. People who are marginal because of gender, race or class. I think that's very important.

RUSSELL HOBAN

The Bear in Max Ernst's Bedroom

 he symbol of the Manitoba Writers' Conference is the Fool of the tarot deck conceived by Arthur Edward Waite and drawn by Patricia Colman Smith. To begin with we might well have a look at Waite's own *Pictorial Key to the Tarot*. The Fool's card is unnumbered, it is designated Zero, and Waite says of it:

> With light step, as if earth and its trammels had little power to restrain him, a young man in gorgeous vestments pauses at the brink of a precipice among the great heights of the world; he surveys the blue distance before him — its expanse of sky rather than the prospect below. His act of eager walking is still indicated, though he is stationary at the given moment....

There at the brink of the precipice but not stepping over the edge I'm going to leave the Fool for the present; I'll come back to him later but first I'd like to fool around with various thoughts that, taking advantage of this chance at an audience, have thrust themselves forward.

In H.P. Lovecraft's novel *The Case of Charles Dexter Ward*, there appears a letter written by one Jedediah Orne to Joseph Curwen who was doing some really exciting things in his basement workshop. In it Orne says to Curwen:

> I say to you againe, doe not call up Any that cannot put downe; by the which I meane, Any that can in turn call up somewhat against you, whereby your powerfullest devices may not be of use. Ask of the Lesser, lest the Greater shall not wish to Answer, and shall Commande more than you.

Joseph Curwen and his descendant Charles Dexter Ward called up entities and forces that threatened to destroy not only the world but the solar system and the entire universe. The book is a deliciously cosy read, offering such handy calling-up formulae as:

Y'AI'NG'NGAH
YOG-SOTHOTH
H'EE-L'GEB
F'AI THRODOG
UAAAH

Even on the printed page the words reek of horror; saying them in a circle of the lamplight on a winter's evening is a real pleasure. After all, it's only fiction. Just imagine living in a world in which people called up that which they could not put down. It scarcely bears thinking of, does it?

We know what fiction is but it isn't all that easy to know what reality is. What we call reality doesn't seem to be the same for everybody; it doesn't even always stay the same for one person. What's real? Is reality a matter of choice? Maybe you're eating a little something, a little pastrami on rye with french fries on the side, and maybe later you pick up some Chinese takeaway and a couple of missile bases, maybe one or two long-range nuclear-missile submarines, and you say to

yourself, "Cholesterol isn't really real. Nuclear missiles aren't really real." And everything's all right for a while but all of a sudden you're in a strange bed with a nurse standing in front of you all crisp and fresh and smelling nice and the nurse says, "Well, Mr. Schlemiel, now you've got to shave all down the front of you because they'll be doing your bypass operation first thing in the morning." And while you're shaving very carefully all down the front of you somebody else's long-range nuclear missile drops in and says, "Let's boogie."

"Just a moment, please," you say. "This isn't real. I'm not accepting this as reality."

Nevertheless as you stand there with nothing left of you but a white shadow burned into a wall you must admit, however grudgingly, that reality might quite possibly not be a matter of choice, that it might be there whether you look at it or not. But it's not only cholesterol and nuclear missiles that can make trouble — there are all kinds of things that have no name and can't be described, really scary dreadful things that live in the mind and maybe you say, "They're only in my mind." Then suddenly you find that you yourself are in your mind with them and there's no escape.

"O God! How did I get into my mind! Please, please let me out!"

And God smiles and says, "Sorry, your mind is the only place there is."

And perhaps you say, "I don't believe that. What about Borneo? What about the headwaters of the Amazon? What about the New York Hilton?"

And God says, "Go where you like, it's still your mind that you live in."

"But God, all these really scary dreadful things in my mind, surely they aren't real."

And God says, "Whatever is, is real."

"Go on, what about all those horrible nasty thingies that Joseph Curwen and Charles Dexter Ward called up, Yog-Sothoth and that lot?"

And God says, "Look around you."

Because Yog-Sothoth and any other unwelcome dropper-in you can think of is here. If it wasn't you that called them up then somebody else did — it doesn't matter really, we're all in this together, offering in our various fashions on our various altars. An altar doesn't have to be a piece of furniture — any special field of attention is an altar. The big CERN particle accelerator at Geneva is an altar, the Pentagon is an altar, drawing boards and computer screens all over the world are altars, the brain itself is an altar, and on it are offered the thoughts and wishes that call up what cannot be put down, gods and demons and unnameable presences hungry for their moment, and every single one of them is real.

At this point people sometimes stop me and say, "Hang on, are you saying that these gods and demons actually have an independent reality outside your mind?"

And I say, "You can't speak of a reality independent of the mind, the mind is the only perceiver of reality there is. We all belong to one mind and everything that's ever happened or been thought of since the beginning of the universe is in that mind and it's all real. I can't always get to it and if I do I can't always put a name to it but it's all there and it's all real: the chair is in my mind and it's real; the table is in mind and it's real, the birth and death of this universe and other universes are in my mind and they're real. And the great blubbering blue fnergl is in my mind and that's real too."

"Aha!" says my questioner. "The great blubbering blue fnergl may be real to you but it isn't real to me."

And I say, "Not only is it real but you're standing neck-deep in fnergl shit at this very moment and you refuse to take any notice of it."

That's where the questioner and I usually walk away in opposite directions shaking our heads.

I've always found reality a risky business but different people deal with it in different ways. One drizzly November evening, I think it was in 1958, I was at the Five Spot in Cooper Square in New York City. Ornette Coleman was playing that night; his altar was his saxophone and he was offering. His music was strange, squawky, Proustian, elliptical, he called up a dark and smoky tohu-bohu, a kind of friendly chaos in which his musical sentences trailed off into three dots, disappeared round the dark side of the moon, and came back, renewed like the corn god in the spring, to the immense relief of all of us listening. We hadn't been sure they ever *would* come back but here they were again and we clapped like anything.

In a break between sets I saw Don Cherry nearby, he'd been playing a pocket trumpet, and I said to him — it isn't something I'd say now but I said it then — "I like the way you're taking risks with your music."

He looked at me in a certain way, then he said, "Man, we ain't taking no risks — however we're blowing, that's how we're blowing tonight."

I staggered back, annihilated. It was as if he had taken the Protestant work ethic and broken it across his knee like a cheap fiddle. "That's how we're blowing tonight." There are many ways to blow and one is as good as another and that's how we're blowing tonight. Well, I thought, there it is: The Decline of the West, anything goes, no more standards and everyone can do as he likes.

I liked the music but I didn't know how to deal with the world-view apparently expressed by the words. I pondered those words over and over and I never could quite get my head around them. Risk-taking was a big thing in my mind at the time. Only a year before that I'd left my TV art director job at J. Walter Thompson to become a freelance illustrator. That was a risk I'd hesitated to take: I had a wife and three children and a mortgage, I was a responsible citizen with a lot to lose. One evening coming home on the train I'd said to my friend Harvey Cushman, who worked at another advertising agency, "When I have $10,000 in the bank and a couple of steady accounts I'll do it."

"You'll never do it then," said Harvey. "I've heard lots of guys say the same thing and somehow the time never comes. If you're going to do it you'll do it without the $10,000 and the steady accounts."

So I did it and I prospered and I was confirmed in my belief that the human animal is a hunting and finding and risk-taking animal. Finding work was a risk-taking thing and so was doing the work: there were safe ways and dangerous ways of going at a job of illustration and the dangerous ways might result in time and money lost and the work rejected. What defines risk, after all? Risk is when you have something to lose.

When I said that Ornette Coleman was taking risks what did I think he risked losing? Music that worked artistically, music that was a successful product. Now thirty years later I think that Ornette Coleman and his colleagues weren't blowing product, product was no part of their blowing. I think they were blowing process; they were blowing this is where we are at this moment, they were blowing the long dark and the wandering night, they were blowing find it and lose it and keep moving and find it again. Or something else. Or not. They were blowing metaphysical rambling shoes and quantum physics midnight specials and the uncertainty principle. Process, not product. No product to lose, no risk. Only the process of being and un-being. Many worlds, and this is the one we're blowing tonight. I saw a film about Ornette Coleman recently. In it he recalled hearing some Nigerian musicians when he visited Africa: "I said, 'I gotta go and play with these guys,' because I could see that for once I would be able to play whatever passed through my heart and head without ever having to worry about was it right or wrong."

That's how it is for Ornette Coleman. Is it like that for a writer? Certainly when you've got to where you know how not to get in your own way you can tune in to things and write whatever passes through your heart and head without having to worry about whether it's right or wrong. The process itself becomes the product, and are there then no risks?

Well, here I can only speak from my own experience. I find that in order to tune in to things I have to spend about ten hours a day at my desk. I have to stay up late and let the night into me so that the bricks of reason move apart and the other comes in through the cracks. The electric light changed a lot of things. It was an Irish writer, maybe Padraic Colum but I'm not sure, who said that traditional storytelling had to do with the circle of firelight and the night all round. When electricity banished the night something was lost. So you have to let the night back in and you have to listen to what wants to speak to you. Maybe sometimes you even have to call up what can't be put down, you have to talk to demons and horrors private and public; you must remember that all of us collectively have called up what can't be put down, we have pre-empted Armageddon and it wants to be talked to in the night, it has many things to tell us, many things to whisper and shout and shriek in the silence of the night. Sometimes the voice is that of Beelzebub, sometimes that of Eurydice.

The writer has to listen to those voices because the straight people seem not to have the capability of living in full reality. The straight people live in a limited-reality consensus in which the chair is real, the table is real, the airplane is real, the summit meeting is real, but what is inexplicable and ungraspable and nameless isn't real. So the writer has to find names and handles, the writer has to find words to make it real. And yes, there are some risks: you might ruin your health or your wife or husband might leave you or you might write yourself beyond the point of no return and get altogether lost in the dark. But if that's your thing you have to do it. Don't do it if you can stand not doing it, but if you can't stand not doing it, then do it. Because there's so much that needs tuning in to. Why are we what we are? And before you can ask that question, *what* is it that we are? Why do we have some of the thoughts we have? When I find myself standing on top of a tall building or on the edge of a cliff why do I have the urge to throw myself off? Our Fool who pauses so grandly on the brink, does he possibly have that urge? Has anybody else in this room ever had it? I'll be very surprised if I don't see a fair number of hands. Is that urge included in the limited-reality consensus? When Reagan sits down with Gorbachev does Reagan's interpreter say to Gorbachev's interpreter,

"Tell me, Mikhail, when you stand on the edge of a cliff do you have an urge to throw yourself off?" And does Gorbachev's interpreter reply, "Funny you should mention that, Ron, because I do have that very urge. Do you?" And does Reagan's interpreter say, "Yes, as a matter of fact I do"? And does Gorbachev's interpreter then say, "Maybe we're all a little bit crazy, do you think? Maybe there's a craziness in the human situation?"

I doubt that they talk about those things. But the reality of it is that all of us are more than a little bit crazy and there is indeed a craziness in the human situation. The ancient Greeks put a name to that craziness, they called it Dionysus, and having given it a name they could take it into account. At the Pentagon I don't suppose they talk about Dionysus very much but they do have a strategy called Mutual Assured Destruction, of which the acronym is MAD. If it's mad why have they got such a plan, you may well ask. They've got it because there is a madness that lives in us, even the Very Important People in the Pentagon and the Kremlin. The following is from *Dionysus, Myth and Cult*, by the religious historian Walter F. Otto:

The elemental depths gape open and out of them a monstrous creature raises its head before which all the limits that the normal day has set must disappear. There man stands on the threshold of madness — in fact, he is already part of it even if his wildness which wishes to pass on into destructiveness still remains mercifully hidden. He has already been thrust out of everything secure, everything settled, out of every haven of thought and feeling, and has been flung into the primeval cosmic turmoil in which life, surrounded and intoxicated with death, undergoes eternal change and renewal.

But the god himself is not merely touched and seized by the ghostly spirit of the abyss. He, himself, is the monstrous creature which lives in its depths. From its mask it looks out at man and sends him reeling with the ambiguity of nearness and remoteness, of life and death in one.

What Otto is saying, what I'm saying, is that it's a strange and frightening thing to be a human being, to partake of the mystery and the madness of human consciousness. Listen to what George Steiner says in his book *The Death of Tragedy:*

Tragic drama tells us that the spheres of reason, order and justice are terribly limited and that no progress in our science or technical resources will enlarge their relevance. Outside and within man is *l'autre,* the "otherness" of the world. Call it what you will: a hidden or malevolent God, blind fate, the solicitations of hell, or the brute fury of our animal blood. It waits for us in ambush at the crossroads. It mocks us and destroys us. In certain rare instances, it leads us after destruction to some incomprehensible repose.

Dionysus and "the other" are outside us and within us. So is Hermes, the Priapic god, the thief-god, the god of roadways and night journeys, of chance and change and all kinds of shadowy connections. Here I quote myself, from *The Medusa Frequency:*

Hermes is a mode of event, a shift in the relativities of the moment, a new disposition of energies. There's what you might call a frequency of probability when complementary equivalents offer and anything can be anything.

The nice thing about Hermes is that it likes change, it enjoys alternative universes in which alternative people do alternative things like not destroying themselves. Our Fool on the brink has a strong Dionysiac element in him but he's got a lot of Hermes as well — our Fool is a wender of many ways who always finds new ways, a chance-taker who finds new chances.

Dionysus and the other and Hermes account for some of the action that keeps us popping like popcorn in a popper but there's no end to it, really, and no end to the names and words that need to be found to provide handles for it, and all of the names and words are out in the real reality beyond the limited-reality consensus. We haven't got a lot of time, the world is being destroyed by people to whom hairspray is real but the ozone layer is not, people to whom dogs and cats are real but whales are not, so they kill the whales to feed the dogs and cats, people for whom the sea is not real so they fill it with poisons and garbage, people for whom the rain forests are not real so they cut them down and put in European-style farms that fail. The survival of the human race depends on a realer grasp of reality than we've been capable of so far. The survival of the human race depends on recognizing what lives in the human mind and learning how not to be annihilated by it.

There have been attempts in the arts to go further and deeper than the limited-reality consensus. There was Dada. In Europe it began in Zurich in 1916. "The Dadaists," says H.H. Arnason in his *History of Modern Art,* "felt that reason and logic had led to the disaster of world war, and that the only way to salvation was through political anarchy, the natural emotions, the intuitive and the irrational." New York Dada had begun earlier, in 1913, and later the American and European movements merged. The Dadaists were out to produce anti-art art, and they did it in every way they could. In addition to anti-art drawings and paintings in the traditional media they made anti-art out of snippets from newspapers, bits of photographs and fabrics, and unlikely objects of all kinds, the less artistic the better — a urinal was featured in one exhibition. Marcel

Duchamp did a now-famous drawing titled *The Bride Stripped Bare by Her Bachelors, Even*. It looks as if it came from the desk of a physicist or a mathematician or a mechanic; the shapes and ciphers have at first glance nothing to do with brides, bachelors, or stripping bare.

All sorts of reasons can be brought forward to account for Dada and I'm sure they're all perfectly valid. It was a time of disillusion and cynicism and disgust with all established authority both political and artistic. But all of the reasons for it add up to one reason: the reality consensus of the time was incapable of dealing with the realities of the time so it had to be expanded. Everything that went into Dada, all the snippets and bits of all kinds of things, all the imagery of shock and surprise, of paradox and unreason, all of that is really only part of the ambient uproar that goes on in anybody's head at any time, even when stripping the bride bare. To the contemporary mind, continually bombarded as it is by high-velocity data of unlimited variety, Dada oughtn't to be surprising and it no longer is.

The art world applied itself diligently to the further expansion of the reality consensus: surrealism followed hard on Dada's heels with Dali's soft watches and Magritte's strange castle-bearing planetoid rock that hovers forever over a grey sea. André Breton said that the purpose of surrealism was "to resolve the previously contradictory conditions of dream and reality into an absolute reality, a super-reality." By now surrealism has been absorbed into realism along with Sigmund Freud and our wildest dreams; what was strange has become familiar, and the familiar in strange contexts no longer startles us.

The Dadaists and the surrealists wrote a great many manifestos but no novels that I know of. The fictional opening-up of acknowledged reality jolted forward with a great bump when Sylvia Beach published James Joyce's *Ulysses* in 1922. I feel that I ought to say something about this book but the fact is that — when I tried to read it at the age of seventeen — I found Buck Mulligan and Stephen Dedalus dead boring and I never got beyond the first chapter. Having another go at my present age of sixty-two I found them freshly boring and got no further than the first time. I accept that the book is a literary landmark and I move on to the bear in Max Ernst's bedroom.

This bear lives in a collage done by Ernst around 1920 with gouache and pencil. The picture is a straight-ahead perspective of a long room with a floor of bare boards. The walls are bare except for an indistinct picture on the wall to the right. By the back wall Ernst has glued on a sheep and a bear. These and the other animals and objects in the room all seem to have been cut out of some old schoolbook. Towards the right foreground are a dining table, a bed, and a wardrobe. In the left foreground a brown-coloured whale swims through the floorboards near a bat and a fish and a coiled snake. The right wall is a sickly grey-green; the rear wall is a pinkish grey; the left wall is pale greenish-grey. The floor is grey with great blotches that look like tear stains. Above the picture is written a caption in German, below it the same caption in French: *Max Ernst's bedroom — it is worth spending a night in it.*

"One might define a collage," said Ernst, "as an alchemical composite of two or more heterogeneous elements, resulting from their unexpected conjunction, due either to a will orientated — for the sake of clarity — towards a systematic confusion and the disordering of the senses or to pure chance, or perhaps to a will favouring chance."

I showed my nine-year-old son Wieland a reproduction of *Max Ernst's bedroom* and asked him what he thought of it. "It's very nice," he said. "I like it when the different parts of a picture don't have anything to

168

do with each other." Wieland is comfortable with the alchemy of that particular collage, I'm not. For me there's something so very bleak, so very dismal and dreary in that room. It's some kind of paradigm of an aspect of things I'd rather not know about but how can I not know when it's in my mind? Maybe it's the shape of the room or the greyness and the greenness; maybe it's the eyes of the bear, they look as if something's been done to them, as if the bear might have been blinded. Nobody knows the shape of the universe, nobody knows the infinite regress of that bear into the distances and the depths of the mind perceiving it. I was in the hospital recently for heart surgery, and while recovering I was on five or six different drugs, some of which made me dream repetitive dreams of a dismal and tedious character. Obviously there had to be a place in my mind for those dreams to come from, and it's to that place that *Max Ernst's bedroom* takes me. I think I must have spent many nights in that room, and when I'm there I suppose I'm glued on the same as the sheep and the bear. Perhaps one morning the paper bear will have a bulging belly and I'll be just a few glued-on paper bones and scraps on that tear-blotched floor.

There are many such places in the mind, places of bleakness and horror and despair. How could there not be? Look at our history. There are also places beyond bleakness and horror and despair, places where there is neither reason nor fear, where there is only the sea of whatever is, and the swimmer swimming in that sea. These places are beyond all known edges and off all charts, they must be found again and again and claimed and named by the mind that goes in fear and trembling, but goes to where its being takes it.

Now let's come back to Waite's words about the Fool whom we left on the brink of the precipice:

... His act of eager walking is still indicated, though he

is stationary at the given moment; his dog is still bounding. The edge which opens on the depth has no terror; it is as if angels were waiting to uphold if it came about that he leaped from the height. His countenance is full of intelligence and expectant dream. He has a rose in one hand and in the other a costly wand, from which depends over his right shoulder a wallet curiously embroidered. He is a prince of the other world on his travels through this one — all amidst the morning glory, in the keen air. The sun, which shines behind him, knows whence he came, whither he is going, and how he will return by another path after many days. He is the spirit in search of experience. Many symbols of the Instituted Mysteries are summarized in this card, which reverses, under high warrants, all the confusions that have preceded it.... I will give you these further indications regarding the Fool, which is the most speaking of all symbols. He signifies the journey outward, the state of the first emanation, the graces and passivity of the spirit. His wallet is inscribed with dim signs, to show that many subconscious memories are stored up in the soul.

I must say that this Waite/Smith fool seems a bit of a poseur to me. I prefer French and Italian versions of this card in which the Fool is altogether a sturdier sort of vagabond who carries a stout cudgel as well as his wand. Of the Fool's attributes the one that interests me most is the wallet that hangs from the wand over his shoulder. I myself am a great accumulator of bags and rucksacks of all kinds, I don't feel right unless I'm somewhat burdened. I'd even go so far as to say that a writer needs to be burdened — the writing is after all the unburdening. To my way of thinking our Fool may flaunt himself on the brink as much as he likes but eventually he must discard the rose, must leave the flower of his youth behind to wilt in the sunshine while he takes his burden and climbs laboriously down into the abyss to get to work. His number, after all, is Zero, a round nothingness which he must fill with the world of his perception.

The wallet is a magic one, he himself doesn't know what's in it but it's heavy with the past, present, and future of the universe; in it is a jumble of unformed words and images, of colours and sounds and strangeness, continually arranging itself in new combinations wanting to be worlds. His real journey begins when he opens the wallet and it swallows him up in its darkness where he must make his way through time and chance, must keep himself empty and knowing nothing so that in that magic darkness the universe can continually fill the Zero of him with itself. He must persist in his folly until, as William Blake said, he becomes wise. And that wisdom lies in knowing how and when to know nothing and be open to everything.

Sometimes the question arises: what's it all about, where are we going and is there any point to the whole thing? Thinking isn't much help, you have to fly by the seat of your pants, you have to feel it. To me it feels as if all of us inhabit and are inhabited by one universal mind, we are all receptors of a universal transmission. Some of us tune into more of it, some less, but it wants to be received, it wants to be perceived and we are its organ of perception. Surely we haven't yet received the whole transmission, surely we haven't tuned into all of its frequencies.

Here we are on a planet that was clean and beautiful and we've defiled it; we're killing the world-child, we're committing terricide. Perhaps this earth will last long enough for the first space colonies to be founded and send their probes farther and farther out into our galaxy and beyond. We planet-killers are the seekers and the finders and we've got to go on finding, inside and outside the self, what it's all about. We must go into the dark and magic wallet of time within which we shall find that bleak and dreadful room where the paper bear waits to gobble us up. We must go into all the scary places to find ourselves, we fools, we must encounter all that lives there, and if we never find our way out again it will still have been a risk worth taking, more than that; it's the risk we're born for, made for. It's the risk we owe to ourselves to take. We've called up what we can't put down and now we've got to look into its eyes and talk to it.

It would be quite natural at this point if you rose up and demanded to know what this exhortation is about in pragmatic terms: what do I want from you? I want to encourage you, if you're not already doing it, to help enlarge the limited-reality consensus. I don't read much contemporary fiction so I'm not really qualified to have an opinion, but I believe that too much of it is simply the conveying of chunks of experience wrapped up in some kind of story. What the world needs more of, although my royalty statements indicate that it doesn't yet recognize the need, is writing that tries to find out what's what by paying attention to the images that live under the picture-cards that we conventionally exchange and the images that appear beyond where we ordinarily look, the occulting glimmers under the reasonable thought and beyond the ordinary range of thought, the words that twist and moan and dance and sing behind the words that go out through our mouths and the unknown words that we sometimes almost hear from far away, the mysteries that move us, and the patterns of the dance that lives us.

I'm encouraging you to have a go because I think — and I could well be wrong — that some writers are afraid to let themselves go that way. Years ago, when I sometimes did workshops, I found people who were quite good with words but they clung to safe structures, they remained unobsessed, they were not driven to write. To do the kind of writing that extends the recognized boundaries of reality you have to be

A writer sitting at a desk is nothing very heroic and yet you have to find ways of feeling heroic because the effort required certainly is. I want a heroic image to end this with, so out of the dust of mortality and the darkness of the magic wallet I bring a column of horsemen borrowed from the end of one of John Wayne's best films, *She Wore a Yellow Ribbon,* John Ford's wonderful elegy for the U.S. cavalry (with screenplay by Frank Nugent and Laurence Stallings from the story by James Warner Bellah). Listen to the music, listen to the sound of their hooves and the slap and jingle of harness as the horsemen pass by and the voice-over narrator says:

> So here they are, the dogfaced soldiers, the regulars, the fifty-cents-a-day professionals, riding the outposts of a nation from Fort Reno to Fort Apache, from Sheridan to Stark. They were all the same, men in dirty-shirt blue, and only a cold page in the history books to mark their passing. But wherever they rode and whatever they fought for, that place became the United States.

Well, here we are, Manitoba writers. The bugle is sounding boots and saddles, it always is. So climb on to your horses and be the kind of writing fools of whom it can be said: wherever they wrote and whatever they sought for, that place became the world.

obsessed, you have to let ungraspable ideas take you in their jaws and shake you around, you have to try all kinds of things, most of which don't work, to get them down on paper, and when you do get them down on paper you'll have to rewrite them fifteen or sixteen times because they won't be right the first time. And very likely you'll have to do something else to pay the rent. I could never have afforded to write novels if I hadn't built up an economic base with children's picture books; there simply aren't that many people who want to read the kind of thing I write, although there are more now than there used to be.

ALBERTO MANGUEL

Jorge Luis Borges on Film

ilms always interested him, even after his blindness. I accompanied him one afternoon in 1982 to see the Australian film *Gallipoli*. Borges sat in front of the screen he couldn't see and listened to the sounds and the dialogue, while I tried to give him an idea of the images. "There's a soldier coming into the room now ... She turns and gives him an ugly look ... It's an extraordinary sunset."

His visual memory was prodigious, which is why, he said, he liked films. He enjoyed walking along the Pasea Colon, a covered sidewalk that used to hug the docks in Buenos Aires and which today houses some of the tallest, most American-looking buildings in the city, and describing the scene as if he were seeing then and there. "Here's where that infamous gang led by Bebe Taboada had their little gatherings to collect votes for the congressman of their choice ... This is where a celebrated and very old hoodlum, whose name I don't want to remember, met a bunch of thugs half his age, and wielding a respectable knife in his right hand, his left arm wrapped up in his poncho, cut two of them and stabbed the third, all the while complaining in a fake whining voice, 'Oh, I'm so afraid, what will this old man do against such strong brave boys?'" He would point out the brothels, the cafés, the houses with cool patios and large whitewashed flower pots, which in the eyes of everyone else had disappeared more than thirty years ago. He said that he had tried to capture that Buenos Aires in stories, but his friends told him it was not believable. So he wrote a fantastic mystery, "Death and the Compass," and invented a city with French names, and his friends told him that at last he had re-created the Paseo Colon in its tiniest detail, and who was he trying to fool by calling it "the dingy rue de Toulon"?

In his introduction to *A Universal History of Infamy* (Buenos Aires, 1935), Borges acknowledged his debt to the films of Von Sternberg; in later life, among the films he preferred was *West Side Story* which he "saw" four or five times. He never liked the adaptations made of his own work: the two versions of the story "Emma Zunz," the film of "Streetcorner Man."

He used to say that, curiously enough, many filmmakers don't trust the language of film and rely instead on spoken explanations. He also missed in many "modern" films, especially in Argentinian films, the

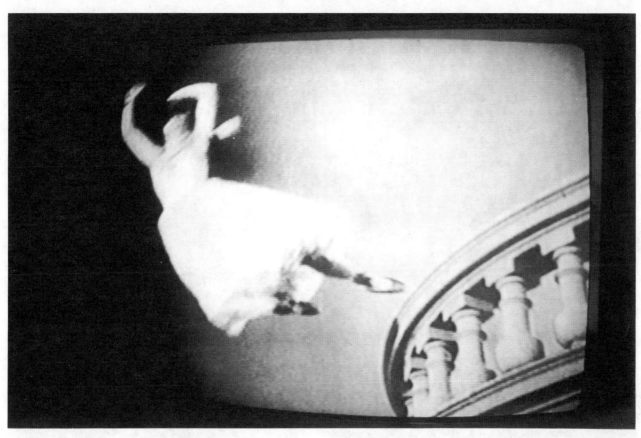

possibility of humour.

His own humour was something akin to that of Dr. Johnson, whom he so admired. When the Argentinian novelist, Ernesto Sabato, had his first novel published in France with a band around it that read "Sabato: Borges' only rival," he commented: "How intelligent. I would never have thought of a band that read: 'Borges: Sabato's only rival.'" During the Falklands War he wrote that no Argentine general had ever heard a bullet whistle past his ears; a certain Argentine general wrote to the paper furiously declaring that he had, indeed, heard a bullet whistle past his ears in battle. Borges published a letter of apology in which he declared his mistake, saying that yes, indeed "one Argentine general has heard a bullet whistle past his ears."

His humour is evident in most of the pieces he wrote. He saw writing and reading as pleasant, happy occupations, "perhaps," he once said, "the only truly happy occupations to which a man can aspire."

Anyone wanting to know anything about Borges' relationship with films should consult Edgardo

Cozarinsky's superb *Borges In and On Film*. For several years before he went blind, from 1931 to 1944, Borges reviewed films for a few Argentine magazines, notably for Victoria Ocampo's *Sur*. A selection appears in a couple of Borges' collections; most of them are annotated in Cozarinsky's book.

Other than reviews, Borges also wrote screenplays (some with Adolfo Bioy Casares) of which two were made into films by Hugo Santiago: *Invasion* (1968) and *The Others* (1973), and several essays touching on the subject of film.

Rommel

174

MARY MEIGS

Interval

The writer and painter reflects on her experience
as an actor during the filming of Company of Strangers.

 lack-water, the period between tides, slack-time, waitlessness. Our school bus is stopped out in the field enclosed in fog; we are sitting in silence waiting for the signal for Michelle to start the bus. We will roll through fog, down a hill, and disappear from the view of the camera.

In the course of shooting, re-shooting, the sun comes up and gradually rolls the fog towards the edge of the field where it lies like a long satin ribbon, floats a hilltop on a white pillow, sharpens the outlines of distant spruce-steeples, puffs up the maples, glinting with autumn (it is September 10, our last day), sends slanting pink veils of fog over mountains, trees and down to the drenched grass. The crew stands in the damp stillness with the sun on their backs and their hands in their pockets. The camera waits.

Time has no gravity in waitlessness, does not pull you from second to second into the future. In the beginning I am a slave to watch-time. "Sometimes I think an hour has gone by," I say in my journal. "I look at my watch and it's only ten minutes." Little by little I learn to unhitch certain terminals in my brain that compel me to glance down at my wrist, where a second hand is hopping its way around the face of my watch. I begin to float in time.

July 7: "I've lost track of minutes, of hours, of morning and afternoon, of the day itself. The day is eternal; it's like being high over the earth as it turns, in eternal daylight."

We are at the second location; the lake is glassy, scarcely ruffled, a burning sun is diffused through the clouds. There are trance-like silences, two crew-members move across the mirror of the lake on a raft pushed by a tiny silent motor. The hours are pulled out, as fine as spider-silk.

"If you'd kept on good terms with time," says the Mad Hatter to Alice, "he'd do almost anything you like with the clock." Time for filmmakers stands still or runs backwards, moves the end to the beginning, the future before the past. They are magicians. Everybody knows this except me, it seems, for I am struck with delight when we are shown a first version of the film and the apple we have cut up and eaten reappears, whole, in a later scene.

An oversight, of course. For me it was a magic apple, the symbol of *us,* who started in pieces and came together as a whole. I was sorry that the recomposed apple had to be cut out, a victim of clock-time, which now and then asserted itself in the editing-room. But ... "you should have cut it into eight pieces," says Sally. "We all forgot that. In the end nobody noticed." Nobody noticed the liberties taken by time and logic, which would have been pounced on in any other kind of film.

Finally, not even the things which had seemed so important out there — correctness decreed by clock-time: the length, the colour of hair, for instance, were among the things not noticed. Perhaps only the apple and our clean and dirty clothes belonged to clock-time; our clothes had a clean before, and an after of grease-stains (Catherine), mud-stains (Michelle), grass-stains (Alice). They show that time has passed, but how much? How many days and nights go by? The hours seem to be stalled in some kind of magic circularity. Perhaps it was in obedience to this concept of circularity or stillness of time that a scene in which Catherine is rubbing castor oil on her feet, in preparation for her thirty-kilometre trek to get help, was cut (in the final version this scene is there again), and our little rescue plane simply comes down from the sky with Catherine aboard. "I did it!" she cries, and we are left to imagine what she did.

The editors have assumed that the audience is capable of making leaps of imagination by filling in the open spaces of time, that they don't need a spoon-fed narrative. When Sally says, "In the end, nobody noticed," she means that nobody noticed what didn't matter. Ordinary time stops when our bus dies; the bus was a vehicle for carrying us forward, to an appointed time in an appointed place, and now we are held in slack-time, spellbound. The story of the film is the story of the eight pieces of us coming together, an invisible and motionless progress, a gravity pulling us towards the still centre which is the place of art.

Certainly it was not planned — the mutual spin-off between off- and on-camera in slack-time, which couldn't have happened without taking us away from our city lives and putting us together in a melting pot. The three fates must have watched our melting with fascinated surprise, how it was happening both off and on. Though they couldn't see that a "story" was developing until they watched the rushes, saw that what was going on off-camera was being translated (a kind of sign language?) into our film selves. The Château Borghese (one of the unfilmed locations) mirrors the circularity of the film. The end of the day is the beginning in reverse; at the crack of dawn we sidle carefully down the stone steps, hanging on to each other, someone below to form a human cushion in case of need; at the end, in the fading light, we help each other up. Silences, perhaps, both at beginning and end, a few heartfelt groans, expressions that speak volumes. These are all part of the language that forges tiny new bonds between sunrise and sunset, that speaks of a consensus — of assent.

Dream (June 10, 1988): My bell rings; I open the door. My cleaning woman, her two daughters and her mother are there, all sobbing uncontrollably. The mother is curled up on a bed. She says, "Take me in your arms." She is old, skinny, almost toothless. I embrace her tenderly with my face close to hers. She is myself, I decide when I wake up, and I'm instructing the dreamer to be kind to herself (myself) as an old woman.

It turns out that the film has the same message: Be kind to yourselves as old women and to each other.

Or do we give *it* the message by responding to the directors' apparent belief that we are only semi-old (they don't like the term "old women")? So it moves in a benign circle: to be thought of as semi-old, even to behave at times (too much, Constance thinks) like semi-children. The camera, too, is in on the conspiracy, though we wear no make-up. Once we have lost our fear of its big eye, we trust it to see us, not *exactly* like ourselves, but the way we feel, i.e. semi-old. We begin to feel almost friendly towards it without knowing what it's up to, for when it seems to be at a safe distance, what it sees may be only a few centimetres away.

We were semi-old. It was a lovely illusion that got us through long days without falling in our traces like decrepit cart-horses. It was the reason for our refusal to be in a nude scene, for wouldn't this have proved that we weren't semi but *old?* Young bodies should be celebrated and old bodies derided, according to society's dictum, proclaimed in books, films, advertising, television. We did not mind being filmed behaving like children in the splashing-scene, but wanted our bodies to stay hidden in semi-reality, protected by clothes from the camera's (and cameraman's) eye.

But ... amendment (February 10, 1990): "No, no, no," says Cynthia, "it wouldn't have been that way." (The way I feared, walking into the water naked with the usual male crew-members on hand.) We were to walk into the water wearing our bathing suits; a cam-era-*woman* was to film us with our backs to her, after we had dropped our bathing suits into the water. The set to be cleared; no men, that meant. But weather didn't permit and the lake got too cold. The seven of us in the calm lake with our backs turned — that was Cynthia's vision.

So now (in the present) I telephone Winnie. She says yes, she'd understood all that but what would be the point of showing our old bodies? "Cynthia says we're *not old*," I say. "But we *are* old," says Winnie. "I'm seventy-nine, Cissie is seventy-six, and so on to Catherine, the youngest of us, still in her sixties." Catherine, given all those conditions, might have been willing, says Cynthia. She mourns again, imagining her beautiful scene of our backs. She has to believe what she says, "But you're *not old!*" since she knows (and I know) that it would have been a beautiful scene. "Backs stay young," she says. But I'm secretly glad that the matter was settled by the impersonal decision of the weather.

But, I think, younger people can't tell us that we aren't old. We know better. Is my body the shapely one I see in this photograph of a young woman sitting on the edge of a swimming pool forty years ago? Far from it. What's more, I don't know when the process of irrefutable ageing began; I didn't notice until it was too late. The screws of old age turn so slyly that it takes you by surprise. We stick with an interior image — the young woman sitting at the edge of the pool, even when her hair turns grey, then white. We select the photographs of us that make us look young, and hide or tear up the others.

"Do I look like that? You've made me look so old," said Constance about the watercolour I did of her. "Am I so old?" asks a wrinkled Masai warrior I saw on television, looking at himself in a mirror for the first time, with a puzzled smile.

When we see the film, we suffer the same shock as the Masai warrior. So that's the way I look! "That dreary old woman," says Constance. For the first time in our lives we are separated from our mirror images, the ones we can control, and have become Others. I see a tall woman dressed in pink and white, a little bowed, with a lined face, a toothy smile, hair as white as new-fallen snow. To the others, evidently, she looks just like me, as they look like themselves to me. And aren't our images of others more stable than those we make, from second-hand evidence, of ourselves? It must be so, for there are friends I haven't seen for twenty years who look at me and say, "You haven't changed at all." Is this because a pattern-face, the one which makes us recognizable, has swum up and taken over? Unless one has changed beyond recognition, this pattern-face will be superimposed on an older face — wrinkles, crepey neck and all, a kind of mask with the power (as Proust points out) to make old friends look as though they've been made up for a much older role. It only takes a few minutes for the face from twenty years ago to sink below the new one, to show through in familiar old features — scrunched-up eyes, an assertive chin. The young person then has a new life in the old person, even if the old person is bent double with arthritis or has put on fifty pounds.

Childhood photographs, however, are merciless, and with unarguable clarity state the passing of time. We dig them out of our archives, learn how we were as children, as young women, and, too often, do not recognize each other. I ache with the pain of seeing what we were long ago, when every one of us was beautiful with the beauty of a child or a young person full of careless energy. But if I study them at length, each merges mysteriously with the present friend in full colour, as Beth has merged, for the child and the young woman are both undeniably the Beth we know. And Cissie's round, puckered face, forty years ago, can only belong to Cissie.

And Catherine? Long before her vocation changed the shape of her life, she looked as she often looks now, like a grinning tomboy free as a bird. But we have all entered the cage of time and have been changed by the lives we haven't lived and by the one life we have lived. Conspicuous (the unlived lives) in the childhood photographs. Is this little blonde angel (Constance) strong enough to contain her future? I see eighty-eight years (ninety now) and a big slice of Quebec history packed into a body no bigger than a microchip; a long life, intelligence, beauty, energy, all are there, and the rest will fill up the minute spaces, and the little angel will turn into a poised young woman who looks familiar to us. Of all of us, Constance hates most being perceived as old, and recoils from her mirror-image. She tells me about the stranger next to her not long ago on a department-store escalator, a well-dressed, attractive woman who looked like herself and to whom she turned at the ground floor. She felt that she knew her and wanted to greet her. The woman had vanished; she was Constance's mirror-image. She realized with surprise that her mirror-image could please her as long as she was a stranger.

Out on the set, except for the fact that there is always someone to catch us if we stumble, or someone to set up folding chairs for us between scenes, we are beneficiaries of the semi-self which denies the passing of clock-time. There is nothing to remind us that we are old except direct comparison with all those staff and crew members who are young. In the outside world an old person is, all too often, either invisible to a young person or perceived as an obstacle or a doddering idiot. On location we are the centre of attention; all that paraphernalia is dragged around, set up, the sun is made to shine or the rain to rain, in order to make a beautiful picture of *us*. Of course, anything or anybody being filmed gets the same attention, even a puppy gobbling up Purina dog chow in a one-minute commercial. But we can bask in a whole summer of attention, we are acting out the myth of our ideal selves, off- and on-camera, and we come to believe in our new reincarnations, there in the centre where the perspective lines meet. It doesn't matter that we, flesh and blood old people, are being translated into a film-language that expresses old people (us seven, at least) to Cynthia, Sally, Gloria and the others. They evidently want to show that old women don't necessarily dodder, quaver and shuffle. The attention so soothing to our egos, even if we know that it is the impersonal attention necessary to all filmmaking, is an exercise of their group will; all of the people standing and watching us are willing us into our semi-selves, until our image of how we'd like to be coincides with theirs.

Supposing — to make the film more conventionally dramatic — we'd had a nasty fight, with hair-pulling, screaming, insults. Fights between women are part of the staple diet of sitcom television. But we don't fight, we don't say mean things about each other, we are, by and large, our best selves. I took my best self back to Montreal with me and was surprised when she was displaced by the old self, subject to the usual fits of crankiness. Almost as if the old self said to the best self, "Who do you think you are? I'm still here." Like an old cat growling at a new kitten.

In the first rushes, Sally says, we seemed (as we were) almost strangers to each other. Our becoming friends off the set changed the nature of the film

and made scenes of discord or violence impossible. Or a death scene. Any kind of pretence, and, above all, a pretended death, would be false to the spirit of the film. But before this process began, of our helping to determine the direction of the film, Gloria had written a scene in which Constance dies. "Constance: Not asleep," she wrote. An evasion? Even then Gloria felt the danger in the words for the end of life: dies, death, dead, could not spell them out, could not fix the spell on one of us.

During the entire filming we are invisible to ourselves, but each must have had a private image different from the one we see when we are shown the film. How strange she is, I think of the Mary I see; she ha\s a slow, creaky voice and a face like her mother's crackleware teapot. Because we are sealed into our bodies, we are surprised by things in ourselves which we have never noticed and which now seem exaggerated and slightly embarrassing. We are seeing new selves — the real ones or the ones that others see? It

must be this, for the others don't seem strange to us, as each of us is strange to herself. Constance and I feel a little guilty; we've been pretending to be something we're not, i.e. younger, and now the secret is out. The camera doesn't lie.

But the second time we see the film (Constance and I) we are less embarrassed by these other selves; we almost like them. Constance still grumbles about herself, to be sure, but with a hint of reconciliation. A kind of focussing is going on, a lining up of self and film images, which will perhaps merge and become one so that we can see ourselves with the same eyes that see others. We have to learn this, and learn to let go of all our preconceived ideas, both about how we look and about the nature of the film. "Nothing happens," says Winnie. I tell her that *we* are what happens. The film is about seven semi-old women and a young woman happening.

Constance begins to doubt the existence of the film. "They've let it go," she says. Mirage-like, it moves away from us; it will be shown this fall, next year, in January, April, or June. Montreal, the place of ordinary relentless time, strewn with doubts and fears and thoughts of death. Our fragile film, lost somewhere in the entrails of the National Film Board, how can it possibly survive peristalsis, "the peculiar worm-like motion of the intestines … forcing their contents onward" (Webster's)?

It is moving, Cynthia tells us in November at Constance's party, for we gather together now and then for proof that most of us are still alive, still fond of each other. (But Gloria is dead, Cissie is fading away in a rest home and Catherine has moved to California.) "The editing is all done," says Cynthia, and we take heart again.

We are asked to think of titles: *Over the Hills, Swan Song, Autumn Leaves* … The last two are Constance's and reflect her preoccupation with old age. "The film is full of bird songs," says Cynthia, meaning that a swan song would be redundant. I remember when Winnie and Edna whistled bird songs at dinner. I remember Winnie's story about her fifteen-year-old budgie. "The dog opened his mouth to yawn," said Winnie, "and the budgie flew in straight as an arrow." "Was he dead?" asked Cissie. "Dead as a doornail," said Winnie, solemnly. Everybody at the table laughed helplessly; we were weightless then and semi-old.

"I've turned into a couch potato," said Winnie the other day. Out there we had a holiday from growing old; here we are moving along on a conveyor belt like luggage at an airport, see in front of us the place where the luggage passes through a curtain of plastic strips and disappears into darkness. Perhaps that's why Beth would like to do the film all over again, to get off the conveyor belt, step out of time. To be protected from time.

"It's awful to grow old," says Constance with angry energy. How can young people understand how awful it is, she says, to have lost control of your body, which changes for the worse without permission? With stubborn courage, Constance cooks, gives parties, plays bridge, reads, discusses books with unfailing alertness. Cissie went on gardening until she was stopped by an aneurysm. Beth and Winnie walk a lot and Winnie's schedule of activities would do me in. But "getting old is the pits," she says. She has had cataracts removed; so has Constance.

I'm another couch potato, and dream about old age and death, dream metaphors that are crystal clear. I want to get rid of my Toyota and get a Studebaker (I had one thirty years ago) or I run my car into a snowbank, can't go an inch further. "It's not funny to be old and vulnerable," says Constance. She wears a beeper around her neck to summon help if she needs it. I think of her dream, of her standing at night in the empty street, waiting for a bus that does not come.

P. K. PAGE

Company of Strangers

*Company of Strangers is a film directed by Cynthia Scott
for the National Film Board of Canada*

othing prepared me for *Company of Strangers*. In Victoria, news reports rather than reviews preceded its opening. We were told it was the most popular film at the Vancouver Film Festival. But what does that say? It might even be reason enough to stay away.

I went because I was curious. I had known a Constance Garneau — slightly — in Montreal in the forties and had read two books by Mary Meigs. To the best of my knowledge neither of them acted. There could, of course, be two Constance Garneaus but surely it was beyond probability that there were two Mary Meigses. What kind of a film was this, anyway?

The Roxie Cinegogue where the film was showing is an old quonset hut with some garish drawings in black and red on one of its side walls and two rows of rather seedy-looking loges at the back. It provides us with our only alternate cinema — film festival movies,

National Film Board movies, *The Rocky Horror Picture Show*. Its audience is almost a community; you are bound to see someone you know as you wait for the lights to go down. People wave, swap seats, chat. The noise level is high.

It is perhaps for this reason that the sound is often too loud at the beginning of a show. The night I went to *Company of Strangers* was no exception. The female voices raised in song in the opening scene were deafening. As were the blasts that announced the demise of the bus and the screams from the driver who got out to examine her vehicle and tripped and twisted her ankle. I missed some footage immediately after that because I went into the lobby to ask if the projectionist could turn down the sound. Back in my seat I imagined I must have missed the explanation as to why these curiously ill-assorted women were on the bus in the first place. But the second time — for I saw the movie a second time and may well see it a third — although I stayed in my seat from beginning to end I was still none the wiser. Thinking about it since I realize that the open-ended beginning is essential.

RON DIAMOND

Cissy Meddings and Winifred Holden in *Company of Strangers*

Essential? Why? I don't quite know. Perhaps for no other reason than that it balances the beautiful title shot of the group of women materializing mysteriously and slowly out of mist. And yet I think there is another reason. Maybe it will come to me.

We get to know these women as they get to know each other. Constance Garneau, eighty-eight, with a cane, walking with Mary Meigs, seventy-one. The bus driver, Michelle Sweeney (a jazz and gospel singer and the only professional actor) limping along on her wounded ankle. The two elderly English women —

Cissy Meddings, seventy-six, and Winnie Holden, seventy-seven, and Alice Diabo, seventy-four, a Mohawk from Kahnawake. (I give their names and their ages. Anything less would belittle them.) The third English woman, Beth Webber, eighty, and Catherine Roche, sixty-nine, a Catholic nun with the Order of the Sacred Heart, are not among the vanguard setting off across the green field to the wonderful house Constance has promised them — Constance so filled with memories of place. We are in Laurentian country, *en plein été*. The white-throated sparrow is singing its high

182

needle-sharp song.

Nothing happens and everything happens. They find the house which is not the house. They share the remains of their picnics — one apple cleverly cut into seven sections by Mary Meigs, some Chiclets, half a sandwich, an orange. They take their pills — for arthritis, bladder, angina. Drink water from the lake where, at dusk, the swallows skim its surface for flies. Sister Catherine Roche tinkers with the engine of the bus as she listens to "Jesu Joy of Man's Desiring" on her Walkman and sings along. (She, by the way, has a Ph.D. in music education.) And Beth Webber, young for her eighty years and holding onto her youth with a bright desperation, stays aboard the broken-down bus in preference to venturing into the unknown country.

The women improvise beds, settle down. As perfect day follows terrible night, they search for food, create fish traps from panty hose, birdwatch, paint — or Mary Meigs paints. She is marvellously inquiring, humorous, self-contained. The world for her is full of interest. They are short of food, deprived of comforts, forced to come to terms with their circumstances, with each other, themselves.

The wonder of it is they are not acting. They are playing themselves. They are inventive, good natured, adaptable, humorous — Cissy, whose adoring husband, now dead, helped her learn to walk again after a stroke; Winnie who had been a belly dancer in her youth; Alice who worked in a bottling factory; Beth unable to speak of her grief; and the nun, bride of the church, cut out for sacrifice and joy. They laugh. They tell their stories. They talk of love. Of grief. Of fear of death. But how can I tell you their conversations? Some things are trivialized if retold. They have to be heard the first time. They have to be exchanged. That is it — confidences have to be exchanged.

If I think of the film in one way, I see it as a long green flowing continuity — a kind of banner with birds and music, splendid music. If I think of it in another, it is a series of perfect vignettes that re-create whole lives for us, that remind us of our friends, ourselves. I think of the back view of Constance as she walks alone through the field towards the lake, uncertain of her footing. Of Constance laughing — her girlish delighted laugh — when she bluffs in a game if cards. Of Cissy and Alice — their shared grief and their recovery from it. Of Winnie conducting a movement class and the extraordinary snake-like sinuosity of her arms. (According to the release that accompanied the film, Winnie is said to have "spent much of her free time on set knitting snakes for the rest of the cast. That's right, *snakes*.") Of the nun and Mary Meigs talking about prayer. Of Beth in one blinding moment, helped by Michelle to remove her mask. And perhaps most moving of all, of Constance and Mary Meigs and the song of the white-throated sparrow.

So this is human existence, we say to ourselves as the credits roll. How wonderful it is. How valiant we are. How beautiful.

Are men and women really the same?" a child asks in James Reaney's *Colours in the Dark*. For answer, imagine *Company of Strangers* with a cast of eight men — an eighty-eight-year-old with a background in radio, an elderly gay, a widower recovered from a stroke, a Mohawk, a priest, a salesman and two less easily categorized. What kind of a film would this have made? I get quite lost in the possibilities. Of one thing I am certain. It wouldn't have been remotely like *Company of Strangers*.

ELEANOR WACHTEL

An Interview With Grace Paley

It's been almost thirty years since the publication of Grace Paley's first book of short stories, *The Little Disturbances of Man: Stories of Men and Woman at Love*. Fifteen years later came a second collection called *Enormous Changes at the Last Minute,* and then in 1985, *Later the Same Day*. Not much volume in three decades, but some of the most remarkably memorable stories you're likely to come across. Paley writes in an idiosyncratic style about women and their children, lovers, husbands, aging parents and friends. Many of the stories are about a woman named Faith, something of an alter-ego to Grace. The stories are told in perfect pitch.

Grace Paley is sixty-five. She grew up in the Bronx — her parents were Ukrainian-born Jews who emigrated to New York early in the century. She still has a residual Bronx accent although she's lived most of her adult life in Greenwich Village. Her second husband, a landscape architect and writer, is a Vermonter and they spend six months of the year there. When she's in one place, she thinks about what she's missing in the other. In Greenwich Village, she wishes she's in Vermont, planting or something. She took up gardening two years ago. When she's in Vermont, she thinks about all the exciting things her New York friends are doing.

Grace Paley has warm brown eyes and a shock of thick, short, white hair. She's five-feet-one. On the day I interviewed her she was wearing a pink blouse under a purple cardigan, dark purple skirt and dark stockings. A thin green-brown agate hung from a chain around her neck. When the publicity director for the 1988 Harbourfront International Authors Festival asked if she wanted the same room at the Harbour Castle Hotel she had earlier in the day, she said: "Okay, it was clean." He led us to the room. It was large, with a view of the lake, but stale cigarette smoke lingered in the air. The publicity director mentioned that one of the writers said that if he had to choose between death and living in that hotel he'd choose death. "With death as the alternative," said Paley, "sometimes you change your mind. You remember that there's a gift shop downstairs." We sat at a small table. She kicked off one shoe, looked me in the face and said: "Ask me anything."

Wachtel: Why did you start writing short stories?

Paley: I'd been writing poems for a number of years — in fact for most of my life. But they weren't doing the work I wanted them to do. So I felt I had to try to see what I could do with the story form.

Wachtel: When you say the poems weren't doing the work that you wanted, what do you mean?

Paley: I mean a couple of things. I couldn't use people in the way I was really interested in doing. I began to think about language and sentences, and using other voices. And I had also become oppressed by my worries, my feelings about women's lives. That was in the mid-fifties. I began to hang around with women, doing the mundane things that most people don't enjoy too much but which I really loved. I liked working in groups. I began to feel a great deal of pressure on my soul about women's lives. A lot of them, even then, were women alone with kids. My kids were in day care. Also it's as though some kind of sound in the air had begun to be heard by other women and by me, even though we didn't know what it was.

A lot of this began to bother me. It wasn't just a question of women. There were my aunts, my mother, et cetera. I had to find a way to write about them. My husband was really good about this. He said, "You have a sense of humour and it's never in any of these damn poems." And it's true, it wasn't. "And you're interested in people." All of this was true and I was also interested in myself as a Jewish woman, which I had not really thought about particularly or read about in literature. So all of that came together at one particular time and I began to write stories. Once I started I was lucky. I was sick that year. As a result I had to be home a lot and the kids had to be away a lot, so I had a couple of months in there — maybe two months — in which I could really carry one or two things to completion. Getting that done was important. Actually beginning and finishing the two stories in my first book — "The Contest" and "Goodbye and Good Luck" — was great.

Wachtel: What kind of voices are you referring to when you talk about the use of other voices in your work?

Paley: For me, you don't get to your own voice until you use other people's voices. I mean, you're not going to get that gift until you have paid enough attention. And maybe in the use of other voices, in that kind of dialectical experience, something happens so that your own voice comes through, almost in opposition. It sounds peculiar, but I think I'm probably right. That's what I was interested in when I wrote those two stories — one in the voice of an aunt who's totally invented and the other in a man's voice.

Wachtel: Your writing style is very original. Were you conscious of going your own way when you began writing short stories?

Paley: I was conscious in this sense. I had gone to school to poetry, I hadn't gone to school to fiction. I'd gone to school to poetry to learn how to write, so I had the habits of a poet, which seem original maybe in fiction. That's part of it: the kinds of jumps and leaps and liking of language that a poet has. The other thing was that I didn't like literary life. I was afraid of it. I didn't want to be part of it in any way, so that must have entered into the way that I began to write. I was afraid of being cut off from my own life by going into another world that was more literary. But I didn't think, "Oh, I'm being original."

I had done a lot of imitating. Not on purpose, though. I didn't even know it when I was imitating someone like Auden and writing with a British accent. Not on purpose, but because this tune was in my ear and I couldn't get my own tune going until I wrote stories. I wasn't so much aware of it as I felt something peculiar was happening. I'm probably doing something wrong, I thought. I was writing about those lives that no one would be interested in. I was putting in all those kitchen scenes that no one would care about. And I was writing in a funny way that probably nobody would like. But I had a great commitment to finish.

Wachtel: To some degree you write the way people talk. You have syncopated rhythms of speech. How do you do that?

Paley: I don't know. I just listen to people. If you pay attention you get some things right. I also rewrite a lot. I don't get it the first time. It can take me a helluva long time to get even the simplest dialogue right. Just an exchange between two people in four lines can really drive me crazy before I get it right.

Wachtel: A lot of people say they write to create order out of chaos, but you let a certain amount of chaos into your stories. Everything isn't tidy and ordered. Things jump from one thing to another.

Paley: That really comes from the poetry. Once you write poetry you get a certain courage about jumping and making leaps. You don't feel you have to put in five paragraphs of transition every time you go from one room to the next. I don't know if one makes order from chaos, it's such a general statement. I've said it myself, to tell you the truth. But it seems to me that that's just one way of looking at it. You might just as easily and with as friendly a tone of voice say: "I'm here to make disorder from excessive order. I'm here to bring a little bit of noise into this quiet place." Why not? Why not say that too?

Wachtel: Where do you start with a story?

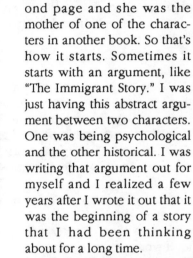

Paley: It could be anything. It could be a sentence. I'm thinking of a story called "Distance," which begins: "I was the lady who appreciated youth." And I just put that sentence in. I was thinking about something. I didn't go on with it for a long time. Then I wrote another paragraph. Then I realized I was writing about this Irish woman and it was her voice I was writing in, which I didn't really know until I was well into the second page and she was the mother of one of the characters in another book. So that's how it starts. Sometimes it starts with an argument, like "The Immigrant Story." I was just having this abstract argument between two characters. One was being psychological and the other historical. I was writing that argument out for myself and I realized a few years after I wrote it out that it was the beginning of a story that I had been thinking about for a long time.

Wachtel: Do you recall what it was about women's lives that you particularly wanted to write about?

Paley: In my first book — I guess it was in my mid-thirties — I was trying to understand men's attitudes towards women, which I had begun to dislike very much, after years of liking both men and their attitudes. I had lived in army camps years earlier with my husband who was a soldier when we were kids — I mean we were in our early twenties, maybe nineteen. And I liked men pretty well in those days and I like them now, but there had begun to be something very wrong. And I had begun to be aware of it in a way that a lot of women were — suddenly feeling a discomfort

— even women who were presumably happily married or who had not seemed terribly dissatisfied. I had not been very ambitious, so I can't say it was because suddenly I realized I couldn't be a lawyer or a doctor or something. It was nothing like that. I didn't want to be anything. I didn't even want to be a writer; I just wanted to write. I liked having kids, I liked all that very much. But I became very resentful of the general attitude of men towards women and maybe getting older had something to do with it.

Wachtel: Where did your feminist consciousness, or whatever you want to call it, fit into your general political awareness?

Paley: It didn't for a long time. It did to this extent: that I worked a lot with women. Women, in general, have been the main workers in local organizations, even the local organizations of great big centralized organizations. But forget that. Think of ordinary things, like getting a light at a crossing. I worked for a long time, at a time when Jane Jacobs was in New York, at keeping a road out of Washington Square Park. Lots of things like that. PTAs were almost entirely women. A kind of sisterhood was happening inside local work — a lot of which involved children, but not all. And then finally, when the Viet Nam War came, there were men working with us too. We had a local [Greenwich] Village centre, but women were still doing a tremendous amount of the work.

Wachtel: To what extent do you draw on your own life? The work *seems* autobiographical.

Paley: Basically I don't, or basically I do. My life is totally different from this woman Faith's. I lived with my children's father for twenty-two or twenty-three years, whereas she's really alone. My children are different. And so in every particular way, in every accountable way, it's not my life. But on the other hand, she could be a friend of mine. She could be some friend who hasn't been registered yet.

Wachtel: Do family or friends think they appear in your work?

Paley: Actually, much less than you'd think. I had to point out to a couple of my friends that I had really jumped off their backs. That's what you do: you get on the back of a person or a sentence and you jump. Sometimes they are very close to life. I have a couple of stories, like "Friends," which I wrote in memorial for a friend of mine who died, so that happens sometimes.

Wachtel: In that story about the death of friend, you write that you, or the character telling the story, are "inventing for my friends and our children a report on these private deaths and the condition of our lifelong attachments." Is that your purpose as a writer?

Paley: I never really think about my purpose as a writer. If I did, my standards would be so high that I would never reach them. If you said, "What should be your purpose as a writer?" I'd think something noble and gallant and great. But as it is I write because I want to tell you something. I write because I don't understand what's going on. And I begin to barely understand my writing. In that particular story, I was trying to understand all our difficult relations, not just with the woman who died, but with the other women. And another reason you write — it's just what every writer does — you simply illuminate what's hidden so in that way you become a person who makes some justice in the world. Every writer does that who's serious, but you do that by accident.

Wachtel: You equate illuminating something with justice?

Paley: Yes, if you have lives that are hidden, where nobody wants to talk about them and you shine a light on them then the world sees that light for the first time. You see that in all new work. We began to write about women and put it in the same scale as the life of men. Black women, Native Americans, different classes. The middle class shone a light in the nineteenth century or earlier, saying: This is how we live, not just the nobles. We're this rising middle class, get a look at us, we're having a good time, we just invented capitalism.

Wachtel: Is it difficult or problematic to try to integrate politics into writing without being didactic?

Paley: No, it's not difficult in that sense. It's something that for me is maybe a little easier than for someone who doesn't do a lot of politics. I really want to write about those people who think about it and talk about it. And I really believe that more people think and talk about politics than writers let on. Writers don't let them talk about anything mostly. So it's not hard. And as for being didactic, you want it to be part of the form of the story and one of the things that the story is about. So that to leave it out would be much more noticeable than putting it in.

One of the things that you try to do when you're writing — you can't really do it — but you try to give as much primary experience as you can. That is, you want people to respond to what you're writing in a way that is as close as possible to the way you yourself responded to the event. But the only way you can do it is by not telling them how to respond, because once you do that they won't. People are very stubborn. There's no dealing with them. So what you try to do is be as primary as possible — really really do the event somehow. You might do it in a very surreal way, I'm not talking about naturalism or realism. You may go way out and yet the reader knows what you're talking about. But if you start telling people what to think they get kind of

grouchy. My characters' political nature just means that they're aware that they live in the world.

Wachtel: What can a writer do, while functioning as a writer, to have some impact on the world politically?

Paley: It's kind of mysterious. I don't even dare to think in those terms because it's too great a dream to think that you could be that useful. Everybody longs for that. And yet we know that there are writers who have been able to speak for different classes or groups or colours. The success of a lot of Black women writers has been empowering to women, whether they mean to do that or not. I think partly you write to give yourself a sense of possibility. In the sense that you strengthen others, you can be useful. You give courage. It's the thing writers think about a lot. And you don't really know who's the boss of beauty.

Wachtel: Who's "the boss of beauty"?

Paley: Who's the judge? Who's the critic? Who are they to say you can be political or you can't? Who knows in what way other work will come forward that is both didactic and beautiful? Who's in charge?

Wachtel: You have this line in a story called "Anxiety" [from *Later the Same Day*]: A woman is leaning out from her window and talking to a young father she doesn't know and she says, "Son, I must tell you that madmen intend to destroy this beautifully made planet. That the murder of our children by these men has got to become a terror and a sorrow to you, and starting now, it had better interfere with any daily pleasure." Is that you talking?

Paley: It's me talking, but you don't see me doing that ... Think of people who are doing really outstanding political work, for example in Central America. People who really decided that they're going to put their lives into trying to prevent a war down there. Take a guy like Ben Linder who went there to build dams, and to help construct — not protest — but construct a new society. These people make up their minds to put away certain daily pleasures. I'm sure they have had a great time — in fact, Linder's a clown from before and rode a monocycle and did wonderful things with children. You can't live without joy and pleasure. But there have to be a lot of serious people around, of whom other people say: Tsk, they never think of anything else. What's wrong with them? There have to be a lot of people who never think of anything else any more.

Wachtel: Are you one of them, or have you been at different times in your life?

Paley: No, I never have been totally. During the Viet Nam War, I spent a helluva lot of time doing all kinds of work, and I do again, now and then, but I'm a writer too and I have to do that. I have strong feelings for happiness.

Wachtel: How can you maintain your optimism?

Paley: Who said I was optimistic? No, I happen to have a cheerful disposition. But I'm not optimistic. I think we just may kill ourselves ecologically before we kill ourselves with nuclear war, so that's a great piece of anxiety. But at the same time, you do see — I think some of my early political struggles had some success. The little ones, the small ones, really, that shaped the city, that helped make parts of the city decent, which most of it isn't, New York, I mean. So you have some of those successes and they shape you a little bit, they give you courage for the future. And I think the United States would be at war right now in Nicaragua if it weren't for the breadth of the anti-Central American War movement — if it wasn't for that, and if it wasn't for the fact that we worked so hard during the Viet Nam period. So in general, Americans no matter how often they vote for Reagan really don't want to go to war right now. They've lost their taste for it. I'm happy that I was a little tiny part of helping them lose their taste for war.

Wachtel: Are there other American writers you have an affinity to who are writing political fiction?

Paley: There are many different kinds of writers who are thinking about these things. There's a young woman, Irini Spanidou, who isn't writing about the U.S. at all, she's writing about Greece. She has a book called *God's Snake* and it's all about women. Then there's E.M. Broner who's a very interesting writer. Mary Gordon thinks about these things a lot. There are a lot of women writing about women, but in a very narrow kind of way, in a way that is so classbound. I really don't know how to describe it because although it does what I believe in doing, it describes the lives of women, which I'm interested in, I don't really care about that particular middle class or upper middle class of woman and marriages and infidelities and stuff like that. It's a little too late for that. There's got to be more of a move. Marge Piercey has given herself the great and serious task of covering all the bases, and there are people I really love like Tillie Olsen and Kay Boyle who are still writing away there — Kay is in her eighties — fierce and amazing women.

Wachtel: Are you conscious of apportioning your time towards writing or political action or happiness?

Paley: No, I'm just pulled one way or another: writing, politics, house and family. That's all right. It's an idea of life. If you can take it, and you don't feel guilty. Feeling guilty is what's wrong. I tend to be pulled without an excess of guilt — just enough so I know something is happening to me. I'm a writer but I'm also a person in the world. I don't feel a terrible obligation to write a lot of books. When I write, I write very seriously and I mean business. I write as well and as truthfully as I possibly can and I write about the things that have created a good deal of pressure in my head.

Wachtel: Who are the people who you hope or imagine will read your books?

Paley: The whole world. I'd like everybody to read them. Sometimes I'm surprised by the people who read the books. Without the support of the women's movement the response might be different. I'm very conscious of the fact that there exists a movement, a political and women's movement that supports all women writers, no matter who that writer is, even if she says: "I hate feminism and I don't really like women too much." Even so, that woman, whether she knows it or not, is supported by the historical fact of the wave of the women's movement. So that exists for all of us women right now and we're very lucky.

Wachtel: Do you think of yourself as a realist writer?

Paley: No, I don't think about where I'm lodged in the house of literature.

Wachtel: How do you want to be remembered?

Paley: I don't know. I just don't think about that. We all throw ourselves into the hearts of our grandchildren and luck.

191

ROBERT KROETSCH

The Half-Imagined Land

ike fans of the Saskatchewan Roughriders, I stick with my team through thick and thin. I've been a fan of American writer John Hawkes for twenty years. In those years he's won a few of the conventional literary prizes. But he's written some of the most exciting prose fiction to appear in this half of the twentieth century.

John Hawkes is an example of an American writer who's better known abroad, particularly in France and Germany, than he is in his native country. Hawkes belongs to no particular school or fashion in the United States, and that makes it difficult for the critics to peg him. I'm tempted to say he's a direct descendent of the Brontë sisters, via Franz Kafka. But mostly he's a writer of astonishing originality.

Hawkes was born into a comfortable family in Stamford, Connecticut, in 1925. Ten years later, his father took the family off to Alaska, intending to get rich as a prospector and businessman. The experience was exciting and terrifying for the young John Hawkes, and that combination is examined often — even

obsessively — in Hawkes's fiction.

After five years and, not surprisingly, no fortune in Alaska, the family moved to New York. John Hawkes published a small book of poems the year he graduated from high school. That was in 1943. He entered Harvard, then left college to work as an ambulance driver for the American Field Service in Italy and Germany. After the war he returned to his studies at Harvard, where he managed to get into Albert Geurard's creative writing class — a class, by the way, that also graduated the poets Frank O'Hara and Robert Bly and the novelist John Updike.

Hawkes tells a wonderful story about walking into the first class meeting and seeing a young man there, in a trenchcoat, and thinking, now there's a *real* writer.

Perhaps I sympathize because I had a similar experience — at the University of Alberta. I talked my way into Professor Salter's famous writing class — and at the first class meeting I was so intimidated by the other students — one was an ex-newspaper editor, another was an ex-bomber pilot — that I left the class and raced down the hall and dropped the course.

Hawkes wasn't so easily intimidated. He has since then published a dozen works of fiction. In 1961, twelve years after his first story appeared, he published his first truly major work, *The Lime Twig*. It was that novel that turned me into a rabid John Hawkes fan.

The Lime Twig is a takeoff on the popular thriller — complete with a gang of thugs, a rigged horserace, violence, orgies, murder. It's set in an England that's half imagined and half real, and has to do with a scheme to steal a racehorse and run it in a famous race.

The scheme is introduced by a man named William Hencher. We first meet him when he's looking for lodgings — and the characters in a Hawkes novel are often looking for lodgings — or for home. Hencher is a man of immense loneliness. He can just barely tell dream from reality. And he knows his dreams have a way of turning into nightmares.

He finds lodgings in a sleazy place run by Margaret and Michael Banks. One morning, in this bed-and-breakfast place, *he* makes breakfast for *them;* he enters their bedroom with a tray and on it, as only Hawkes can say, "a teapot small as an infant's head":

The door was off the latch and they were sleeping. I turned and touched it with my hip, my elbow, touched it with only a murmur. And it swung away on smooth hinges while I watched and listened until it came up sharply against the corner of a little cane chair. They lay beneath a single sheet and a single sand-coloured blanket, and I saw that on his thin icy cheeks Banks had grown a beard in the night and that Margaret — the eyelids defined her eyes, her lips were dry and brown and puffy — had been dreaming of a nice picnic in narrow St. George's Park behind the station. Behind each silent face was the dream that would collect slack shadows and tissues and muscles into some first mood for the day. Could I not blow smiles onto their nameless lips, could I not force apart those lips with kissing? One of the gulls came round from the kitchen and started beating the glass.

"Here's breakfast," I said, and pushed my knees against the footboard.

It was a small trouble. And not long after — a month or a fortnight perhaps — I urged them to take a picnic, not to the sooty park behind the station but farther away, farther away to Landingfield Battery, where they could sit under a dead tree and hold their poor hands. And while they were gone I prowled through the flat, softened my heart of introspection: I found her small tube of cosmetic for the lips and, in the lavatory, drew a red circle with it round each of my eyes. I had their bed to myself while they were gone. They came home laughing and brought a postal card of an old pocked cannon for me.

It was the devil getting the lipstick off.

But red circles, giving your landlord's bed a try, keeping his flat to yourself for a day — a man must take possession of a place if it to be a home for the waiting out of dreams.

That's a great line, breaking through there, it speaks to the root of me: "… where they could sit under a dead tree and hold their poor hands."

The hesitation in the language, the mixture of richness and delay, might make the reading a bit difficult at first. But the poignancy breaks through like a delayed bud turning into a rose.

The Lime Twig came out in 1961, but I didn't read it until 1968. One of those small accidents that shape our lives. I was living in England, working on my third novel, *The Studhorse Man*. I started out to read *The Lime Twig* simply because it was set in England and written by a writer who at the time, so the story had it, hadn't laid eyes on England.

Before I finished the book I was hooked. Hawkes has a great sense of how horses occupy our imaginations, and I liked that. I liked the way he connected horses with dreams, with nightmares, with our sexual energies and fantasies.

William Hencher joins up with Michael Banks and his gang of horse thieves. They succeed in stealing the horse called Rock Castle. But that dream of horse, become real, turns into a nightmare.

The stolen racehorse kicks William Hencher to death. And by then Michael and Margaret Banks are too deeply into their get-rich scheme ever to escape. They must go through with it. And just as our innocence turns to nightmare, so, in the middle of our nightmares, we remember our lost innocence. Michael Banks, as the fixed race begins, decides he must interrupt it, and he runs out onto the track:

The green, the suspended time was gone. The chill pounded on his heart with anonymous rhythm and he found that after all he had been fast enough. There were several seconds in which to take the centre of the track, to position himself according to the white rails on his right and left, to find the approaching ball of dust and start slowly ahead to encounter it. Someone fired at him from behind a tree and he began to trot, shoes landing softly, irregularly on the dirt. The tower above the stands was a little Swiss hut in the sky; a fence post was painted black; he heard a siren and saw a dove bursting with air on the bough. I could lean against the post, he thought, I might just take a breath. But the horses came round the turn then and once more his stumbling trot was giving way to a run. And he had the view that a photographer might have except there was no camera, no truck's tailgate to stand upon. Only the virgin man-made stretch of track and at one end the horses bunching in fateful heat and at the other end himself — small, yet beyond elimination, whose single presence purported a toppling of the day, a violation of that scene at Aldington, wreckage to horses and little crouching men.

The crowd began to scream.

He was running in final stride, the greatest spread of legs, redness coming across the eyes, the pace so fast that it ceased to be motion, but at its peak becomes the long downhill deathless gliding of a dream until the arms are out, the head thrown back, and the runner is falling as he was falling and waving his arm at Rock Castle's onrushing silver shape, at Rock Castle who was about to run him down and fall.

"... the blighter! Look at the little blighter go!"

At the end of the novel, two very incompetent detectives are trying to figure out what happened — their incompetence matched, fortunately, by that of the criminals. I like this parody of all the braininess of detective stories — and in my novel, *Alibi,* where I work with parody and the whodunit, I suspect I'm still indebted to John Hawkes.

Is it influence, or is it the recognition of a kindred spirit? I'm not sure. I do know that Hawkes, with every book he writes, reminds me of something I knew in my body but never quite spoke — something about the nature of daydream and desire.

In 1970 I was again knocked over by a new and major novel by Hawkes. In that year he published *The Blood Oranges,* the first novel in a trilogy, followed four years later by *Death, Sleep and the Traveler.* And two years later he concluded with the novel, *Travesty.*

Hawkes is always the novelist of love. He has a wicked eye for comedy, along with its tenderness. He sees its mixture of bravado and terror, its self-deception and its grand satisfactions.

The Blood Oranges is set in a world that's Mediterranean — vaguely Greek. This coastal paradise is called Illyria in the novel. The narrator, Cyril, begins with the claim that "Love weaves its own tapestry, spins its own golden threat...." and we as readers — perhaps as lovers ourselves — never know for sure if love is weaving us or we are weaving love.

One of the great scenes in the novel takes place when Cyril goes snail hunting with his cook, Rosella. Rosella speaks a language of which he does not speak a word. And yet Cyril is persuaded that *passion* is the real subject, while he and Rosella fill their pot to the brim with snails:

> Moments later I was once more able to enjoy the sound of heavy snails falling into the wide-mouthed pot. In the twilight we were side by side, Rosella and I, kneeling together at the edge of a small rectangle of pulpy leaves. The snails were plentiful and the sticky silver trails crept down dead stems, climbed over exposed roots, disappeared under black chunks of decomposing stone. Everywhere the snails were massing or making their blind osmotic paths about the villa, eating and destroying and unwinding their silver trails. They were the eyes of the night, the crawling stones.
>
> "Faster, Rosella," I murmured, "a little faster."
>
> She was backing up. Her haunches moved, her thighs began to work; again one of her sandals cracked against the pot, and suddenly one hand reached behind and tugged up the constricting skirt of her hemp-coloured dress. Rosella, I saw, was moving backward. And smelling the gloom of the funeral cypresses, I laughed and, despite the rules, thrust out my hand so that in another moment my hand might have confronted her flesh and staved off the now partially exposed buttocks, though even my hand pushed hard against her buttocks could not have prevented us from tangling in what would have been a kind of accidental Arcadian embrace. I lost hold of the pot and tipped it over. Rosella looked at me, and in the clear rose-tinted twilight and amidst small noises of grass, brambles, stones all disturbed by our movements, I thought that Rosella's eyes reminded me of the bulging eyes of my

> little long-lost golden sheep. And then we stopped. Stopped, waited, listened, heard the ticking of the grass, the brushing sounds of a few small birds, the slow dripping of contaminated water and, from somewhere in the increasing shadows, footsteps.
>
> "Someone's coming. Hear it?"

This first volume in the trilogy is Hawkes's look at our impulse — or our attempt — to create a paradise on earth. He gives us the lyric beauty of that vision.

My own work is full of gardens, I discover, after years of writing. Part of that comes, I suppose, from my having been the gardener on a farm in rural Alberta when I was a boy. I was passionately the gardener, growing twice as many vegetables as ever we could eat, growing flowers, planting trees on that prairie landscape. I was in my early teens then. No wonder gardens came to haunt my imagination. In fact, this past summer I once again retreated to a Greek island.

Hawkes showed me how that garden world is connected with daydreams and fantasy and the erotic. He pictures love's tapestry with all its birds and flowers — and snails. And then he shows us the other side of the cloth.

Death, Sleep and the Traveler reverses the picture we saw in *The Blood Oranges*. This second novel in the trilogy is set in another of our dream places — this time it's a cruise ship.

The cruise ship is, again, a place of erotic fantasy. But now it's a place of imprisonment as well as freedom — as anyone knows who's gone on a cruise.

The hero of this novel, Allert Vanderveenan, has been sent on a cruise by his wife, who is in the long process of leaving him. He is nothing if not clumsy and, setting out, he quickly discovers once again that what he's best at is standing still. Early in *Death, Sleep and the Traveler,* Hawkes has his hero awaken in his berth:

I awoke. The porthole was half open and, in the moonlight, was streaked with salt. But so too were my lips, the clothes piled on the nearby chair and flung on the floor, the sheet that was stiff and the colour of silver on our two bodies. Salt-encrusted and bitter, all of it, as if we had slept through a violent storm with the porthole open.

I was awake, my left leg was bent in a cramp, the body next to me was small, the cabin was not mine. The darkness, the glint of a brass hook near the louvered door, the girl whose naked sleep I could feel but not see, and the salt, the moonlight, all of it made me more than ever convinced that the small unfamiliar stateroom in which we lay had momentarily been

emptied of black sea water. The pillow was damp. But what else? What else?

"Good God," I whispered, "good God, we have stopped again. The ship is not moving."

"We are becalmed," I whispered. "I must go on deck."

She curled still closer and spoke though she was quite asleep. Then she took nearly half of my finger into her mouth. Suddenly, marvellously, I understood what she had said and felt through all my weight and cold musculature the heavy slow rumble of the engines and the unmistakable revolution of the great brass propeller blades in the depths below us. The distant vibrations were all around us, were inside me, as if my own intestinal centre was pulsating with pure oceanic motion and the absolute certainty of the navigational mind doing its dependable work. Our arms were crossed, my fingers were tentative yet firm, the girl's dreams were in my mouth. But the sea, I realized quite suddenly, was not calm, as I had thought, but rough.

Hawkes here makes the novel work wonderfully like a play. When the young woman, Ariane, takes Allert's finger into her mouth, worlds, as Hemingway would have it, move. The great ship starts to life. Rumbling engines and brass propeller blades speak to us of mystery and release.

When I was a young man I worked on riverboats on the Mackenzie, in the Northwest Territories. I know those shuddering sounds of engines and propellers — and I know the solitude that gives them meaning. Unfortunately, I was on a boat that carried freight, not passengers. I wrote my first novel, *But We Are Exiles,* out of that experience. I hadn't at the time read Hawkes. I suppose he'd have made me write the book differently. Hawkes is that kind of writer's writer. He tells us how to hear the reverberations of experience. The resonance. I was, believe me, an innocent kid, looking at the violence and rawness of that riverboat life. Hawkes as a young boy went to Alaska. As a young man he worked on a power dam construction site in Montana. He knows the collisions that take place within us of innocence and the lived life. The fine and dangerous edge between the two goes on fascinating me, and Hawkes has a lot to say on the subject.

Allert, in *Death, Sleep and the Traveler,* balances precariously between his own dream of love and the actuality of the encounter. He finds Ariane on the cruise ship. She comes to his cabin. She too is involved in a love triangle, because she loves the ship's wireless operator as much as she loves Allert. Allert claims he isn't jealous. But the ending of this love affair suggests, as I hinted earlier, the dark side of the tapestry:

In my arms she was like a small child struck by an auto. Together in the dark we swayed on the deck as if I had just dragged her in from a wreck at sea. I was holding her horizontally in both my arms. Her eyes were glazed, she refused to speak. The white officer's cap had fallen from her head only a minute before the white tunic fell open from her nude body like the remnant of some outlandish costume from a masquerade, which indeed it was. She was limp but watching me, though the eyes were glazed and she refused to speak. The moon was a streak of fat in the night sky. I could not feel her weight. I heard a shout. I turned. I heard a splash. The deck was a hard crust of salt. The night was cold. I heard the splash. I could not feel her weight. And then along the entire length of that bitter ship I saw the lights sliding and blurring beneath the waves. Clumsily, insanely I wrestled with a white life ring that bore the name of the ship and that refused to come free. I saw the ship's fading lighted silhouette beneath the waves.

Who is safe?

Who *is* safe?

John Hawkes won't let any of us feel safe, and perhaps that's why he has never appeared on the bestseller list in the back pages of the *New York Times Book Review*. But he has been reviewed on the front page, which is about the only place where most of the bestsellers don't appear. Hawkes is reviewed by the best reviewers, and by his fellow writers, in the United States and in Europe. He stays alive by teaching at Brown University in Rhode Island and, like his own characters, he finds himself spending more and more time in France and Greece — his own life imitating his art.

He is seen as a major writer who elects, by the richness of his prose and the dark hint in his vision, to stay on the edge. On the edge of popular success. But on the cutting edge of where fiction is at these days. I suppose I should admit that I admire that about him too. He listens to his own drummer, and in the process gives a gift that is unique and liberating.

JOHN RALSTON SAUL

We Are Not Authors of the Post-Novel Novel

he English and Americans write about English Canadian writers. The French write about French Canadians. This division of tasks is perfectly logical given the established empires of language and their healthy disdain for political borders. The Canadian case is complicated, however, by the possession not of a major and a minor tongue, but of the two great western languages, with their endless, mutually exclusive trains of literary, social and historical baggage. There is no precedent for a long partnership between the two. Outside of Canada, no other large French minority has lived for two centuries in complicated but peaceful co-operation with an English majority, who are themselves a small minority obliged to maintain a daily resistance — intellectual and practical — against the American domination of North America.

Any literary analysis of Canada which is done by separate linguistic groups inevitably deforms this reality of a nation of two minorities, who have been fixed into approximately the same constitutional and legal arrangement since 1850 — that is to say, subject to the rules of what is now the third oldest constitution in the world. Mythology, after all, is the irrational expression of experience. And the Canadian experience, linking the two minorities, is now one of the longest stable experiences in the modern world. The resulting mythology — spoken, unspoken, denied, conscious, unconscious, whatever — is there, and there in a unified, distinct pattern. English critics nevertheless are still looking for ex-colonialists, Americans for some subclass of Americans, and the French either for distant cousins or for Americans who speak French.

Elements as simple as the vast role played by a savage and unforgiving nature in the Canadian novel render the separate linguistic approach irrelevant. Outsiders insist on discovering in this nature remnants of the English rural novel or of the American frontier tradition or a sort of Rousseauean romanticism gone wild. But the nature flowing through Margaret Laurence's *The Stone Angel* or Marion Engel's *Bear* (in which a woman carries on a metaphysical and physical love affair with a bear) or Matt Cohen's *Salem Novels* or Rudy Wiebe's *The Scorched-Wood People* is neither a romantic decor nor an element to be subdued. Nature is not a background in the Canadian novel. It is one of the principal characters. Even in urban fiction — Margaret Atwood's *The Edible Woman* or Mavis Gallant's short stories — where nature is not overtly mentioned, it is there, rushing through the sensibility of the characters and their actions. In that sense, if Canadian fiction resembles any other, it is Russian, where even if a character stays in bed, devoting himself to philosophical self-doubt, his geographical condition will remain central to every thought, as if each were the result of conscious physical resistance.

This sense of resistance — moral as well as physical — runs through the fiction and poetry, giving it a kind of Third World aggressivity quite unlike anything American or European, unless it is Eastern European, where industrial civilization has been mixed with a primal need to resist. Canada was created, after all, out of a conscious desire not to be American; a desire to reject the American and French revolutions. Those who believe the two revolutions to be landmark, positive events — and that is the reigning international mythology — assume the Canadian refusal was merely a negative reaction, dictated by an inability to free ourselves of colonial values. The American and French mythological propaganda is still so strong that Canadians have never been able to clearly assert their own position abroad or, for that matter, at home. We tend to blame this uncertainy on the confusion within our own myths. But this is a masochistic interpretation of events. The reality is that our situation is unprecedented. No other western nation has had to deal with the free and aggressive operation of outside cultures inside its borders, particularly of cultures so contradictory to its own. After all, the result of both revolutions was a centralized, single-note mythology which rejected the idea of accommodation between minorities.

The original Canadian refusal of the revolutionary option was produced in large part by a middle-class obsession with avoiding violent or abrupt methods which would disturb the delicate relationship between the minorities. An integral part of this — and it is one of the most original characteristics of Canadian civilization — is a profound distrust of heroes.

The philosopher George Woodcock, in his biography of Gabriel Dumont, explains why this rebel Métis general has not become the sort of mythological hero who would have been inevitable in Europe or America. Canadians reject the strong hero who dominates in order to lead. They search out endurers and survivors.

In *Survival,* Margaret Atwood writes of a people who see themselves imposed upon, distrusting the individual hero, searching out a kind of collective heroine. "The truest democracy," Woodcock has written, "is that in which minorities are allowed to flourish, even at the expense of the patience of the majority." So the aggressivity of Canadian fiction is complicated by the endless refusal of individuals to act in a manner befitting the age of individualism.

The individual act, they believe, will lead to violence and violence will destroy everything. Thus, over the last century, while the Americans and various European nation-states killed tens of thousands of their own citizens in civil wars, coups d'état and racial outbursts, the Canadians, despite an apparently impossible combination of minorities, killed about seventy-five of their own. With the inescapable clarity of small numbers, these few deaths became symbols of what would happen if the individual decided not to restrain himself. Such constant, conscious self-control produces fictional characters quite unlike the overflowing American model, whose lavish extremes seem to Canadian eyes to be part of a profound and dangerous disorder. Timothy Findley in *The Wars* created the archetypal controlled Canadian individual, who is subjected to the lunacy of an uncontrolled world and is therefore destroyed. Stephen Leacock, before the last war, did much the same in books such as *Arcadian*

199

Adventures with the Idle Rich. He wrote with a black, semi-lunatic humour which is frequently used by Canadian novelists to expose the discomfort of their condition. Poet and novelist Dennis Lee has done much the same thing today, as has William Rowe in *Clappe's Rock*.

Western Europeans and Americans often look at Canadian fiction and judge it limited by newness, bereft of mythology. They are really saying they do not understand a modern western mythology which has no need of the rampant Hero — the individual as monster quite apart from whether he is a moral or immoral monster. Again, the Canadian resistance to this unchaining of the single will is part of our character as a Third-World nation. It is our situation which dominates, and not the individual.

A key factor often overlooked when trying to understand this approach is the role of the Native population. In the first two Canadian wars — 1776 and 1812 — there was a curious and unexpected alliance between the British and French settlers. The third and essential partner in that alliance was Native. Faced by a militaristic and conquering American nation, which was driven by uncontrolled individual privileges, the aboriginal civilization, based as it was on a group ethic, allied itself with two small European settlements who also sought to work in groups. That part of the alliance later turned sour as the Europeans took advantage of their own growing numbers and of instability in the Native community to deform the intent of the treaties which bound them together. But the original tripartite approach was nevertheless integrated into the Canadian myth. This may explain why the public has responded so rapidly to a whole new generation of Native writers led by playwright Tomson Highway.

The Canadian is also a stubborn sort of person, certain of hidden collective truths. His middle-class stability, combined with the requirements for surviving several centuries in an unforgiving place, has produced a form of collective action — what is called Red Toryism: middle-class, anti-revolutionary and socialist. This social democratic structure began developing from the mid-nineteenth century on without any serious reference to European ideas of class struggle or of capitalism versus the state. Curiously enough, whenever Canadians write about this phenomenon, they insist upon finding external roots — Disraeli conservatism or French-Catholic reformism, for example. But these roots are, in fact, tacked on after the event. The truth is that the Canadian model, mixing conservatism, socialism, middle-class values, God and minority rights, is entirely the result of the Canadian experience. In Canada the model was the middle class and the result was a sort of conservative socialism aimed first at protecting the British and French minorities, then extended, not without problems, to the endless groups that began arriving — the Ukrainians, Mormons, Jews and Chinese through to the Spanish, Italians, Hungarians, Pakistanis and Jamaicans of the last few years.

All of this produced an obsession with the difficulty of communications between groups and individuals — a slightly pessimistic but stubborn obsession. The classic vision of that shared isolation is Hugh MacLennan's *Two Solitudes*, written in 1945 about the French and English in Montreal, a decade before the nationalist movements got seriously under way in both English and French Canada.

Part of the obsession with communication was the inevitable result of a small population spreading itself out across an enormous space, cut off from each other in summer, triply cut off in winter; turned in upon themselves with the Chekhov-like precise fatalism of Alice Munro's stories or those of Guy Vanderhaeghe. But it is also the isolation of people dug in to resist external forces. A few decades before Braudel began in France, Harold Innes was describing Canada in terms of great commercial movements which held the isolated groups together — a form of concrete, practical communication. Marshall McLuhan was his disciple and when his vision of a planet of global villages and of hot and cold mediums of communications broke upon the outer world, it was the first wide reverberation of the Canadian view of peoples dealing with each other from semi-isolation.

The master of the restrained, hidden character is no doubt Robertson Davies. Behind a classical style he describes apparently straightforward people who gradually slip into a world where secret, mystical themes overwhelm them. In his *Deptford Trilogy*, small-town boys somehow end up in a world of magicians, Jungian manipulators and saint worshippers. This magic realism appears again and again in the Canadian novel — in Jack Hodgins's *The Resurrection of Joseph Bourne,* for example, or Graeme Gibson's *Perpetual Motion* — and is not too distant from that of many South American writers. B. W. Powe, one of the most interesting of the new thinkers, has drawn the themes of isolation, leadership and secrecy together in a book called *The Solitary Outlaw,* which compares Glenn Gould, Pierre Trudeau and Marshall McLuhan.

One of the driving forces behind Canadian fiction is that its role is not the same as that of the novel in other western countries. The novel in most places has been pushed off the centre stage of communications and ideas by the various electronic arts. Novelists, and even more so poets, have withdrawn into more private considerations and adopted a less accessible, sometimes private language. In their writing they have abandoned most of the public concerns of the nineteenth and early twentieth centuries. The electronic media in Canada, however, are dominated by the United States and by France. The Canadian — English or French — does not find him or herself reflected daily or hourly in the dramas of television or of the cinema.

Even the magazine shelves are filled with foreign products. The novel and the poem have therefore remained the privileged place of public debate, just as they have in Eastern Europe and Latin America.

This sense of being at the centre of a nation, which is itself not at the centre of a world civilization, has had a series of unexpected effects. For a start there is the great public strength of poetry which has lost so much of its audience elsewhere. Al Purdy, Irving Layton, Leonard Cohen, Michael Ondaatje, Margaret Atwood, Dionne Brand all hold wide audiences.

Consciousness of not being at the centre has also made the writer turn outwards — first in a practical way to ensure he is published in London and New York. Because he is more likely to avoid a private language than those who come from the great centres, he is relatively more successful than the British and Americans are in each other's markets. He also turns outwards in search of subjects, so that a large number of Canadian books are not about Canada. Some of them come out of the immigrant experience — Michael Ondaatje's *Running In the Family,* for example, or Michael Ignatieff's *The Russian Album* or Josef Skvorecky's *The Engineer of Human Souls.*

There is also the phenomenon of anglophone writers seeing themselves as defenders of French Canada before the English population. And, finally there is a related element which is best described as the spirit of minority. In a definition which would certainly have pleased Flaubert, Robertson Davies once described to me the enormous advantage of having come from the provinces, because it allowed one to write about the whole world without the curiously provincial limitations of believing one was at the centre. This might be called the mythology of the anti-myth. It is a decentralized vision produced by the scribes of a decentralized people.

PAUL WILSON

Keepers of the Looking-Glass

Some Thoughts on Translation

"When the shoe fits, the foot is forgotten" – Chuang Tzu

hen I was translating Josef Škvorecký's novel *The Engineer of Human Souls,* one of the greatest sources of energy for me was the fact that the hero's dilemma was the same as my own.

Škvorecký's narrator, Danny Smiřický, is bursting with memories of his childhood and youth in Czechoslovakia: of playing forbidden music — jazz — during wartime under the Nazis, of engaging in a suspect profession — writing — under the Communists, and finally leaving his country in 1968 in frustration and fear when the Soviets invade and occupy it. When he washes up in Toronto and finds work as a professor of English literature at Edenvale College, Danny discovers — as almost every immigrant to this country does — that he cannot communicate that wealth of experience to his fellow Canadians, in this case his students and colleagues. He tries every means he can

think of overcome the barrier. He reads them a Soviet translation of Poe's "The Raven," even re-translating the Russian version back into English in the hopes that something of the infinite sadness and terror of his own reading of Poe will get through. He draws their attention to passages in Hawthorne and Twain which show how profoundly those writers, without benefit of totalitarianism, had understood the kind of fanaticism that leads to it. He argues that Crane's *The Red Badge of Courage* presents war as it really is, and that Conrad's *The Heart of Darkness* prophesizes future totalitarian rule. But his students remain puzzled, bemused, uncomprehending and hostile, and when they are forced to express an opinion, they fall back on academic or political clichés.

At the root of Danny's frustration — understandable enough in anyone but doubly so in a writer in exile — is the problem of language itself, or more specifically the problem of translation. Danny may write a novel about his experiences in Czechoslovakia and Canada, but as long as it remains in Czech or, to put it another

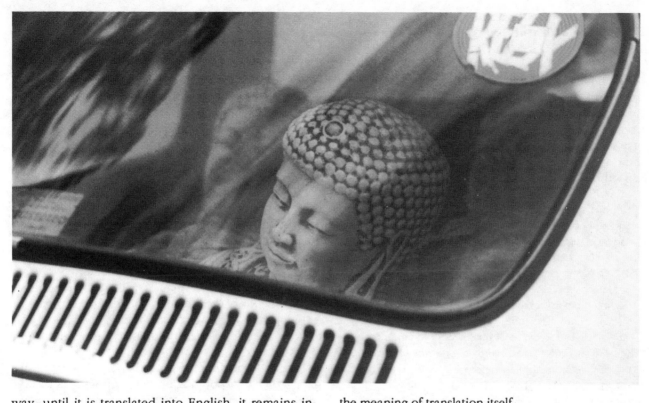

way, until it is translated into English, it remains incomplete. The problem is that much of Danny's experience — "how life feels to him," as the Czechs say — is beyond the reach of translation, and thus the book acquires a meta-significance: it is "about" the impossibility of conveying, in English, the experience of what life feels like in a modern tyranny.

Translation is a strange, self-effacing craft in which perfection is unattainable and the ultimate sign of success is not to be noticed.

On the other hand, translation requires an almost obsessive attention to the problem of meaning, and it would be strange, indeed, if some of this did not spill over — in the translator's mind — into reflection on the meaning of translation itself.

First, an ego-boosting (and sobering) truism: though invisible, the influence of translation in our culture is profound, all-pervasive and not always benign. Many of the words, expressions and concepts we use in everyday speech were brought into English by translators who needed to fill a gap in the language. The word "ego" itself, for example, came into popular use thanks to translations of the works of Sigmund Freud. The propriety of those translations, however, has recently been challenged by Bruno Bettelheim (in *Freud and Man's Soul,* 1983), who pointed out that in the German original the word was "das Ich" — "the I" — and therefore much closer to ordinary German than "ego" is to colloquial English. English has had its revenge and made the word commonplace, but Bettelheim's point remains: in English we perceive Freud's thought as more abstract than it really is.

Another example: translation was a major factor in the spread of Christianity. The Dark Ages, as I see them in my mind's eye, were actually alive with flickering light — the midnight lamps of translators busy rendering the Bible into the many vernaculars of non-Roman Europe. My authority for this is Edward Gibbon:

> "Ulphilas, the bishop and apostle of the Goths, acquired their love and reverence by his blameless life and indefatigable zeal ... He executed the arduous task of translating the Scriptures into their native tongue, a dialect of the German or Teutonic language; but he prudently suppressed the four books of Kings, as they might tend to irritate the fierce and sanguinary spirit of the barbarians. The rude, imperfect idiom of the soldiers and shepherds, so ill qualified to communicate any spiritual ideas, was improved and modulated by his genius; and Ulphilas, before he could frame his version, was obliged to compose a new alphabet of twenty-four letters; four of which he invented to express the peculiar sounds that were unknown to the Greek and Latin pronunciation [from Vol. IV of *The Decline and Fall of the Roman Empire*].

Ulphilas flourished in the fourth century A.D., and Gibbon wrote about him from the commanding heights of eighteenth-century England. Today, of course, the shoe is on the other foot: Gibbon's "prudent suppression" would now be "blatant bowdlerization" and we are far more inclined to believe it is our own rude and imperfect idiom that is ill-equipped to express the complex spirituality of peoples Gibbon would have unabashedly called barbarians. Indeed,

there is (or was, for these are the 1980s) some hope that our lives — if not our language — might be improved and modulated by the genius of Native people.

A third example: the spread of Marxist ideology. According to UNESCO, Vladimir Ilich Lenin is the world's most translated author. Much has been written about the mischief totalitarian ideas have caused, but not enough has been said about the damage they do to the languages into which they are translated. Among other things, official Marxism makes skillful use of figures of speech like the oxymoron — pointedly absurd phrases like "democratic centralism" and "the freedom of necessity" — and pleonasm, my favourite being the epithet "people's democracy." Expressions like these are more than just an insult to logic and common sense; their final effect is to undermine the original meaning of the constituent parts, thus allowing the new phrase to be defined and redefined at will, according to the political needs of the moment. The real evil of ideological language — imported or home-grown — is not that it is used to tell lies, but that it is, in itself, meaningless.

When I was teaching English in Prague, one phrase that kept popping up in textbooks was an obvious translation from Russian: "an exchange of experiences," as in, "Last summer, I went to the Soviet Union for a three-week exchange of experiences with comrades in the Komsomol." I would explain to my students that in English, you can exchange hockey cards or telephone numbers or wedding rings but not experiences. The most you can do with your experience is learn from it, or give someone else the benefit of it, and I insisted that "an exchange of experience" was a bad translation because it wrenched the English out of shape. "How should we translate it?" my students asked. I suggested "visit." "But that's not what it means," they replied. When I asked, naively, what it *did* mean, I was told, "Political instruction."

So there it was.

One final illustration of the pitfalls of translation: the German philosopher Heidegger once made the astonishing claim (in "The Origin of the Work of Art") that when the Romans translated some basic notions from the Greek into Latin, they bungled it. According to him, the Greeks experienced a thing, its essence or core, and its characteristics as an indivisible entity, even though they had a separate word for each of the parts. The Romans translated these notions as *subiectum, substantia* and *accidens*. "This translation of Greek names into Latin," Heidegger remarks, "is in no way the innocent process it is considered to this day. Beneath the seemingly literal and thus faithful translation there is concealed, rather, a *trans*lation of Greek experience into a different way of thinking. *Roman thought takes over the Greek words without a corresponding, equally authentic experience of what they say, without the Greek word*. The rootlessness of western thought begins with this translation." [from *Poetry, Language and Thought,* translated by Albert Hofstader, Heidegger's emphasis.]

Heidegger is right, we should pause for thought. A bad translation made several thousand years ago led to a grammar of perception, persistent to this day in English as well, in which things are treated as subjects with predicates — accidental qualities — tacked onto them, rather than entities that simply *are* wholly as they appear to us. This way of perceiving reality allows us, conceptually, to manipulate things (and people) and to fiddle with their integrity, but at the cost of our "rootedness." Whether we agree with Heidegger or not about where it comes from, it is not hard to agree that much of what passes for thinking these days does have a rootless, drifting and purposeless quality about it. We have gained dominion over nature. But where has it got us?

Heidegger is right about one thing, though: language — non-ideological language — is not a just a tool of communication, it is a repository of human experience. And Heidegger even suggests a reason why experience, which is difficult enough to convey within the limits of a single language, cannot be "transcribed" or carried over into another: because experience is a *substantia,* not an *accidens* of language. The idea sounds complicated, but it's not. The English word "February," for example, arouses in us none of the feelings, associations, memories and emotions aroused in a Czech by its dictionary equivalent *Unor.* Capitalized, the primary meaning of *Unor* is not the month, but the Communist takeover of Czechoslovakia in February 1948. It means the division of the country into "the victors" and "the vanquished," and what it signifies after that depends on which side you were on, or sympathize with. For the majority, the word has mostly negative associations. The "official" associations (enforced by law, of course) are all positive. Yet this fact, too, adds its own special colouring to the word.

Czech has evolved in conditions that are far removed from those in which English developed. Historically it is about as old as English, but unlike English it has not enjoyed seven or eight centuries of uninterrupted evolution. In fact for two hundred years the Czech language was suppressed and survived only as a peasant dialect, to be revived and re-created in the nineteenth century by nationalist scholars, poets and writers who believed that if Czechs were ever to be masters in their own house, they would need a language that could handle the complexities of life in a modern nation state. Between the two world wars, Czechoslovakia enjoyed a brief, bright twenty years as an independent liberal democracy, but from 1939 on, the language developed under specific and unprecedented pressure from two totalitarian regimes — one German and the other Russian. The Czechs have not had an easy history.

There is another factor in the evolution of their language, however, that may be as important as history: Czech is spoken by about ten million people, all of whom love to talk. In fact, like the legendary Inuit words for "snow," there are dozens of words in Czech for "conversation," each one expressing a slightly different shade of meaning, from idle chit-chat to serious debate. I mention all this because conversation for the sheer joy of it is, like uncultivated nature, a rich spawning ground for new evolutionary forms: new words, new turns of phrase, new slang, jokes, insights and gossip, new perversions of grammar, decorum and good taste, new sins and new abuses — in short, all the things that keep a language alive. And the Czechs have not done too badly. My unabridged Czech dictionary, *Ottův Slovník Jazyka Českého,* covers three feet of shelf space. Most of its tens of thousands of entries have come into the language in the last two hundred years, and only a small percentage are loan words.

The pressure of tyranny and censorship forces language underground, but its evolution does not stop, it merely takes specific turns. Written literature, of course, suffers, but oral forms flourish — for a while, at least. The language develops antibodies, an immune system. Words the regime means to be taken seriously are travestied in jokes and puns that rapidly become common property. "Capitalism is the exploitation of man by man, communism is just the opposite." Marx, brought back from the dead by the wonders of Soviet medicine, declares on national television: "Workers of the world, forgive me." *Bons mots* flourish: "Nothing surprises me any more, yet I never fail to be amazed." Optimism finds a curious refuge in cynical wit: "It can't get so bad that it couldn't be worse." Language sprouts verbal equivalents of the shrugged shoulder. The dominant feeling is absurdity, the absence of meaning, and the burden of meaning is shifted to sub-text, to the unspoken parts of language. The works of Kafka — when people can get their hands on them — are read for comic relief.

Writers such as Škvorecký and Bohumil Hrabal (author of *Closely Watched Trains*), like their famous predecessor Jaroslav Hasek (who wrote *The Good Soldier Švejk*), draw much of their inspiration and power as writers from the subversive language of everyday Czech, just as much of their material and their raconteurial style comes directly out of the Czech passion for storytelling. Their boon is my bane, for although there are oral traditions here to draw on, they tend to be regional and therefore unsuitable for use in translation. It would not have done, for example, to have Danny's friends in Kostelec speaking like baymen from Placentia, though I was not above salting in the odd pungent phrase where I thought I could get away with it, or even using expressions that popped unbidden into my head, if they seemed right. Nadia, for instance, calls Danny a "windsplitter," meaning she thinks he's quite a guy. I'm not even sure if the word exists or what it means, but it seemed to convey what she wanted to say, so in it went. Malina, the foul-mouthed factory worker who terrorizes the latrine seminarians with his enormous hoard of zoological insults, was great fun to re-create in English. Once, on a drive back from Kingston, I batted around obscenities with two fellow translators, Ray Ellenwood and David Homel, and some of their suggestions went in. An element of competition even crept in, for I was certain — and still am — that when it comes to ribaldry, English can still go head to head with Czech without fear of losing face, as it were. (There is a fine tradition of linguistic rivalry in translation. One of the best translations of any book into English, Sir Thomas Urquhart's seventeenth-century version of *Gargantua and Pantagruel,* deliberately sets out to be more

Rabelaisian than the original. Wyndham Lewis called it "a miracle of a kind that could only happen once or twice in the history of letters," and at a certain stage in any translation, I go to Urquhart for sustenance and inspiration.)

Understandably, political jokes and slang present a more difficult problem. A constant figure in Czech literature of this century is the *fízl* (which rhymes, appropriately, with weasel). A *fízl* is an informer, a plainclothes policeman, a stool-pigeon, a secret agent, a narc, or even a uniformed cop on the beat. He may be someone who works with you, or a professional busybody on the street, or just some poor sod who was nailed on a trumped-up charge and then agreed to spy in exchange for his so-called freedom. The common denominator is that they all report what they see and hear to the secret police. There is no single word in English that can quite convey the ominous threat that *fízl* conveys in Czech, even to law-abiding people, or the sense of disgust that goes with the label. At one stage in the translation, I was tempted to try and bring the word into English, as Solzhenitsyn's translators have introduced the word *zek,* but something held me back, a superstitious fear, perhaps, lest the word foreshadow the reality.

Related to the omnipresence of authority in a totalitarian state is the barely subliminal paranoia that surrounds the ordinarily trauma-free experience of meeting someone new, or the subtle process of "feeling out" that goes on in casual conversation. Even among old friends, discussions of art and politics take place in a kind of short-hand that leaves much unsaid. Needless to say, there will be a lot missing in verbatim translations of material like this into English, and so wherever appropriate, I tried to convey associational content by using a device Czech translators call "internal footnotes," a kind of invisible mending technique whereby information the reader needs to appreciate what is going on is woven into the text without his being aware of it.

I hope it is clearer now what I meant by saying, at the beginning, that my dilemma, in translating *The Engineer of Human Souls,* was the same as that of the hero.

Danny's unspoken thesis is that the benefit of his experience under totalitarianism cannot be passed on to those who have never lived under it. But he tries anyway, knowing he will fail. The challenge to the translator is to prove Danny wrong, knowing it will be impossible to do so. In that sense, there was a deep harmony between the author's intentions and expectations and my own.

There is no way of knowing whether I succeeded or not. The target has no bull's-eye. All a translator — all any writer — can do is provide material for the imagination to go to work on. After that, it's up to the reader to complete the work, and make of it what he will.

The experience of reading *The Engineer of Human Souls* is not, and cannot be, the same as the experience of reading *Příběh inženýra lidských duší.* But this is not to say translation is impossible. That would only be true if the ideal were perfection, a perfect unity of source and target. In a way, translation is the most human of arts because it must learn to live with its shortcomings. To paraphrase Chuang Tzu, the desire to be perfect drains a translator of power. And if there were a zen of translation, it would be learning how to shoot at a target that has no bull's-eye. To change the metaphor, the mirror translation holds up to nature may be one in which the reader appears to see himself, but in fact, it is more like Alice's looking-glass: the reader steps through into another world, where the forms, the shapes, the words are all familiar, but the substance — the experience and the atmosphere — is different. Translators are the keepers of the looking-glass.

Remembered Conversation

I interviewed Anne Hébert in Toronto, but after speaking with her for an hour in her hotel room I discovered in the elevator that my tape had been thoroughly chewed by my new recorder and nothing on it could be saved. I entertained the idea of going back to her room to ask if we could start over, but I was haunted by the words of a character in one of her early plays, *Le temps sauvage:* "The greatest accomplishment would be to stay totally secret to all and to one's self. No more questions, no more answers...." The integrity and shyness that Anne Hébert projects make it difficult to face up to one's own temerity, so in exasperation I retreated to the hotel bar.

A meeting with Anne Hébert, however, is not an event that simply evaporates. Her willingness to co-operate while retaining a private distance, the guarded precision of her answers, the radiance of her remarkably strong and youthful face at the age of seventy-three, all linger for days. I keep reconstructing the interview in my head. I reread her books, some of which I've already read several times.

I first came across Anne Hébert's work shortly after my parents finally rescued me from eight years in a convent. I was struck by a familiar oppressive aura that permeated her first novel, *Les Chambres de bois.* The setting of the novel, the massive silhouette of the seigneurial manor, was not so different from the massive silhouette of a building that housed two hundred French-speaking Catholic girls and nuns.

I continued to read Anne Hébert for many reasons. I admired her accuracy and economy of language. Unlike myself, she never neglected her French roots. Also, there exists in her novels, as in much of the literature of Quebec, a collective consciousness awakening to its own voice after centuries of submission to a pervasive religious, cultural and sociological structure. It is undoubtedly a measure of her talent that her work sometimes reflects a society which is so unflattering that a few Quebec critics have refused to recognize it as their own. Yet her female characters never give the impression that they are the mere personal invention of an author. They are, for the most part, rebellious women who no longer fit the mould of such characters as Maria Chapdelaine and Angéline de Montbrun. No longer able to conform to the model life prescribed by their church and culture, her female characters are caught in a process of fragmentation, *dédoublement,* that is all too familiar. I remember the distinct effect of Elisabeth's words the first time I read Hébert's masterpiece, *Kamouraska*. "The moment has come when I must detach myself from who I am. I explore the pleasure of pretending that I am not here. I learn to withdraw myself from my words and gestures without betraying that I am doing so."

Between Anne Hébert the author, one of Quebec's most renowned writers, and Anne Hébert the gracious woman dressed in the natural woollen greys and blues one usually associates with woven fabrics from Quebec, distinct patterns began to emerge.

Her most recent novel, *Le premier jardin,* published in 1988, addresses the search for a child and a return to a place of childhood. It is a theme that recurs in various configurations in much of Hébert's work since her first poems, plays and *Les Chambres de bois,* in which a brother and sister attempt to protect themselves from the outside world by recapturing the innocence of their past.

"I don't want to compare your novels to Marguerite Duras'," I tell Anne Hébert, "yet I discern in *Le premier jardin* the same kind of fragmentation and doubling that one finds in some of Duras' novels, such as *L'amant,* where the main character has the impression of having been someone else. Could we say of Anne Hébert, as Flora Fontanges says in your novel, that she needs a constant coming and going to and from a place of childhood, or perhaps a constant return to who she once was?"

"I made Flora an actress who returns to Quebec from Paris, because an actress has that ability to let herself be invaded by different characters, different periods and places, but she could just as well have been a writer," she replies.

Anne Hébert's first literary love was not poetry or novels but children's stories and plays. It was a tradition in the Hébert household that the children offered, as their Christmas gift to their parents, a play that Anne had written. It wasn't long before she was also appearing on the stage of the local parish hall, with her cousin Hector de Saint-Denys Garneau, in such classic roles as Angélique in Molière's *Le Malade imaginaire*. Shy to the point of virtual speechlessness in social situations, she would lose all inhibitions when it came to the theatre. "I've never understood it," she says.

"And the theme of childhood that keeps recurring in your work, why is it so important to you? What does childhood represent to Anne Hébert?"

"My youth was my most important period, it is childhood that forges us. Everything that comes later is an extension of that."

Anne Hébert was born in 1916 in Sainte-Catherine de Fossambault in the county of Portneuf about twenty-five miles west of Quebec City. It was an attractive village populated by a French gentility who resided in ancestral stone manors that dated back to the seventeenth and eighteenth centuries when the seigneuries that formed Quebec's social structure were established. These manors, referred to in history books as "les résidences de nos grands bourgeois," were the residences of an upper class made up of small communities of people who were often related. Anne's father, Maurice Hébert, was the neighbour and "a daily friend" of his cousin, the poet Hector de Saint-Denys Garneau, who was only four years older than Anne. It was in Sainte-Catherine that Saint-Denys Garneau wrote much of his poetry, critical essays, journals and correspondence, all of which would eventually become an integral part of the literary history of Quebec.

Saint-Denys Garneau was continuing a family tradition. His great-grandfather, François-Xavier Garneau, was the historian who wrote *Histoire du Canada,* which many French-Canadians still regard as their most important historical record. The poetry of Alfred Garneau, Saint-Denys' grandfather, figures in all the anthologies of early French-Canadian poetry.

As described in Saint-Denys' journal in 1929 when he was seventeen, Sainte-Catherine must have offered an idyllic setting for any child or young adult:

Sainte-Catherine is a small village scattered along the back of the Jacques-Cartier river. Although the river runs through a plain that isn't very fertile, there is an abundance of spectacular views. The surrounding countryside unfolds in cultivated fields of varied velvet swatches under a lively autumn sun, some green, some golden and others as fawn as the skin of lions. Surrounding these expanses are vast woods of green firs, white birches, wild cherry trees with silver barks, black-boughed pines that stand gigantic as mountains against the sky. Blue waves carve the horizon in irregular swells to the east, to the north and to the west.

Where the road of the village meets the trail that leads to the fields, there is a sand path that stretches between some pine and blue spruce trees, then disappears beyond a curve. If you look up, on a green plateau under a cluster of hundred-year-old black-boughed pines, you will see the long-standing manor of the ancient seigneury, pink under the sunlight. Among the gigantic pines, the pale red manor house looks like a winsome flower. This is where I spent my childhood and this is where I return each time summer turns green again.

"You were greatly influenced by your cousin, Saint-Denys Garneau." It is more a fact than a question since the similarities between their first collections of poems have been widely recorded.

"Yes, he was a great influence on me."

"Could we talk more about that? How he influenced you and your relationship as you were both growing up in Sainte-Catherine?"

"I don't think that's necessary," she replies and smiles.

The 1942 publication of her first collection of poems, *Les Songes en équilibre,* was instantly compared to her cousin's *Regards et jeux dans l'espace* which had appeared in 1937. The landscapes of both books reflect images of water and light, secure family circles, cloistered houses and rooms often impenetrable to exterior forces, birds trapped in cages, exploration of the self, a nostalgia for the days of childhood games and freedom.

In a recent book of essays by Patricia Smart, *Ecrire dans la maison du père,* there is a chapter on the poetry of Hébert and Saint-Denys Garneau entitled "Le Fils détruit, la fille rebelle." Smart examines the way the two young poets reacted to the stifling cultural atmosphere of Quebec in the thirties and how the publication of each of their first books paralleled two important stages in the history of Quebec, that of

HARRY PALMER

alienation from the ideals and rules of an old regime and the onset of the transitional period towards more freedom from those rules. She concludes that while Saint-Denys Garneau, who died in 1943 at the age of thirty-one, was irrevocably marked by the cultural and religious restraints placed upon French Canadians before the "quiet revolution," Hébert's salvation came through rebellion and writing.

I mentioned Smart's book to Hébert. "When you began to write, did you have the impression that you were writing, in Patricia Smart's words, within your father's house and that you consequently had to rebel against it?"

"No, not at all," Hébert replied. "On the contrary, I was always encouraged by my father. He was responsible for much of my education. Our house was full of books and my mother was also very interested in literature."

For reasons of health Anne Hébert did not attend regular schools except for a few short stints at Notre-Dame-de-Bellevue college in Quebec. She completed her studies at home. Through her parents, she received, according to several biographical sketches, a remarkable education as well as an extraordinary exposure to and deep understanding of the arts. Her mother came from a very distinguished background, her family long established in the seigneuries of Kamouraska, and like Saint-Denys' mother she was well read and interested in literature and the arts. Anne's father, Maurice Hébert, was a published poet and a literary critic. A review of one of his books of literary essays on French-Canadian authors, *De livres en livres,* in the January 1930 issue of *La revue scientifique et artistique,* noted that Monsieur Hébert had a deep love for Canada as well as a decided taste for and knowledge of literature and the French language. "He is a stylist: he loves words for words' sake, for their consonance, their rhythm."

It's clear throughout her work that Anne Hébert shares her father's love of the French language. In its economy of words, its lack of flamboyant and ornamental adjectives and awkward arabesques, her language is absolutely concrete. Unlike many Quebec authors of the past forty years who have adopted *joual* to convey the realities of what they perceive to be a true Quebec voice, Hébert's French, except for a few colloquialisms, is classically flawless. The French poet Pierre Emmanuel, a member of the prestigious Académie Française, speaks of her poetry as "austere, curt as if it is about to snap and so carefully devoid of lyricism it's as if the tip of a dagger traced itself on the bone."

"Many women," I said, "especially in France, find the language they speak is sexist and there is a need to feminize the French lexicon. Since you manipulate language so well, do you feel there is a need for such a change?"

"No," she says, drawing out the one syllable as if to emphasize the futility of such a project. "Ça donne une langue lourde."

In spite of her claims that she didn't need to rebel, many of her characters are unable to exceed the constraints imposed by their environment and when some of them do the results are often violent and chaotic. Most of them live in communities limited by boundaries, either geographical or cultural, and many eventually stray towards some form of alienation or madness, symptomatic of those societies that eventually consume themselves in their isolation.

"So why is it that you left Canada? Was it for personal reasons that you decided to live in Paris permanently?"

"No, it was professional. It became increasingly difficult for me to get published in Quebec. I had great difficulty in the forties finding a publisher for *Le Torrent,* for example. The violence shocked them; one didn't publish that kind of literature, it wouldn't sell."

In *Le Torrent,* Hébert's first collection of short stories, which was written in the winter of 1945 but not published until 1950, the violence done to the mother by her would-be priest son has often been regarded by reviewers as a symbolic, rebellious act of a dominated son towards "la mère patrie," the mother country or even the mother church. I also think of Nicolas Jones, the minister in *Les fous de Bassan,* who tells his flock to "honour thy mother and father," while he and the entire congregation so carefully protect themselves against outsiders who have come to the small village to investigate the murder of two young girls. I think of her most famous character, Elisabeth of *Kamouraska,* who exceeds all limits in an attempt to escape her confinement.

"Do you return to Canada often? You must have to spend a fair amount of time here if only for the research required in several of your books, such as *Kamouraska."*

"When I first went to Paris in 1961, I travelled back and forth from Paris to Quebec but since my mother's death in 1977 I've lived there permanently and come back for only a few weeks every year. *Kamouraska* didn't require as much research as one would think. The basic story was part of my growing up. The character of Elisabeth was based on an aunt of my mother's and she became a family legend that my mother spoke of often."

"Would you come back to live permanently in Quebec? Now that you're so well established as a writer you could publish anywhere?"

"Probably not."

"Why?"

"Montreal has become too American and Quebec City is too small. And after twenty years abroad, I've concluded that nothing's really changed."

"What really impressed me about your last novel is how the main character, Flora, not only finds the daughter who had disappeared but she also finds herself as a mother. As if the search for the child was a mapping for the discovery of her self both as mother and woman."

Hébert adds nothing to this statement. She only nods. I sense that I've stayed long enough. I glance out the large window and comment on the panoramic view of Lake Ontario. It is a brilliant day, the sky an unusually crystalline blue with large cumulus clouds suspended over a few sailboats. "A northern sky that one never sees in Paris," she says, and for a few minutes she speaks of the distinct light of Canadian cities.

Earlier that morning the moderator of a panel on which Anne Hébert was participating asked if the panelists didn't think that perhaps writers were, after all, only voyeurs. Anne Hébert paused for a few moments and in her typical precise manner she replied that perhaps some writers were *voyeurs* while others were *voyants.*

Anne Hébert has always had that rare quality of seeing beyond surfaces. The intensity of vision throughout her work could not possibly be compared to the writing of anyone who fits the category of *voyeur.*

As we stood at the window a gull swept by and I was reminded of the many images of birds in her early work, many of them confined to cages, songless birds, dead birds. But as she watched the large movements of the gulls and as she continued to comment on the quality of Canadian light, it occurred to me that although her writing holds so much memory it has also become a mediating element between the opposing forces of the past and the present. It holds the memory and the progression of Anne Hébert and of French Canada.

HECTOR DE SAINT-DENYS GARNEAU

On David Milne

Translated by Lola Lemire Tostevin

hroughout his writings and his art, the poet, artist and critic Hector de Saint-Denys Garneau (1912–1943) seems to have had a fascination with the theme of space, as the title of his collection of poems, *Regards et jeux dans l'espace,* published in 1939, would indicate. The following commentary on the Canadian painter David Milne is an excerpt from a letter to Garneau's cousin Maurice Hébert. The letter appears in Garneau's *Oeuvres.*

April 29, 1935

Dear Maurice

I went to an exhibition of a Canadian artist who vaguely takes after the Fauves, or so they say, for I know little about the Fauves. It is one of the best exhibitions I've seen here.

David Milne is an Ontarian who retired to the woods so he could give himself to his muse, fill his eyes with the display of nature, wild and ragged, and conform it into strange paintings that reflect an extremely subjective vision.

When you first enter the room, nothing extraordinary strikes you. You're only aware of a vast emptiness, a desolate monotony. It all escapes you and you don't know what to look for. Here, a jumble of houses, all the same red with the same green roofs: a white sky above: empty spaces with patches of raw canvas. Over there, fields that ripple in green lines and a few trees contoured in black which separates them from everything else. All this without intelligible order, again with large empty spaces and skies smeared lightly so as not to cover the canvas completely. It's all very pleasant and you go around the room several times, let your gaze wander, let it rest haphazardly here and there. And little by little, everything starts to sing, vibrate and come alive. Where it all seemed monotonous and similar, each painting acquires its own vitality and autonomy and radiates beyond the frame. Each one summarizes its own world, each one a point of departure, a centre of radiance.

Gradually you begin to understand why each

painting, so different from the other you can't walk by without astonishment, initially gave the impression of uniformity. It is because they have not been painted in *relief*. The colourings extend beyond the frame but none springs out from within the frame or sinks into the wall: they are flat. They are without contrast: only a simple juxtaposition of colours and empty spaces on a flat background. The subject is so unimportant that many of the canvasses could be turned upside down. To do so would merely displace their centre of gravity and change their sense of balance.

Yet these are not merely empty spaces. Mr. Milne is not a fraud. His intensity asserts itself as you penetrate its expression and begin to understand the vision that informs it. Milne is partly impressionist but his is not an instant impressionism. One senses behind each painting an accumulation in which resides an anterior meaning: an accumulation of nature, of landscape, which has become part of the man, until his vision conforms to it and informs his art. The impression is long and lived. It is not intellectual art: it is untamed with a sense of fatalism in its sweeping accumulation; but all this is felt by the artist, or rather it is subjected to a profound intensity. Some critics insist that it is instant impressionism, even whimsical, but I find quite the opposite to be true. Each landscape is but a spark through which a profound spirit finds a pretext to express itself: an untamed spirit not entirely aroused by nature and chaos but not entirely free of its appeal.

The subjects, the pretexts for these paintings are limited in number. Fields populated by a few trees where green waves overlap. A bare elevation around which curves a railway track. A small black town made up of black and grey cubes with a few lively touches of green and red as if dreamed, as if lost at the edge of a wilderness under a stark white and leaden sky. A street whose grey makes the red and green of the sharp angled houses sing. Or a street bordered with grey houses against a canvas that is half grey and half pasty white; a few olive leaves as a reminder that there is life in this gloom. Winter in its last stages; white spaces surrounded or scattered with branchings, leaves about to sprout, or a network of trunks in tangled violent lines; roots half-buried in snow; chaotic desolate spaces where all vegetation is banished and only a ray of light survives. The shock of an orange earth and a grey sky that explodes like a bomb; sharp mountain ridges under clouds of firm broken lines. All this apprehended rather than seen, like an unarticulated song that lingers long after it has ended.

You could summarize the range of this artist by two or three dominant moods: endless bleakness and desolation; clash of elements with little relief, radiant and explosive joy. And always, behind these, there is an infinite, permanent nature (perhaps all of nature but certainly what is most characteristic of our own landscapes) and the sharp perception with which it is emphasized.

His technique, which is most interesting, has been reduced in order to render more effectively the elementary impressions of a universal spirit: wonder, desolation, joy.

His colours, like the emotions expressed, are not varied. They can be placed within three categories, each one corresponding to a state of mind and which, according to the prevalence of one or the other, establish the mood of the painting.

Lead grey and black — orange, green and red — blue and lighter grey; a few violet, mauve and fawn derivatives. And some white, to blend, isolate or lighten. For a town of lively houses, he uses grey as foreground which accentuates the cheerful harmony of green and red with sunny touches of orange against an empty white sky. He often isolates elements with a heavy dark line so that there is no relation of perspective. A few grey spaces and a succession of cube houses in blotches of green, as if to summon light, are scattered throughout a dark town emphasized by a stark white sky above.

Milne is unconcerned with subject matter and approximates the last stage of Matisse's art in that the symmetry of his paintings resides in the distribution of colour and the arrangement of empty spaces and filled areas instead of subject matter. Milne sometimes uses empty space excessively, but he nevertheless obtains striking results. He creates an affinity between two colours as if they had joined hands and were singing a duet across the emptiness, like two melodies that extend themselves by offsetting each other. This prevails especially in the relation of lines that separate the empty spaces: the coloured areas could be compared to musical chords, not the full chords of a Chopin or a Beethoven, but a modern harmony where two notes answer each other from two different clefs, either in harmony or in dissonance or even in the style of Bach's fugues where the melody is elaborated in bounds and rhythmic succession. All this is accomplished through very careful proportions, although at times the spaces are not filled in relation to two forms, two tones or lines and the effect can simply be barren and excessive.

Just as colour yields a sense of impression, a line expresses rhythm. In Milne's paintings, the two often merge, as in Bach or Stravinsky's last works, when the line, a progression of strokes, a surge of colour, surrounds emptiness. Long, sinuous and repeated, the lines overlap and give the impression of expanse and boredom and recall Baudelaire's "the deserted plains of profound boredom." And how deserted! The violent and hard broken lines, the outbursts are as sharp among clouds as among rocks, the clashes. Or the lively rhythm of jostled houses and trees that erupt like laughter, and the gradual but sure awakening of slow curves.

What I like in all this is how the purity and strength of Milne's technique reflects certain aspects of nature as we know it. I don't know if I have spoken to you about the difficulty I've experienced in trying to capture our wilderness without weighing it down. I've been experimenting with a form that approximates the predominance of the mystical line in Chinese art, where colour, the material mass, is indicated only by a contouring line. Well! I have now come across a most interesting realization of this vague dream. Milne has communicated to me how to fill empty space which had become my greatest obstacle.

Undoubtedly the technique is incomplete. It seems to me that the arrangement of the subject should not be entirely without importance, but rather should determine colour and space. Also it lacks the elevated and mystic elements that I'm searching for, that fine point of awareness that moves the line towards the intangible as in a melody by Mozart. There is, however, great strength and the technical elements, reduced to their essential, summarize a purity, a primitive asceticism.

All in all it is a captivating exhibition. Something new and good at last. A tragic and untamed simplicity.

St-Denys

STAN DRAGLAND

The Bees of the Invisible

"things that could never be told, / so we gave words instead."

friend of mine opened *Kerrisdale Elegies* in a bookstore, read a few pages, replaced it. Maybe he noticed the reference to Rilke in Robert Kroetsch's blurb on the back of the book; anyway, he detected Bowering poaching on *Duino Elegies* and it put him off. Like any good browser he was looking to fall in love at first sight. Which is how *Kerrisdale Elegies* took me. What I liked first was the voice, curiously unRilkean, unless we were to imagine how a Rilke reborn and settled in present-day Vancouver might sound. That voice has its modulations, but one very important thing it does is swallow all influences. Therefore *Kerrisdale Elegies* is not like, say, *Burning Water* or *Allophanes*, into which Bowering introduces undigested chunks of other books. In the novel, shifts of style are the only signals that the ground has changed. Of course that's for fun. Nobody whoops it up in an elegy. *Duino Elegies* and *Kerrisdale Elegies* are really like night and day —

caught at the same hour on the same globe. Despite the powerful presence of another powerful poem in it, I still read *Kerrisdale Elegies* every time with admiration for its originality.

We are not talking about *Duino Elegies* as a general influence or model, as for Dennis Lee's *Civil Elegies*, Jan Zwicky's *Wittgenstein Elegies*, Stephen Scobie's *Dunino* — Rilke has certainly had his effect in Canada — or Jack Spicer's unfinished group of elegies. *Kerrisdale Elegies* is actually, in part, a free translation of *Duino Elegies*. At times the two poems go along together almost line for line, though Bowering makes changes no translator would be permitted. A translator doesn't substitute a baseball team for a family of acrobats, as Bowering does in "Elegy 5." A translator doesn't all but throw out Rilke's angels, dispersing their function among humans, as Bowering does. Amazing but true, the spirit of *Duino Elegies* doesn't evaporate as Bowering writes his own time and place, his own life across it.

It's impossible to show all the sorts of difference between the Rilke and the Bowering in a short parallel passage from each, but the opening of each poem might illustrate some of the things I've been saying. The Rilke is in Stephen Mitchell's translation:

Who, if I cried out, would hear me among the angels'
hierarchies? and even if one of them pressed me
suddenly against his heart: I would be consumed
in that overwhelming existence. For beauty is nothing
but the beginning of terror, which we still are just able
    to endure,
and we are so awed because it serenely disdains
to annihilate us. Every angel is terrifying.

(Rilke, "The First Elegy")

If I did complain, who among my friends
would hear?
              If one of them
amazed me with an embrace
he would find his arms empty, his own face
staring from a mirror.

Beauty is the first prod of fear,
                         we must
live our lives in.
              We reach for her,
we think we love her, because she holds the knife
a knife-edge from our throat.
                    Every fair heart
is frightful.
              Every rose petal
exudes poison in bright sunlight.

(Bowering, "Elegy 1")

We recognize the Rilke in the Bowering here, though a divergence has already begun. Bowering's personified beauty is more concrete, more secular, his generalization therefore less sweeping than Rilke's, to mention only one thing. *Duino Elegies* is a sort of core text which Bowering courts in a rhythm of departure and return. Sometimes he is quite near; sometimes he moves off where there is no Rilke to follow. Since there is always something more than translation going on, Bowering is always in dialogue with Rilke. Sometimes he explicitly interrogates his source. But always there is this sense of vindication of the essential vision of Rilke, always the feeling of homage being paid, and ultimately of two powerful voices contrapuntally celebrating life lived in the shadow of death.

Bowering's poem is full of his own versions of Rilke's "Things" to be valued and praised for themselves, and also as part of the rich ensemble of life so loved that the prospect of leaving it is agonizing — until pain is recognized as a principle of that life.

                    How we squander our hours
    of pain.
How we gaze beyond them into the bitter duration
to see if they have an end. Though they are really
our winter-enduring foliage, our dark evergreen,
one season in our inner year—, not only a season
in time—, but are place and settlement, foundation
and soil and home.

(Rilke, "The Tenth Elegy")

                    Precious
agony.

    How we threw away half our lives
waiting like cows for better weather.

                         Suffering
is our winter of bare branches,
                    our secret abode.

(Bowering, "Elegy 10")

Bowering sparely endorses Rilke's conviction that the world is re-created and sustained in the eyes of the

218

committed beholder. That is their answer to mutability. It takes hold, as these passages from "The Tenth Elegy" and "Elegy 10" begin to say, when we stop trying to leave our home in suffering.

Bowering's type of this committed individual, more explicitly than Rilke's, is the poet, and the poet at the centre of the poem is quite like Bowering himself. *Kerrisdale Elegies* is an unchronological portrait of the artist in formation, but Bowering manages to handle the autobiographical element impersonally and with self-irony. He doesn't grandstand. If he did, the reader would not feel invited to share the immensely difficult task of sustaining the spirit of the things that are.

So what is Bowering in *Kerrisdale Elegies* — an audacious pirate or a self-effacing participant in tradition? He is surely both, and if I stress the latter mask it's to argue for the seriousness of his wonderful poem. The fact that it *matters* could easily be lost as critics move in on the question of influence. A reader needs to be relaxed about what Bowering is doing, and that means first simply responding to his words. Then one can safely enter the labyrinth of influences. Holding on to what the words actually do, wherever they came from, one never gets lost.

Am I the only reader who almost prefers to get his Rilke in Bowering's words? I don't read German and it's unsettling to go from translation to translation. Something of great poetry comes through and the something is probably Rilke's, but there's no definitive Rilke in English, whatever various publishers and reviewers claim. This is Bowering's opportunity. Released from the impossible demands of exact fidelity to the German he can make real poetry in English.

Anyone who studies the intertextuality of *Kerrisdale Elegies* needs to delight in seeing double. Such a person will also want to remember the context of Bowering's other writing — like *Allophanes*, whose playful intertextuality throws out this manifesto-like unattributed line from Yeats: "Talk to me of originality / and I will turn on you with rage." Why not take Bowering at Yeats's words? — which might mean reading *Kerrisdale Elegies* alongside *Duino Elegies* the way scholars read Malory's *Morte Darthur* as both an original text and an edited translation of French originals, an origin Malory doesn't hide. Even the idea of offering under one's own name a text borrowed from a writer in another language is far from new, and there are modern precedents like Pound's "Chinese" poems.

Kerrisdale Elegies sounds nothing like *Duino Elegies*. The two poems look completely different too, and at one level the arrangement of the poem on the page controls how it sounds, but this is not so much in the way Bowering effortlessly catches the idiom of his time and place. He never speaks "poetically," in fact he never raises his voice, and yet he comes across with authority, speaking levelly and conversationally to his peers, with confidence that people will listen. His language is bare of artificial ornament, there is no straining at figures of speech; quiet conversational rhythms carry much of the effect, while avoiding the banal or monotonous. In everything from the brief burst to the drawn-out periodic sentence (see the last page of "Elegy 5"), in tones from jaunty to hushed, diction from correct to slangy, *Kerrisdale Elegies* strikes the ear in an authentic North American accent. The lines are as natural as speech, if you imagine speech that is everywhere active, like a chord augmented with a fifth or a seventh note — on its way somewhere else. There are examples on most pages. One of my favourite active colloquialisms (oxymoronic, in this case) is from "Elegy 9" and is an attempt to persuade the reader to make his or her own joyful noise.

> The ghastly dead will never applaud your imitation of
>   them,
> your beautiful silence.

                    They wrote the book on silence.

Bowering's voice could not be colloquial in the same way as Rilke's, given the gap between their time and place and language, but there is an even greater disparity in the deeper principles of sound and sense caused by Bowering's distinctive notation, with alternation between full lines and stepped half lines and shorter units. Bowering makes the page a unit of composition and his page might show a number of opened-up couplets or tercets or longer staves. Visually there is a lot more open space than there is in *Duino Elegies*. The amount and disposition of space is not constant; it depends on the words it surrounds. These are all arranged along the traditional horizontal axis, though the stepping introduces a degree of verticality into the wordscape, but they do sometimes seem to rise and float on a white ground. There is almost the feeling that if the page weren't opaque you could see past the words to something else. Writing or typing out the lines makes you feel their physicality, their almost sculptural interaction with white space. That is also an interaction between sound and silence. Variations in these, together with subtleties in the use of traditional schemes of sound arrangement like repetition and refrain, give an improvisational feel to the music of the poem. It never settles into a predictable pattern.

Rilke is the most important literary presence in *Kerrisdale Elegies*, but by no means the only one. In all of Bowering's elegies but the third, adding up to the "magic number" of nine, there suddenly appear a few untranslated and unattributed lines of French poetry. None of the passages sounds like Bowering (and none of them reads like any other) but the French lines are not out of place in terms of content. Sometimes the lines follow the sense of what Bowering has just been doing, so that a bilingual reader will feel only an enharmonic change of language; sometimes the lines are not locally related but pick up or point ahead to something elsewhere in the poem. Occasionally, freely translated phrases from the French passages appear in Bowering's text proper (though the more we look into this matter, the fewer words we find that seem to be merely Bowering *propre*). A further advance in understanding the French presence in *Kerrisdale Elegies* requires finding out where the passages come from. There are orthodox ways of doing this, with concordances and so on, if you know the authors' names, but it doesn't hurt to get lucky.

I was reading *Kerrisdale Elegies* on the plane to Winnipeg where I spent some time with other readers and it occurred to me to ask if any of them knew anything about the French in Bowering's poem. Yes, said Smaro Kamboureli, she'd asked Bowering about it for an article she was writing on the *Elegies* and Dennis Cooley's *Bloody Jack*. Bowering might appreciate this "chance" encounter because in *Burning Water* he tells the reader how infallibly his choice of apparently unlikely writing venues produced "something for his book."

But I wonder how Bowering, this burier of things he's not sure he wants his readers to find, liked his critic's direct approach. "For me to know and you to find out," might he not have whispered to himself? The peekaboo poet bearded by the audacious critic. Sic 'im, Smaro!

Who generously shared with me all she worried out of the poet. We still haven't located the Rimbaud-sounding lines in "Elegy 10," but here are the sources of the other passages:

"Elegy 1": Baudelaire, "La prière d'un paien."
"Elegy 2": Villon, *Le Testament.*
"Elegy 4": Hébert, "Le Tombeau des Rois."
"Elegy 5": Apollinaire, "L'Ermite."
"Elegy 6": Beaulieu, "Rémission du corps enamouré."
"Elegy 7": Mallarmé, "Petit air."
"Elegy 8": Nerval, "Vers dorés."
"Elegy 9": Laforgue, "Complainte de l'oubli des morts."

This is a sampler of French poetry; fragments from a whole tradition of "dead poets" implicitly acknowledged as Bowering's ancestors by their mere presence in a poem saturated with literary tradition. A reader bridges two languages in coming to terms with them, and two Canadian cultures as well, because Anne Hébert is a Québécois poet, as was the late Michel Beaulieu.

Searching for Bowering's French sources and finding them often in literary territory new to me was a pleasure in itself (finding not only Mallarmé's "Petit air," for example, but the holograph version illustrated by Maurice Denis) and I often felt like lingering there whether or not it would help me with Bowering. But questions remain about their place in *Kerrisdale Elegies.* How far do we push the relevance of each whole poem from which Bowering selects? Is the volume it appeared in relevant? The writer's other work? His/her literary milieu? The answer is probably "It depends." Take the Villon:

Si me soubmectz, leur serviteur
En tout ce que puis faire et dire,
A les honnorer de bon cuer.

("Elegy 2")

This works beautifully as a comment that could easily be Bowering's on the lovers he has observed "on each other in a lamplit Chevrolet." He is their servant. He submits himself in all that he may do or say to honour them with open heart. The lines are wrenched from their context in *Le Testament,* and that might seem to rule the context out, but the forms of testament and elegy are joined through their inspiration by death. That helps me to notice Bowering actually verging on the testament form in "Elegy 9," where the explicit homage to Rilke appears:

On my dresser upstairs you'll find a limestone pebble
I brought across the sky from a cliffside path
at Duino.

I'll leave it here when I go,
along with
everything else.

Of *Le Testament* and (stretching a point) of *Kerrisdale Elegies* it could be said that each is both testament and bequest. Bowering actually addresses "Dear children to come" in "Elegy 7." And the work of all the writers Bowering draws by various means into his text is both cultural inheritance and reassurance to him of the enduring value of a trade which calls out loving acts of response to forebears:

Dead poets' voices I have heard in my head
are not terrifying.
They tell me like lovers
we are worth speaking to,
I am a branch
a singing bird will stand on for a moment.

Like a singing branch I call out in return. How
do otherwise?

("Elegy 2")

Whatever one makes of the French poets, adding their presence to that of Rilke, both sorts of source make sense as part of an intricate web of conscious intertextuality that includes the epigraph stanza from Emily Dickinson, reference to H.D., quotation of Margaret Avison, dedication of "Elegy 8" to Michael Ondaatje, general references to famous dead poets in "that great anthology," allusions to and echoes of all sorts of specific poets, vestiges of Bowering's other work, even the poem's doubling back on itself as it reconfigures certain clusters of thought and feeling in refrain and self-quotation. The self-reference works us back towards the central figure of "Bowering" and his poem as the container of all that tradition. A highly self-conscious poem, at times about itself. So the reader is entertained with a view of the writer writing — discovering the poem — and is shown certain pressures of the passage of time on the very lines being read. In the postmodern way, then, the reader is shown the process of poem-making. In the case of *Kerrisdale Elegies* that means watching the tip of a living tradition unfold.

It isn't easy to summarize what happens in *Duino Elegies* because the writing is so volatile, to borrow Robert Hass's term for it in his lovely introduction to Stephen Mitchell's *Selected Poetry of Rainer Maria Rilke*. It's even harder to offer a general account of *Kerrisdale Elegies* because, as Borges might say, Bowering's elegies contaminate each other. We aren't reading a general "argument" punctuated by elegy-examples so much as a metamorphosing field of images that roll, not without hesitations and detours, towards a hard-won and convincing affirmation. *Kerrisdale Elegies* has the mitigated coherence of the long poem, its structure interwoven, partly, of repeated motifs. The line, "Beauty is the first prod of fear," for instance, appears as the poem opens then reappears in subsequent elegies, prodding the reader with new faces for beauty and fear, becoming a cluster of associations. Let's be bold and call this cluster a symbol. There are other refrains too: "Being dead is no bed of roses," "Lightning and love," "Half the beautiful ones I have known are gone." And there are other sorts of gathering through the poem. (See what is done with "glistening with creation" in "Elegy 2," "Elegy 7" and "Elegy 10.") The poem doesn't shake out into stiff categories, but once the sense of shift in it has been remarked it seems worthwhile to offer an overview of its shape.

It's tempting to see "Elegy 5" as pivotal because of its middle position and since it's the most uniform of all the elegies, being about baseball from beginning to end. About doomed physical grace and beauty. "Elegy 5" is the home, as it were, of all the references to baseball elsewhere in the poem. Baseball is the "game of boyhood." The ballpark is "the fancied green of our wishes," and watching the game in such pastoral surroundings creates a moment of equilibrium that transcends the game.

> I sit in section nine and sometimes wonder why,
> but know I am at ground zero
> where art is made,
>
>   where there is no profit,
> no loss.
>
> The planet lies perfect in its orbit.

This moment of peace (and potential, "ground zero" being the point of explosion) almost divides two movements of the *Elegies*. The first plays over childhood and youth, the nurturing of a poet by parents and ancestors under the open skies of all time and space. The voice is that of an adult, of course, and his perspective is that of one who has lived half his life, much of it as a poet. Therefore he can look back on his work in lyric forms as juvenilia, as a stage outlived, presumably on the way to inhabiting a form with an amplitude and seriousness capable of containing more mature thoughts on love and time and death. A long poem composed of elegies might qualify. ("Elegy 7" picks up the outgrown lyric and plays it in a different key, a farewell to love songs; elegies are paired in certain ways.) The most traditionally elegiac material in *Kerrisdale Elegies* appears in "Elegy 4," in Bowering's moving lament for his father (the theme of two earlier longish and deeply felt elegies, "The Descent" and "Desert Elm").

To regard the first four or five elegies as a single movement is to register an awareness of certain matters present in them which don't really slip into fine focus until "Elegy 10" has been read. Quiet intimations of immortality prepare for the dramatization of entry into the afterlife in "Elegy 10." Retrospectively, then, one understands a certain blurring of identity between the dead and the living in early elegies, as well as the serious side of an amusing deadpan picture of spooks with deadlines ("Being dead is no bed of roses, / you have so much work piled up in front of you / before the long weekend"). Why death is not the release it's cracked up to be we have to read on to discover.

Beyond the "Elegy 5" watershed, "Elegy 6" is an extended treatment of a figure whose presence is felt throughout the poem — the "bright flash," the hero who dies young but leaves his name behind as he blazes into a star (looking towards a more sedate and mournful transformation of the heavens in "Elegy 10"). And then the turn of the sequence is reached in "Elegy 7." This is not consolation, in any traditional terms, because it doesn't reaffirm a pre-existing truth, such as that those lost to us find a home in God or in some other welcoming bosom. Rather it begins to show, and "Elegy 9" and "Elegy 10" continue to reveal, that we

make our own consolation and that there is no harder work. This requires an extraordinary devotion to loving, praising the world, a superhuman direction of attention to what will pass if not rebuilt, piece by piece, inside, by people become poets, in thought if not in word. "Elegy 8" is a relapse of sorts, an upswelling of the feeling of foreignness on the planet that raises its head in other elegies, a feeling, here, of inferiority to dumb animals. Even a robin

> will eat and fly and die,
>   and reach eternity
> without naming it.

Nothing in *Kerrisdale Elegies* is easy. Naming is a curse, like the consciousness it serves, but refined to hair-trigger sensitivity it's also the only blessing that can repay the gift of being. Readers will recognize Rilke in all this, but it should be clear by now that there is more than Rilke here. It certainly isn't the usual contemporary poet's stance and address, is it?

The least Rilkean lines of *Kerrisdale Elegies* appear in "Elegy 8":

> Oh oh, says the anxious reviewer,
> this poet is not in control of his materials.

This one-time break with decorum is actually much more jarring than any of the French passages. The lines that precede it, about the difference between the way humans and animals meet the world, are unlikely to create much anxiety. The "materials" in them seem controlled enough. So what do we do with this brief taunt? It almost seems snipped out of one of those other Bowering poems that take a consistently provocative/challenging stance towards the reader. "Uncle Louis," the long poem about Louis St. Laurent, has a running gloss written in the point of view of a debunker of the poem; *Allophanes* has a string of self-reflexive passages, including this one:

> (Shit, shore up the fragments
> for yourself, don't expect
> a fullness here, I'm only
> one pair of ears)

The question of what belongs in a poem was always less complicated for a loving reader than for the critic who theorizes reading, but in recent years it has become critical "policy" not to risk homogenizing a heterogeneous poem by presupposing that everything in it, however hard to connect, was tailored to round out a whole. That saves us all sorts of stretching and squashing in the service of an obligatory organic view. Now critics are allowed to delight in strays and anomalies. Some like such passages best and use them as keys to wind up an argument aimed at undermining the whole poetic edifice. But you have to get up very early to catch a postmodernist poet in full stride.

The passage in question can be annotated with the help of sources elsewhere in Bowering's work, all right, but it's just as interesting to think of it as a mild slap of the reader's face which might ("I needed that") jar him or her out of an illusory feeling of following everything that has been going on in the *Elegies*. There is certainly a forward thrust of an almost narrative sort (a multiple story is being told, with "Bowering" at its core; an accommodation with mortality is being negotiated); we can almost make a map of the cosmos the poem assumes, and almost paraphrase an argument, particularly in the last half of the poem. But look more closely at the poem's small units — half lines, lines, stanzas, sections. "I'm always quoting Mailer who quoted Gide, who probably quoted somebody else," Alden Nowlan once said, indirectly addressing his own readers in an interview, "please do not understand me too quickly." One can too quickly bridge the spaces in *Kerrisdale Elegies*, join the units too facilely, ignoring leaps and dislocations that in fact are more of its energy-source than what makes immediate sense. The weave is visually and otherwise extremely open ("refusing / a closing couplet," to adapt something Bowering says about the immortals in "Elegy 10") and the spaces are packed with mystery. Why not think of that odd reflection on the reviewer as merely the most overt of the signals that poetic not logical sense will be made here? This poem will not work unless it pitches the reader into mystery, into the "open" on the road between the stars where the immortals are.

It won't work unless it makes the reader believe in busy ghosts. Argument alone can't do that; technique must. Linger with the smallest units of the poem, then, and see if their relatedness doesn't swim in and out of focus, like the identity of the "speaker" which metamorphoses through "I," "he," and "you," offering a subject–object gamut where we normally find a stable identity. This slide happens to various other characters in the poem too, most obviously the women, who are both many and one. The poem is full of small exciting bewilderments of easy meaning, though the units themselves are crystal. This adds up to a palpable presence greater than anything that greets the eye or ear — something huge between the lines, just out of range.

So much for the oblique approach to that little assault on the reviewer. A reader gets various other passes at it, since Bowering likes to recycle some of his nuggets (a quotation from Heraclitus — "Men who love wisdom should acquaint themselves with a great many particulars" — appears unacknowledged in "Desert Elm," in *Autobiology IX*, and then, identified, as epigraph to *Curious*), and I linger on this one because it turns out to touch much of what Bowering feels poetry and his relationship to it are. One other pass, in a fairly early poem called "Single World West," doesn't help much: "Right now / are you wishing I had more control / over my material?" Others, in Bowering's *Open Letter* interview of Frank Davey and in the *Outposts/Avant-postes* interview of Bowering by Caroline Bayard and Jack David, do:

I know that the main danger to that [energy source] is my trying to control the material, me trying to tell it what to do. You know that old thing, that newspaper reviewers always say, "He doesn't exhibit enough control over his materials," right? Well that's what I don't want to happen.

The last sentence is ambiguous. Bowering is talking about "capital D dictation." "I just get into that space and the writing comes through from somewhere else." So there's an irony: the obtuse reviewer inadvertently damns the poet's very aesthetic. This reviewer seemed to me like a straw person until I read Keith Richardson's book on *Tish* and Terry Whalen's article on Bowering's *West Window*. Both, participating in the irony unawares, chastise the poet for his lack of control over his materials. Shirley Neuman, by no means an anxious reviewer, approaching *Kerrisdale Elegies* profitably with the "concept of meaning residing in the relation of words to other words and not in the relation of words to referents," finds Bowering's breach of decorum "silly," and says that "the poet is not living up to his materials." Maybe not. But he hasn't just suddenly lost it either.

"If there is a place in poetry for discipline and control," Bowering says, "they are to be applied to the poet by himself and not to the poem or its subject material" (*Craft Slices*). Relaxing control means submitting to a deeper discipline, to something — Bowering calls it language-larger than yourself.

No artist can really create. He gathers and arranges materials found at hand — pebbles on a beach, song from the boughs, bright colours from the veins of the earth, those materials that Nature shares with Herselves. The artist excels as he enters, not as he controls. He arranges himself among the particulars

(*Craft Slices*).

"There was a discipline," Frank Lewis says, thinking back on the art of his colleague Buddy Bolden, in Michael Ondaatje's *Coming Through Slaughter* ("There was no control except the *mood* of his power"), "it was just that we didn't understand."

Bowering says himself that there's no point in trying to take dictation before the poet is ready with craft. That is a precondition for receiving, or at least for doing something with what you get. Control in that sense is important. And then after you've got something it will probably need to be reworked. There's nothing very wild about all this. It is mysterious but it needn't be mystified, and Bowering doesn't want to do that. It just means that intuition not reason moves the words into place; the poet shunts his daily self out of the way of the self with antennae. Bowering's breezy comments about the process in the interview are nowhere near as convincing as a passage in "Elegy 4" that comes in after the elegiac words for his father:

> I am staring at this sound
> coming out blue, so hard,
> another voice
> must mix with its own,
> a dead poet or father.

What is it about those words "blue" and "hard," as gnomic as they are simple, that seems so right? Some focussed flame, something anthracite. Something is missing from the interview: mixing voices is not like mixing drinks; it costs to be the conduit. Bowering draws back from the subject of his father into a related subject, the poem he's writing. There's no relaxation of intensity as he reveals his lack of control over his materials. What is being dictated, here, has to do with dictation. The sharing of astonishment at what is coming through reminds us that the writer is the first reader of his/her own work, a fact Daphne Marlatt makes much of. For her, writing *is* reading. There would be no point in doing it if you knew what was coming.

The poet is not always passively surprised as he watches the words appear; he also questions, comments, exclaims, in a range of response to the influence of Rilke, the most important dead poet in the mix. "Is this true?" he asks (do dogs have memories?). Or later, "Is this possible?" (that things want "to disappear / and live again in me"). "Am I going mad in Kerrisdale?" Or, about these lines: "Those lovers in the car / are seduced not by each other but by secret earth / filled with proper desire for transfiguration": "That I should say such a word in a poem." Or:

Corny, isn't it?
      The world turns with us,
while we transform it,
         fancy words but true,
sweetheart.
              ("Elegy 7")

These various tones, from the awed to the laconic (Bogart at the end of that last bit?) are responses not only to the words that emerge. We are also hearing something like "My god, look what I turn out to believe!"

"I"? "I" slides into other persons in the poem, as I said, and at one point the "I" darkens its own identity in a way that seems like a more cynical take on the mixture of voices:

I am not I here,
             but the burglar
of your past.
              ("Elegy 4")

"You"? The most obvious victim of theft is Rilke, but the reader seems implicated too — our common past is being plagiarized and the theft disguised. At any rate, between this passage and the one about the hard blue words lies a range of moods in which the writer catches himself thinking about making the poem — is it collaboration or ripoff? And that sentence about the reviewer is not as isolated as it first appears.

Kerrisdale Elegies radiates from a house at West 37th and Larch Streets in the Kerrisdale neighbourhood of Vancouver, where Bowering lives; it issues from the study of that house where, with his "toys — a pen, some lined paper, / my books open around me" ("Elegy 4"), he writes. The physical place, with its particular streets, trees, bushes, its human and animal denizens, is effortlessly established in brief strokes.

This sense of locus is necessary to set up one of the surprises for the speaker/poet near the end of the poem: the Vancouver neighbourhood which seemed so independent of him (and he — communing with dead heroes — aloof from it) actually needs him. That's not how it seems in "Elegy 4":

These high chestnut branches along Larch Street
fade above the streetlights,
             live without me.

Through much of the poem the speaker wonders intermittently about his relationship with the world he lives in. At times he feels implicated with the alienated human exploiters of the earth, "late in the machine age," those with too much consciousness and too little conscience. Always looking for something better, never getting it, wasting valuable time out of the now.

> Stupid fate,
> to be nothing more than this,
> a foreign timetable,
> an unwanted designer trampling the woods.
> ("Elegy 8")

But this is the ironic stance, only one way of looking at it. By "Elegy 9" that mood has given way to the realization that a poet, an ephemeral human being, has a function in the world:

> Because here this once I can be bound to
> meaning,
> because it looks as if the world wanted me,
>
> this disappearing neighbourhood needs my step.

One chance — one life, one blank page to fill — and it's over so quickly. But at least there is the once chance. So one speaks, names things.

> To count them and bind them to life,
> to praise
> them and energize the earth.
> ("Elegy 9")

Now the chestnut trees are like the ash trees along Larch Street, like the whole neighbourhood, they

> turn to me for their life,
> to this ephemeron in running shoes.
> ("Elegy 9")

"Death is the side of life that is turned away from us and not illuminated," Rilke says in a letter, and he elaborates in another, written to his Polish translator about his *Elegies*:

> Affirmation of *life-AND-death* turns out to be one in the Elegies…. We of the here-and-now are not for a moment satisfied in the world of time, nor are we bound in it; we are continually overflowing toward those who preceded us, toward our origin, and toward those who seemingly come after us. In that vast "open" world, all beings *are* — one cannot say "contemporaneous," for the very fact that time has ceased determines that they all *are*. Everywhere transience is plunging into the depths of Being…. It is our task to imprint this temporary, perishable earth into ourselves so deeply, so painfully and passionately, that its essence can rise again, "invisibly," inside us. We are the bees of the invisible. We wildly collect the honey of the visible, to store it in the great golden hive of the invisible. The *Elegies* show us at this work, the work of the continual conversion of the beloved visible and tangible world into the invisible vibrations and agitation of our own nature … (Mitchell).

This is the argument of *Duino Elegies*, beautifully paraphrased. Reading *Kerrisdale Elegies*, you feel some understandable resistance to Rilke's certainty, some space of irony between Bowering and his forebear, but "Elegy 9" comes around in amazement to accepting it, the view of life lived *with* death (but not as a dead end) in the lure of the open.

For the dead as for the living the open is perpetually out of range. We feel near it making love, in dream sometimes, sometimes in writing. Dream returns us to a home prior to our earthly home, among the "gruesome gone" who in Bowering's poem are located among the stars. Perhaps everyone invents his or her open, those at least who feel its pull. The pattern is Rilke's; Bowering illustrates it with a small sector of the open, the road between the stars made of dead poets' voices.

In "Elegy 10," in a bar on Hastings Street, there is a woman who has appeared in different form in other elegies — a mysterious young woman clad in a "diaphanous comet tail dress." Earlier she has been mother, lover, reader, muse, *Deêse*. She has been the world. In "Elegy 10" she is too good for this cheap bar, and a Dad who's been drinking the golden stuff they serve there considers trying to pick her up. She's not for taking, though. Her home is on the road between the stars, as becomes clear when she begins to shed her earthly guise just as mythological goddesses used to. She is a goddess who enters Bowering's poem through Rilke's, Bowering's version of Rilke's "Sisterhood of Laments," and she leads a "newly dead" "young visitor" into the afterlife, showing him a very familiar neighbourhood — Kerrisdale — turning spectral. It seems he might spend his death there, where he and the other dead would rub elbows with the living if there were any tangible substance to them. This departure/arrival happens, in an atmosphere of poignantly beautiful melancholy, in both Rilke and Bowering, but Bowering uses a metaphor whose effect is opposite to Rilke's — an erasure of life as it slips into death, the unwriting of a poem. This is "decreation," possibly attended by a shade of Robert Kroetsch, though the word is Simone Weil's for the absurdly generous act of love that imitates God's absence, "the death of the thing within us that says 'I'." The Guide offers the young man

> a short poem of unwelcome comfort,
>   a direction
> to read where reading erases the words
> line by line,

street by street.

> Till the last page opens onto the earth
> beyond his darkened acres,
>   above invisible branches.
>
> Every star becomes a coal as he reads it,
>   figures
> turning to ashes:
>   the Archer, the Scribe,
> the one he's always called the Infielder, to the south
> the Triestino,
>   quickly followed by the Coyote,
> the Wine Glass, Erato, the three-armed Saguaro.
>
> Last to go,
>   drawing his reluctant gaze,
> the clear white diamonds of the Number Nine.
>   ("Elegy 10")

Rilke makes his own quite different list of stars, but his are "the new stars of the land of grief" that the Laments conduct one to, not the symbols of a life that blink off as they're bid goodbye. (Not for good. They "come on again inside the committed dead" ["Elegy 10"], and this seems to fulfill a promise made to the one who fills his or her single page in "Elegy 9": "No eraser can undo your visit.")

Who is that dead youth? He has no name, but he is perhaps becoming a "ghost of the dying young," the hero of "Elegy 6," one of those

> few who sprout flames in the dark before morning,
> lighting the air we've only learned to breathe,
> their godlike voices singing from their still skinny bodies.

The dead youth can't exactly be Bowering, who has lasted into middle age, admiring movie heroes like

James Dean, Marilyn Monroe, Fred Astaire and Ginger Rogers, besides his baseball players and poets, long enough to need the music of lament that the young can't hear, except when the theme is love. But the dead youth is looking at Bowering's stars, a sort of constellation of Bowering's life and work, so he is a mask of the writer after all.

The list of stars is interesting for the image-shapes and for the sounds of the words and for the traces of the *Elegies* that gather in them — the appearance they offer of summarizing what has gone before in the poem. So they have a function and a resonance beyond the merely private. At the same time, as will be clear, it isn't easy (for me) to speculate further about them without straying into the arbitrary.

The Archer, the centaur Chiron, might be found in the Greek skies and in the zodiac. He is Sagittarius, Bowering's sign. The Greek background with heroes-become-stars that both Rilke and Bowering inherit is most often touched in Bowering's "Elegy 3," as in the allusion to Mount Cyllene, where Hermes was born and where, to shorten a long story, he made the first lyre by stretching the intestines of sacrificial bulls over the shell of a tortoise. A scribe is one who writes down the words of another, a poet taking dictation, like Yeats, Spicer, Bowering. Saguaro is one of those huge armed cacti that have become cartoon shorthand for American desert. Quite exotic to most of us; not to Bowering, who has some poems about the Southern U.S. and Mexico in which Saguaro appears — by name in "American Cops." The Triestino? I'm not sure. Bowering went to Trieste to begin writing *Burning Water*, rather perversely travelling about as far east as he could to begin his novel about George Vancouver's far-western exploration. There is a polyglot Triestino, Everyday Luigi, in Bowering's *Caprice*. But maybe it's more important that Duino Castle, where Rilke began the *Elegies,* is near Trieste. There is a wine glass in a Bowering poem called "The House," but that's a weak guess at the source of the Wine Glass. Mount Cyllene was one of the mountains Pan particularly liked to wander, but I doubt that he bothered with a glass.

Of Coyote, Bowering says in "The smooth loper":

He was my favourite animal
but I didn't know
I imitated him
till recent years.

(*Smoking Mirror*)

Bowering doesn't imitate the lope, as far as I know. He would be thinking of the coyote's sly resourcefulness, and beyond that of Coyote in Indian legend and of Coyote's place in Sheila Watson's *The Double Hook*. Essays on this novel, especially those by Kroetsch and Bowering, have turned Coyote into a figure of the postmodernist writer as ambiguous shapeshifter and trickster whose pranks sometimes rebound on him. "Do you know I am keeping secrets from you," Bowering says to his reader in *Allophanes*, "& I want you to discover them & I will be disappointed with myself if you do." *Kerrisdale Elegies*, as already mentioned, is full of the metamorphosing or disappearing I. The poem opens with it, in fact, and one remembers, reading an enigmatic play with persona in "Elegy 2," that Bowering's collection of essays on fiction is called *The Mask in Place*, after Roland Barthes' observation about writing in the novel: "Its task is to put the mask in place and at the same time to point it out."

Does a mask
feel the touch of a mask;
does the face
beneath the mask feel the mask?

The Infielder and the Number Nine pick up threads

229

from the baseball elegy and, very indirectly, so does Erato (who also recalls the "team of womanly figures" in "Elegy 7"). Bowering's passion for baseball is no secret to his readers. In *Baseball: a Poem in the Magic Number 9*, he names, under "today's lineup," his ideal team:

lf Terpsichore
2b Polyhymnia
rf Clio
1b Erato
3b Urania
cf Euterpe
ss Thalia
c Melpomene
p Calliope

Playing First and batting cleanup, the muse of erotic poetry. She is chosen for the All-Star Team of *Kerrisdale Elegies* to represent the metamorphosing selves of the Desire who's not for taking home, not for keeping.

From contemplating the stars one always returns, the writer who is alive, and his reader, to the dear surroundings we desire to perpetuate, saying

chestnut tree, laurel bush, cherry, front porch, eyes open,
    to tell bird, window, lover, determined insect
happily burrowed in the earth round these gladiola.
                                             ("Elegy 9")

These are Kerrisdale Things, modelled on Rilke's different ones, that Bowering praises to bind them to life. We have met each of them elsewhere in the *Elegies*, so the list is an earthly gathering to parallel the heavenly bodies in "Elegy 10." The poem compacts a cosmos of flowers and stars — a double cosmos, because homely flowers and exotic stars do not cease to matter to the dead. In "Elegy 10" there is that amazing shadow-Kerrisdale held together by sorrow.

Borges's Pierre Menard duplicates in the twentieth century, from scratch, part of the *Quixote*, and Menard's biographer (the narrator of the story) prints side by side a passage from the original and one from the new version. The two excerpts are identical, but the biographer claims that the latter is infinitely richer, given the complex circumstances (including all the history between the seventeenth and twentieth centuries) it sprang from. The idea is hilarious, but the story still teases the mind to see double in a way whose ramifications somehow exceed the humour. Bowering is hardly Menard to Rilke's Cervantes, but he has achieved a not dissimilar doubleness. Bowering's complicated but unqualified affirmations are in a way more remarkable than those of Rilke. We don't want to underestimate the opportunities for despair in Rilke's age, but he was not writing in the shadow of nuclear annihilation. Bowering is, and the understanding is there between the lines of his poem. For Bowering, though, despair bottomed out among the literary modernists, and his own age is — *has* to be — on the rebound. He says this about fiction in "Sheila Watson: Trickster," but it fits *Kerrisdale Elegies*: "... the postmodernists live in a second stage of twentieth-century irony, and they are interested in some kind of reconstruction beyond despair — that is why their fictions are characterized by both laughter and non-realistic treatment" (*Mask*).

Laughter and comic endings, accommodations with existence, are nowhere in a bland text, of course. The consolation of the traditional elegy had to be wrested out of the pain of loss made palpable in words, or no one would care. Bowering still has to earn his consolation, his affirmation. So he wraps the commonplace of impermanence in the new words needed to make us feel it. Here he makes a grab at a couple of moments, and misses:

What happened
to that smile that was on your face
a minute ago?
God, there goes another breath,
and I go with it,
I was further from my grave
two stanzas back, I'm human.

("Elegy 2")

O Heraclitus! Suddenly time is racing by. Yes, beauty is the first prod of fear. We never love anything that isn't disappearing. No wonder we generally ignore the seconds and pay attention to the hours and days that can actually seem like solid blocks of time. No wonder we panic noticing that whole years have slipped away, and search the past and the future for meaning. Both Rilke and Bowering reconcentrate the attention on the here and now to bring the beauty of it burningly home. Both poets offer the vision of existence as a continuum joining life and death, past and future, but in the poems of both everything intensely crucial is now. There is unpatronizing pity in both poems for those Bowering calls "poor *insensatti*," the ones who see nothing of life as it passes. "The optic heart must venture," says Margaret Avison in words that Bowering folds into his poem.

Dear children to come,
remember this word above all else:
what you live all your live to be,
you are now.

("Elegy 7")

"These are the good old days," as the song says. We need reminding.

It is lovely to be here.
Even you know that,
you women lost in your familiar
dirty coats in front of a broken door,
a pissy hotel
on East Hastings,
rain on passing cop cars, somewhere
you know it.
For each of you there was an hour,
there was a long minute,
a time I can measure
with half a line,
when your eyes were wide enough
for your soul to leap out,
stand and say
yes,
here I am,
I am.
Entire.
You felt it beating
against your nerve-ends.

("Elegy 7")

Grief is the sharpest reminder and we shun grief like passing time. Rilke and Bowering practise a discipline of grief that dilates the optic heart, that imprints the here and now, transforming it inside, preserving it "where it will never be razed, invisible." This is a communal work carried out in individual cells by those who care, and the results are shared. Each observed death, like that of the youth in "Elegy 10," makes a difference.

as he goes,
his going lifts our eyes;
we see
a little more from time to time.

...

each quick appearance is a farewell.

The single events that raise our eyes and stop our time
are saying goodbye, lover,

goodbye.

Kerrisdale Elegies ends in a paradox of stopped time and farewell.

Yes, I'm going to die; no, it's not out of my hands. You have been reading words written on my "one page." I wrote them not for money or fame but because *Kerrisdale Elegies* moved me and raised my eyes. How could I help but sing in return? It makes a thin sort of melody, spinning the poem out like this, but everybody ought to do a little something around the hive.

Selected Errata

n the theatre, each member of the audience sees a different play, because no two people are sitting in the same seat. This is much less true of a movie because the camera is in the middle, seeing for your eye. Those in the front of the movie theatre will feel a greater loyalty, perhaps, to a segment of the screen, but not much. Now, what about the reader of literature? A Montrealer reading *The Stud-Horse Man* probably sees it as a kind of more recent western; it happens (oh yes, mythically) out *there*. But an intelligent reader in Leduc knows better than to look out the kitchen window for Demeter riding by; but her "out there" means outside the house. People who posit ideas such as the Canadian Tradition or the Northern Experience should travel less and spend time in more places.

People often ask, "What audience are you writing for?"

But how can one write for an audience? One can read poems or stories to an audience. If one had the talent one could sing and dance for an audience, especially north of the fifty-fifth parallel. But when one is writing there is no audience there; at the best of times one is alone. Or nearly alone. There is no audience, but there is the text; one is alone except for the text. So one writes for the text. This is for you, one says, and one really hopes the text likes what one is doing. It is not, perhaps, the judge; but it is the significant and growing discernment one has to be aware of as company. When one happens to be the reader, producing the text that way too, one is also alone with the text. For instance, *Surfacing:* one is there, and the text is there — no one else.

The art in fiction, as in poetry, is that part of language that is not communication. In conversation (with my wife, for instance, she of the prodigious memory) I am often embarrassed by my failure to remember what happens in a novel I have read a year or two ago — *The Manticore,* for a recent example. Yet the half of me that likes to speculate in writers' theory says that such forgetting is not important. Although recent novels by Robertson Davies may be described as page-turners, really it is the flavour of the mind we (not remember, but) remember tasting. How hopeless it is to try to convey that! Cole's Notes will never manage that experience, and neither will any film "version" of a novel. Communication works best when there is little sign of art. The Grecian Urn was more beautiful before John Keats got hold of it.

Here is the difference between the serious artist and, say, the politician, the businessman, or the social scientist: the more the serious artist gets to know about people, the less able he is to manipulate them. The realist writers always used to pretend that they were not manipulative; they used to say that their "characters" lived lives determined by environment and accumulative incidents, while the author only stayed around to observe. What a boon to their illusion were the clinics of Vienna and Zurich! But the best of them did not seize upon language as a tool to manipulate their readers, as Winston Churchill did with his evasive and hortatory abstractions or metaphors. Margaret Laurence, in *The Fire-Dwellers,* exhibits a great fondness for the words we have been gifted with, even while revealing the horror of their use by official terrorists.

If you will look at page 199 of the Bantam Books edition of Ross Macdonald's *The Chill* (1965), you will find this: "It was a well-worn copy of Yeats' *Collected Poems,* open to the poem, 'Among School Children.'

The first four lines of the fourth stanza were underlined in pencil, and Bradshaw had written in the margin beside them the single word, 'Tish'." We published *Tish* from the fall of 1961 till the summer of 1963, when we were schoolchildren at UBC. Among our favourite predecessors in poetry was William Butler Yeats. Ross Macdonald went to a different Canadian university, one I was to attend after finishing at UBC. This is how intertextuality works best, as a series that looks accidental, that makes an order by apparent coincidence, synchronicity, let us say. But it is still unlikely that you will find a clue about *Tish* by reading those lines from Yeats. I dont remember checking.

I dont want to read first-person narration in which the "I" is not writing. I see no point in the narrator's adopting the persona of a letter-writer, say, unless what I am reading is presented as writing done by that "I." If it's dictated to a scribe, okay. In the latter days of realism too many authors quit paying attention to the world as referent. A similar thing happened in poetry when poets got so inattentive that they paid more attention to allusions than to vowels. I like *Famous Last Words* because I believe that I am reading silver words on resort walls. I know that both authors are writing as well as they can because of the problem of getting the words down and up. Some modernists retreated from plot and went inside the head, into a faked "stream of consciousness," for example. They never bothered to tell us how we readers got in there. They didnt seem to care about us readers.

Suppose that you are writing a novel. Let us call it a book. Let us suppose that like many writers, like Ethel Wilson in *Swamp Angel,* for example, you are trying to get the world right in your book, or, say, right into it. But really, if you should succeed in getting the world right in your book, you cant do it again that way, because now the world contains that book you have been writing. You would have to get the world, including now that book, right in that book. And you were probably not intending that at all. But at first the world did not contain that book and now it does. Your book, accepting both worlds, becomes discontinuous and plural; but is a world you are trying to get right like that? Maybe you can get the world right in your book for one sentence, and (but) then the world changes sentence by sentence because now your sentences are in it. I think that that is probably true, and it is exciting, a reason to go on in the world.

When people talk about discontinuity, disjunction, disruption, and so forth, they are really remarking a break with habitual reading. Claude Simon has correctly pointed out that the real discontinuity was to be found in the long nineteenth-century realist texts, in which the narrator declared a distance from his own writerly concern, set the notion that the story he was telling was interchangeable with actuality, and then broke his characters' lives into little pieces with gaps between them. If the attention, as in *The Palace,* for instance, is given to the progress of the sentences rather than the events befalling the referent, there can be no question of discontinuity. Sentence follows sentence. There is no meanwhile, no later the same year, no in another quarter of the city. The next sentence is the next sentence to read, continuity, conjunction, narrative.

Dont get me "wrong" — I am not on a crusade against Realism. Realism was a brave adventure, and I was thrilled as I read the story of its course. There has never been anything wrong with Realism; only with what people thought it should try to do. What is important in the fictive event is not the possibility that it could happen in Chicago, but that the reader can imagine its happening in the book. That is what makes text. The reading, not the world, is the context. I read *The Pegnitz Junction* while I was living in Europe, but I had only the murkiest notion about where that train was. The story proposes destinations but nobody gets to them. However, we learn some fictive couple's real estate, even while the questions of residence and property are problematic in at least two "outside" worlds.

Writing on "The Dead," Richard Ellmann referred to modernism, as practised by T.S. Eliot and James Joyce, as "the imaginative absorption of stray material." When I read that phrase I took to it immediately. It posits by omission the notion of the individual creator, but it does not concern itself with him. In fact the grammar of the phrase leads right to the incoming. It lies just this side of Spicer's "writing from outside," and gives no validation to the personal unconscious at all, as far as I can see. Furthermore, it does not rank resources — so I would recommend it to my friends and relatives who accuse me of being a packrat of the trivial. Any stray material, once absorbed, becomes part of the solution. But there is something in postmodernist

Tisb Editorial Board, 1946
Standing: bpNichol, Fred Wah, Robin Matthews, James Joyce. Sitting: George Bowering, Alice B. Toklas, Frank Davey.

composition that welcomes the stray material, as an object among objects, not the solution, but one of the undissolved.

The difference between a long poem and a long novel is the application of the word "long." A long poem is like a long play — it is the same length for all members of the audience, except for those who sleep or bolt the theatre. The so-called long novel is like a long corridor — some people will amble and others will dash its length. Rather, it is like a mansion of rooms — the tourist will decide not only how long to spend in it before going to the nearest café, but also how many rooms to visit and to some extent in what sequence to visit them. For this argument, _Wacousta_ is an apt example. That is to say, or rather to repeat, a poem is a temporal event and a fiction is a spatial event. So the colloquial expression is more apt — a fat novel. In the event of a poem the time is determined and the space varies; in the event of a novel, the opposite is our experience.

If, in the making of your book, you indulge the language's whims rather than your own plan for dominance, some moron in the public press will call you "self-indulgent." Probably some semi-amateur reviewer took on Robbe-Grillet's *Jealousy,* that amazing feat of making a first-person novel without a reference to the first person, and labelled it "self-indulgent." It appears that champions of authoritarian convention reach without analytical thought for authoritative clichés of the reviewer's trade. The enemies of "self-indulgent" writing favour standard practices, including things like description. In my opinion, that is where self comes to the fore, in the decision to present some referent in the author's power. There the author has to exhibit control over the other of language in order to dominate and represent the other of "landscape," his term for places and people.

I am just working away contentedly in my avant garden. We always have to put up with the social responsibility of the terms — how they would sneer when they assigned you to the "avant-garde," or the "experimental." Now we have to decide whether to blush when they say "postmodern" and so on. "Post-everything," they say. I have known the name of Gertrude Stein all my life, and have read her seriously for twenty years. I guess that when all is said and done I will settle for what they gave her: I will be someone who did not write books like *Fifth Business,* to be placed in the mainstream of Canadian literature, but all the same someone whom they cannot write a history without mentioning. He was always pottering around in his garden, they will say, and once in a long while someone would come around and, well, not really admire, but perhaps enquire about the odd-looking shrubs.

When I was young and intending to be a writer, and writing stories and probably poems, I continued the contrariness I had always practised as a kid. It seemed the logical way to escape common thought, which must be not good enough, and it was an instinct. So I instinctively distrusted the satisfaction of understanding. Now I know how to practise and describe a *méthodos,* so I say that I function by and through misunderstanding. Maybe I should say dis-understanding. I know that my favourite books have always been the ones I could not really understand but which I could see immediately and could immediately see would last all through my life. An example would be *The Unnameable.* I really understand detective books, so now I cannot remember them. I feel a similar way about writing. I dont even mind if my readers think they understand, as long as they do not really understand the most important stuff.

What does one want one's readers to learn and know? Is it the world, pictured and referred to? Is it details of one's childhood and defloration and problematical present life? No, they already know all that, or they can easily find it elsewhere, in or out of books. Here is what one wants his reader to learn and know: that writing and imagining can be done, can still be done. One wants them to notice thinking, not buy thought. That's thinking, not thinking about. If I remember anything about my favourite books, such as *Tristam Shandy,* it is not what objects had things happen to them, or what people did what. I can usually remember next to nothing about what people mistakenly say is the action of the novel. But I always remember what was actually happening — language tracks that told me there was a really interesting kind of thinking going on. Those tracks are still here.

I guess I write to trick reality into revealing itself. I dont think that I can do that by using realism. Realism is a belief as well as a practice, and reality is aware by now of how it approaches, and thus where to go and hide. You have to treat reality like a cat. Chances are that a dog will come, like confessional description, when you call it; but to entice a cat you have to appeal to its curiosity, or make it think that it is making the approach. Artists and writers, and even philosophers have been after reality for centuries. Sometimes they find it and get a good look. They got a good look and told about it in *Sister Carrie.* But reality has learned their approach, so no writer will ever be able to use Dreiser's method again. If you use Dreiser's method now you will end up with novels such as those written by Arthur Hailey.

I have recently read that two hundred million years ago a considerable land mass completed a voyage from the South Pacific, to fetch up against us and become Vancouver and Quadra Islands. Yet some people less than a century old are still criticizing me for not knowing deeply the human writing (for instance, *The Heart of the Ancient Wood*) that makes up their version of the Canadian tradition. I tell them my biographical and geographical reasons for my ignorance of their regional literature, but their response is that I should strive to overcome the accidents of my birth and rearing. I recognize their attitude. I used to hear it (and still do hear it from immigrant academics) from purveyors of British folkways in my various B.C. homes. But tradition, in the post-Victorian age, is not even determined any more. We now choose our traditions. The International Modernists, who were neither British nor Canadian, showed us that. I do not give up my birthright when I choose Ruben Darío over Charles G.D. Roberts, or Kingsley Amis.

I have always been impatient with the easy use of the term "experimental" as it is attached by reviewers and others to unorthodox writing. When Zola used the term in his famous essay, he was firm in his analogy with laboratory science, and his emphasis was upon the experimenter's detachment. An experiment proceeds from a theoretical position, and results most often in a mental product to be discarded or amended. Experimental writing, most often, should not be published, though a report on the experiment might be. I am often an experimenter. During some years, for example, I planned to try a story based on the fact that the Italian word *stanza* means room. In the story a traveller would be shown into a room, and would confront all the material in a stanza of a famous poem. Then I elected to try one of Ezra Pound's cantos instead of a stanza. I experimented with every canto, and found out that this experiment, like most, clarified the question by failing.

"Memory," wrote Roland Barthes, "is the beginning of writing, and writing is in its turn the beginning of death (however young one is when one undertakes it)." Barthes said that in a particular context, in his great essay on Chateaubriand, but I believe that it applies wherever you will look, even to the antehistorical beginning of all writing (which, I believe, follows reading and precedes speech). My first unpublished novel, the 550-page *Delsing,* grew (and foundered) on my perfect recall of all sensations to the time at which I wrote it, in my early twenties. I then forgot nearly everything up to that time — my childhood and adolescence were dead. As soon as one looks at life, reads it, and then writes *about* it, it is a corpse. That is a great story. The novelist, then, lives the rest of his deaths, and may dedicate himself to the life of our language.

I like photographs rather than paintings or drawings, rather than art, to decorate my books. On the cover or inside, I prefer photographs. Photographs happen now, and then, now and then. But art always happens when. No matter how active, art comes from somewhere like eternity and is pointing its nose, and ours, toward eternity. The photograph is "taken" or made, in perhaps one five-hundredth of a second. Think what a second is to eternity, and then think of five hundred

possible photographs in that time. My books are that far away from the perfect. But look how much light there was available in one five-hundredth of a second! It is not that a photograph is more real than a drawing — it is only that you know it was made more by light than by you. I keep hoping that that is true about my books — or something that feels like that. Writing can be so nice when it is a snap.

Italo Calvino, in his marvellous essay on the combinative process, said that the author is in charge of a machine without knowing how it works. That is perhaps how I drive a car. The author is looking a little way down the road his sentences are becoming, and gliding with a kind of hip *gnosis*. Not to get somewhere, let us say, but to be getting there. Scholars make much of Joyce's multi-tiered allusive structures, but surely the joy in reading Joyce is in sharing his pell-mell plunge down the sentence and knowing that neither of you understands how the thing keeps going. There is gravity, and finally the thing falls into the bookseller's hands or onto the critic's desk. One knows that a writer like Robertson Davies, for all his scholarly spooks, does not want to drive over the speed limit. But while one is reading *Beautiful Losers* one is aware that Leonard Cohen does not know what in hell he is doing so damned well.

Once I was looking at a man sitting at a coffee counter in the Ottawa airport. A flight number was called over the public address; he pulled out his ticket and checked it. Later a name was called over the p.a.; he pulled out his ticket and checked it again. Here was a man bedevilled by uncertainty, and not put to any comfort by authority, an authority he wanted to consult. He could have been a conventional reader forced to play a role in postmodern fiction. If *Gone Indian* had begun in central Ottawa's airport instead of marginal Edmonton's airport, that man would have been a marginalized central character, at least for a small scene. What does he mean? In my notebook I have been wondering for ten years, while the Ottawa airport has been displaced by the new Ottawa airport. Robert Kroetsch said, "The minute you ask answerable questions, you're beat as a novelist." There's hope in that.

When I was a kid, and was trying to know what people who knew know, I was always told about writing that the best was that that was very clear and seemed effortless, and that that was good, that the writer should be congratulated if he could pull it off. So I believed it. But for some reason I didnt practise it in fiction, though I certainly did in poetry. In fiction I kept giving in to those things that were fun, and of course I felt guilty about roiling the surface that was supposed to be limpid. That was their favourite word: limpid. I always suspected that word somehow. People who said always seemed so much pleased with themselves. So I wrote prose that was not like *The Heart of the Matter*. I confess it: I like to make the craft visible and the referent invisible.

A small number of us on the West Coast make much of what we call dictated poetry. It is something we cherish as against the exploitive will, against the order of subjective description and anecdote. Of course we recite the examples Rilke, Yeats and Spicer. But of course we are not mesmeroids; we are more likely to be scholastics of verse practice. In an essay called "Concerning 'Adonis'," Paul Valéry probably most honestly or accurately put our case: "The gods in their graciousness give us an occasional first line for nothing; but it is for us to fashion the second, which must chime with the first and not be unworthy of its supernatural elder." In this way, failing or not, we turn our ears to the poem — it is its turn to take our attention. We will insult that first line the second we turn our hungry regard upon some "subject." We are priests, not monarchs. We have no subjects. A gift from the gods is not a licence to rule.

I never wanted to write an autobiography. I think that certain works I have done with what looks like my life story should be called biotext. The problem with the historians, or let us say the way they chose to work, is this: they did not study what people are, but what they did. They were more interested in time than in place. So literary historians did not much address what books are, but rather who wrote them and how they fit into the time of their societies. Hence the deprivileging of literary form — the very place where the writer of the poem or the fiction found himself. Michael Ondaatje, in "Rock Bottom," created biotext, or it created for him. Readers of *Running in the Family* know right away they are not getting history, not getting autobiography. Autobiography replaces the writer. Biotext is an extension of him.

There are two different reactions by peoples who have come to find themselves rejecting their images as historical victims. In the East the Easterners try to get their own history. In the West we Westerners try to get something else. In Montreal they want their young to read and live the new history of Quebec. In Toronto they want the history of Canada instead of the appendix to the history of Britain or Babylon. In the West we make *Tay John,* the West Edmonton Mall, and bill bissett. We think we live west of history, so when we write historical novels, their heroes are born out of ground rather than time. We tried history, and it beat us; that's why we came here. If you want to enter the West you have to check your history at the door. Easterners, also known as realists, tell us that if we dont stay in their history the Americans will get us. But just as the Romans learned their subjects' languages the better to rule them, so the Americans will try to learn your history. Better not have any.

The best poetry is written in fear. I dont know about the best fiction; maybe the best fiction is the best poetry. But the best poetry is written in fear. When it has a good reader, the best poetry is read in fear. When I was a child I did not believe that a dog could have eyes as large as millstones, but when I heard the words telling about it, I was scared smaller than I was. And by something mainly prose. All that subjectivist descriptive poetry filling the Ontario poetry papers and quarterlies could not scare anyone, certainly not the poettes. Great poetry does not tell you things about some poet's day or family. But *Duino Elegies* and *The Triumph of Life* gather up as much skill as the human soul can muster and leave safe soil behind, to lay human song at the doorsill of the gods' music room. There, there is no courage, no time for courage, no space. Only the fear. Only the beloved icy torrent of fear.

I suppose that "setting" in a fiction is not truly equivalent to a set on a stage, a stage set for a play. But many of us can be persuaded that some such equivalency will serve. Thus the author of *Two Solitudes* will spend a leisurely page setting the stage, or let us say describing the location before he puts his characters into it. But there is another, basically phenomenological, view that would not be able to conceive or perceive a horizon even theoretically independent of the human, character or narrator. This view does not like perspective much. The place, the "out there," is not prior to human perception or activity; it is the result of someone's being in the world. "Environment" is not possible, because one cannot be surrounded by something he is part of. The writer's words call the fictional place into being. The human being's presence is the first language.

DEREK COHEN

Athol Fugard and the Liberal Dilemma

 n 1962, when I was a student at Rhodes University in South Africa, two friends and I got into a heated argument about what we called the meaning and, quite probably in those days, the message, of Athol Fugard's play *The Blood Knot*. The play had caused a huge stir in South Africa; in part this was because in that rather Victorian atmosphere of white culture, the sheer Beckettian non-realism of the play challenged everyone's idea of what a play ought to be. More important still, Fugard made it a condition of production that *The Blood Knot* be played before a non-segregated audience only: after all, one of the two characters onstage was a Black man, being played — unusually for that time — by a Black man. This is not to say that the audience were very mixed; they were largely and primarily white.

But Fugard had refused to allow the play to be performed in theatres which denied admission to Blacks. The theatre community, being then, as now, somewhat more progressive and tolerant than the rest of society, co-operated. It was the political authorities who created difficulties merely by insisting on obeying the laws of apartheid. And besides, who was Athol Fugard in those days? A white man who had written two relatively unheard-of plays about Black township life. As a result, venues were found for performances in English-speaking universities and in the halls of liberal, usually Anglican, churches.

I can well remember being an excited schoolboy usher at one of the church halls in Pretoria, my hometown. I remember meeting Fugard, the brilliant writer and actor in his own play, who had been confidently authenticated by the pundits as a home-grown genius — "world-class" was the term being chucked about. He was and is an energetic, intense man, full of vitality and enthusiasm. I remember clearly and vividly the wonderful — to me, then and forever — and actually unremarkable opening lines being spoken by Fugard and Zakes Mokae, as the Zakes character — Zack — stumbles into the house after a hard day's work as a watchman, sits heavily down, dips his feet into a chipped enamel basin of warm water, and loudly complains: "Not as hot as last night, hey?" To which the nervous white brother Morrie — played by Fugard — whines: "But last night you said it was too hot!"

It was a dynamic and historic moment, a dramatic

exchange fraught with a significance no non-South African could have comprehended. A Black man and a white man together on a public stage for perhaps the first time in South African history; certainly it was the first time that a play which commanded such attention in the white community had broken the colour bar. My memory of it is bound up with my own memories of those wonderful South African accents — white and Black — of the rich tones Fugard and Mokae projected into the auditorium, of the inspired poetry and zany comic games that filled the air.

The argument that I and my friends were having was about what the depressing, futile ending of the play meant, as the brothers, defeated and penniless once more, talk about starting over. For there was a very interesting irony that surrounded the reception of *The Blood Knot*. While the English, liberal critics and newspapers hailed the play as a "searing indictment" (favourite phrase) of apartheid, the Afrikaners, recognizing or acknowledging their own ambiguous kinship with the Cape Coloured South Africans — represented in their darker form by Zakes and their lighter form by Fugard — saw the play as a profound, artistic vindication of apartheid. It is safe to say that there have been few profound artistic vindications of apartheid, and this seemed at last to be it. To them the play demonstrated in moving and heartbreaking ways that, after all is said and done, Black and white people cannot live in harmony together.

The liberal critics were offended by this appropriation of their ideology and one of their heroes. And, as history can record, they were able to sit back and watch as the play became a hit in the liberal capitals of the world. In London and New York, and all over the continent, *The Blood Knot* received the seal of approval. It was demonstrably a liberal play. It indicted apartheid, and it blamed apartheid for the failure of the two brothers to be able to live in honesty and tranquillity together. And that was that.

Our argument at the university took place, however, before the experts (London and New York) had pronounced on its political purity. Two of us were sure that the play attacked apartheid; the third — and the cleverest of us — argued, vehemently and heatedly, that the play was reactionary and that, for all its liberal sensibility, it ended up sustaining apartheid's ideology, playing into the hands of the dominant culture. I truly loved that play then, and would have none of this argument.

At about eleven that night the three of us jumped into the crock of a car one of us owned and drove to Port Elizabeth (some eighty miles away) to talk to the author himself. None of us was from that city, we were drunk, we got lost, and Athol Fugard was spared an undoubtedly obnoxious visit. This all took place in the days when it was possible to be certain about what things meant. A play meant one thing or another. It was in the days before the glories of ambiguity had been celebrated and before the uncertainties, deferrals and displacements of deconstructionism.

Last summer, in Toronto, I saw Fugard's latest play, *My Children, My Africa*. And a couple of days later I heard Fugard read from his one novel, *Tsotsi*. Both occasions confirmed me in my skepticism of liberalism, especially of the white, South African variety which advocates a transition to majority rule that seems to me designed to leave most power in the hands of those who presently possess it; a huge majority of the population will end up inevitably poor and exploited as before. This time there will be a sizable number (perhaps even a majority) of Blacks among the exploiters of the poor along with the whites, but nothing structural or essential will change with a liberal government.

The serious flaw of liberalism, as I see it, is that the South African liberals believe in the transition to majority rule by the use of constitutional means; i.e. by

means which by definition exclude the participation of the very majority for whom they claim to be speaking.

The new play is, as may have been noted by the critics, a little dated — an unimportant but interesting point. At the end, its young Black hero heads north to join up with the freedom fighters — probably the ANC. The events of the last few months have made such tendencies and impulses redundant at least. It is now possible to join the ANC in Johannesburg. The troubling politics of this play are the same politics that troubled my friend twenty-five years ago in Grahamstown. They derive from an embedded doctrine of liberal ideology which lies at the core of the play. There is, however you cut it, and however much it is debated, finally a kind of Christian optimism that clouds the hard political issues.

Fugard's plays derive from and feed directly back into a Christian guilt, which also becomes the paradoxical source of salvation of South Africa and South Africans. *Tsotsi,* his novel about Black hooliganism in the townships which movingly and effectively constructs the life and mind of the frightening Black thugs to whom killing is a way of life, features a looming church as the symbol and overt means of spiritual salvation. The novel includes a beautiful and innocent Black Madonna who redeems through love and charity. It is the work of a much younger Fugard and its Christianity is more palpable than in the plays, but it offers a clue to the politics which Fugard has persistently supplied as a kind of moral underpinning to those of his South African plays which include whites.

This is, ironically, a politics of optimism. For all the bleakness of Fugard's work, for all the violence and destruction that surround and invade the action, there is a constantly present "villain" whose demise could bring salvation. Apartheid itself is represented as a kind of anti-Christ within the dramas. It is a force that stands as the opposite to that meaningful church in *Tsotsi.*

Fugard's South African plays (he has written non-South African dramas), like South African life, are heavy with the permeating presence of apartheid politics. The humanity of his characters is inescapably linked to that fact, and their redemption is somewhat too closely tied to the possibility of the extinction of apartheid's ideology, making quasi-morality dramas out of complex and traumatic facts of life. It is this occasional simplification which arrests the humanity and the dramatic resilience of *My Children, My Africa.*

The title, *My Children, My Africa,* poses questions of its own. Whose children and whose Africa? Are they Mr. M.'s, the aging Black schoolteacher whose grief is contained in the words? Or is it Athol Fugard's voice uttering the moving words?

The title is curious; it is both humble and arrogant, mournful and celebratory. It refers to the two young people — one Black and one white — whose lives are being deformed by apartheid. It refers too, to Mr. M., whose solution to the racial crisis in South Africa is an ideology of togetherness under the banner of nineteenth-century English romanticism where conflict is resolved through passion, brotherly love, and Byronic heroism. His solution in action, rather than in abstraction, is to go to the police with information about the political radicals among his students so that he can return to the business of providing them with as good an English education as he can; the action, coupled with an adulation of Byron, exposes a contradiction that the play does not appear to recognize.

The radicals discover this treachery and attack Mr. M. in the street and set him on fire. At the end of the play, the young white girl returns to white life, mourning for the death of Mr. M.; she is changed, but the politics of apartheid go on. The young Black man, Mr. M.'s prize student, leaves South Africa to join the resistance. The two have been united for a short time by Mr. M. and English literature. But, as was true of *The Blood Knot,* the South African reality makes such unions temporary and unsustainable.

The play is a construction of the specifically South African solitudes inhabited by three essentially compatible people. A white, eighteen-year-old schoolgirl, intense, intelligent, progressive, is brought to a Black school to debate the leading Black male student on the subject of the equality of the sexes. The debate is managed by the Black teacher, Mr. M. When it is over he proposes that the two young people, who have much in common and who like each other, team up for a literary contest and share the prize between their two schools. He will train them for the competition. All goes well until the unrest begins in the Black township and the students commence a boycott of the schools in protest against the oppressive Bantu Education. The competition dwindles into nothing, a delusory memory of what might have been.

It is, however, the relationship between Isabel and Thami that the play explores most fully, both in itself and as a demonstration of the polluting power of apartheid. It is upon this relationship, too, that the play falters. The liberal tendency of the play is its underlying proposition that if it were not for apartheid, these two promising young people would be made for each other. They are both fiercely intelligent, passionate, energetic, committed, and they obviously share the same goals, the same belief in social justice. And, finally, they like each other.

Something, however, is seriously missing between them that the play only once addresses, and then only in a fleeting and throwaway fashion. An eighteen-year-old woman and an eighteen-year-old man are brought together in a tense and charged atmosphere; they compete joyously with one another in impassioned debate; they slowly develop a powerful friendship; their attraction for one another is spontaneous and electric. And yet nowhere and not once does sex come into their feelings. Not once, even in the fulsome soliloquies, is the sexual relationship between them brought up. Isabel could as well be a boy as a girl. So singlemindedly does Fugard direct his drama to its crashing finale that he omits the most explosive and devastating and obvious issue of the relationship.

The greatest of all taboos in South African life is the taboo against sexual relations between Black men and white women. It occupies an unacknowledged prominence in the minds of South Africans, a prominence that is, perhaps, more vivid in South Africa because of its racial obsessions. This is not news in a world that seems increasingly to be trapped in racial crisis. This sexual prohibition looms large in the practice of apartheid, which has until recently had Draconian laws to support it.

As in *My Children, My Africa,* when a young couple like Isabel and Thami are thrust into the artificial proximity of an interracial relationship predicated upon a debate and then a literary competition, the sexual element of that relationship necessarily becomes foregrounded, just *because* it is forbidden and unmentionable. The only sexual allusion in the drama occurs with far too little fuss; it is made and dropped again, suddenly, as a kind of authorial acknowledgement of its — inconvenient — presence. Remarkably, however, sex is not mentioned or dealt with or discussed by the young students, even though one of them, a sophisticated and ardent young woman more of the world than she admits, can curse South Africa in a burst of passion as "This fucking country!" The word fucking — used just once in the play — is obviously carefully chosen by Fugard *and* Isabel as a means of revealing a kind of sexual awareness in Isabel. It is an awareness that has no other outlet in the drama.

After Isabel and Thami have been practising for the literary competition for a while, she issues an invitation to Thami and Mr. M. to come and meet her parents on the following Sunday.

ISABEL: Would you like to come to tea next Sunday to meet my family? It's not a polite invitation. They really want to meet you.

THAMI: Why? Are they starting to get nervous?

ISABEL: Oh, come off it Thami. Don't be like that. They're always nervous when it comes to me. But this time it happens to be genuine interest. I've told you. I talk about you at home. They know I have a good time with you ... that we're a team ... which they are now very proud of incidentally ... and that we're cramming like lunatics so that we can put up a good show at the festival.

It is possible, probable even, that Thami's question which elicits such an agitated response from Isabel refers to the unspoken fear of sexual relations between them. The phrase "Oh, come off it," means stop kidding around. It refers here to something that may not be acknowledged, that causes embarrassment to Isabel and must be avoided. She is apparently attempting to urge him back to the real subject under consideration — tea with Mom and Dad. He is making a covert but specific reference to a sexual relationship between them which, surely, everyone in the audience is wondering about. But that is the sum total of sexual life in the play, notwithstanding its clear demonstration of the real possibility that the two young people are in love with each other.

My point is not simply that this is a calamitous omission in a drama of human relations — though it is that — but that it undermines rather than sustains the political isolations of the drama. Like so many of Fugard's plays, *My Children, My Africa* is an allegory of South Africa. Its context is not universal, it is specifically the recent political context of South Africa, with its various political colorations taking form in the actions and decisions of its three characters. The young white liberal woman, Isabel, starts out hopefully in pursuit of liberation through education, and believes that the nation's ills can be cured by good will. The young Black man, Thami, is driven to radicalism by apartheid; his love of culture and literature and liberalism itself are destroyed by the oppressive white regime. Finally, the old schoolteacher is excited by the possibility of defying the system through the agency of education and liberal ideology.

All three argue passionately for their own politics of survival. Isabel and Mr. M. have a common belief in the humane values they find in rationality and romantic literature. They appear to believe that rationality can be defined through romantic literature. This is the liberal fallacy: that political action and political ideology are best achieved by the rationalized consequences of benign feeling.

Thami's potential strength — which the play represents as a lamentable inevitability of apartheid — is his redefinition of political action as a meeting of apartheid on its own terms of equal and opposite violence. The consequences of violent action are vivified in the terrible necklacing death of Mr. M. at the hands of a mob.

There is a way in which Isabel is almost redundant from the start. The real conflict of the play is between the two Black men. The play commences as a debate with Isabel giving a deeply impassioned but rather banal defence of the equality of the sexes. Thami's response, redeemed by its humour, is an ironic defence of the traditional tribal values which require the subservience of women. She offers a specifically white and, again, white liberal perspective on the conflict. She sees, but she does not ultimately comprehend, the forces that wrench the Black community. Here, perhaps, is the difference of this play.

Isabel and the white world in which she lives and whose privileges determine its perspective are ultimately outsiders in this conflict. Their perception of the Blacks and Black difficulty is hollow and useless.

She can only fall back on romantic clichés about brotherly and sisterly love, about peace and decency, fairness, self-help, tolerance. Her argument, though unassailable, loses enormously from the context in which it exists: a clever, privileged, white teenager with perfect English, lecturing Black teenagers for whom English is a second language on their duty to modern progress is a rather unlovely sight. The initially grudging but ultimately enthusiastic participation of all parties in the experience is a measure of the play's devotion to what seems to be a rather condescending white rationalism.

For Isabel's experience as a white liberal has limited and narrowed her imagination. If *she* can be accepting and tolerant and generally nice, why can't Thami? But as it is all very well for her to blather on about friendship across the colour line, she is not really capable of seeing that her perception is utterly, finally, and completely tied to the fact that she is white; that her whiteness alone makes it possible for her to enjoy the luxury of liberalism. She is a voyeur in this township; she risks nothing by being here, among the Blacks. For her this is an intellectual exercise, a kind of literary slumming which she aggrandizes as friendship. Here is Isabel making one of the more passionate pleas in the play:

> I'm sure it's just my white selfishness and ignorance that is stopping me from understanding *but it still doesn't make sense* that we have to break up like this. Why can't we go on seeing each other and meeting as friends? Tell me what is wrong with our friendship?

The answer, as she does not recognize, is what they each have at stake, what each has to lose by the friendship. In short, the inherent and invincible inequality of that friendship. And one keeps wondering how this supposedly intelligent girl can be so blind. In several ways, the answer to her question comes down firmly on the side of rhetoric. The other side which argues that discourse itself — moral and intellectual — has failed is made concomitant with the failure of all sides in the debate. But South Africa is *not* a debate, as Thami sees. Mr. M. and Isabel are different from Thami in one important particular: they believe in the power of words to heal and overcome.

This belief is nowhere more eloquently and passionately stated than in the encounter between Mr. M. and Thami after it has been revealed that Mr. M. is an informer — albeit a well-intentioned one. He believes that the disruption of education, that is, the school boycott, is destructive to his hopes for the Black people. He goes to the police with a list of names of troublemakers in the hope that this will help to end the strike. Confronted by Thami, his justification of his act and of his life provides the dialogic centrepiece of the play. The moment is charged: Thami has come to the school to warn Mr. M. that his life is in danger. While they are talking, a stone comes through the window sending shards of glass in all directions.

> MR. M.: You haven't come for a lesson have you?
> THAMI: No I haven't.
>
> MR. M.: Of course not. What's the matter with me. Slogans don't need much in the way of grammar do they. As for these … [*the stone in his hand*]. No, you don't need me for lessons in stone throwing either. You've already got teachers in those very revolutionary subjects haven't you. [*picks up his dictionary — the stone in one hand, the book in the other*] You know something interesting Thami … if you put these two on a scale I think you would find that they weighed just about the same. But in this hand I am holding the whole English language. This … [*the stone*] … is just *one* word in that language. It's true! All that wonderful poetry that you and Isabel try to cram

into your beautiful heads … in here! Twenty-six letters, sixty thousand words. The greatest souls the world has ever known were able to open the floodgates of their ecstasy, their despair, their joy!… with the words in this little book. Aren't you tempted?

This speech occurs in a context which the play fails to acknowledge. On one level it stands as a ringing assertion of traditional, liberal western value and morality whose touchstones in South Africa are specifically English culture. The value of that language is claimed to be its capacity to open the floodgates of ecstasy and despair. What Mr. M. cannot see; what Thami cannot see; and what Isabel's limited imagination prevents her from seeing is that this language and these values which include and express such feeling are also and simultaneously the very means by which Black South Africans like Thami and Mr. M. have been held in slavery and bondage. They fail to acknowledge the ideological component of language itself. They fail to acknowledge the ideological nature of culture. Aren't ecstasy and despair, etc., ideological, especially as constructed by the adulated Romantic poets of Act 1?

I was rather shocked during the performance to see the Mr. M. character, played by John Kani, speaking with such uncritical and unseeing admiration about the language which had been the instrument of his own suppression. His own English is thick with his Bantu accent; yet there he stood, proclaiming the superiority of the language and literature which he had been taught *was* superior. The choice between a book and a stone is not axiomatically a dramatic or rhetorical triumph for the book, however much it implicitly condemns the politics of violence. It is quite decidedly a triumph for the English language and, by extension, colonial civilization. In the midst of the bleak and colourless poverty of the Black township, in the ill-equipped and sterile classroom, the image of a poor

Black teacher urging obedience to the ideology of an alien and, even, enemy culture is fraught with ironies, the greatest of which is the victory of a liberal ideology which has historically and inevitability protected the dominant interest.

In this moment of the drama, Mr. M. possesses impregnable authority. He has endangered his life by going to the police on behalf of his belief in education as the means of liberation of his people. His love of his students, his love of liberty for Black South Africans, is not in doubt for a second. Indeed, that stone rocketing through the window is a message of doom for him.

And he faces his doom with heroic acceptance, absolutely certain of the moral and political rightness of his action. For the violence spells death to his values of liberalism and reasoned peaceful political change. Where he is blind, where even his loving adversary the young student Thami is blind, is in his failure to recognize that the cultural value system for which he is fighting and arguing, the system of rationality and liberalism, has succeeded in sustaining the very political structures which have oppressed his people. Mr. M. — and perhaps Fugard — fails to see that the very breadth and flexibility of liberalism, its infinitely elastic capacity for tolerance and accommodation, have absorbed the discourses of Black dissatisfaction and given them a place to exist *within* liberalism itself. Thus the beautiful and sincere eloquence of the choice of the stone and the book is determined and contradicted by the context.

The African teacher, holding up an English dictionary with its sixty thousand *English* words is a terrible and brilliant icon of the terrible triumph of colonialism in its most subtle and pernicious sense. The context of this sacrifice is the more tragic because Mr. M.'s borrowed culture has triumphed over him utterly. The greatest victory of colonialism is to have convinced its colonized populations of its moral superiority and, by extension, their dependence and inferiority. To put it crudely, Mr. M. believes everything he reads, which is as dangerous a practice as believing nothing.

The play ultimately confirms and sustains a rigid dichotomy between an ethic of mindless violence and one of humane, liberal western values — the stone and the book. Like all of Fugard's work, it is unequivocal in its detestation of apartheid. But it seems to see apartheid as a deformation and perversion of western values and not, as I would argue, a logical product of those values within the context of the capitalist economy of South Africa. Even Thami's courageous and inevitable decision to join the freedom fighters is represented as a tragic failure; he gives voice to the passions and imperatives that drive Black people to desperate acts of killing, but then, having described these motives to Isabel, he is later forced to repudiate them:

I don't call it murder, and I don't call the people who did it a mad mob and yet I do expect you to see it as an act of self-defence … listen to me! … blind and stupid but still self-defence. He betrayed us and our fight for freedom. Five men are in detention because of Mr. M.'s visit to the police station…. What Anela Myalatya [Mr. M.] did to them and their cause is what your laws define as treason when it is done to you and threatens the safety and security of your comfortable white world. Anybody accused of it is put on trial in your courts and if found guilty they get hanged. Many of my people have been found guilty and have been hanged. These hangings *we* call murder!

Try to understand, Isabel. Try to imagine what it is like to be a Black person, choking inside with rage and frustration, bitterness, and then to discover that one of your own kind is a traitor, has betrayed you to those responsible for the suffering and misery of your family, of your people. What would you do? Remember there is no magistrate or court you can drag him to and demand that he be tried for that crime. There is no justice for Black people in this country other than what we make for ourselves. When you judge us for what happened in front of the school four days ago just remember that you carry a share of the responsibility for it. It is your laws that have made simple decent Black people so desperate that they turn into "mad mobs."

Sidestepping the question posed by the phrase "your laws," Isabel asks Thami if he participated in killing Mr. M. That is, as "your laws" makes Isabel a collaborator with apartheid, she is motivated to discover how far Thami collaborates with the mob he has just defended. Thus another of the play's ways of vindicating the values of Mr. M. — or liberalism — is to have Thami confess to Isabel that he not only did not participate in this execution of a traitor, he actually tried to stop it. There is a clear implication in having Thami, the young Black radical, depart from the world of education and restraint for the world of necessary violence and revolution: what is represented as tragic about this development is the unwilled betrayal of the *liberalism* of Isabel and Mr. M. which consequently receives a powerful extra fillip. What is represented, therefore, as wrong with South Africa in this and other plays is that it has become inhospitable to the really saving ideology of liberalism. The so-called outmoded and outdated ideas of Mr. M. are not themselves outmoded, it is merely that South Africa has traduced the basic canons of western civilization, kept alive only by such old-fashioned practitioners as Mr. M., and, in a sense, doesn't deserve them.

All narrative is dialectical, but this drama in particular tends to depend upon dialectical conflict for its momentum. Its discursive structure is palpably that of the dialectic: and it includes lengthy and pungent soliloquies which advance this process. *My Children, My Africa,* like most of Fugard's South African plays, is specifically about South African politics and their effects on the individual. Obsessively over the years Fugard has been driven to this issue. In South Africa racial politics is a constant, omnipresent and ubiquitous fact of life in the Black and white worlds alike. Simply put, it determines everything, from how you hold your fork to where and with whom you will sleep at night. Fugard's obsession is the more understandable once this fact is properly grasped.

Athol Fugard has been wrestling with the relationship between the individual and an oppressive politics for his whole writing life. His ideological response to the matter has, perhaps unfortunately, become predictable and formulaic. His self-declared liberalism has become rather too palpable, rather too quick a fix for the tragedy submerged beneath the lives of his characters. While *The Blood Knot,* thirty years ago, in the profoundly different political climate and context of those days, could provoke healthy confusion — was its ending optimistic or pessimistic? — there is little to ponder in the last speech of his latest play. The speech belongs to Isabel as she addresses the spirit of Mr. M.; it looks forward with a chastened optimism that vindicates and elaborates the title:

You gave me a little lecture about wasted lives … how much of it you'd seen, how much you hated it, how much you didn't want that to happen to Thami and me. I sort of understood what you meant at the time. Now I most certainly do. Your death has seen to that.

My promise to you is that I am going to try as hard as I can, in every way that I can, to see that it doesn't happen to me. I am going to try my best to make my life useful in the way yours was. I want you to be proud of me. After all, I am one of your children you know. You did welcome me to your family.

[*A pause.*]

The future is still ours, Mr. M.

It is well known in South African writing circles that Athol Fugard opposed the world-wide cultural boycott of his country from the beginning. His view has been that access to ideas is *always* desirable, that blocking that access plays into the hands of oppressive regimes. This position of principle, shared, incidentally, by some organizations to the left of the ANC, caused Fugard a good deal of pain. Before he became established as he is today, he was vilified by pro-boycott writers.

Especially difficult for him must have been the scorn and anger of Black South African writers who were virtually unanimous in support of the boycott. His position derived from his humane liberalism, his deeply held conviction that ideas can liberate.

It is curious and strange that today the ANC itself has modified its own stand on the boycott. It has declared that the cultural boycott is no longer in effect under the same conditions as previously. Work — imaginative and scholarly — that contributes to the undermining of apartheid, as Athol Fugard's most certainly attempts to do, is exempt from the restrictions of the boycott. Scholars and artists may now obtain an ANC clearance to travel to or have their work shown in South Africa. For years Fugard has laboured under a kind of anathema because of his defiance of the boycott. There is a curious parallel between this cultural politics and the events of the drama. Though he is an informer, Mr. M. is an informer for the sake of his beliefs. He derives no reward from his political betrayal of the school boycott, beyond the vain hope that he will get the children back into school where they belong. In a sense, then, he is a martyr to his passionately held belief in liberal and humanistic values promulgated and advanced from a white world from which

he is excluded. It is for these that he dies.

Fugard too has been called a traitor to the cause for defying the cultural boycott of South Africa. One may fairly assume that the writing of the play is a means of dealing with some of these questions, albeit in a more extreme context. Interestingly enough, all this has now changed. And, in a sense, the Fugard position has been vindicated by the softening of the ANC position to one of compromise and accommodation. All this in the midst of a rapidly polarizing situation of violent confrontation on many sides. It is perhaps revealing that as in this matter the ANC and Fugard appear to be closer than before, so in the matter of extra-literary political realities, the ANC is looking remarkably like the defunct South African Liberal Party in both economic and political ambition.

Nelson Mandela himself has stated that the ANC is not wedded to socialism. This will come as no surprise to those who have watched during the last few years as the ANC has entered into negotiations about a non-racial South Africa with the moguls of big business in South Africa, whose object is of course to ensure that they and their business interests survive.

It seems, in short, that the liberal capacity for accommodation has been borrowed by the revolutionaries and the businessmen and has tempered their fervour. Liberalism has become the site where agreement has been thought possible.

The ANC/government negotiations are looking more and more like a victory for de Klerk and white nationalism. The liberal solution of avoiding revolution through negotiation appears to have played into the hands of white South Africa and the ANC is looking less like a revolutionary force. Fugard's position has become the ANC position. Whether it will be justified in the end must remain in doubt for the time being.

251

Brick readers since 1976

JOYCE MARSHALL

Remembering Ethel Wilson

She talked as she wrote. This comment, slipped almost in passing into *The Other Side of Silence,* Mary McAlpine's biography of Ethel Wilson, brought not the slightest hint of surprise. Of course she did, one thinks — or at least I thought — for there has seldom been a writer who seems more one with her books, not like those autobiographical writers (Thomas Wolfe comes at once to mind) who write always of themselves and the events of their own lives but in the sense that it is clear almost from the first sentence that the writer's entire nature is in the books, in the style and in the attitudes, and that one knows her. Though we were both members of a writers' group that presented a brief to the Massey Commission and corresponded on one occasion, I never met Ethel Wilson in person. Yet to me she seemed, still seems, a known if somewhat mysterious person whom I might walk in on at any time and resume a conversation only briefly set to one side. For though she died in 1980 and had not published anything since *Mrs. Golightly and Other Stories* in 1961, she persists, which is strange in view of the short time she was with us as a writer. Apart from three stories in the *New Statesman and Nation* in the 1930s, which most of us in Canada did not know about, she produced only six books, four novels, two novellas — "Tuesday and Wednesday" and "Lilly's Story," printed together as *The Equations of Love* — and the stories mentioned above, all between 1947 and 1961, the rather brief space of fourteen years.

When *Hetty Dorval* appeared in 1947, we were still hungry for writers, in a way it is hard for younger people to understand — hard even for me to remember. As a fairly young beginner, I was conscious always of having not very much behind me and precious little around me. I felt that I lived in a very large (in fact a little too large) country, which despite its size and its variety didn't really exist because not enough writers had gathered up our various landscapes and found words for them, thus making them real. Even in childhood I often wished that some of the stories I read happened in places I knew. (Children are so precariously situated on the earth on which they find themselves. They need to be told that others have been where they are before they came.) By 1947 only a few beginnings had been made — Grove, MacLennan,

Callaghan (though he has never been much for landscapes and tended till that time to set his novels in Anycity). Gabrielle Roy's *Bonheur d'occasion* of 1945 had established streets in my native Montreal that I could have traced with my own feet but even so I still found trying to be a writer as fearsome and as painfully obvious as trying to mark a path through snow.

I knew, of course, that our landscape, once made real by writers, would have to be peopled and there was a great deal of talk at that time (how footling and time-wasting this seems now!) about "Canadian themes." How were our writers to find them? Was there indeed such a thing as a "Canadian" theme? Canada was not a "major" country. We had lived, by fortunate accident, to one side of the great "causes" of our time. Curious as this now seems, people spent a lot of time wondering whether Canadian writers could possibly have anything to say that would be listened to elsewhere. I remember remarking during one such discussion, "Well, I guess that leaves us stuck with the human heart," for I'd already begun to feel, as I still feel, that the human heart is pretty much the same wherever it beats. (Mine, I may say, was not a popular opinion and it did nothing to stop the questioning.)

So here in 1946 was Ethel Wilson beginning to — what word should I use for this very complicated activity? "establish"? "claim?" "possess?" — at any rate mark out what can now be clearly recognized as "Ethel Wilson country," the upper country of British Columbia, in this case a community where two rivers come together but do not blend. (I knew about that sort of thing; as a child, a passenger in my father's canoe, I'd been shown the line where the brown of the Ottawa River meets the green of the St. Lawrence and they continue, distinct and unblending, side by side, but I needed Ethel Wilson to tell me that this was extraordinary.) To tell me and all of us also that there need not be all this fussing about "Canadian themes."

A fine writer of great individuality, the first Canadian writer of my acquaintance who did something quite idiosyncratic and even unique with the English sentence, she wrote quite coolly of the human heart and human entanglements, leaving the great world themes of depression and impending war (*Hetty Dorval* is set in the 1930s) on the edge of these human entanglements where they belong.

Hetty Dorval's theme, plot, call it what you will, might in other hands have been so commonplace: a young girl is charmed by a beautiful, lazy, utterly amoral older woman, eventually sees through her and at the last bests her, sending her off to vanish into Austria just weeks before the Anschluss. The book is flawed. The culminating scene — in which Frankie confronts the soft slipper Hetty — requires more, and more sophisticated, insights from young Frankie than most teenagers could accomplish, but the prose is so lovely to the ear, at once so innocent and so worldly, so simple and tricky, tipping us from time to time, and when we least expect it, to one side, that we forgive its author anything.

I at any rate was hooked and, ever after that, the announcement of a new Ethel Wilson book always sent me out next day to a bookstore, even the year I lived in Copenhagen and had to order *Mrs. Golightly and Other Stories* from the English bookstore there, my last chance, though I didn't know it then, to order an Ethel Wilson book. (It's a source of modest pride to me that as reader for the radio program "Anthology" I was the first "professional" reader of the magnificent but neglected story of possession across the centuries that she called "Haply the Soul of My Grandmother" and "Mrs. Golightly and the First Convention." I remember laughing aloud when poor shy fumbling Mrs. Golightly kept forgetting that she'd already introduced herself several times to Mrs. Grampus. I still laugh whenever I think of it.)

All this is in the past, the rather distant past. But as an inveterate rereader, I've continued to read the Ethel Wilson books, finding new delights each time, finding also that her essence as a writer, her peculiar quality and attitude, its freshness, its surprises, is as hard to entrap in words as ever it was.

And here she is back with us again in 1988 — the centennial of her birth though no one to my knowledge has mentioned this, nor the fact that she shared this centennial with T. S. Eliot — in a selection of her papers, *Ethel Wilson: Stories, Essays, and Letters,* chosen by David Stouck, and in Mary McAlpine's loving if perhaps not overly analytic biography. A real feast when we'd thought there'd be no more for us. The papers are particularly rich. Most of the unpublished stories were discarded for good reason but they still bear the Ethel Wilson stamp and can be read with pleasure. And the book includes the strange eerie dream story, "A Visit to the Frontier," which, though it had appeared in *Tamarack Review,* she did not include in *Mrs. Golightly and Other Stories.* Perhaps she found its picture of death and desolation too painfully prophetic. And there is a selection of her lively and characteristic talks and essays, all so wonderfully and slyly titled — "Cat Among the Falcons," for instance, in which she claimed, among other heresies (Earle Birney never

forgave her for this), that university teaching of "creative" writing would lead only to "guided mediocrity."

Mary McAlpine knew Ethel Wilson in person for many years though she admits that she didn't "really know" her. Wisely then she has told much of the story in Ethel Wilson's own words. In consequence this is not a psycho-biography, if that's the right term. There are no shocks, no scandalous or even surprising disclosures, no answers to burning questions — just the facts, fleshed out by reminiscences from surviving contemporaries and younger friends and extracts from Ethel Wilson's own letters and essays. In fact, and this suits the sort of person and writer Ethel Wilson was,

she has controlled the whole thing. Before her death she destroyed most of her personal papers — all but a few of the letters written to her, a scattering of unpublished stories and a final novel that never saw the light of day. She disliked and usually avoided the mechanics of publicity. I wonder what she'd say if someone tried to launch her on a transCanada book tour. (No, I don't have to wonder, I know. "I find writing to be a private and avidly solitary affair," she wrote, "which I do not disclose even to my nearest and dearest one.") She chose to keep her own secrets, to tell only the truth she chose to tell for, as Audrey Butler, who as a teenager was a "war guest" of Ethel Wilson and her husband, put it, though she would never lie "she might swing away from a subject."

As for her life and the way that life affected her (and thereby her writing) the books give abundant clues, reticent clues but clues nevertheless. She was born in Port Elizabeth, South Africa, in 1888 and had no memories of her mother who died before Ethel was two. Her father, a Methodist missionary, took her back to England and himself died when she was nine. In a "story" given with a doll to Mary McAlpine's daughter, her godchild, she spoke of her "smashed-up" feeling after his death. Even in old age she remembered their laughter together. She used to roll on the floor with merriment, she wrote, and "never never laughed so much ever again." She was shuttled from one relative to another till her grandmother came to take her to Vancouver where she was brought up in a household of older women — the grandmother, an aunt, a great aunt — and very much loved, she maintained. In fact, the circumstances of her life were much the circumstances of Rose's life in *The Innocent Traveller*, her second novel. When she was fourteen she was sent to boarding school in England, returned four years later to Vancouver, qualified as a teacher and taught until her marriage in 1921 to Dr. Wallace

Wilson, a distinguished physician who became president in turn of the British Columbia Medical Association and of the Canadian Medical Association. They were "oh so happily married," she told Mary McAlpine and his death in 1966 marked in a real sense the end of Ethel Wilson's life — as a writer and, almost one might say, as a human being. The last of her letters — the last at least that have been preserved for us and printed — are almost inarticulate with grief. The final years are shadow.

It now seems an impertinence to say of such a secretive, or at least guarded, person that she never recovered from the early loss of her parents but even a cursory glance at her novels will show that this is so. All the women she wrote about are orphans or quickly become orphans. Maggie in *Swamp Angel* is the most bereaved of all; before we meet her she has lost not only her father (her mother is not mentioned) but her husband and her child. Frankie in *Hetty Dorval* and Gypsy in *Love and Salt Water* have parents but soon lose one or both. It was as if she could not imagine the endurance of a complete family. The dark side of life was too close to her — "the dreadful private casualties of life," as she expressed it, and again "the irrelevance of cause and effect amongst us."

It is as important, or at least as interesting, to notice what she didn't write about. Apart from the ruefully gentle hints in *The Innocent Traveller*, there is nothing about the real emotions, what Mary McAlpine calls "the furies," of a child growing up through adolescence into maturity in an old-fashioned, somewhat muted household of considerably older women. And there's not a word anywhere about the years she spent teaching what was then called a Baby Class — fourteen years after all — in the Vancouver school system. She clearly disliked the work and always answered questions about those years rather snappishly, in monosyllables. And in a letter to Margaret Laurence,

one of the many younger writers she encouraged, about *A Jest of God*, she wrote, significantly, "I, as a young teacher once, understand Rachel's school life." She was so endlessly curious. A conversation with a gardener, a face glimpsed at a bus stop (some such vague encounter, I believe, was the seed for "Tuesday and Wednesday," Ethel Wilson's favourite of her writing, and sometimes also mine) could lead to an entire imagined life, relationships with other lives imagined for other faces. Yet she never wrote of the child-teacher or teacher-child relation. Were those years so stultifying she couldn't bear to write of them? Or did she simply find them dull because she'd have preferred to be doing something else? Practising to be a writer, for instance?

It suited her, publicly and also with her friends, to present herself as someone who just suddenly, and rather impulsively, became in later middle age a writer. Dr. Wilson had been elected president of the CMA. She would have to appear with him, in a semi-official wifely capacity, at a large convention. The thought terrified her. She had been trained in social poise and decorum, and was always lovely to look at — some people found her a bit gushing at social functions and remembered her "extraordinarily bright and sharp blue eyes" — but she was also, and this may explain the gushing as well as the sharpness, somewhat diffident. She wanted to make something for herself, perhaps more accurately establish herself as herself, before she had to plunge into those social horrors. So she went off alone to Lytton in the B.C. upper country and in three weeks produced what she called "a small amateurish piece of work" — the vivid and elegantly structured novel *Hetty Dorval*.

So much for the public persona: a housewife who at the age of fifty-seven became, almost whimsically, a writer. But there were those stories in the *New Statesman and Nation* during the thirties. Among the few papers she preserved are twenty pages of notes dated September 1930 for what was to become *The Innocent Traveller*. She corresponded during this decade with Simon and Schuster and with Houghton Mifflin about the possible publication of a series of sketches. In 1944 she sent some bits of *The Innocent Traveller* to Macmillan of Canada and requested two days later that they be sent back to her. Ellen Elliott, then editor at Macmillan, had time to read the pieces and asked to see any future writing — and did see and so published *Hetty Dorval*. And there was an earlier piece of "writing" — a children's serial called "The Surprising Adventures of Peter," written as a sort of advertisement for the family tea-importing business. Even as a child she had a writer's curiosity — and a writer's obsession with words. "Papa, what is a 'the'?" she asked her father when he was teaching her to read. She was fascinated by the chain gang laying sidewalk planks in Vancouver and tried to look at the men's faces, and she was so amazed by the sight of men chewing and spitting tobacco that she ventured a chew of it herself. (She found it disagreeable and was relieved to learn that ladies didn't chew.) All her life she was, informally at least, a storyteller. Her companions during the ritual "crocodile" walks at her English boarding school were enchanted by the stories she told them. Friends of her maturity remember her telling them stories which they claimed they later read in print "in the same words."

Was she simply a natural writer, prevented by modesty and the circumstances of her life and of the times (there were so few writers then) from seeking publication till so late? Is there such a thing as a natural writer, a person gifted with a sense of language, a marvellously precise ear for speech, a capacity for close observation of things and persons far beyond her own rather restricted milieu, who could be content for more than half her life simply to play with these gifts? It's known that she used to sit in her husband's car making notes when she accompanied him on his night calls to patients, but if there was early and continuing practice in writing Ethel Wilson has made sure we'd never see it. I admit to curiosity about this. I'd like to know. But does it matter really? She remains to an extent a mystery as perhaps she should be.

She was unique, remains unique, in our literature. For her style, for one thing — an ability to make sentences so light and quick (with some of the lightness and quickness of Virginia Woolf's sentences, as Gabrielle Roy, to whom I introduced Ethel Wilson's writing, expressed it), so marked by the Ethel Wilson stamp and personality, that twisting and turning at unexpected moments, that I'd recognize one of her sentences, I've always felt, if I found it scrawled on a barn door. (In fact when I was rereading a letter she sent me in 1962 before sending it away for safekeeping, I found that I knew most of it by heart though I hadn't looked at it for years.) She possessed, in her own words, "a reverence for the English sentence that is nearly worship." Again and again, in her letters and essays, she speaks of "the sentence" as the essential tool of the writer. She was given a firm grounding in the English language and in the classics of our literature at the Vancouver girls' school and especially at the English boarding school where she spent her high-school years. "Our education at this English boarding school," she wrote in a letter to Desmond Pacey, "was rigorous, almost Spartan, sound and often very amusing." Note this last. If Ethel Wilson hadn't found it amusing, one feels, it wouldn't have taken.

It is this that indicates part of her uniqueness — a strict, almost classic sense of language (though on the surface so modest — she was at first unwilling to have her name appear as author of *Hetty Dorval*, conceded finally that it might be printed "in very small letters" — she could be quite fierce with editors in her insistence that her choice of word, and even comma, should be respected), combined with a thoroughly modern mind, a mind moulded by the great world catastrophes (two wars, the Depression) through which she'd lived and the sense her own life had given her of personal desolation, "the irrelevance of cause and effect." It is, in fact, her attitude to the incidents she writes of that marks her as modern. Sean O'Faolain called her writing "original and unspoiled." It was. But it was also highly sophisticated. She was fascinated by the human personality and the way it can clash or only half mesh with others, a fascination that could include such unlikely figures as Mort, Myrtle and Victoria May Tritt of "Tuesday and Wednesday" and Lilly of "Lilly's Story," that slut turned devouring mother who longed only that her daughter should be "like folks." (It's interesting to note that a radio adaption of this novella, with its thesis that great good can come, even to the liar herself, from lying, caused a scandalized outcry in the Canadian Senate.) Ethel Wilson's attitude to these and her other characters can best be described as a sort of mocking love. Even Maggie's crass crude deserted husband in *Swamp Angel* is allowed to have his say and become pathetic. She had quirks and wasn't afraid to show them. She delighted, for one thing, in a particular sort of warm expanding (in flesh and comprehension) older woman — Nell Severance in *Swamp Angel*, Mrs. Emblem in "Tuesday and Wednesday." Her writing is so seductive, so strong in personality and conviction, that we allow her to break the rules and intervene again and again as herself, to say of Mrs. Emblem, "She really was a darling" and to insert into *Love and Salt Water* a page-long digression about a happy family, simply because these people pleased her and she wanted to include them.

Her books could be called small, slight, even minor. She suspected this herself. "I only wish," she wrote in 1961 after she was awarded a special Canada Council medal, "that my attainments were greater and more pertinent." "I was aware," she told a CBC audience, "that if I had talent ... it could be measured with a teaspoon, not even with a liqueur glass — that would be too heady — whereas I know other talents that flowed with the power of a river." The novels are certainly not very bulky, appear to be simple. But try to sketch the plot of, say, *Swamp Angel*, which is perhaps the best known, certainly the most studied, of her books. Maggie leaves the man she'd married in grief after the death in war of her first husband and the death of their child. She takes a bus up to the B.C. upper country where she gets a job at a failing fishing camp. The place begins to flourish. The owner's wife becomes jealous of Maggie's efficiency and warmth, so jealous that she tries to kill herself. Well and good. But we've left out Maggie's dear friend Nell Severance and the warm but heavy past she carries with her. We've left out Nell's daughter's marriage to ... We've left out the little revolver called the Swamp Angel which in the book's final scene Maggie flings into the deepest part of Three Loon Lake. We've left out all the resonance, all the implications, all the things not said or merely hinted (or said slightly askew) that exist in the real story, the one only partly present on the page. In fact, we've left out almost everything. "I know myself," Ethel Wilson wrote, in a letter to Desmond Pacey, "to have a small talent only of a certain sort." But any effort, by Ethel Wilson or me or anyone else, to sum her up, or sum up even one novel or one story, will always be short of the mark, will come, to borrow the words she used as a title for one of her talks, only "somewhere near the truth."

KEVIN CONNOLLY

An Interview With Don DeLillo

merican Don DeLillo began writing professionally when he was in his mid-thirties, beginning with *Americana* (1971). Since then, he has published nine novels, including *Players, Great Jones Street, Running Dog, The Names,* and *White Noise,* which earned him the American Book Award for 1985. A writer of unusual range, DeLillo has tackled topics as diverse as rock 'n' roll, terrorism, pornography, international intelligence, and college football in styles which often blur traditional boundaries between genres — from psychological drama to political thriller, science fiction to satire. Much admired by his peers, DeLillo has a reputation for being largely indifferent to commercial success. Until recently, he has enjoyed a degree of privacy uncommon among writers of his stature. DeLillo's novel *Libra* promises to change all of that. The novel deals with a topic for which the public, after twenty-five years, still has an insatiable appetite: the November 1963 assassination of U.S. President John F. Kennedy. In creating *Libra*, he has invented characters to complement his fictionalized versions of the key figures, but in most significant respects the novel draws on detail which is consistent with the facts, as we know them. Given the sheer volume and inconsistency of these facts, that in itself is no mean feat.

DeLillo was interviewed by Kevin Connolly in Toronto in 1988.

Connolly: I wanted to ask you a little about research — the effect of research on what you've taken pains to point out is a novel.

DeLillo: Well, I did do extensive research, and the heart of it was the Warren Report and its twenty-six volumes of testimony and exhibits. The first fifteen volumes contain the testimony of hundreds of people, ranging from witnesses to the assassination to people who knew the main figures involved. It's like an encyclopaedia of daily life. You learn a great deal which has nothing to do with the case itself, ranging from interesting regional speech patterns to the particularities of occupations. What it was like to be a train man in Fort Worth in 1963. Waitresses, stripteasers, private detectives, all sorts of people trot out their lives, their theories, and so forth. So it was not only an education in an immediate sense, it provided a nice background on the fifties and sixties in many ways.

Connolly: And gave you the type of detail you needed for the novel.

DeLillo: Not only the detail but also the voices of certain characters. The Marguerite Oswald in the novel is, in most important respects, the Marguerite Oswald of the Warren Commission report. She spoke to the commission lawyers for a number of days and for hundreds of pages. So I found out a great deal from this, not only about her life and about Lee's life, but about how she speaks, how she thinks, and so on. It's interesting that her conspiracy theories have been borne out, if not in fact, then in that so many serious commentators on the case ended up coming to the same conclusions she came to instinctively and maternally. I also travelled to New Orleans, Dallas, Fort Worth, and Miami. Seeing the places where Oswald lived was particularly haunting. They're old houses that are in much the same condition as they were twenty-five years ago, and they stand in a kind of haunted aura, full of mystery and regret. I felt a similar sensation in Dealey Plaza itself. It's the loneliest place in Dallas, even with all the traffic buzzing past it. From my hotel window I could see tourists standing on the lawns and gesturing up to the sixth-floor window of the Texas Schoolbook Depository and down towards the triple underpass, and it was eerie. Like a kind of local tai chi exercise.

Connolly: Did you find anything in your research that you found burdensome as a writer, details you felt you couldn't omit, things you wish didn't exist?

DeLillo: No. In fact I found the research invigorating. It was the factual detail that drove the novel forward, that provided a motor. In important ways all I really had to do was follow these lives onto the pages in my typewriter. Aside from the fact that I needed a great deal of factual information to drive the book, the simple reality that these lives were so interesting came up. Not only Oswald and his wife and his mother, and

Jack Ruby; but many other peripheral characters as well. Characters some readers will assume are fictional are in fact straight from the pages of history.

Connolly: Was there anything particular that you ran into that you remember as being important in producing the novel *Libra* as opposed to any number of possible novels you could have written when you were starting out?

DeLillo: I think what made the novel what it finally became was not anything I learned from my research so much as themes which began to develop themselves as I continued to work, chapter to chapter. It seems to me, finally, that what this book is about is history and dreams. Dreams meaning all those forces in our lives that are outside history. Most importantly, coincidence, for example. There is coincidence in the story itself, but it didn't suggest itself as a major theme to me until I was well into the book. I think the character of Ferrie impels Oswald toward that moment in history, in trying to convince him that he ought to step outside history to find his self-fulfillment. In 1963, Oswald committed two acts of violence. He also took a shot at General Walker, a famous right-wing figure in Dallas, and this was an act informed by a strict political motivation. I think that by the time Oswald fired at President Kennedy he had begun to unravel. I think the assassination was a much more complex act, driven, in the novel in any case, by coincidence and by fantasy to a certain extent. In this respect, Oswald predates other would-be assassins like John Hinkley Jr., who took a shot at President Reagan, and Arthur Brimmer, who tried to kill Governor Wallace. Young men acting out of a backdrop of fantasy and disaffection.

Connolly: One of the characters in the novel comments on these kinds of people, saying that they no longer have to live "lives of quiet desperation …"

DeLillo: Yes. Suddenly it is possible to shape your desperation, to find a destiny for it. It didn't have to be quiet. You suddenly *could* enter history, as long as you were willing to spend it in prison.

Connolly: The character of Nicholas Branch interested me from an authorial point of view, not just because he is also a writer, but because he almost seems to be a nightmare image of you, had you tried to write something that was historically accurate.

DeLillo: He had a tougher time than I did. Of course he was writing history and I was writing fiction. But what I was trying to express with Branch was, I guess, two main things. One was the enormous amount of material that the assassination generated, material which eventually makes Branch almost impotent. He simply cannot keep up with it: the path changes as he writes. The material itself becomes, after a while, the subject. The other thing I wanted to do with Branch was to suggest the ways the American consciousness has changed since the assassination. I think that what has been missing for the past twenty-five years is a sense of the coherent reality most Americans share. It's almost as if we enter the world of randomness and ambiguity. Branch himself refers to this as an "aberration in the heartland of the real." Even after all these years we still can't agree on the number of gunmen, the number of shots, the time span between the shots, the number of wounds on the President's body, the size and shape of those wounds. And even beyond this confusion of data there's a sense of the secret manipulation of history. This has certainly entered our mass consciousness. Documents are lost or concealed. Official records are sealed for fifty or seventy-five years. A curious number of suspicious murders and suicides. And I think this current runs from November of 1963 right through Viet Nam and Watergate, and into Iran-Contra.

Connolly: It's almost as if these hearings have become societal rites of passage. They seem to pop up every ten or fifteen years.

DeLillo: Exactly. But it's something we have to go through almost as a token of memory, as a memorialization of the first time it happened.

Connolly: I was wondering if you had been watching the Iran-Contra hearings while you were writing *Libra?*

DeLillo: No.

Connolly: Because the first things I thought about when I ran into the people in your book were the impressions I had while watching those hearings. What struck me first was how mundane and toothless these people seemed to be — people like Secord and North and Poindexter. They came across as completely unremarkable people. The other thing I noticed was how compelled I was to watch something which was essentially boring, in its presentation, and everything else. It became almost an unconscious pursuit of secrecy.

DeLillo: Someone said to me that to find the roots of the Iran-Contra all you had to do was look at *Running Dog.* A CIA proprietary becomes a way to generate vast personal profits. A fake company set up as a conduit for espionage becomes a vast profit-making apparatus on its own, which may have been what happened in Iran-Contra. Many people think it obviously did.

Connolly: Terrorism and intelligence become business.

DeLillo: Yes, exactly.

Connolly: A lot of people would think that that kind of thing must have something to do with ideology.

DeLillo: I don't think it's nearly so much about ideology as it is about succeeding in the world. Personal power and profit.

Connolly: One of the things I've noticed in your work, and in particular the novels which touch on covert action, is the presence of faith as an issue. In the new novel it's a little bit different from novels like *Players* and *Running Dog*, I think. And I understand that your background is in theology and philosophy. Selvy, for example, in *Running Dog*, is described by one of the other characters as a "believer," someone who would do clandestine work for nothing. But when you are confronted with Selvy's character, he seems to be indifferent to ideology. His faith expresses itself more in things like how to fire a handgun properly.

DeLillo: Exactly. His faith is in tradecraft. But in the world of *Running Dog* I think the only true believers are the Mafia. Because they're a family in the general and the specific sense of the word. This is what binds them, a sense of blood relationships and a very long tradition of doing what they are doing. But there's a surge of acquisitiveness in *Running Dog* which peters out as soon as all of the players get their hands on the object. They seem immediately to lose interest. I think this was a feeling I had about the country in those particular years, in the late seventies. It was interesting that some years after, after the Hitler diaries surfaced, there was the same kind of acquisitiveness going on, but on a much larger scale. In a way I was naive about what might happen if this Hitler film [in *Running Dog*] suddenly surfaced. When the diaries surfaced there was a much greater reaction. Entire publishing empires went totally berserk over these fake diaries. And it died out immediately afterwards.

Connolly: I can see a similarity between Selvy and some of the characters you have created in *Libra*. Why the interest in people whose lives are so focussed on secrecy, people who in many ways are completely divorced from any real sense of community?

DeLillo: Most of my novels seem to turn on a character who ends up alone in a small room. I don't know why that is exactly. And it's curious that in moving towards the assassination I finally came up against a *real* character who spent a significant amount of time in a small room alone. Of course that was Oswald himself, who planned the murder of General Walker in a room only slightly larger than a closet, who spent time in the brig [in the Marines], who lived in a rooming house in Dallas in a room about the size of a jail cell, and who finally ended up in a real jail cell, before he himself was killed.

In *Libra* I tried to trace secrecy back to childhood through Win Everett's daughter, Suzanne. Win thinks about secrecy in terms of a child's secrets and how important they are to her. He thinks it's dangerous to give up your secrets because in doing so you lose some of your identity, some of your grip on the world. It seemed to me that secrets — the pleasure and the conflict of secrets — remained the same through your entire life. I think it was Octavio Paz who said that man spies on himself, and eventually I think this is what happens to Win Everett in *Libra*. He begins to examine himself as a subject, as someone in the third person.

Connolly: At the end of *Libra* you've included an author's note, but despite what you say there, and what you've said to various people in articles about *Libra* being a novel, and how it should be treated as such, you still have people writing letters to the *New York Times* complaining about your accuracy on certain counts.

DeLillo: I've answered that letter, which is just a misinterpretation of what happens in the novel. The fellow who wrote the letter was assistant counsel to the Warren Commission, and his feeling is that Jack Ruby's murder of Oswald could not possibly have been carefully planned, for reasons he details in the letter. And in fact, in the novel, it is not carefully planned at all.

Connolly: It's a coincidence.

DeLillo: Yes, it's more or less a coincidence. Ruby, obscurely motivated as always, was more or less on his way to send twenty-five dollars to one of his

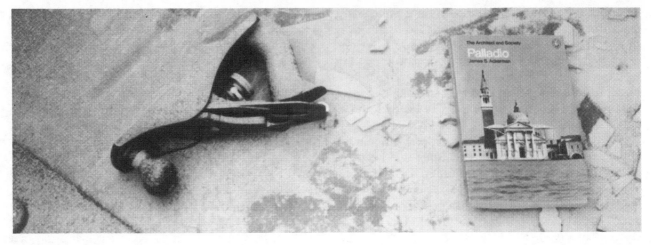

stripteasers and/or to shoot Oswald.

Connolly: Are you surprised about the direction in which this issue of accuracy has gone since the novel was published? I guess what I want is for you to expand on that tantalizing remark you make at the end of the author's note to the effect that fiction can be a kind of refuge from the uncertainties of fact.

DeLillo: I'm not so sure now that was such a good idea. The afterword is really a dressed-up legal disclaimer. Possibly I shouldn't have dressed it up. But I didn't want one or two stark sentences disclaiming any resemblance between characters in the book and certain living characters. In a theoretical sense I think fiction can be a refuge and a consolation. In *Libra* the national leader still dies, but for one thing, at least we know how it happens. Beyond that, fiction offers patterns and symmetry that we don't find in the experience of ordinary living. Stories are consoling, fiction is one of the consolation prizes for having lived in the world.

Connolly: It seems as though you've anticipated the fact that with a thing as naturally paranoia-producing as the Kennedy assassination, people are going to come up with their own answers for what might have happened. It could be as simple as saying, "Oh, Hoover had him killed, it's obvious." It seems in the afterword you've anticipated treading on other peoples' fictions.

DeLillo: I suppose I was saying to people who've read lightly in the non-fiction end of the spectrum that it's possible to imagine the assassination having happened in this way and therefore to move to the edge of the spectrum other obsessions and other possibilities. Doing this helps us to understand not just the characters in the novel but character itself and human motivation, and the forces of chance and coincidence on the way characters act.

Connolly: Something that would be lost if you were simply faced with all of that information.

DeLillo: I think so. None of the material I've read has ever attempted to enter the minds of Oswald or Ruby, and none of it treats them as flawed humans. They're always treated as people who would automatically move from spot A to spot B in the straightest possible line. And the reality is that these were the last two men in the world who would ever behave in that way.

This is in fact what is behind Ruby's shooting of Oswald. All the junk and torn newspapers in Ruby's consciousness are not only part of what he was, but probably the major part.

Connolly: I wanted to ask you a little more about history. In recent years there has been a spate of films, books, short stories, and so on, trying to deal with recent history. Viet Nam is the most obvious example. And it seems to me the way you've approached recent history is different from the way most other artists appear to be approaching it. There seems to be a kind of moralistic digestion of the Viet Nam experience, an interpretation of what it means on extremely simplified levels.

DeLillo: You're thinking of *Platoon*.

Connolly: Among others. One of the blurbs on the back of the paperback edition of *Running Dog* praises it as one of the best novels about Viet Nam. It had never occurred to me that *Running Dog* was about Viet Nam in anything but a peripheral way. Given all of this appetite for commentary on recent history, I was wondering if you think about your own responsibility as a fictional interpreter when you are dealing with material which is so current?

DeLillo: Yes. First, in writing *Libra* I did feel a strong sense of responsibility. Much more I think, than most novelists feel while writing a particular novel. But I never forgot that I was doing a novel and not a piece of history. In a way *Libra* is about history. But it certainly is not history itself. I tell people, when they want to know what to call this book, that it's a novel. I don't think of it as a non-fiction novel or a "novel-as-history," or any of those designations which have been used in the past. Or even as a historical novel, which technically I suppose it is.

To me the history seems too recent for that. It's about history in a way. It's also about fiction, about plot-making, and the relationships between plots and deaths, something which I first encountered while I was writing *White Noise,* and which I've developed somewhat in *Libra*. Mainly through the character of Win Everett, who thinks that the more tightly one plots a story, the more likely it is to end in death. Detective novels most often have a corpse turn up at some point. And so the plot Win devises in the larger world will turn out the same way. Even though he does not want a death at the end of it, it will naturally happen that way because this is the nature of plots; they move inevitably towards death, both in the world of books, and the world outside books.

Connolly: The novels I've read of yours have a much greater emphasis on plot or storyline than a lot of literary fiction these days. They are also psychological studies, but I think plot is always prominent. Do you prefer to work with plot; do you like to keep the reader hooked that way?

DeLillo: I think the reason is partly the novels you've mentioned. They are all more carefully plotted than my other novels, simply because they are about conspiracy, or about terrorist plots, as in the case of *Players*. When I started writing *Players* my only plan was to write a novel about the way people naturally talk to each other, all the time, and in particular people who are intimate with each other — as it turned out, Pammy and Lyle. The whole novel was simply going to be dialogue between two fairly typical New Yorkers of a certain age. Certainly Pammy is, Lyle is a little stranger, not really typical of anything. But very early on, I abandoned this. I found a murder taking place on the floor of the Stock Exchange and I followed that path. This automatically supplied me with a sense of plot I had no intention of producing earlier.

Connolly: It took me a while to get used to the way your characters speak; I think it might take a lot of people who are used to traditional literary dialogue a while to get a sense of where you're coming from.

Your dialogue is clipped and idiosyncratic to fit the way people actually speak. You explained where it came from in the new novel, from the Warren transcripts, but from reading some of your other work it's obviously not a new thing. Is duplicating actual speech something you are interested in?

DeLillo: The only time I consciously tried to do it was in *Players*, again because the novel started as endless dialogue between a husband and wife. I wanted to get it the way people actually spoke it. It is my theory that if you record dialogue as people actually speak it, it will seem stylized to the reader. It will seem like a conscious attempt to shape dialogue when in fact it's *literally* the way people speak to each other. I listened to people very carefully around the period I was writing *Players*, and the result is what you see on the page. Of course it's the dialogue of certain people; it's not the way everyone speaks. But there's a certain strata of New York society in which people speak the way they do in *Players*. As far as I'm concerned it's word for word, literally like that. In *Libra* I had the benefit of printed dialogue in which people were talking, I think fairly comfortably, to Commission lawyers. And I got much of that, particularly Marguerite Oswald, right out of the Warren Report.

Connolly: Some people would argue that you can't do that and expect to get literate dialogue. I think it's a bit of a shock to people what it actually looks like transcribed. You do what playwrights often do, taking advantage of the verbal accidents that clipping sentences and colloquialism create.

DeLillo: Right. This is something you could study for the rest of your life and attempt to write properly for the rest of your life. And you'd probably never do it the same way from book to book, because real dialogue, as spoken, is always a little different as you move one millimetre from one social strata to another. It changes so much that you could develop a whole

new theory of it just by listening to it.

Connolly: Are you especially conscious of what your writing is doing as you're writing it? Do you usually structure your novels in advance?

DeLillo: No. Not at all.

Connolly: It's more organic than that?

DeLillo: Yes, absolutely. Again, *Libra* is an exception because the life of Oswald and the other characters suggested a kind of sequence that I'd have to follow.

Connolly: You have an obvious point to which everything moves.

DeLillo: The two streams actually converge. The Oswald chapters and the conspiracy chapters actually converge at the end of the long New Orleans chapter when Ferrie talks to Oswald. He in fact explains the plot of the book in explaining that what they in fact want from him is for him to assassinate the president. He is actually laying out the plot for the novel *Libra* there because they turn out to be the same thing, these two streams converging: one, Oswald's life; two, this plot against the president's life.

Throughout the novel, Oswald's viewpoint is predominant in the Oswald chapters. In the conspiracy chapters, Oswald is only talked about or distantly glimpsed. Once the two streams merge there is no longer this chapter-by-chapter sense of a separation of viewpoints. Oswald appears in what were essentially their chapters. His viewpoint is suddenly introduced into other people's chapters, and vice versa. The book becomes one headlong scream towards November 22.

Connolly: The scene immediately following the assassination, after the shots were fired. How much of that is imagination, and how much of it is what you actually know? It's a part of the novel I admire a great deal. It's got the literary equivalent of a handheld camera feel to it.

DeLillo: That's a good description of it. It all

happened, I mean I actually walked the route he most likely travelled in the neighbourhood of his rooming house in the Oak Cliff section of Dallas. Nobody knows why Oswald shot patrolman Tippet. Anti-Warren people think that Oswald in fact did not shoot Tippet, that somebody else shot him, or that there were two people shooting. But I'm convinced that Oswald killed him; the gun was found on him when he was captured. It's all true as far as Oswald is concerned. What happened in the theatre is also true except for the presence of Wayne Elko, a fictional character, in the back row.

Connolly: The symbol of the woman's shoes left on the hood of patrolman Tippet's car ...

DeLillo: This happened.

Connolly: It struck me as extremely important as you set it up in the novel. Where your novel is satisfying as an explanation, albeit a fictional one, of the assassination is that it acknowledges the almost mystical presence of coincidence. And the woman's shoes seem to incorporate that mystery. Because there turns out to be a perfectly natural human reason for them being there, but at the time they're found it's almost spooky.

DeLillo: Think of the cops standing around the car wondering where this pair of shoes came from. [The woman who found Tippet was a nurse and she left her extra pair of work shoes there in the confusion.] It's totally bizarre. But it did happen. When this is first introduced at the beginning of the novel in a scene with Nicholas Branch he thinks of it as a "holy moment." You used the word mystical. And that's what it is to me too. It's a kind of accidental holiness, a randomness so intense and surrounded by such violence that it takes on nearly a sacred inexplicability. And as you noted it's so strangely real at the same time. That's what I was aiming at.

Connolly: The structure of some of your other

works interested me as well. *Libra* is traditional in the sense that you build towards a climax and then there's a dropping off near the end. But most of your novels seem to use non-traditional structures. *Players*, for example, seems to dissolve rather than build to a climax. Plots are initiated, and then seem to untie themselves towards the end. There's a scene at the end of *Players* in which Lyle lies on the bed in front of a motel window. The light's pouring in and you get a vision of him breaking into pieces in the light.

DeLillo: The novel is also breaking apart in order to regenerate itself. At the beginning of the novel we hear a discussion about motels, which is where the novel ends. I think there's also a blinding flash of light which anticipates the one at the end of the novel. That seems to happen in my books, and I wasn't really aware of it until somebody pointed it out. There's a looping action from the end of the book to the beginning.

Connolly: That feeling of things breaking up, everything moving towards entropy, seems to connect with some of the ideas in *Libra*. All of that information which swallows Branch becomes so rationally overwhelming. Is this something you believe in general, about life or American society?

DeLillo: No. I don't know why certain currents run through my books. They're not necessarily based on logical convictions I have about the world outside the novel. Some of them are almost abstract patterns, like the way painters repeat lines or colours. I repeat them, and I'm not always conscious that I'm doing it.

Connolly: You're not compelled to pull it apart rationally?

DeLillo: No ...

Connolly: Is that a superstition you have, or is it just something that doesn't interest you?

DeLillo: It's not a superstition. But I don't try to do it because I don't think I know how. I wouldn't be able to do it if I tried. And if I thought I could, I probably wouldn't do it anyway. So maybe it is a superstition. [*laughs*]

Connolly: The other pattern I wanted to ask you about, and I guess this is also specific to your novels about intelligence agencies, is the tendency of things, once they become extremely sophisticated, to turn the motivations of their users or creators towards the primitive. The whole set-up of the PAC/ORD company in *Running Dog* seems to reflect that tendency. For example, Selvy's self-worth is based on very primitive impulses. He's like an animal in some ways.

DeLillo: People are sometimes reduced to their essentials in my fiction. *White Noise,* if I had to summarize it briefly, studies the idea that the more advanced technology becomes, the more primitive our fear becomes. In *Ratner's Star* there is a much more elaborate discussion of the connection between modern minds and the primitive, mysticism and science, and how one curiously begins to shade into the other. I think one of the effects of solitude is that you are eventually reduced to a more essential being, and this does happen to Selvy in *Running Dog.*

Connolly: Characters in your books also tend to emphasize the importance of naming things. Lyle experiences it, and certainly Oswald does. Oswald is constantly writing in his diary and trying to actualize things he dreams about by using the words. Lyle does it in *Players,* he focusses intensely on names and numbers, as if he were getting a kind of primitive understanding from that.

DeLillo: I think naming things helps us hold the world together, almost literally. Without naming I think it would all fall apart. Names are the sub-atomic glue of the human world, and for a certain type of mentality, the clandestine mentality like Lyle's or like Oswald's, naming becomes a secret act, secret and obsessive. I think people do it as a way of keeping their grip on the world, and I think Oswald's dyslexia made it a problem for him to see the world as a coherent set of facts and words and ideas.

Connolly: It's interesting that something which he has so much trouble with becomes so important to master and control. Even when he doesn't understand the Marx he is reading he's absolutely convinced of its importance.

DeLillo: Yes, and he didn't know that he was dyslexic. Nobody knew, apparently. It wasn't until after he died, after the psychologists studied his writing that they could tell he had this problem. He felt that he knew things, yet they continued to elude him. He just couldn't get a grip on them.

Connolly: Critics I have read who are equivocal about your writing — there was a review of *Libra* in a recent issue of *Mother Jones* that was like this — tend to admire the craft and the technique while complaining about what they see as a lack of depth in your characters. Other people take the approach that the writing is paranoid. In a recent article in the *New York Review of Books,* Robert Towards called you the "chief shaman of the paranoid school of American fiction." And I was wondering what your reaction is to this kind of criticism.

DeLillo: It didn't annoy me. I could take it as an observation about *Libra* and not disagree strongly. I don't consider myself paranoid at all. I think I see things exactly as they are. William Burroughs has said that the paranoid is the man in possession of the facts. Once you know the facts, people who don't think you're crazy. It's impossible to write about the Kennedy assassination and its aftermath without taking note of twenty-five years of paranoia which has collected around that event. This is one of the major functions of Nicholas Branch in the novel, of Marguerite Oswald as well. Simply to give the reader an idea of the psychic energies which have flowed from November 1963. One of the major energies is paranoia. But you don't have to be paranoid to write about this, or to understand it.

So that's my answer to that statement, which was probably meant as a compliment. He did mention me with Pynchon and Mailer, and that's pretty good company.

Connolly: I'm wondering if you've thought about the relationship between your writing and your politics. Because there are certain things you write about that other people might consider paranoid for political reasons.

DeLillo: I certainly don't try consciously to make political statements or to include political material. It depends on how you define politics, I suppose. In a way everything we do is politics. Very few critics have commented on *Libra* in those terms. The one who did, though, was very adamant about it; I was virtually an agent of Moammar Ghaddafi. [*laughs*] I don't know how to respond to that, because it's certainly not surprising that you learn something about a novelist by reading his fiction, without hearing any of his public utterances. Of course you do; what I write is what I am. Aside from the fact that it must naturally flow into one's books, I certainly don't have any political program. Not only for my books, but for my life or for the life of my country.

Connolly: I guess if you grapple with a topic you are interested in, people are always going to fall on one side or another of you.

DeLillo: Especially if it's a famous and tragic event as the assassination was. People will object to the fact that in the novel the CIA, at least renegade agents from the CIA, are to some extent behind it all. But it's hardly a leftist position to think that.

DeLillo: The effect of film on your writing: I noticed it in the film that begins *Players,* the film which is the object of the pursuit in *Running Dog.* Most notable for me was the realization I came to while reading the assassination scene in *Libra,* about how my perception of that event was so completely determined by film, the amateur footage that was shot of the assassination, and so on. And I think you consciously worked that perception into the pacing of that scene.

DeLillo: Yes. Sure.

Connolly: Do you look at film technique and try to find an equivalent technique in your writing?

DeLillo: I've never thought about applying it to writing, but I was a very avid filmgoer through the sixties. That was my personal golden age of movies: Bergman, Antonioni, Godard, and several other people. I haven't been nearly so enthusiastic since those days. But I never thought of a novelistic counterpart to certain types of filmmaking. If this has seeped into my work, that's fine, but I've never taken a conscious crack at it.

Connolly: Have you had film producers interested in your work?

DeLillo: Now and then, yes. Usually someone in a borrowed office phones up and says, "You know, *Great Jones Street,* boy that's somethin'. Wow, let's have lunch." [*laughs*] Things like that. People have taken options and written screenplays, but I've never wanted to write screenplays for my own books. There is serious interest in *Libra,* but I don't know what's going to happen there. One of these days someone is going to ask me if I want to write a screenplay for *Libra.* I guess I'll decide then.

bpNichol

The Dart, Its Arkness

David McFadden's *The Art of Darkness*

he title of this essay is a little overly contrived perhaps, but to the point. David McFadden never just throws straight at "the truth," as though only a bull's-eye will do, he keeps hitting at it from various sides and angles. And along the way the arcs of his imaginative flights illuminate whole arks for the soul, places you can enter, come in out of the rain, the storms, and claim as your own.

A case in point is his absolutely marvellous *The Art of Darkness* (1984), a book which I've kept by the side of my bed, taken with me on buses, subways, trains, planes, etc., constantly since it first came out, a good two years ago. And here I am only now taking the time to sit down and tell you about it. It's full of so many wonderful moments, wonderful hours, that I've barely known where to begin writing about it. I'm a fan. I've fallen in love with it. I've lost my heart to the way the mind is led through and into new areas of the imagination, and that's because it's a book for the

mind *and* the heart. There's a lot of stuff passes for poetry in Canada these days, and very little of it is for the intelligent heart or the feeling mind. But *The Art of Darkness* is.

There are, of course, as we've come to expect almost as our right, what we might call the "usual" McFadden poems, those marvellously witty juxtapositions of ordinary events with profound insights. Take, for example, "Country Hotel in the Niagara Peninsula," which begins with an incident in a pool hall and ends with a precise definition of the act of writing. There are funny poems which talk of deeper things, like "Velma's Giant Cinnamon Buns," poems which remind me of the time McFadden said to me, after a particularly successful reading in the late sixties, "I can make them laugh, now if I could only make them cry." And then, as if addressing that very statement I have just quoted, there are poems of such incredible frankness, such openness, like "Letter to My Father," that we wince to read them. Or poems full of the contradictions of being, like "Kitsilano Beach on a May Evening," poems that call into question the too-simple images we throw onto the screen of the word "poet."

But having said all that is only to begin to suggest the richness that is available to any reader in this wonderful book. And having said it, I want to focus on the two long poems within which the rest of the book is contained, the poems that open and close the book, "Night of Endless Radiance" and "Country of the Open Heart" — because in these poems in particular something very special is happening. I want to try to articulate my sense of it, leaving open, of course, the question of whether my sense is the author's sense.

There are a few lines in McFadden's introduction that set up what I want to explore, the essence of these two poems and, I think, the book as a whole:

Anything but total absorption in the insanities of the surface seems cowardly....

And a little later:

Love isn't all but it must take precedence over all, no matter how difficult, fraught with indignities, embarrassing and unfashionable it may be. Now as never before it's our civic duty as citizens of the world to subject ourselves to ecstasy, to go beyond and discover the new oceans of ecstasy that lie waiting for the pure pilgrims of love, and to return and talk about it indiscriminately, passionately, like a fundamentalist doorknocker.

Passion is the keynote in this whole book. McFadden's voice has often been misheard as being laconic or whimsical, but here he wears his beating heart on his sleeve and the reader can't miss it. There's a tone of high moral outrage fuelling the writing. Not that it comes through in terms of some shrillness or scolding that informs the voice-voices in these texts. Far from it. But what I mean is there's a sense of not settling for the safe line, the too-pat perception, or the recycled psychological insight. McFadden's going for the jugular in every line, and if your jugular can take it it's exhilarating. Particularly in the two long poems, where something amazing is happening. Each is concerned with the heart, as metaphor for the emotions, as beating organ, as central point, as a word among the quest for true spirituality and a coming to terms with both those terms in the lived life. But as the line quoted earlier suggested, a lot of where that's happening is right on the surface of the poem. I said he was wearing his heart on his sleeve and I meant it literally. So does McFadden. It's the country of the open heart after all. Oh!

I need to quote a long chunk of "Night of Endless Radiance" to illustrate what I'm talking about. From Part IX:

The night is afloat in the mind of the dreamer
and the one-eyed light of an approaching train
becomes an illuminating flower from heaven
and the world is a station where such glorious light
shines through occasional chinks to illustrate
the halls of hell. The radiant flower was warm,
with a passion that plunged forth courageously
into further dimensions of *awe* (the sound
the heart makes as it opens a little further).
Every day you age two days
and every night you become one day younger
for time stops when the sun goes down
and the dreamer's life falls apart
for there are too many patterns to smash
and the one pattern she wants can never be found
and the quiet path through the quiet woods
keeps branching and before the branches
reconverge her life will be all but over,
and as soon as one path is chosen it too branches
until she becomes trapped in her own originality,
lost in a grain of sand inexhaustible as a star.

For the mind works better when completely naked,
solemnly flashing in the middle of the night
like a beacon of incredible flesh, a wild blossom
blinking music into deepest space.

And the dreamer is afloat in the radiant night.
Even her phone is off the hook....

If we track the surface of this excerpt from the text we can see very clearly what's happening in both these poems. In the first place night is afloat in the mind of the dreamer. But at the beginning of the next stanza the dreamer is afloat in the radiant night. Again, at the beginning of the stanza night is afloat in the mind of the dreamer and through this night the light of an approaching train is seen. This transforms into an illuminating flower from heaven. But then, even though night is inside the mind of the dreamer, the world (presumably the one in which the dreamer sleeps) is a station (and therefore, presumably, the destination of the train) where such light shines through the chinks in the walls and illuminates the halls of hell, which are in the world which is in the mind of the dreamer. Even earlier, in Part I of the poem, the writer has described images as being:

like rays of light from stars viewed
by people on a train heading into the northern night

And this is literally true of course. Images are passed onto us through light, are part of that branch of physics, and are, at the same time, a physik for the soul. But the point is, there's that train and there's that light. And going back to that earlier notion of the station there's the statement in Part V that

... no one listens
not even the whispering crowds of time travellers

masquerading as rosy velvet puffs of consciousness
in the middle of Service Station Nightmare.

And we know the Time Traveller could be the dreamer for whom time has stopped, "for time stops when the sun goes down." Everything is part of something else. "Country of the Open Heart" first occurs as a phrase in "Night of Endless Radiance." And then the poem begins with the line: "When the phone rings in the middle of the night." Naturally there's a sleeper dreaming there whose dream it enters. Because at the end of the book, as the poem says:

... the human race has awakened and now
must reverse itself and fall asleep again —

But even though "Country of the Open Heart" grows out of "Night of Endless Radiance," "Night of Endless Radiance" is embedded within it. That earlier poem is changed by our reading of this later poem and vice versa.

It is this very porousness, the way in which images shift and transform, that allows the light in McFadden's poems to shine through. The chinks are created and through them illumination pours into the halls of hell. And McFadden is dealing with illumination, spiritual and physical, and he breaks new ground in talking of it, rhyming metaphors with a casual bravura and punning in high seriousness. When he talks of light-hearted dreams, we know what he's talking about. And when he talks of thought as "the thin king ... thinking," we see and hear the play of intelligence. McFadden doesn't just talk about *his* visions, he presents visions to us. We are not just readers then, in some old sense, but rather seers, witness to the miracles played out in front of us.

The way that phrases keep returning, as images, as new similes, is also the way in which McFadden keeps us most on our toes and teaches us to teach ourselves.

The world is transforming around us daily. It's all happening there right on the surface. Don't retreat from it. Deal with it. Or deal with whatever it is right now because tomorrow it may be different again. No such thing then as final answers. Or no easy way to blame anyone else. As McFadden points out in the fourth part of "Country of the Open Heart":

... thus in the sea, when tides are strongest,
the surface often shows its calmest face
and the agony of cruel crucifixion
lies behind the saint's beatific smile
as your writing, when it appears to be
pretending to reflect spiritual truth,
is merely moving through the nature of itself
like a snake awakening on a mild spring morning.

Let's take one other example, an example which illustrates why I'm hesitant to take this essay much further. In his introduction to the book, McFadden says, "Analysis of these poems is strictly forbidden." And in truth I've tried not to analyse the poems but rather to deal with my responses to them, what it is in them that keeps me excitedly rereading the book. But McFadden himself does not suggest a strategy for reading. At the end of the first part of "Night of Endless Radiance" the poet writes:

And there is only one test for true minds:
if they were to jump in the sea en masse
would dolphins save them
and with them on their Quasimodo shoulders
disappear in the moonless night
bound for Ancient Isles of Splendour?

And in the very next part says:

Miscellaneous crowds of apes swarm
in and out of the night like schools of dolphins
crossing imaginary equators....

I don't think there's any doubt who the apes are, but let's press on. Subsequently the poem says of the mind:

... It has an ability
to disappear, a love of appearing and disappearing
here and there....

Now I'm drawing these lines just to suggest how the mind must operate to read these poems. The true mind needs to take the leap and see if it's carried, dolphin-like, plunging into the depths, above the surface, through it, crossing imaginary equators or, as stated later, "sobbing with incontrollable sorrow." I don't think it's reading into the text to suggest that what McFadden's trying for is that interplay between surface and what lies below the surface while at the same time avoiding the locating of the term "depth" in any naïve geographical or physiological location. The very way the location of the mind shifts in these poems suggests that.

It's human passion this work is full of. McFadden doesn't want the poem to be just one thing, he wants it to be all things full of feelings, good and bad, of wit, wisdom, spiritual revelation, of detestable emotions you'd rather hide under the nearest rock. He knows you need to admit them all if you want to break through into the country of the open heart.

"You need another line here. That'll do."

LAWRENCE GARBER

Looking Back at James Jones

n *Viet Journal,* the second-to-last work James Jones published before his death in 1977 at age fifty-five, there is recorded one of the most poignant moments in modern American literature. Poignant, that is, for Jonesians everywhere. On his way home from a writing assignment in Viet Nam where he witnessed the final phase of U.S. involvement there — an old soldier assessing a new kind of war — Jones made an unplanned stop in Hawaii. It was late March, 1973, thirty-one years since he had last seen these islands as an infantryman at Schofield barracks, twenty-two years since he had made claim to them as his own mythical territory in *From Here to Eternity*. He was nearing fifty-two, already beginning his slow death of congestive heart failure, a craggy, middle-aged ruin of the fierce cock-of-the-walk he had once been; and this was his *nostos,* a return of Odyssean magnitude to the one spiritual home that had permanently scored his consciousness (and ours), that had made all his literature possible, that had set his attitudes for life.

It is not given to many to have such a place to return to, one that resonates so clearly and painfully with a sense of genesis, and Jones records the compulsion to re-enter his past as if under the sway of siren-songs: "I had not been in Viet Nam more than a week, before I knew I was going to do it. And once I had made up my mind, it seemed I had known all along that I would go. That I could not not go. A sounding of Recall. The song 'Jamaican Farewell' was much in my mind...." In *The White Album,* Joan Didion has written that Hawaii belongs to Jones in the same way that Kilimanjaro belongs to Hemingway and Oxford, Mississippi, to Faulkner: places not only of sources but of recapitulations, terrains for discovering where we have gone *because* we have never quite left them. In Honolulu, on Waikiki, at Schofield barracks, Jones retraced his steps, seeking out what remained of his youth, "a certain twenty-two-year-old boy, walking along Kalakaua Avenue in a 'gook' shirt." It was something akin to the seven stations of the cross for the man who had written the finest army novel in the language while still in his twenties: the Royal Hawaiian Hotel (preserve of officers), the New Senator Hotel (where Lorene in *Eternity* had worked as a prostitute), Wu Fat's Chinese restaurant (where Maggio had gone

HAWAIIAN MAIDENS.

increasingly depressed as he saw how the landscape had altered, the farms and cattle ranges gone, the bulldozers and earthmoving equipment at work extending the Lunalilo Freeway. It had been at Makapuu Point in November of 1941 — a month before the Japanese attack on Pearl Harbour — that Jones's F Company had dug five pill-boxes into the cliff rocks, and now, suddenly, as Jones got closer, "the constantly starting and stopping cars ... seemed no longer to be there.... A curtain had dropped behind me, cutting me off from them, and with a kind of frightened, awed wonder I stood looking at a scene that had not changed one grass blade since I had last looked at it thirty years before." Then a further miracle of sorts happened and Jones was not merely encountering the landscape of his past but, for a brief awesome moment, reliving it as the young man he had once been:

My feet started carrying me up the complex of faded paths as surely as though they knew the way before my eyes did.... They were all there. All five of them. I stood in each of them a long time, looking out and remembering times when late at night I had sat behind machine-guns in all of them, staring out into the dark toward Rabbit Island and the beach that faced it. When I came up out of the last one and started back down, I looked down and automatically placed my foot on a natural step in the rock that we had always used to climb in or out. It was still there, unchanged, uneroded, unchipped. And my foot still knew where it was. I stood staring down at it for several seconds, shocked, and when I looked back up and looked down the hill at the tourists and the clustered cars, it was as if I were back in 1942, when the overlook was empty, peering forward into an unforeseeable future when it would be open and crowded with sightseers, as it was now. The only thing that was different was that I was alone, that there was nobody with me.

off guard duty and into the stockade), the Waialae Golf Course (where Prewitt had been killed trying to return to his unit), the Post Library where Jones himself had first read Thomas Wolfe's *Look Homeward, Angel* and knew instantly that he had been a writer all his life without having yet written a word. One has to understand that Jones's return at fifty-two to the setting of his first novel was a return for all of us who had been moved and turned by that great work: a kind of communal *nostos* for a generation that had discovered in Jones the perfect voice of revolt and conscience.

But during this tour, Jones was disturbed, too, by all the things that had changed of the world he had known and understood and a profound sense of futility and loss shades his account. Something to do as well with the scorched veteran of life he had become, with the personal and literary wars he had fought and lost and drawn since the heady days of his first success. Then, on the day of his departure, the climactic moment: that morning he drove out to Makapuu Head, for "something kept telling me I shouldn't miss Makapuu." On the way there, Jones became

276

But Jones wasn't alone. As one of the millions of readers who had read *From Here to Eternity* in the fifties and thrilled to its realistic depiction of the peacetime army and the tragic rituals of honour and comradeship, and as one of the considerably fewer who held onto the faith over the years that Jones was unique, an American original, whose gifts were instinctive rather than learned (like a Joe Louis, a Rocky Marciano), I like to think that Jones's lonely *nostos* was a shareable thing, that he had built a spiritual landscape in his work so textured and tactile that it could be inhabited permanently like all the great houses of fiction. The real estate of Elysium. Many would disagree, and I must admit that my own perspective on Jones and his accomplishments has long ago passed beyond the critical and into something resembling a personal graph. In the way of an unofficial apostle, I tend to see all of his many flaws and complexes and limitations as the weaves in a larger, bolder tapestry. Certainly, after the great success of *Eternity*, his reputation suffered considerably (the price for writing an early great novel must always be paid in America, Jones himself knew); from *Some Came Running* onwards, critical perceptions of his work were variously lukewarm and cruel, and eventually dismissive. The point has always been, though, that either Jones's impact on his readers was immediate and personal, or not at all. It has to do with the kind of writer he was, digging directly into his own wounds for material, making absolutely no attempt to compromise or camouflage his own obsessions, never playing it safe. That, above all else, is why he appealed so powerfully to me and a whole generation still in their teens when *From Here to Eternity* appeared in 1951. Even then, at the height of his early fame, winner of a National Book Award, the last author to be edited by Maxwell Perkins at Scribner's, growing rich, there were those who thought of his world view as basically adolescent,

filled with half-baked philosophies, narrow macho codes and the residues of his own sexual frustration. The truth was that at the deepest psychological level he had tapped into the fundamental crises of untried youth and the response, particularly of my generation, had been profound and overwhelming. No other novel of the time was more fantasized over than this one.

I can remember bothering my father to drive me down to Coles bookstore at Yonge and Charles in downtown Toronto when I was fourteen to buy a copy of the first paperback printing of *From Here to Eternity* with its famous black-and-red bugle cover. I knew that they would not have sold me, over the counter, this hesitant, skinny kid with brushcut and glasses, such a sizzling work, and my father had to go in to buy it for me. I sat in the car waiting, with the motor running. I can to this day still inhale the smell of that fresh Signet pulp paper, like the scent of oil on leather. I remember the following summer when I first tried my hand at a novel, a fifteen-year-old's version of Jones's epic, sitting in our backyard on Rostrevor Road, writing in longhand on long yellow sheets an army novel called *The Boovermak Episode,* which ran to three hundred pathetic pages and managed to recycle every relationship, incident and tragic nuance of the original. I remember that when I first went to Paris in 1962 I would gravitate regularly to the Ile St. Louis where Jones and his family lived in a remarkable apartment at 10 Quai d'Orleans overlooking the Seine; circling the area, I would sometimes linger in the narrow rue Budé in front of the heavy entrance doors wondering if I would ever muster the courage to push the buzzer and pay my respects. I never did, though Jones was known to be a notoriously easy touch and extraordinarily generous to people like myself, aspiring young writers without credentials. I became an habitué of Shakespeare and Company, an untidy little bookstore across the river, because I knew that Jones sometimes dropped around to scour the shelves or attend cocktail parties in the upstairs quarters. George Whitman, an American, who still runs it, was equally generous to young people going for broke in the land of Hemingway; there was free coffee on a hot plate upstairs, chairs and sofas for reading, corners for down-and-outers to sleep in overnight; if you reshelved a book with your bookmark still in place George wouldn't sell it until you had finished. The sort of place Jones would've liked, unpretentious, fundamental, open-ended. I met him there one afternoon, at last, as he browsed along the narrow corridors of shelves. He was square-bodied, lantern-jawed, fierce-looking: not a big man but he gave the impression of compacted power that went all the way to his eyes. I managed to push out something, half-greeting, half-tribute, and he nodded, and that was it, sadly. And I remembered an hour's conversation with Mary McCarthy in London, Ontario, a few years after his death, when she spoke of his problems as a writer and virtues as a man. I ought to have paid him a call in Paris, she said; he was good at that sort of thing. Strangers who buzzed him up from the rue Budé often stayed for dinner.

After the terrific impact I had experienced with *From Here to Eternity*, I took to following his career as closely as I have any writer's. At the broadcast publicity level, that wasn't difficult since Jones was perhaps the first post-World War II writer to achieve international celebrity, to sign blockbuster multi-deal contracts, to live out the dream of the rich and famous American artist living in Europe, wintering in Klosters, Switzerland, scuba-diving in Greece and the Bahamas, establishing at his residence in Paris a gathering place for expatriates where the weekly Saturday evening parties were legendary. He was regarded as a cultural phenomenon by the media right from the start, good copy this heartland American ex-soldier boy who

marched brashly into Max Perkins's office at Scribner's, carrying his manuscript in a box, demanding attention; who had written the most exciting novel of the decade while crossing America in a trailer; who kept a vast collection of guns and knives and knew how to use them; who boxed for real, and was photographed by *Life* in his fencing outfit, daring the fates to take him on. Norman Mailer called him the most naturally gifted author of his generation, Ed Murrow interviewed him on "Person to Person," and the somewhat misleading myth of the noble savage who had seized his moment and confounded the establishment began. It was a trap the extent of which Jones only realized later, but it was the sort of story — helped along at the time by Jones himself — that proved as fascinating to the public as the big novel he had produced.

And, of course, every subsequent book he wrote I bought and devoured, even when the reviews ran thin and wicked: the 1,266-page *Some Came Running* (1957), the most exhaustive study of mid-western America in the language; the jewel-precisioned war novella, *The Pistol* (1959); the scuba-diving study of masculinity and its illusions, *Go to the Widow-Maker* (1967); the short-story collection, *The Ice Cream Headache* (1968), containing some pre-*Eternity* material that dealt with the pain of coming of age in the middle of America; his misfiring novel built around the Paris student revolution of 1968, *The Merry Month of May* (1971); his gutsy excursion into the hardboiled detective genre à la Chandler and Hammett, *A Touch of Danger* (1973); and his two non-fiction war books, *Viet Journal* (1974) and *WWII* (1975), the latter an informal history of the war ostensibly written to accompany reproductions of war art but containing perhaps the best account of the Pacific theatre from the combat soldier's point of view. Most of all, there was the war trilogy, the first and final books of which enveloped his career and defined his life. Eleven years after *From*

Here to Eternity came *The Thin Red Line* (1962), considered to be the best combat novel since *The Red Badge of Courage,* and then the last book of the trilogy, so long delayed, that he was so desperately working on at his death, *Whistle* (1978), published posthumously, its final sections dictated on his deathbed. Fearing not death so much as *not finishing*.

But there was a lot I didn't know about Jones that anyone interested in the significance of his life and work would want to know. Frank MacShane's biography, *Into Eternity* — the first full biography — gives a needed shape and scope to that life and measures the man and the oeuvre in a way which makes no larger claims than his achievements justify or that Jones himself would have wanted. "The Life of James Jones, American Writer" is the subtitle of MacShane's book, and it is in Jones's quintessential Americanness, in his roots and in the curve of his career, that MacShane finds his theme:

> James Jones's story is American to the bone.... [There was an] almost mythic quality [to] his rise from obscurity.... He had appeared like a comet from the heart of America, and he wrote with a directness and a truthfulness that recalled such distinctly American writers as Walt Whitman and Mark Twain. No one before had quite expressed Jones's vision of America as a country of people torn between optimism and cynicism.... Jones felt the naked and desperate energy this fundamental schism created in American life, and he was therefore able to evoke a response in his readers that few of his contemporaries could match.... A man with the most ordinary of names, he was interested in the most ordinary of people.... The intimacy of the provincial world in which he grew up made him see how intensely emotional human relations really are.

Yet while in large part MacShane's biography is a

tribute to the kind of man and writer Jones was, it is by no means a panegyric; if Jones was a diamond-in-the-rough, a forceful, compelling literary jock, his character was nevertheless deeply flawed. He was obstinate and crude, fascinated with violence, obsessed with the reaches of his own masculinity, individualistic to the point of dismissing most received wisdom on principle, irretrievably suspicious of intellectuals and of all forms of political activism (one cause of his falling out with Mailer), a drinker, a fighter, a bully, scornful of writers like Proust, Lawrence or James whom he considered "effete" and corruptive (his favourites were Kipling and Conrad), and mistrustful of women (he married at thirty-six, before which he preferred the uncomplicated company of prostitutes). MacShane's ordering of his materials demonstrates not only how Jones combatted and struggled through these warps and limitations in his personal life, but how, at the bravest level of self-awareness, he utilized them as an integral part of his work. Indeed, Jones is frequently depicted as a classically fissured personality, a textbook American paradox in whom toughness and generosity, sentiment and cynicism, conservatism and rebelliousness, compromise and integrity operated in uneasy, troubling relationship. No one was more personally respected and admired among his contemporaries than Jones, a man of deep emotional attachments and loyalties, of roisterous charm and genuineness; yet his volatile nature also rendered him unpredictable and capable at times of surprising meanness and impatience. Jones's personality was in this way a battleground, an explosive field of shifting, contrary pulls: a war within that permitted him to understand so well those other wars he fought as soldier and author. The appeal of such explosiveness and self-division to a generation born into blandness is obvious. Equally appealing is that throughout his career Jones attempted to resolve this fissure by creating in his books two central figures who could represent his own disturbing two-sidedness: Robert E. Lee Prewitt and Milt Warden, Dave Hirsh and 'Bama Dillert, Jonathan Hartley and Harry Gallagher — idealists and cynics, rebels and compromisers. Jones even resurrected his three major figures from *Eternity* (Prewitt, Warden, Stark) and made them principals (under new names) in his other trilogy novels in order to trace their development and, by implication, his own in terms of the conflicts that had shaped his life. Mac-Shane views this as an imaginatively creative act, a refusal to let go of the demons; and it is certainly true that few writers have been as scrupulous in confronting the big existential issues on the one hand and the narrow psychic debilities on the other that make humans perform as compulsively as they do.

MacShane's treatment of Jones goes some way towards solving various puzzles that have always mystified me concerning his entrenched attitudes. Why are Jones's fictional women, for instance, so unfinished as characters compared to the intensity and depth of his male figures? A soldier's world, of course, is a predominantly male realm, but even in his "civilian" novels like *Some Came Running* or *The Merry Month of May* women are dealt with in remarkably stereotypical terms, often as insidious Circe figures, endangering masculine honour and integrity. The facts of Jones's background and rearing explains a lot here. He was born on November 6, 1921, in Robinson, Illinois, to parents already in their mid-thirties. As a boy he was neither as large nor as athletic as his older brother Jeff, had weak eyes, wore glasses, failed at organized sports and possessed small hands; he "quickly found that the best defence was to be aggressive and he began to abandon his natural gentleness for a more aggressive attitude." Out of frustration and anger, he became a rebellious figure at school where "he was unpopular with his classmates ... because he always

RIDING THE SURF WAIKIKI, HONOLULU

compared unfavourably with his brother," a naturally gifted athlete. The cult of masculinity that pervades his early work can be seen to have its origins here, in his need to prove his strength of character, and to turn his essential loneliness and sense of inadequacy into a principle of independence. His relationship to his mother is another key to his attitudes regarding women and sexuality, for one of Jones's greatest themes revolved around the notion of American sexual maladjustment. She was tough on him from the first and he disliked her intensely. In a letter to his brother in 1967, he remembered her as "totally selfish, totally self-centred, and totally whining and full of self-pity ... she was also basically stupid." MacShane writes that "in later years, Jones went out of his way to make sure he did not emulate her in any way and occasionally blamed her for shortcomings in his own life. Undoubtedly she affected his attitude towards women, making him cautious and mistrustful." When he was dying of congestive heart failure (she had died of the same disease in 1941), he went so far as to curse her memory for having willed him what he considered to be a hereditary weakness. Her influence on his sexual attitudes was even more direct:

> One day, discovering that he was masturbating, she told him that if he continued to do so, his hand would turn black. For a while he stopped, but as the fear of his hand turning black receded, he started again. After discovering him in the act one night, his mother waited until he fell asleep and then went into his room and rubbed black shoe polish into the palm of his hand.

It is a curious thing, though, that however much he found commitment to women difficult, they tended to direct his life in powerful ways. The second important woman whose influence shaped his attitudes was Lowney Handy, a figure who is one of the more bizarre minor footnotes in the history of American literature, and out of whose character Jones later drew a devastating portrait in *Go to the Widow-Maker*. Also a resident of Robinson, Illinois, she was forty years old, seventeen years Jones's senior, when he moved in with her and her husband in 1944 following his discharge from the army. Lowney saw in Jones the makings of a great writer and herself as a kind of midwife to literature whose essential task was to provide the proper atmosphere and training for her protégés, of which Jones was the first. She became his mistress, apparently with her husband's approval, not so much out of love or even promiscuity, but as "a charitable act," servicing Jones's sexual needs so that he could give his full attention to his writing. This was typical of Lowney's views regarding the creative imagination and she was, in every way, a woman of fixed, dogmatic ideas concerning art, sex, philosophy. Her plan from the beginning was to develop Jones as a person "so that he would be capable of writing the novel she sensed was in him, struggling to get out." She was self-taught, attracted to the individualism of the American transcendentalists, convinced that only the most spartan regimens could push an artist into producing great work. For fifteen years she dominated Jones's life and thinking, taught him how to overcome and re-channel personal bitterness and private anger, and managed to transform his earlier "adolescent" yearning for an ideal woman's love into something pragmatic and cynical: "Under Lowney's tutelage, he lost his former yearning for a woman to love, and now looked upon sex simply as a biological urge that needed occasional tending." Women, love, marriage, were the enemies of artistic freedom, she counselled, entrapments that diminished male energy, sapped and distracted from creative power.

After the enormous success of *Eternity*, Jones helped Lowney found her famous "Colony," a barracks-like compound in Marshall, Illinois, where aspiring young writers were made to live in austere, minimal conditions, follow her instructions to the letter and go through a form of physical and mental training devised to release their fundamental masculine nature (belching, farting and coarse language at the table was encouraged). The Colony and its rules became legendary and *Life* magazine did a nine-page spread — called "James Jones and His Angel" — on the experiment. It was run on Spartan principles reminiscent of the army: there was a special diet for colonists based on Lowney's study of Yoga, 6:30 a.m. rising, lights out at 8 p.m., no newspapers or radio, no women members or female visitors, physical labour in the afternoon, exercises in copying out word for word the published works of masters like Hemingway, Faulkner and Jones himself (a practice based on Lowney's theory of "osmosis"), and fifty dollars a month for a trip to the whores in Terre Haute. This "literary boot camp" was intended to purge the colonists of ego, to develop the discipline and self-knowledge necessary to write important work which meant, Lowney preached, ridding themselves of all external relationships and ambition. She encourages her young men to renounce family, marriage and emotional relations and all "sissyfying" Proustian impulses were discouraged by the threat of instant expulsion. Jones was, of course, cock of the walk at the Colony, absolved from many strictures, and at the centre of a world he could control. *Eternity* was, naturally, the model all colonists aspired to. But gradually even he began to realize Lowney's limitations and the limited life that was offered there — a perverse extension of the regimentations of the Schofield barracks — an escape from the sort of emotional responsibilities that came with fuller, freer relationships he had been schooled to mistrust. And for all Lowney's messianic zeal, history will record that not a single significant novel ever came out of the Colony; only Tom Chamales' *Never So Few* is remembered at all.

Jones's escape from Lowney's domination was one of those difficult, bloody breakouts that characterized most of his choices; but the woman who replaced her, actress Gloria Mosolino, whom he married in 1957, gave a domestic and social order to his life that broke

ROYAL HAWAIIAN BAND·

the pattern of barracks regimentation he had compulsively maintained since his army days in Hawaii. Gloria was a beauty (she had been a stand-in for Marilyn Monroe during the filming of *The Seven Year Itch*) from a slightly shady Mafia family in Pottsville, Pennsylvania; she was stubborn and strong in the Jones mould, a party-girl and gambler, and there is something of Bogart and Bacall in the fireworks they generated in their first years together. That marriage brought out new and surprising aspects of Jones; it certainly gave him a healthier perspective concerning his own masculinity, muted the violent streak in him, and established him at the centre of a more stable circle than he had ever known. Paris became their home for seventeen years where Jones discovered himself playing mentor and pater familias to countless expatriate Americans passing through. And because of his own unstable childhood and lack of strong bonds with his parents (his father had committed suicide when Jones was in the army), he was determined to provide a settled, happy environment for his own two children, Kaylie and Jaimie. In this phase of his life, grounded in a kind of island domesticity, Jones was able to push beyond the sacrosanct rituals of male bonding in his work and in *Go to the Widow-Maker,* his fourth novel, he could take an ironic and even comical view of those macho codes and anxieties that had been so deeply embedded in the sweats of *Eternity.*

But as MacShane's skilled deployment of his materials shows, Jones, for all the powerful women in his life, had been shaped by the army and it never left him. His work ethic and discipline were impressive; the collection of knives and guns was oiled and tended with the fastidiousness of a man who still needed to believe that his survival depended on them; the Friday evening poker games that eventually replaced the Saturday night parties at 10 Quai d'Orleans were boisterous and risky and in them was something of the gambling pits that he had known in Honolulu and at Schofield barracks. Yet if he had been shaped by war, he also knew how to revise that experience, how to give heroism another name. He had won the Purple Heart at Guadalcanal but he had never been under any illusions about the nature of courage. A Japanese soldier he had bayonetted to death had caught him unawares defecating in the jungle and their grapplings had a dark gallows humour to it; the "wound" that brought him home in the middle of the Pacific campaign was a bad ankle suffered during a football game scrimmage; his discharge from the army in 1944 had been prompted by a series of psychiatric reports that found him mentally unfit for further combat. Like Stephen Crane before him, Jones was determined to be absolutely authentic in his report of similar men in extremis, to see fear and hopelessness as the twin dynamos that propelled millions of infantrymen through the shadow of the valley. The interwoven subtitle to *WWII* is "Evolution of a Soldier," and Jones's war novels can themselves be seen to evolve from prelude (*Eternity*) to combat (*The Thin Red Line*) to aftermath (*Whistle*). In each case, heroism suffers a further diminishment from its customary meaning. It is a cynical view that less and less romanticizes its own sense of grief; and in the final pages of that last novel at the end of his life, the recycled version of Prewitt, Warden, Fife and Stark find no way out of their misfit states except through suicide and madness.

MacShane offers a further surprise to those (myself included) who always viewed Jones as a primitive operating on a gut instinct for the authentic in human relationships. It had long been a cherished belief of mine that Jones was a natural in every sense, that even his trademark stylistic awkwardness was somehow a confirmation of the instinctive straight-shooter I conceived him as being. It turns out, however, that Jones's conscious literary ambitions were much higher than most gave him credit for. In preparing for *From Here to Eternity*, for instance, he steeped himself in Tolstoy's *War and Peace* and Stendahl's *The Charterhouse of Parma*, turning to epic models where the army itself had served as a microcosm of society. "He was eager to render the modern army as they [these authors] had rendered the armies of the preceding century. He knew that in the modern age military conflict had to be presented in modern terms, but he wanted to preserve the scale of the great nineteenth-century novels to which he hoped it would compared." He also experimented with language in *Eternity*, dispensing with apostrophes to get closer to the spoken language "where punctuation marks dont exist;" and he deliberately devised an ungrammatically awkward prose to reflect the characters of his men and the world they inhabited, "to achieve a rhythm that would carry the emotional burden of what he was saying."

Jones's literary ambitions were certainly never small; only Thomas Wolfe before him in this century had possessed such an epic impulse for the grand, sweeping view. In *Some Came Running,* Jones claimed that he wanted "to do for the great American myth and illusion of romantic love what Cervantes did for the myth and illusion of chivalry." When he finished that work, he posed for *Life* magazine with his twenty-three-hundred manuscript pages: "It was more than two feet thick, and Jones could barely hold it." For Jones the epic vision had to be made a tactile thing, dependent as much on literal weightiness as on great designs. Jones called this work his most misunderstood; no work by an author has ever received more vicious reviews. Yet *Running* is technically his most adventurous novel. Who would have guessed, for instance, that Jones had been influenced by the impressionist experiments of Flaubert and Ford Madox Ford? Yet Jones attempted to work a variation of *le style indirect libre* into his narratorial strategies in *Running,* using devices "intended to break down the barrier that traditionally exists between the language of the narrator and the language of the characters. He believed that the abrupt change between colloquial dialogue and formal narrative was jolting, [and] he tried to reproduce in storytelling the quasi-grammatical circumlocutions he thought typical of midwestern speech and thought." MacShane ranks *Some Came Running* — despite its structural flaws and tonal inconsistencies — with the work of Andersen, Wolfe and Steinbeck in portraying "the feelings and beliefs of a hitherto unrecorded segment of the American population ... allowed to speak with an honesty and directness" uncommon in literature. In fact, every novel that Jones wrote was carefully conceived at the most erudite levels. *The Thin Red Line,* a combat novel modelled partly on Stendhal and partly on the Battle of Borodino section of *War and Peace,* was "meant to go further than either of those books in emphasizing the absurdity of war while concentrating on the personal side of combat and on enlisted men rather than officers." To capture that personal side, Jones developed another special narrative technique: "The story is told from the point of view of an omniscient narrator; but without breaking the rhythm of the narrative, Jones switches into the head of an individual soldier so that the reader has simultaneously an overall view of what is happening." Jones as a Joycean? The notion is mind-boggling, yet he is revealed as a disciplined craftsman throughout his writing life, charged with the sense of literary tradition, pushing himself into difficult technical ranges, later influenced by the theories of Robert Ardrey and Tielhard de Chardin whose ideas he approached with a freshness and even a naïveté inherent in his larger suspicion of all doctrinaire systems.

As in many an American fable, he came home to America to die. In 1974, he accepted an appointment at the Florida International University (Miami) as part-time visiting professor in creative writing. At a salary of $27,500 (for a writer who averaged between $160,000 and 200,000 a year) he conducted seminars and offered pithy, epigrammatic advice:

Show me the sympathetic insurance man. Everybody suffers.

The key is to catch the main character on the cusp of change.

Keep your first drafts.

A lot of American girls have built-in chaperones.

Jones's decision to return to America was partly the result of having felt himself to have been a tourist in France for seventeen years; he had never learned the language properly, had had little to do with French literary circles (he considered the *nouvelle vague* creatively bankrupt), never troubled to understand the complex nuances of French society, and eventually saw "how artificial his relationship to France had been. Such cultural loneliness has been self-induced, of course; he loved Paris as a city and the life-style it could offer him, but like many Americans living in Europe, he worked around the culture that was not his won, preferring the role of uninvolved witness which is another form of freedom. Eventually, though, that sense of distance — which had produced *The Merry Month of May* — made him anxious to re-enter the American experience which has seeded his finest work, and after Florida, Jones and family settled in a farmhouse in Sagaponack, Long Island, where the race to finish *Whistle* was almost won.

He died at 7:45 p.m., May 9, 1977. All those who had been weaned on his fiction took the loss badly.

The novel that we knew he had long planned on the gypsy jazz guitarist Django Reinhardt would never be written. At the funeral service, old friends like William Styron and Irwin Shaw and Willie Morris delivered moving eulogies. The most highly regarded bugler in the army — arranged for by Senator Edward Kennedy — played taps. It had been a brave death; alert and working on *Whistle* almost to the very end, he had sat on the edge of his hospital bed with tubes attached to his body, knowing that his heart could fail at any moment, dictating to Willie Morris in a faint voice the ends he had planned for those other soldiers, Prewitt, Warden, Stark, he understood so well. Dying himself and swiftly, he guided them into death with him.

There is an anecdote which touches nicely on what Jones means to me. It occurs about two-thirds of the way through MacShane's masterly biography. In Paris,

After a quarrel in the car that made Jones walk away and leave Gloria to drive home alone, she became so flustered that she couldn't get the motor to start. When

a policeman arrived, she explained the situation by saying *"Mon mari est en chaleur."* Surprised, the policeman helped to get the car started and said, "Madame, you are very fortunate. I advise you to hurry home at once."

There is a great deal of truth in that malapropism, for Jones was always a writer in heat, never letting up on the intensity with which he confronted the big issues, never retreating from the larger questions a writer can ask. If he lacked the smoother skills of his immediate contemporaries, the daring political consciousness of Mailer, the narrative controls of Styron, the stylistic graces of Capote or Mathiessen, there was still a genuineness, a largesse, a particular rage to his work that made him an American original. What Thomas Wolfe had been for Jones, Jones became for much of a generation growing up in the fifties.

I definitely should have pushed that buzzer in the rue Budé.

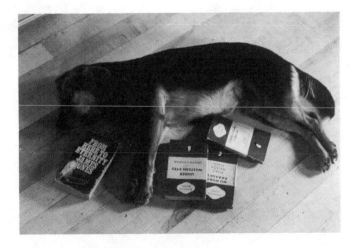

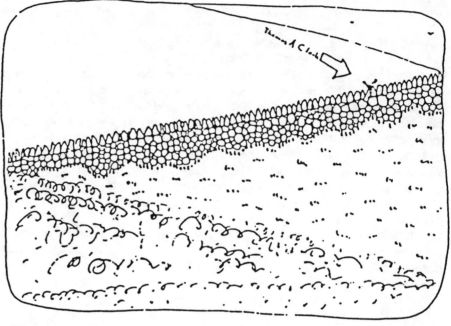

ECSTATIC VICTOR THOMAS A CLARK IS

SEEN HERE AT VICTORY MOMENT ON ROCKNESS HILL
IN NON-ANNUAL GLOUCESTER FOUND ODE CONTEST.
A LOST BOTTLE OF COLOGNE PROVIDED CLARK WITH
THE CRUCIAL PUN FOR HIS MARCH 31st 1979 TRIUMPH.
OTHER CONTESTANTS INCLUDED LAURIE CLARK, JOHN
FURNIVAL, ASTRID FURNIVAL + FRENCH HOPE HENRI
CHOPIN.

•3 in a series of lively literary events

C'MON KIDS! CLIP THEM! SAVE THEM! TRADE THEM!

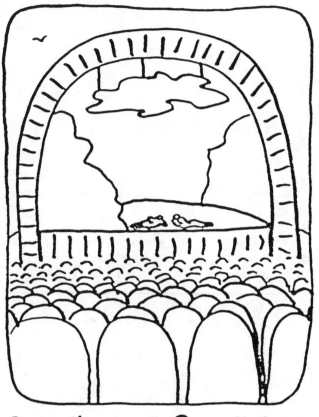

David Young and David McFadden relax on stage between rehearsals of their "Meeting Gene Kelly" number from the stage version of BRUSHES WITH GREATNESS. #7 in a series of Lively Lit Footlites. Save The Set!!

bill bissett is lone attendee at the Hundred Mile House's Syntactic Drift and Other Mush Colloquium, February 1988. #8 in the collectible series on our Lively Literary Legacy.

An Interview With Alice Munro

achtel: I'd like to go right back to the beginning. What is your earliest memory?

Munro: It's such a rural memory, you'll think I'm making it up. I remember standing — I was too small to look over the wall of the pig-pen, but I had climbed up on the boards, and I was peering over, watching my uncle feed the pigs.

Wachtel: You grew up on a turkey and fox farm.

Munro: It was a fox farm when I was a very small child. Then it became a fox and mink farm. After World War II, people didn't wear fox furs any more. Nobody minded the idea of wearing fur, but fox furs became unfashionable. So we went out of business, and my father became a poultry farmer — chickens, then turkeys.

Wachtel: When did you know you wanted to be a writer?

Munro: I really can't quite remember. I think when I was about ten or eleven. Before that, I would tell myself stories a lot, and I would make up endings — for stories that didn't satisfy me.

Wachtel: These were stories you were told or that you read, and you didn't like the way they ended, so you —

Munro: *The Little Mermaid* is the one I chiefly remember, because it has a *horribly* unhappy ending. She changes into foam on the sea, she doesn't get a soul — she doesn't get the prince *or* a soul. I thought that was just very hard luck.

Wachtel: What did you do to her, do you remember?

Munro: I think I gave her the prince. I don't think I worried about the soul!

Wachtel: Very telling!

Munro: Then I used to think about being a movie star. I used to make up a lot of movie stories that I would be in. Somehow, from the movie-star bit, I slid into the writing-things-down bit. I started writing poetry and then stories. I was into it quite thoroughly by the time I was twelve.

Wachtel: You told me that you come from an environment that is inhospitable to writers, that doesn't honour writers.

Munro: Pretty much, yes. I'm a descendant of a pioneer family. There are quite sensible ideas in such families, that it's very important for people to know how to do physical work. So I was trained to do domestic jobs, as the most important thing that I would ever have to do. Also I lived in an environment where there weren't labour-saving devices. There weren't for a lot of people. We didn't have running water or anything like that. The idea was that I would have to learn to work hard. We all read in our house, but it was seen as a luxury, something you did when everything else was done. There were stories in the community about women who had become readers, in the way that they might take up drinking. And how the men would come in from the fields, and there would be cold grease in the frying-pan, and no dinner ready, and under the bed there would be fluff-balls as big as your head, and it would all be because the women read! I've no doubt this happened. That kind of reading was probably a total escape. They probably read romances and things about royalty and stuff like that. The sort of stuff I like to read sometimes myself.

Wachtel: So it was very iconoclastic to think you could be a writer, in that environment.

Munro: I didn't think about that. I very early on got the notion that my real life had to be hidden, had to be protected. I didn't think you could go to your teacher or your parents, and tell them what you really thought about anything. I knew that was a bad idea. So I got used to this quite early. I didn't need encouragement or reassurance. I just, I suppose, lived a very deceptive life. But it didn't bother me.

Wachtel: You said once that there's a betrayal involved in leaving home, especially if you're from a working-class family, because you begin to talk differently —

Munro: Yes.

Wachtel: And that you feel guilty about that.

Munro: Certainly it isn't one of my major guilts. I've got bigger ones. But it does make a gap. It used to be, I think, that class divisions were a little more definite than they are now. There is still a different way of talking, though it's not so pronounced. In some places in Britain, for instance, if you left home and got a BBC accent, and then went back, people would not care for that. But you do become a different person in a lot of superficial ways, to make yourself acceptable in the world away from home. You were apt to feel perhaps a bit of a phony, I suppose, when you went back home. Who are you then? Which person? How do you talk? Usually, I take on protective coloration very readily, without having to think about it. So there isn't a big conflict. I generally do what is expected.

Wachtel: One of the titles of your books is *Who Do You Think You Are?* which is a reprimand, about the inescapability of your background or your hometown.

Munro: Yes. I find this very interesting and complicated. I think, in the story, the first time someone says "Who do you think you are?" it's a teacher reprimanding a student in class, for trying to shine, to show off. I was brought up to think that that is absolutely the worst thing you could do. I don't know if this has a Scottish background, or a Presbyterian background or — it seems to me it's rather Canadian. It wasn't confined to my background. So "Who do you think you are?" comes the minute you begin to let out a little bit of who you would like to be, as soon as you start sort of constructing somebody that is yourself. Of course we all construct ourselves. So there's always a little worry about this. Are you trying to shine? I think most of us would rather undergo punishment — up to a fairly severe kind — than ridicule. It's so difficult to think that you may be acting foolishly. I think that keeps a lot of people from trying this self-construction business.

Wachtel: You've had a lot of different jobs on the way to becoming a writer. There are several that surprised me. One was picking tobacco?

Munro: Yes, I picked tobacco. Actually, I didn't

pick tobacco, because I wasn't skilled enough. I would have got more pay had I graduated to being a tobacco-picker. I picked the suckers that grow from the top of the tobacco leaf and prevent the sunlight from getting at the leaf. They have to be plucked off while the tobacco is still growing, before the leaf is ready to be picked. You go up and down the rows of tobacco all day doing that, and black, tarry, sticky stuff comes out of the stem and covers you from top to bottom! Yes, I did that.

Wachtel: When was this?

Munro: When I was at university, one of the summers. And I also waitressed one summer. Everybody's waitressed. One summer before that, when I was a high-school girl, I was a servant — I guess an all-purpose servant — for a family in Rosedale.

Wachtel: Which is a posh part of Toronto.

Munro: Yes. At that time, it was thought that country girls made good servants, which they *did*. I knew how to *do* a lot of things that most sixteen-year-old girls didn't know how to do. I was fetched down from the country. I worked all summer in this environment. I didn't like it.

Wachtel: It sounds like a Victorian novel! Pluck the country girl and plop her into this upper-class home. What was that experience like? Did it get any of your writing antennae sharpened?

Munro: Oh, certainly. It was probably a very important experience that way, because I saw all sorts of class things. I thought I knew a lot, because I had read a lot, but I really had hardly any experience. I was a very naïve person in some ways. Being a servant in a household, for one thing, you see things about you and them — the barrier — which totally surprised me. Then you see things about them that they don't show to people who are their equals, because the ideal servant has no eyes or ears. But I had them!

Wachtel: Did anything you filed away surface later in any of your writing?

Munro: Yes, I wrote a story about that, in *Dance of the Happy Shades*. I think the story's called "Sunday Afternoon." It's a very early story, it's not that great, but it came out of that experience.

Wachtel: You're the eldest of three children?

Munro: Yes, I am.

Wachtel: Did that give you a sense of extra responsibility? How do you think that affected you?

Munro: It gave me a certain amount of bossiness! Which I conceal some of the time. I was five years older than my brother and six years older than my sister. I had a wonderful time. I thought I was bringing them up in the way they should go. They have a different idea about this, I think. I enjoyed it, and I had a sense of power. I had to do a lot of housework, because my mother became ill by the time I was eleven or twelve, so I was doing fairly heavy work in my teens. But that really was fine. It gave me a great sense of achievement, responsibility. Bossing people around, saying "Don't track dirt over that floor, I've just scrubbed it," and all those things. So it was much easier than being a teenager who was expected to do *chores,* under someone's supervision. I got to be the boss.

Wachtel: Like playing house.

Munro: Yes, thoroughly hard, though. You couldn't quit if you got bored!

Wachtel: You said the first *real* story you ever wrote was about your mother. It was called "The Peace of Utrecht." It was about the death of a mother. The title story in your new book, *Friend of My Youth,* is about a woman who's thinking about her mother, who's died young. Or, as it's put in the story, the "bitter lump of love" which she has held in relation to her mother. In fact, *Friend of My Youth* is dedicated to the memory of *your* mother. Can you tell me about that relationship?

Munro: It was a very difficult relationship. Mothers and daughters generally have fairly complex relationships, and this was made much more so by the fact that my mother was ill. She had Parkinson's disease, which was not diagnosed for a long time, and which has very peculiar symptoms anyway, so that it can seem in the beginning like a neurotic, self-chosen affliction. And it *was* seen so, by some people in the family. It also has rather bizarre effects later on. The voice becomes thickened, and eating becomes difficult. There's no control over saliva. There are lots of things that are very difficult for a teenager to face in a parent. All that made me very self-protective, because for one thing I didn't want to get trapped. In families like ours it is the oldest daughter's job to stay home and look after people when they're in this situation, until they die. I, instead, got a scholarship and went to university. There is enormous guilt about doing that, but at the time you're so busy protecting yourself that you simply push it under, and then you suffer from it later on. You suffer from it to a certain extent, but I think if you're realistic at all you also look at what you had to do. There were all these fairly hard problems to solve, when I was seventeen, eighteen.

Wachtel: Do you feel regret now?

Munro: That I didn't take the chance of relating in a different way? Yes, I feel terrible regret, but I also feel that it's practically impossible at that age to do so, so I don't think I feel an unreasonable guilt about that. I wish I could meet my mother as I feel now, but in order to get the confidence — I think this is not just with mothers who are ill, but with all mothers and daughters — by the time the daughter gets enough feeling of herself that she doesn't feel threatened by her mother, that her mother is not going to change her into somebody that her mother wants her to be, then, quite often, the mother is dead. Because to get to be this kind of person, you're probably forty-five to fifty

years old, so while it's something that's part of my story.... You know, I don't think that much about my relationship with my mother and what it did to me — I sometimes just feel terrible regret about her, what her life must have been like. Often, when I'm enjoying something, I think of how meagre her rewards got to be, and how much courage, in a way, she needed to go on living, which she did. I appreciate all that, but I also feel so sad that it had to be that way. Now I think there is more care. In a way, our society has improved. People in her situation, I don't think are quite as isolated as she was. There's more recognition altogether of illness, and that the people afflicted are human.

Wachtel: When I read the title story of this book, *Friend of My Youth,* some time ago, when it came out in the *New Yorker,* it made me feel happy to be alive. The writing is that good. The story is about a woman and her mother, but then it takes off and it allows the mother to tell *her* story, which is an extraordinary story about a love triangle, about two sisters and a farmworker, whom the mother knew when she was young. I got the sense, in reading that story, in the way it circles around, that you were trying to figure something out, when you were writing it. Is that something that happens?

Munro: Oh, yes! I was trying to figure out why I needed to write this story. The germ of it was given to me, in the story about the two sisters and the farmworker. I thought about them and I thought about their self-dramatization, with the aid of their religion, and what happened to them. Then suddenly my mother's story began to weave around it, without me making a decision. When I started, I was going to write about Flora and Ellie. Then I wrote about my mother — sort of circling around the Flora and Ellie story. Then I began to write about writing a story, which is where I finally end up. Then I come back to the mother. I knew I was struggling with the subject matter of my mother, which I hadn't thought I would go back to again. I hadn't thought I'd tackle that part of my life ever again. In fact, when I did that story, I really thought I had moved on from autobiographical or personal stories. What interested me in the story was this idea that, after a while, we don't want the stories changed, even in a better way. The dream business —

Wachtel: This is where the character is dreaming about the mother —

Munro: And the mother appears in the dream — and I did have dreams like this for years — the mother appears in the dream and things aren't so bad. Well, okay, be happy about it. But you've constructed your whole personality and your feelings have their roots in something different, and you can't quite give it up. So I thought this is a really interesting layeredness of feeling, and I want to write about it. Maybe that ties in — it does tie in — with how I would have seen the story of Flora, at first in that very classic way, that the teenage girl imagines the story, as she would write the novel — the classic tragedy. Then it's all turned around by the idea that Flora might be working in a department store and going out with a man or something. Which sort of stirs the ingredients all around, and you've got a whole new world to deal with!

Wachtel: Is that part of writing stories? To try to figure something out?

Munro: Yes!

Wachtel: Are there stories where you already know everything at the beginning and you just put them together?

Munro: That's the kind of story that I don't usually bother to write any more, because it doesn't interest me enough. It works, but it doesn't give me enough pleasure. Always now, when I write a story, it's just going in — what I'm doing right now: trying to figure out what the story is all about. Not how it will work, but what it's really about. This is the pleasure of writing to me.

Wachtel: Many traditional stories lead to a moment of insight, an epiphany, that sort of thing. Your stories have moments of insight —

Munro: Yes, and then they're wrong!

Wachtel: Or there's something that in one instance happens, a moment of accidental clarity — I don't know if they're always wrong, but then it evaporates, they're that ephemeral.

Munro: The moment evaporates, or the insight leads to something else. That's what I meant when I said flippantly that they're wrong.

Wachtel: They're not like the traditional payoff at the end of a story —

Munro: No, I want the stories to keep going on. I want the story to exist somewhere so that in a way it's still happening, or happening over and over again. I don't want it to be shut up in the book and put away — oh well, that's what happened.

Wachtel: That kind of open-endedness also implies that things don't necessarily improve or get better, that there isn't really — as in the title of one of your books — a progress of love.

Munro: I haven't lived a whole life yet, so I can't tell you … We'll do an interview some time later! But that doesn't depress me, that idea, that things don't "improve." It's a funny word. I think, if you ask me what I believe as a person, I'd say I do think life gets better, or one's ability to put up with it gets better. But I think things change. That's really one of the things that interest me so much in writing, and in observing people, is that things keep changing. Cherished beliefs change. Ways of dealing with life change. The importance of certain things in life changes. All this seems to me endlessly interesting. I think that is the thing that doesn't change, or that I certainly hope doesn't change. If you find life interesting, it just goes on being so.

Wachtel: Some readers, some critics, have pointed out about *Friend of My Youth* that they feel it's a little sad, elegiac, that sort of thing. Is it misguided to expect happiness in modern fiction?

Munro: I'd like to think that in the stories there are lots of periods of happiness. I don't think anybody ends up saying: Well, now I'm a lot happier than I used to be and I'm going to go on being this way forever and ever. I think it's all muddled up: happiness, sadness, depression, elation. As I said, the constant happiness is curiosity. I wouldn't set out to write a story that I thought was depressing, because that would depress me. But I notice that sometimes other people's stories, that I like so much, are criticized as being depressing. And I feel very puzzled as to the person who's making this judgement, and what they like to read or what their lives are like. Maybe a lot of people are sort of happy all the time!

Wachtel: I thought it was the other way around — that they weren't happy all the time so they wanted their fiction to be happy all the time!

Munro: Maybe, I don't know!

Wachtel: I want to try a theory out on you: one of the ways you exhibit your great craft as a writer is that you give us in these stories a profound sense of absence, that there are absences everywhere, there are deaths, vanished worlds, missing spouses, broken marriages. One character has a missing eye. What do you think?

Munro: Well, I never think! I can't —

Wachtel: You don't think about it like that!

Munro: I can't deal with theories very well! But, yes, absences certainly interest me a lot. Loss, which everyone experiences all the time … we keep losing ourselves and the worlds we used to live in. Whether this is more a factor in modern life, I don't know. But I think maybe it is. Nowadays people do go from one sort of life to another. It's not uncommon now to go from a marriage to another, or to go from a marriage to being unmarried, or from being one sort of person into being an entirely different kind of person. So you've got all these rooms in your head that you've shut off but that you can remember. I think some people don't really bother much with remembering. It seems a useless activity. But most writers are addicted to it. So I suppose I am, too.

Wachtel: The memory comes through. Your stories are getting very, very complex. It's a bit like a three-dimensional chess game sometimes. There are so many layers of things going on and cross-cutting in time and memory. Or it's like a pile of snapshots that are all shuffled up. Why do you do that?

Munro: I just like to. I can't get a grasp on what I'm trying to talk about unless I do that. I don't do it to make things difficult. I've been doing it as I get older, so you might think it's the challenge of writing this way, but I don't think that's true. It's that I see things now, in this way, and there is absolutely no other way I can deal with the material of fiction. It's as simple as that. It's like having to. You'll have something that is awkward, that is difficult to work in, and why do you need it, and you think, I can cut this, I can streamline this, and it doesn't work. It's got to be got in somehow.

Wachtel: I was wondering if it's a way, if you need the complexity to get a greater emotional honesty, because life is never that simple.

Munro: Yes, well … the complexity does, of course, lead you to realize things that you don't if you put on blinkers.

Wachtel: At the beginning of one of your stories you have a character taking a creative-writing course who is being told not to try to put too many things in at once, and so she makes this long list of all the things she wants to make sure she gets in there, and hands it in as an appendix to her story! Are you just fooling around here?

Munro: Well, no. Of course I haven't done that and haven't known of anybody who did. But it seems to me that if you wrote the sort of story she is advised to write, you'd be very worried afterwards, thinking: But, I didn't mention that, and that was also part of what was going on at that time, and I didn't say that afterwards, and I didn't, and so on. To me, what you have, when you pull all these things out, is not the story. I suppose this is a kind of anti-minimalist way of writing. I can enjoy minimalist stories. They seem to me to have a singular force, but I couldn't enjoy writing one.

Wachtel: That's because yours have a multiple force. You have in *Friend of My Youth* a story called "Hold Me Fast, Don't Let Me Pass," where you — or the voice in the story — ponder questions like: What makes a man happy? What makes a woman happy? Do you know what makes you happy? Are you happy?

Munro: Yes. It's what I said. It's being interested. This is the thing I hope will never leave me. A very high level of interest most of the time. When that vanishes — which it sometimes does temporarily — I think it would be awful to live like this, going through the motions of life. But we all experience times that are like that. It's also very important to me to love certain human beings and be loved by them. Then what happens in their lives is very important. But underneath, the thing that would help me survive anything, I think, would be this interestedness.

Wachtel: In your fiction, there is often sex without guilt. In fact, given the complexity and the attentiveness of all the characters, I was surprised at how little guilt there is generally.

Munro: That's part of being interested! If you find something interesting — really interesting — it's very hard to regret it! You may think, Oh that was frivolous behaviour, and that was selfish behaviour, and that was perhaps damaging behaviour — but wasn't it

interesting! Why would a person who feels this way now about something have felt that way then? Regret fades away in the face of interest.

Wachtel: Why are you so interested in adultery?

Munro: It's kind of like modern theatre, it's the adventure it offers in ordinary people's lives. I suppose it always did, but much more in men's lives than in women's, in days gone by, and more in rich, idle people's lives, than in ordinary people's lives. The opportunities have become much greater. The guilt about it may be less but it's still there. It's a way of people expressing themselves, perhaps, who have no other way, because people get boxed in, in various boxes, and there's this role it's possible to play, very briefly, which gives people a sense of still existing. Then, of course, it leads into all kinds of other things. It's a drama in people's lives that I think a writer is naturally attracted to.

JOE FAFARD

The Pasture

A Proposal to Bring Cows to Downtown Toronto

he plan is to bring five slightly more than life-size silicon bronze casts of a plaster sculpture of a lying cow, each to weigh approximately twelve hundred pounds, by train to Toronto;

The five pieces to be distributed on the grassy area west of the IBM tower in Toronto or according to better possibilities discovered at the time of deposition of the casts in the area. In any case, an atmosphere of randomness rather than a geometric one to be maintained;

A full range of patinas to be explored so that each is somewhat different from the others. Sharp, brassy polish to be avoided. Blacks, browns, reds, greens, blues and yellow to be sought;

Each cast to be anchored in the dirt according to the diagram provided.

The Pasture is based on many childhood experiences. I remember many times achieving some degree of serenity and insight by taking a leisurely walk in the pasture. There I observed nature undisturbed. A small herd of milk cows, quiet and woven into the landscape, was always the focal point. They became the connection between humans and the land. They were part of nature, yet they were ours. We exploited them, yet assured their survival and well being. We spent much of our summer working to assure their food supply for the coming winter. In winter we housed, fed and cleaned them. In return we drew much of our food directly from their bodies. A symbiotic relationship between us and them has been established for thousands of years. It continues today and will continue tomorrow. The city dweller is no less involved, just less directly involved.

For these reasons and others I'm sure, the scene in the pasture has a reassuring effect. It is nearly everywhere. Nearly everyone has seen it. It is timeless. It is as old as the hills, as new as the towers and as likely to continue as humanity itself.

A pasture in the downtown core of a large metropolis does provide some contrast. It can serve as a reminder to the inhabitant of the totally man-made (except for the weather) environment; it reminds the

295

inhabitants that the displayed wealth of the city has its real source in the country.

I have two main concerns about this proposal for the designated site. First, I have not actually seen the site except through a concrete building, but I think I have imagined it fairly accurately. It is a fairly intimate area that invites relaxation and contemplation, being adjacent to a walk-by, but not itself a walk-through. It invites the passersby to stop, wander in, sit and collect him or her self.

My second aesthetic concern is for the individual pieces themselves. I have tried in the model to express my sculptural concerns, especially mass and the weight of that mass.

It has always intrigued me that a large living object reveals more about its sculptural qualities when it is doing what is necessary but not what nature has primarily designed it for. Lying down is a secondary activity that the primary activity (walking about and eating) must accommodate. That which is designed to be suspended hammock style from an articulated frame is, in the state of rest, plopped down on a solid flat surface. The supported bulk becomes, in part, the support for the structure designed specifically to support it and to move it about.

In order to appreciate this it is important to establish separately in one's mind the various components and then reassemble them into a whole. For instance there are solid bones of various sizes and shapes each one attached to another by sinew and muscle. All the parts fit together with beautifully designed and articulated joints. There are muscles large and small distributed all over in various shapes, thick and thin, long and short. The interior has a bulk of organs of soft, tough and elastic tissue full of liquids or semi-liquid matter such as juices, blood and whatever the animal has ingested, ground down and soaked. This body of matter, solids, liquids and even gases is made whole

JOE FAFARD

by being carefully wrapped by the skin that fits snugly and loosely where it must.

Going from this image of the real animal to the model that I have provided, note the tautness and looseness of the skin in various points. It is nonetheless a uniform envelope for the whole structure. It gives the impression of continuing underneath from one side to the other. The skin of the sculpture is meant to reveal the characteristics of what is below it. Also an effort has been made to articulate how the skin is attached at all points — the eye, neck, belly, nose, tail, brisket and legs.

Next consider the skeletal structure. An attempt has been made to reveal it without emaciating the whole. The spine is there and continues into its extensions, the tail and the neck. The tail is defined but inactive, the neck is active (it holds up the head) but immobile; that is, it acts like a cantilever, a crane that can move up and down, sideways and also rotate somewhat. The massive head is the weight that the crane carries. It is mostly solid bone with only the jaw as an articulated joint. Therefore the skin is tightly attached to most

296

of that structure with special considerations for the eye, nose and mouth. The wrinkles and folds of the neck and jaw are there to express potential movement of those parts.

The front legs neatly folded on either side of the massive body are like flying buttresses that keep the whole from rolling over. One leg supports more weight reinforcing the notion of awkwardness and imbalance of a body, at rest in a comfortable position, that was primarily designed to stand up and move about.

The large bone of the back leg acts as a tent pole from which much weight is suspended. A large sheet of muscle drapes over it and spreads out to define the bulk of belly and hindquarter muscle. From that point of stress various other stresses are revealed. (These are more easily looked at than described.) The other back leg finds space underneath the body amongst the soft baggy matter that balloons out where space permits.

The back and sides of the sculpture are stretched taut by the sideways flow of the interior liquidity of the body. This is where the bulk of the mass can be expressed.

The ribs and interior diaphragm continue the bellows function in any position the animal takes. It is one aspect that can only be expressed successfully within the limitations of this style by giving enough life and static dynamism to the whole which results in the impression that breath will come at any moment. The idea is to suspend the object between the inactive and its potential opposite. In my opinion when translating the model into its much larger reality I will have the opportunity to espress more clearly and with greater force those ideas I have mentioned above. I do not intend to simply quote the model in larger letters, but to translate it into a larger language. When scale changes, certain proportions will have to be adjusted to meet expressive needs. I am excited about this opportunity to amplify and articulate my sculptural ideas on a scale that our own bodies can relate to.

If I am selected to do this piece many people will only see bronze cows scattered about a lawn. Some may think that that is enough, others that it isn't. In either case it is possible that something may subconsciously sneak up on them like good architecture does.

Addendum to the Proposal

Ideally seven cows would be the appropriate number for a small herd. Because of budget limitations, I am reluctantly proposing only five — despite the fact that I feel seven would be more appropriate — more impressive visually — more in keeping with the symbolism in the Pharoah's dream as interpreted by another Joseph long ago.

A small herd of seven bronze cows, lying down on a green lawn (or in the snow, in winter) was installed in October, 1985 beside the IBM Tower in downtown Toronto, on the south side of York Street, half a block east of Wellington Street, directly behind the kitchen entrance to the Royal York Hotel.

A Rough Journey and a Sad Heart to Follow It

y journey to Haworth Parsonage, Penistone Moor, and Top Withins really began when I was nine years old. My mother, in idle breakfast conversation, related to me the story of the Mad Wife in the Attic from *Jane Eyre*. It seemed to hold some special significance for her and she told it with such chilling accuracy that, by the time I'd finished my toast and peanut butter, the dark mansion, the lacy wedding gown, the dripping candle and the mad wife herself, had presented themselves, with utter clarity, in my visual imagination. They took up residence there, where they have stubbornly remained to this day.

My subsequent reading of the book brought with it a host of other images to clutter up both my daydreams and nightmares; flaming manor houses, bad-tempered Byronic heroes, dangerous foreign visitors (I *still* can't sit through a wedding ceremony without expecting someone from Jamaica to bring it all to a grinding halt), and, most importantly, those moors — the ones you stagger around on for days and days after something dramatic and tragic has happened to you.

Words like *bracken, bilberry, heather,* and *couch grass* became part of my vocabulary in times of stress. Probably the only reason that I never ran permanently away from home as a child was that there were no moors to run to. I had to content myself with angry winter walks through the deserted fairgrounds of the Canadian National Exhibition. Dreary enough, but somehow, I knew, not the *same.*

So much for childhood. *Jane Eyre* is, I think, essentially a children's book. That feeling of isolation and persecution, of being an innocent victim of corrupt adult circumstances, maintains itself with perfect balance from page one to page five hundred and twenty-five. Even after a child-like Jane has married the tyrannical adult Rochester, I sense that it is only because she is cowed and humbled by blindness and dependency that she is able to tolerate him at all. Militant feminists have a different view of this, but then they have a different view of most things.

Enter adolescence. This is a very dangerous time to be reading any Brontë material whatsoever. My mother, sensing this, produced the Random House hardbound edition of *Wuthering Heights* casually, one morning at the breakfast table, saying, "I wondered, dear, if you might not like to read *THIS*. Perhaps you should look at the pictures first."

It was my introduction to obsession. By the time I had finished my toast and peanut butter, Fritz Eichenburg's engravings had made themselves permanently at home in my brain; all those snarling dogs tearing at the throats and ankles of equally fierce-looking human beings, isolated houses built with black stones, twisted trees, and last, but not least, the picture I turned to again and again, Heathcliff growling and digging up Catherine.

And the moors were there too, in the engravings and, I discovered as I devoured it, in the text of the story. But something had changed. They were no longer a place to wander tearfully around after those Jamaican brothers show up at your wedding, not some place to turn *after* an event of great doleful significance; in *this* book the moors were the setting for the emotions, in fact, in many ways they were the emotions. They caused and outlasted events. They mattered more than anything else.

So there I was, barely fourteen years old, sitting in a sunny North Toronto kitchen with a head full of gloomy burned-out mansions, mad attic-bound wives, snarling dogs and the moors. Talk about handicapped! Thanks Charlotte. Thanks Emily. Thanks Mom.

I struggled through the next twenty years of my life somehow. Occasionally, the Brontë influence waned a little though, whenever I got married, I avoided church

JANE URQUHART

ceremonies and white gowns, convinced that they were certain to cause the arrival of those Jamaican brothers. (Minister: Does anyone know of any reason why this man and THIS woman should not be joined together in Holy Matrimony? Jamaican Brothers: Do we EVER!) I had a child, and even though I called her Emily Jane, I was raising her in a fairly sensible manner. Then, a few years ago, due to a series of circumstances too tiresome to relate, the Brontë influence returned with a vengeance. By last winter I knew, I absolutely *had* to visit those moors.

I was prepared to be disappointed. Living in North America had taught me that most of the past is now covered with condominiums. Mississauga swallowed Jalna, Green Gables is a golf course and who knows how many other literary landscapes have been dredged, bulldozed, paved and built upon. I knew, however, that in Haworth, Yorkshire, the parsonage where the Brontë girls lived and wrote still existed and was open to the public. To gaze upon the couch where Emily Brontë fell down dead (she died standing up) would be enough for me were I to find the moors littered with chemical companies.

So, at the end of a twenty-five year journey, I found myself, last February, climbing up the Main Street of the village of Haworth. I felt like Marco Polo arriving in the Orient. Everything was exactly the way I had pictured it. I could see the surrounding moors, the town was constructed of dark millstone grit, the Black Bull Hotel, where brother Branwell Brontë drank and talked himself to death, beckoned. Dark Satanic cotton mills, built during the Industrial Revolution, decorated the surrounding valleys. It all delighted me, as did the giant mastiffs, straining hysterically at the ends of chains in various gardens, snapping viciously into the air. For once in my life, the way that it was, was the way I had always hoped it would be.

It wasn't that twentieth-century commercialism

didn't exist in the village. It did, in the form of The Land of Gondol Toy Store, Shirley Lane, Vilette Coffee Shop and Keeper's Larder. This latter establishment was a tiny shop filled with pet supplies, various leather goods (mostly leashes, muzzles, etc.), and some cute puppies who would, no doubt, grow up to resemble the monsters with whom I had become acquainted on the main street. I had, upon growing to love Emily Brontë, grown to love Keeper as well and I was pleased therefore, to see his name leaping out from the green sign above the door of this small business.

"Who was Keeper?" you ask.
"Who was KEEPER?" I reply.

Keeper was Emily Brontë's very own snarling dog, her constant companion, quite possibly her only non-blood-related friend. In her *Biography of Charlotte Brontë,* Mrs. Gaskell observed that while:

… the helplessness of an animal was its passport to Charlotte's heart, the fierce, wild, intractability of its nature was what often recommended it to Emily.

Hence, Keeper, and hence all those terrifying dogs in *Wuthering Heights* whom Eichenburg had so graphically depicted and who had assigned themselves various apartments in my own imagination.

Keeper anecdotes abound: the time he attached himself to the neck of a canine colleague of equal size and ferocity on the Main Street of Howarth and had to be removed from there by Emily with the aid of a pepper pot and strength of will, his weakness for soft beds and white counterpanes, and how Emily cured him of that, how he followed her coffin to the grave and lay, for weeks afterwards, moaning outside her empty room. Now Keeper's brass collar, which is large enough for the neck of a horse, occupies its own special display case in the Brontë Parsonage Museum and Keeper's Larder graces the lower end of Main Street. Somehow it all makes sense.

At the beginning of *Wuthering Heights,* the phrase "Other dogs haunted other recesses," almost sums up the tone of the rest of the book and is, I think, a wonderful tribute to Keeper. Heathcliff, himself, is a dog haunting a recess (the barn, the enclosed bed by the window, beneath a table, under a cloak with Catherine on the moors) and he growls and shows his teeth appropriately. Our introduction to his personality in Chapter One is depicted through his dogs. They were his interpreters, and, as he says himself, not kept for pets. The insipid Lockwood comments: "You might as well leave a stranger with a brood of tigers."

Perhaps Emily Brontë was a brood of tigers. Certainly, from what we know of her, her response to strangers, if not snarling and hostile, was anything but friendly. "I am happiest," begins one of her poems, "when most away," suggesting that even human beings with whom she was acquainted held, at best, no real interest for her. Her relationships with her father, the servant Tabby, Branwell and Charlotte, her twin-like intimacy with Anne and her identification with Keeper, seemed to complete her social world. There simply was neither room nor need for anything else. One of the ferocious Keeper's functions was to keep the world at bay, allowing Emily to turn inward and examine and describe the Empires of her own imagination.

Still, over the years, through countless readings of both *Wuthering Heights* and the poetry, I was never able to rid myself of the suspicion that Emily Brontë had a secret lover. How else to explain the emotional energy of the Catherine/Heathcliff relationship; how else to explain lines like:

He comes with the western winds, with evenings

wandering airs
With that clear dusk of heaven that brings the thickest
    stars
Winds take a pensive tone and stars a tender fire
And visions rise and change which kill me with desire.

Surely a young girl, living in a remote Yorkshire parish with no human contact save that of her immediate family, could simply not *know* romantic obsession to the extent that she seemed to (despite genius, imagination, and total immersion in the works of Byron), without some particle of experience on which to feed. It needn't have been much — a glance across a church, the words of a stranger passing through — her imagination was more than able to furnish details. But I felt that a kernel of actuality had to have been there to trigger the immense amount of emotion that pervades all her work. Emily Brontë was not a writer of fantasy, her invented land of Gondol notwithstanding. Her voice reaches right through anecdote and verse form and seizes the heart. Her characters carry passion, sharp as knives, in their pockets. Nothing she wrote was a fairy-tale.

Searching, myself, for some particle of actuality, I spent my first morning in Haworth in the Brontë Parsonage Museum and surrounding graveyard. The latter was a Gothic gourmand's feast; endless dark, dark tombstones leaning in every possible direction, moss covering names and inscriptions. In my notebook, I jotted down lines such as:

Farewell vain world thou shop of toil and pain

and;

Welcome sweet death, thou entrance into bliss
A place of rest! Oh, what a change is this!

Inside the museum I admired Charlotte's mourning gloves, Keeper's gleaming collar, Emily's toy iron. Emily's writing desk was there as well (the small lap variety) with (who knows?) parts of *Wuthering Heights* backwards on the blotter. I got my notebook out again to record the oddly portentious words which were painted on the family teapot: "To live is Christ, To die is gain." Each one of these objects assumed the power of religious relics for me, as charged with evidence and meaning as an authenticated splinter of the true cross. I looked through Emily's bedroom window, the site of much of her poetry, for a long, long time, out across a sea of graves to the path which led to the moors. Then, I decided, as she must have so many times, to go for a walk.

In my back pocket I carried a pamphlet which I had picked up at the hotel and which was entitled *How to Stop Yourself Dying on the Moors*. In it, the writer suggests that anything at all could happen out there; typhoons, floods, blizzards and heat waves, all in the space of one afternoon. It is therefore advisable to take along parkas, earmuffs, raincoats, walking boots, summer shorts and a sun hat when going for a stroll, as well as emergency rations and a tent in case the fog closes in. My only concession to all of this was to change my usual high-heeled boots for a pair of Kodiaks, and to tie, around my neck, a tartan scarf which I hoped would flap dramatically in the breeze.

Weather *is,* however, a central issue in *Wuthering Heights,* something which cannot be predicted and which must be contended with at all times. Interestingly enough, though, weather is not a villain as far as the main characters are concerned. Heathcliff and Catherine embrace wind and weather at least as often as they embrace each other. Catherine, separated from Heathcliff, imprisoned in the safe, calm, sheltered world of Thrushcross Grange, a world totally alien to her true self, actually seeks out weather, flinging open the casement in her sick room, desperate for the wind that blows down the Heights. "Open the window, Nelly," she says, "I'm freezing." And one does freeze in prisons — one becomes solid and immobile, looking in a kind of arctic stasis. Weather fluctuates, moves clouds and grasses, causes waterfalls to thicken or dwindle, shapes the limbs of trees. Shelter encloses, drugs, and inevitably paralyzes those who were not meant to be sheltered. *Wuthering Heights* is a novel concerned with storm, or, more importantly, the suffocating effect of the lack of storm on one of the central characters. Catherine's seduction into order is her fall from grace. Her "self" cannot live at Thrushcross Grange, can exist only in condition of total exposure.

Thinking of this and wanting wild weather, I was slightly saddened to note that a cheerful sun was accompanying me onto the moors. Soon, however, I had to confess that, since I was neither Catherine Earnshaw nor Emily Brontë, and hence was unused to walking for miles and miles in chilly weather, I was grateful for its warmth, and, as I got farther and farther away from civilization, for its constancy. For absolutely nothing else stayed the same in this landscape: acres of unvarying heather were followed by acres of unvarying bog, open pastures were followed by fields enclosed by crumbling, dark dry stone walls. Waterfalls leapt out from cliffs, rocks jutted, a large stone house, gutted and blackened by fire, filled most of a small valley. And the relentless wind was everywhere, coming from all directions, never leaving me alone. This wind had havoc on its mind and I knew it. There was nothing anywhere out there that was not subject to its whims. I remembered Catherine's reference to walking the long path that led from the Grange to the Heights; "a rough journey and a sad heart to follow it." I remembered Charlotte Brontë's statement that in Wuthering Heights' "storm heated and electrical atmosphere we seem at times to breath lightning." I began to recite, mentally, one of Emily Brontë's shortest and most powerful poems, understanding it fully for the first time.

> The night is darkening round me
> The wild winds coldly blow
> But a tyrant spell has bound me
> And I cannot, cannot go.
>
> The giant trees are bending
> Their bare boughs weighted with snow
> And the storm is fast descending
> And yet I cannot go.
>
> Clouds beyond clouds above me
> Wastes beyond wastes below
> But nothing drear can move me
> I will not, cannot go.

My mood began to swing back and forth between exhilaration and fear. There were times, out there, when even the snapping jaws of the killer dogs in town would have seemed familiar, almost friendly.

Top Withins, a roofless ruin four miles out on the moors from Haworth, is vaguely identified as the possible site of Wuthering Heights. Certainly it *is* high, remote, exposed, surrounded on all sides by a sea of moors, with no human habitations in sight. When I eventually arrived there, I leaned against one of the dark walls, warmed a little now by the sun, opened the paperback I had brought with me, and began to read the first page:

> 1801 — I have just returned from a visit to my landlord — the solitary neighbour I shall be troubled with. This certainly is a beautiful country. In all England I do not believe that I could have fixed on a situation so completely removed from the stir of society. A perfect

misanthropist's heaven — and Mr. Heathcliff and I are such a suitable pair to divide the isolation between us.

Then I turned to the last page and read:

> I lingered round them under benign sky, watched the moths fluttering around the heath and the harebells; listened to the soft wind breathing through the grass; and wondered how anyone could ever imagine unquiet slumbers for sleepers in that quiet earth.

I looked out over the long path I had taken to this spot, over the rough road and the sad heart, over the heath and the cliff, and suddenly I knew who Emily Brontë's secret lover had been. By times fierce, by times quiet, relentless, stern, gentle, soft. Always changing; evasive, unpredictable, but constant and enduring. As inescapable as gravity and as inexplicable — this landscape. She lived it and she wrote it. She sickened and pined when she was away from it. She created her characters from its features and her poetry was a metaphysical response to it. Suddenly, her lap desk, toy iron and death couch lost power. Her real world was out here, still changing, still alive.

As Charlotte Brontë stated at the end of her Introduction to the 1850 edition of *Wuthering Heights:*

> With time and labour the crag took human shape and there it stands colossal, dark and frowning, half statue, half rock. In the former sense terrible and goblin-like; in the latter almost beautiful, for its colouring is of mellow grey and moorland moss clothes it and heath, with its blooming bells and balmy fragrance, grows faithfully close to the giant's foot.

I picked some unblossoming winter heather to place on Emily's grave. Then I began the rough journey back.

LEON ROOKE

Rash Undertakings

I discovered Cormac McCarthy in 1970 in Victoria when I stumbled into a bookshop, Poor Richard's this was, began browsing among the rear shelves and pulled down a hardback called *The Orchard Keeper*. It was a first novel, I saw, sent five years earlier for review purposes to the Victoria newspaper. It wouldn't have been reviewed, of course, because in those days the only books reviewed were those having to do with military history. So many books about military history, four or five each week. Week after week, year after year, this and that campaign, this and that war, the autobiography and biography and notebooks of this and that General or Admiral. The mind boggled, but the mind accepted with delicious malignity what the book page maintained: that fiction worthy of notice hadn't been written in this country or elsewhere in 137 years. "If ever anything of note is written," wrote the book editor, "we shall review it." But at least back then the paper had a certain ludicrous character; now the reviews come to us from U.S. syndicates.

It interests me to pursue this gratuitous insult, since McCarthy's newest novel has not been reviewed either, though war is one of its principal topics of discussion. *Blood Meridian* has a pre-Civil War setting and might therefore be called an historical novel; it opens as the American West is being claimed and therefore might be called a western. But it is most assuredly not the West we have inherited through books and movies dealing with the subject and all prior works will seem tame beside it. No one leads a charmed life here. No one is safe, no one stands tall or rides into the sunset, and few are seen as even making the effort. A cutthroat gang, matchless in their depravity, some among them borrowed from historical truth, contracts with a Mexican governor to take Apache scalps at a payment of $100 each, and these men — who are the embodiment of evil, evil endemic now incarnate, juvenescent and rapacious of spirit — swarm through the pages like Armageddon's ardent and armipotent servants, opposed by no visible moral force nor slowed by any of the expected civilized restraints. Inevitably, they soon observe that the scalps of their contractors are not unlike those they have been hired to confiscate.

The terrain we may take to be not unlike that of hell. McCarthy finds no glory in war, no nobility in its endeavours or the West's expansion, precious little even in its victims, and only a stumbling, minute grace for one character at the end; in this book his is a projection of the earth as an expanse of unremitting nightmare, a nightmare ever with us, ever on the meridian. He has offered no more escape for the reader than is granted his characters, both the doers and the done-to — none except language. But he has penned these horrors with the ink of an angel.

Every man is tabernacled in every other and he in exchange and so on in an endless complexity of being and witness to the uttermost edge of the world.

Notions of chance and fate are the preoccupations of men engaged in rash undertakings.

The bodies of the dead were stripped and their uniforms and weapons burned along with the saddles and other gear and the Americans dug a pit in the road and buried them in a common grave, the naked bodies with their wounds like the victims of surgical experimentation lying in the pit gaping sightlessly at the desert sky as the dirt was pushed over them. They trampled the spot with their horses until it looked like the road again and the smoking gunlocks and sabreblades and girthrings were dragged from the ashes of the fire and carried away and buried in a separate place and the riderless horses hazed off into the desert and in the evening the wind carried away the ashes and the wind blew in the night and fanned the last smouldering billets and drove forth the last fragile race of sparks fugitive as flintstrikings in the unanimous dark of the world.

They entered the city haggard and filthy and reeking with the blood of the citizenry for whose protection they had contracted.

Save for their guns and buckles and few pieces of metal in the harness of the animals there was nothing about these arrivals to suggest even the discovery of the wheel.

Who is Cormac McCarthy and is his work always so gloomy? No, his work often wildly funny — there is, in his novel *Suttree,* for instance, a lovable character who fornicates with an entire field of watermelons — though his novels diligently probe the nature of good and evil. McCarthy was born in Rhode Island in 1933, and at the age of four moved to a rural appendage of Knoxville, Tennessee, where he grew up. That's hill country, land of your Great Smokies, your Appalachian chain, homeplace at one time to your Cherokee, Shawnee, Chickasaw and Creek. An area rich in southern yore and lore, famous for Robert Mitchum illicit booze-running movies, next door to your Waltons of TV fame, your Ma and Pa Kettle and other immortals of that stripe. He attended the University of Tennessee and served in the Air Force. He now lives in Texas, where he guards his privacy, I'm told — though it did not seem so to me — with somewhat the tenacity of Salinger.

McCarthy has published five novels: *The Orchard Keeper* in 1965, *Outer Dark* in 1968, *Child of God* in 1973, *Suttree* in 1979 and *Blood Meridian* in 1985. His editor for twenty years has been the distinguished Albert Erskine, who was Faulkner's final editor, as well as editor for John O'Hara, Robert Penn Warren, Ralph Ellison, Eudora Welty and Malcolm Lowry. I asked Erskine how he ranks McCarthy among this literary enfilade. "Of those I've read," he said, "and I haven't read all, of course ... he is the best of his generation.... Let me say this," he went on. "Lowry's *Under the Volcano,* in 1944, was the first novel I sent out advance bound galleys of to booksellers, reviewers and critics. I believed in it that strongly. *The Orchard Keeper,* twenty-one years later, was the second."

Here is the opening page of that novel:

The tree was down and cut to lengths, the sections spread and jumbled over the grass. There was a stocky man with three fingers bound up in a dirty bandage with a splint. With him were a Negro and a young man, the three of them gathered about the butt of the tree. The stocky man laid aside the saw and he and the Negro took hold of the piece of fence and strained and grunted until they got the log turned over. The man got to one knee and peered into the cut. We best come in this way, he said. The Negro picked up the crosscut and he and the man began sawing again. They sawed for a time and then the man said, Hold it. Goddamn, that's it again.

They stopped and lifted the blade from the cut and peered down into the tree. Uh-huh, said the Negro. It sho is now, ain't it?

The young man came over to see. Here, said the man, look sideways here. See? He looked. All the way up here? he said. Yep, the man said. He took hold of the twisted wrought-iron, the mangled fragment of the fence, and shook it. It didn't shake. It's growed all

thue the tree, the man said. We cain't cut no more on it. Damned old elum's bad enough on a saw.

The Negro was nodding his head. Yessa, he said. It most sholy was. Growed all up in that tree.

The Orchard Keeper, though violence is much a part of its tapestry, is the warm and compelling and beautifully wrought story of three linked individuals in remote mountains during the Depression — a young boy, a young man, and a very old man, the orchard keeper of the title, and one of McCarthy's remarkable achievements is that each of these three is perfectly and movingly observed, their story, to my mind, being one of heroic survival, say victory, in an impoverished world.

I'm not going to speak of McCarthy's fourth and longest novel, *Suttree,* except to say that many, Erskine among them, hold it to be his finest. And except to say that its setting is Dreg's Row in Knoxville in the early fifties, and its protagonist, Cornelius Suttree, renounces his "safe" family to take up life and find his transformation among:

... thieves, derelicts, miscreants, pariahs, poltroons, spaspeens, curmudgeons, clotpolls, murderers, gamblers, bawds, whores, trulls, brigands, topers, tosspots, sots, and archsots, lobscots, smellsmocks, runagates, rakes, and other assorted and felonious debauchees.

And to say that this novel contains more sustained comedy than his others, thanks largely to a fellow named Gene Harrogate, your watermelon man, a Duddy Kravitz-type turned upside down and emptied of three-quarters of the sense he never had in the first place, Gene being truly one of the most astonishingly madcap, zany and somehow touching creations in all of twentieth-century fiction.

Let's dip into *Child of God,* his third novel, a

chronicle of the lurid life and hard times of Lester Ballard, backwoods murderer and necrophile, a man of mean spirit and stubborn resourcefulness we come eventually to understand fully, and finally even, incredibly, to identify with.

Here is the tail end of one of that novel's many vivid scenes:

One cold morning on the Frog Mountain turnaround he found a lady sleeping under the trees in a white gown. He watched her for a while to see if she were dead. He threw a rock or two, one touched her leg. She stirred heavily, her hair all caught with leaves. He went closer. He could see her heavy breasts sprawled under the thin stuff of her nightdress and he could see the dark thatch of hair under her belly. He knelt and touched her. Her slack mouth twisted. Her eyes opened. They seemed to open downward by the underlids like a bird's and her eyeballs were gorged with blood. She sat up suddenly, a sweet ferment of whiskey and rot coming off her. Her lip drew back in a cat's snarl. What do you want, you son of a bitch? she said.

Ain't you cold?

What the hell is it to you?

It ain't a damn thing to me.

Ballard had risen and stood above her with the rifle.

Where's you clothes at?

She rose up and staggered backwards and sat down hard in the leaves. Then she got up again. She stood there weaving and glaring at him with her puffed and heavylidded eyes. Son of a bitch, she said. Her eyes were casting about. Spying a rock, she lunged and scrabbled it up and stood him off with it.

Ballard's eyes narrowed. You better put down that rock, he said.

You make me.

I said to put it down.

She drew the rock back menacingly. He took a step forward. She heaved the rock and hit him in the chest with it and then covered her face with her hands. He slapped her so hard it spun her back around facing him. She said: I knowed you'd do me thisaway.

Ballard touched his hand to his chest and glanced down quickly to check for blood but there was none. She had her face buried in her hands. He took hold of the strap of her gown and gave it a good yank. The thin material parted to the waist. She turned loose of her face and grabbed at the gown. Her nipples were hard and bluelooking with the cold. Quit, she said.

Ballard seized a fistful of the wispy rayon and snatched it. Her feet came from under her and she sat in the trampled frozen weeds. He folded the garment under his arm and stepped back. Then he turned and went on down the road. She sat stark naked on the ground and watched him go, calling various names after him, none his.

307

I have a special fondness for *Outer Dark,* McCarthy's second novel, because of its compactness, its conciseness, a dramatic intensity that is practically stereophonic, and because it has a structural form clean as a Concorde jet. The story develops from an incestuous brother-sister relationship, terrain again taking on mythic properties as brother looks to find sister, sister looks to find her stolen baby, and three ghostly murderers stalk the countryside like grim Magi, all journeys eventually converging in horrendous spectacle, emptying finally into these apocalyptic notes:

Before him stretched a spectral waste out of which reared only the naked trees in attitudes of agony and dimly hominoid like figures in a landscape of the damned. A faintly smoking garden of the dead that tended away to the earth's curve. He tried his foot in the mire before him and it rose in a vulvate welt claggy and sucking. He stepped back. A stale wind blew from this desolation and the marsh reeds and black ferns among which he stood clashed softly like things chained. He wondered why a road should come to such a place.

Going back the way by which he came he met again the blind man tapping through the dusk. He waited very still by the side of the road, but the blind man passing turned his head and smiled upon him his blind smile. Holme watched him out of sight. He wondered where the blind man was going and did he know how the road ended. Someone should tell a blind man before setting him out that way.

I reached McCarthy by phone in Texas and put it to him that perhaps the public found his tales a mite bleak. "Jolly tales," he said, "are not what it is all about. My feeling is that all good literature is bleak. When a work gets a certain gloss on it with age and the current reality of it is dulled, then we can say what has and what does not have the true tragic face. I'm guided by the sweep and grandeur of classical tragedy. Mine are the conditions common to people everywhere and finally the work has little to do with any personal aberration of the characters."

I suggested that perhaps one reason his work has not secured its deserved audience was that his characters were indeed cast adrift in some "unanimous dark of the world," within a "lethal environment" which offered neither relief nor instruction, pre-wheel times, time without mercy, time presided over by the implacable face of Nothingness, with a will to survive, fortitude, as the only and last testament. Whereas today's reader wanted events explained, lamented, accounted for: Lester is the way he is because he comes from a broken home, his parents whipped him, he had no shoes until he was ten years old.

"I don't doubt it," McCarthy said. "Modern readers are a lot more familiar with Freud than with Sophocles."

I asked him how difficult he finds it to write these amazing novels. "I work on each for several years," he said, "and am brought to the brink of innumerable suicides. I want, even for the worst of the characters, grace under pressure, some slinking nobility."

I asked him what he had been reading lately.

"I've just finished *Shakespeare and the Common Understanding,*" he said. "And one of your guys, Michael On — ? How do you say it?"

"Datchie."

"That's right. Ondaatje. Wonderful stuff."

So the circle, in this nicest of ways, came round.

A L B E R T O   M A N G U E L

An Interview With Richard Ford

fter three novels — *A Piece of My Heart, The Ultimate Good Luck* and *The Sportswriter* — Richard Ford published his first book of short stories, *Rock Springs*. It's a superb collection: carefully crafted, menacing, moving. The characters are all people on the verge of some discovery which they somehow fail to understand; their landscape is the Montana–Canada border. Ford has been to Canada several times, crossing over from the U.S. into Saskatchewan to hunt geese with Raymond Carver, invited by David Carpenter. But this time it's Toronto, and he reminds one of Sam Shepard, walking carefully as if he had decided, a long time ago, not to move more than one side of his body at a time. His eyes wrinkle when he smiles, and he smiles a lot.

Richard Ford spoke to Alberto Manguel at the Courtyard Café in Toronto on Sept. 21, 1987.

Ford: My mother, she certainly had a lot to do with my becoming a writer. She was a big reader, but not a reader of difficult books. She read things like *The Egg and I,* and *Lydia Bailey,* but she neither encouraged nor discouraged me to read. But she had an intuitive respect for writers, for someone who was a writer. She liked Hemingway's books ... I was on another track: I wanted to drink, steal cars, be with girls, that sort of thing. Writing. Literature. They were far away from me. Sometimes you can be encouraged just by being let alone to like what you will like.

Manguel: Where was this?

Ford: In Mississippi. In Jackson.

Manguel: Had your mother read Eudora Welty?

Ford: I doubt it. She knew Miss Welty was a writer and held her in reverence for that reason. In my mother's allowance it became a creditable thing to me, then, to be a writer. After that first time, whenever we'd see her, my mother would whisper to me, "There's Miss Welty." I know Miss Welty now. After all this time. We just won an award together, in Mississippi. Me for fiction, her for non-fiction. That's odd, isn't it?

Manguel: Did seeing Eudora Welty make you want to read her?

Ford: No, not then. Later it did. When I published my first novel, I used to believe she had read it and didn't like it — because she never wrote me anything. I thought she probably oversaw what young

Mississippians were writing and harboured opinions. That seems stupid now. It was sort of a dirty book, and I thought it might've offended her. She's never delivered an opinion to me on that subject, though she liked *The Sportswriter,* I'm relieved to say. Last year she came to a book signing of mine, in Jackson, and she was kind enough to say so. We also talked about the fact that we'd gone to the same grammar school and actually had the same teacher. Now Miss Welty was born in 1909, and she'd had a third-grade teacher — Louella P. Varnado was her name — in 1917 or '18. And Miss Varnado had been the principal of the school when I was there in the early fifties! "Yesterday I was having my hair done, and Miss Varnado was having hers done sitting right next to me," Miss Welty said and we laughed. This was in 1986, so Miss Varnado must be in her nineties now. She was very stern in the fifties, and Eudora said she was very stern in 1917, too.

Manguel: Was there anything else that happened to you as a child that made you want to be a writer?

Ford: No. I didn't lead an inspired life. I wasn't a prodigy. My mother wasn't too bothered about my education. We lived next door to the school, it just followed that I went. I sometimes think that if I'd never read a book she'd have been just as happy. She believed you occupied a niche in life and strived to make yourself happy in it. I remember she said to me once, "Richard, when will you get started with your life?" That was after I was married to Kristina and was actually writing a novel and was probably twenty-eight years old. I thought I *was* started. But she had a different idea of what life was like. She was, to some extent, a fatalist — although she was a very willful one. My life was certainly a sort of source of new information to her on that subject. Later she asked me, "Richard, are you happy?" — this was years later — "You must make yourself happy." That's actually all I've tried to do, in fact — make myself happy writing. Just a regular wish.

Manguel: When did you get started with your life?

Ford: Not right away, actually. I went to law school, Washington University, in St. Louis. Then one day I heard Stanley Elkin lecturing on literature, right across the quadrangle. And I didn't want to go back to law classes after that. So eventually I quit, went home, or to where my mother was living, in Little Rock, got a job as a substitute teacher, teaching French — a language I had a very casual relation with, though it was better than the students', who were just a bunch of punks. They couldn't care less what they were supposed to be learning. After that I tried a job writing sports for the *Arkansas Gazette,* but I couldn't type very well, plus I didn't know one thing about how you wrote sports. I just liked it; it seemed like it would be interesting — what someone would now call "fun." But there were specific ways to go about doing that job. Protocols. Inverted pyramids. So I failed. Then I tried several other things. I applied for a job in the State Police, even for a job in with the CIA — neither of which is so strange a calling for someone with a writer's temperament, not when you think about it. Anyway, I didn't get those jobs either, and so I was at home with nothing to do. No prospects. I'd just write and apply for any job I thought of.

Manguel: Why didn't you get the CIA job?

Ford: They actually did offer me a job, only later. But I turned it down. In 1968, Kristina and I were living in California — we'd done some moving — and I was in bed watching TV. And I saw the Viet Cong storming the American Embassy in Saigon, the Marines standing shooting alongside these guys in civilian clothes. "Who are these civilian people with guns?" I wondered. And I thought, "Well, of course, they're CIA." I certainly didn't want to do that. I'd always believed doing things for your country was okay. I still believe it. But not that particular duty, in that country. We were all getting smart fast, then. And I was admittedly slow to get smart. Now I see a guy like Oliver North on TV and I say to myself, "I could be him, that could be me." I've made a writer out of myself, but things certainly could've gone differently. Character may be fate on some occasions. But fate often assigns you a character. Isn't that what heroes always say? I bet Ollie himself would agree.

Manguel: Maybe you see North as a character you wish you had invented. He could be a character in one of your novels ...

Ford: Conrad already did him; did him better, actually.

Manguel: Your stories, though, are very different from your novels.

Ford: I suppose so. I wrote half the stories in *Rock Springs* while I was writing *The Sportswriter,* though. Most writers, I think, are more various and versatile in the use of fiction's formal features than it's often convenient for someone taking a cursory look to admit. There seems to be a putative virtue — at least in the minds of some book critics — in superficial "consistencies" in a writer's work: this woolly business of *voice* and *style* — whatever they are. Myself, I've just always tried to find ways to write so as to include as much as I knew or could discover by writing. In the process, I've learned more, and I've used up a lot of things that interested me, and I've tried to write in more than one received form. So, things change. It's not so surprising. Not to me. Where does it say in the manual that things have to be superficially the same? Maybe when I've finished writing — if I'm not finished now — someone will be able to locate what's consistent in it all. I'm sure something will turn up. I did write it all.

Manguel: How do you feel about *The Sportswriter?* It certainly gave you a good name.

Ford: All I really cared about was that people read

that book. I tried to write about the most important things I knew when I wrote it. Beyond that, I know a lot of writers who have not-so-good names, some with disputable names. But people read their books. Likewise, many writers with prestigious names — and wonderful writers, too — don't get read enough. If having a recognizable name could mean that people would read your book, then that's good, I suppose. Anything else it might mean is less important to me.

Manguel: You didn't like being told that one can see Hemingway's influence in your writing.

Ford: No, because I don't think it's true. You would think, from the mass of invocations his work seems to authorize, that he was the first American to write a sentence. But that's just tiresome. It's another book critic's shortcut, whereby the critic makes himself look smarter than the writer whose work is under consideration, while simultaneously locating a way not to read complex work complexly and on its own terms. Hemingway was a fine writer. So was Sherwood Anderson, whom I'm much happier to credit as an all-important influence. Isaac Babel, too — read in translation of course. Chekhov. But Hemingway of all people. I don't even like Hemingway very much.

Manguel: What about "Indian Camp"?

Ford: I was going to say that. With the exception of "Indian Camp," which is a great story. There are a few other really fine ones, too. But I've never thought he was generous enough with language. I just read something Richard Locke wrote in the *Wall Street Journal,* in which he said Hemingway's trademark restraint was really just *faux naïf* — from which I conclude he didn't really tell or find out enough in most of his work to be a truly great and reliable informer for full-fledged adults. I bet if you reread a Hemingway story today, one you remembered liking, you wouldn't like it as much. But try that on "A Guest of the Nation," or "The Lady with the Pet Dog," or "Death in the Woods."

311

There are influential stories, and not for some patina of style, but for all they *do literally say,* what they become aware of and do dedicated language to for our benefit. Apart from that, it's hardly an important admission to say that most of what we read that's good influences us. In a letter somewhere, Delmore Schwartz says it's really only what we find and can make our own — armed as we are with our own inheritances — that will cause our work to be considerable. That premise satisfies me. The anxiety that critics seem always to feel about influence — and I doubt writers share it much — will finally cause them to value only the *appearance* of the new — literary novelty acts.

Manguel: Can you tell if there's a general idea behind all the stories in *Rock Springs?*

Ford: Well, once I wrote them I thought a few of them are concerned with how hard circumstances brought on by fate and character can sometimes be alleviated by brief moments of affection. Although, also sometimes not.

Manguel: Do you write with an idea like that in mind?

Ford: Sometimes. If I know it, or if I can just say that phrase like the one I just said. I used to think I didn't, but I suppose I do. The phrases or words themselves that represent ideas sometimes interest me — and I mean just as raw language — and I'll often try to find a way to fit them into a sentence, which then for me establishes a new set of relationships for that word and for what it represents. I remember in a story I wrote called "Children," the word "conscience" was in my mind, it kept recurring to me, really somewhat outside its meaning — just the word. So I tried to find a way to use it and see what it meant in the context I contrived. I'm sure language often comes into use in just that way in our lives. Somewhat haphazardly and full of surprises. From this I guess you can conclude I don't write a story to illustrate anything. If I knew what to illustrate I'd already know what — as it is, I need the agency of the story to find out. My own sense of any story's necessity — and this is not a new idea — is that you can only know or come to know what the story teaches by reading that story. Or for me, by writing it. It's not knowable otherwise. But back where ideas are concerned; ideas are just words which represent or organize rather disparate experience — details, etc. I'm interested in those details. And I'm most interested in language that gets used to represent experience. Sometimes when there's a dystrophy between those two, that very thing becomes a source of drama in our lives — if we don't agree, say, about what "affection" means or if our experience in life, and the words we have to refer to experience with, don't match. What's mostly the case with my own writing experience has less to do with ideas than with writing sentences that appeal to me, one by one. A sense of rhythm; how many syllables a word contains; whether a sentence sounds right with this or that long vowel sound in it. Niggling with sentences is what I do, hoping to come up with something new to the world. Lowell said that if he wrote a line and didn't like it and couldn't fix it, he'd add "not" in front of the verb. That adds a syllable to the sentence and changes it rhythmically. And of course it also springs the sentence and opens up a new possibility — the opposite to the one you were thinking about. But you *were* looking for something new, right? Often I've found that when a word doesn't come right in a sentence, the problem is not just the word.

Manguel: "Take care of the sounds, and the sense will take care of itself."

Ford: Well, not exactly. I finally have to be responsible for the sense. I have to decide if it's right or wrong.

Manguel: In *The Sportswriter,* the wife's name is

"X" throughout. Why?

Ford: I couldn't think of a name for her as I was writing it, so I just wrote a bracketed "X" in every sentence, thinking I'd fill it later. I thought about that name for two or three years. At last — when I couldn't make myself satisfied with any name, I decided that Frank — in whose voice the novel is narrated — simply couldn't bring himself to say it, and that was why I couldn't find it. "X" was all that was utterable, or it at least stood for his incapacity. Names are of maybe undue importance for me, by which I mean they have a sound that's somehow right to my ear — make some intuitive match with the lines of speech I write for that character. I admit a reader may not be so finicky. But being finicky is my part of the compact, I guess.

Manguel: Your writing has been called "realistic" or even "hyper-realistic."

Ford: And I'm quite sure I don't know what that might mean. It's been called other things, too. Those categories aren't much help in the writing. I know that Montana and Wyoming — where almost all the stories in *Rock Springs* [and also *Wildlife,* Ford's latest book] are set — are real places on the earth, and you don't need to read my stories to know about them. You can get in your car and go there. What I write is something else, again. For one thing, it's made of words and so is a different object entirely. Hemingway — since we were talking about him before — wrote in a letter to Edward O'Brien that when he wrote "Big Two-Hearted River" he was trying to "do" the country — that was his expression — so that you didn't remember the words after you read it — all you have is the country. I guess I'm different. I want you to remember the words. And how much like real life, real place, all that is even further complicated by the fact that my intention is to create something new, a new logic, a new conclusion about life, fashioned maybe on some observable experience, some putative locales and sensations that are already known. That is one redemptive quality of literature — secular redemption, I'm talking about; it creates the new out of an experience that's knowable, or already known.

Manguel: You mean that literature is a way of understanding reality?

Ford: From what I know most, understanding is simply creating some logic which you can believe in and which others will profitably believe in too. Fiction's such a logic. So is the law. At some higher realm, so, I guess, is even mathematics. Understanding isn't passive by this formula. It's active. When I'm asked, "Do you understand your past?" I don't know, I think, but I'll try to invent a logic based on knowable facts that's compelling, convincing, useful. The responsibility of literature, for me, is not merely to portray something as it is, it's to represent what something is or seems to be and to create something more — something intelligent, something touching, something to redeem the species.

This photo of Eudora Welty and me is mostly funny, of course, but it might have emblematic "significance," too. It was taken last spring in the yard of the grammar school where we were both students, thirty-five years apart, Jefferson Davis School. The school is next door to the house where I lived, which was across the street from the house where she lived years before. I think, when I see this picture, that it emblemizes me wondering what in the world there is left to write about, since Eudora seems so much at home.

An odd quality of Mississippi's being the literary landscape it is — so fully imagined and in a way documented by Eudora and Faulkner and others — is that even a native can come to think the place is already completely known. When I began to be an adult I realized that, in fact, a great, great deal of what I thought and remembered and liked and felt was important about Mississippi had come from novels and stories I'd read, and that those books already represented the place perfectly and completely, both as it was or seemed to me, and as it could be represented in literature. I sometimes think that much good writing *to come* got eclipsed by previous wonderful writing, as odd and exasperating and debatable as that for-mula might seem. I do know that among a lot of Mississippians my age curiosity which might've ended in writing got replaced by a sort of literary connoisseurship. For me, I know it's a prime reason I've written about Montana and New Jersey, for instance, instead of about Jackson or that schoolyard. Here's, I guess, a literary influence of a somewhat different nature.

Richard Ford

MICHAEL PFLUG

Life With Christiane Pflug and Her Friends

At the end of the summer she started a night painting. We had seen the black doll standing at night in the light falling out through the kitchen door. Its head was hardly visible against the darkness. Its white dress caught the light. We put the Shirley Temple doll on a wooden children's chair. Both stared into the room. The black doll looked downward, holding her raised hand over the white doll, protective and threatening at the same time.

The nights grew colder. I made a separating wall across the kitchen with a large discarded canvas of mine. I cut out a window. Christiane sat behind it protected from the cold and looked on her motif through the cut-out canvas. A lamp on the fridge behind the canvas shed its light on the balcony. The open door framed the subject. Heinz loaned us a white porcelain electric stove which Christiane put at her feet. She wrapped herself in a blanket and started to paint after supper, working into the morning hours. She got up in the morning to prepare breakfast for Esther, who went to kindergarten at Brown School, and for Ursula, who would get up on her own and play through the house while Christiane went back to sleep.

This new rhythm was incorporated into Ursula's story: the hen got up when the sun shone brightly through the window, combed herself, brushed her teeth, then prepared the meal for the little chicken who had stayed home. Christiane enjoyed the close association with her.

I slept for an hour when I got home, then returned to my books. Sometimes I got up to watch Christiane. As the painting progressed, she was consumed by the effort of finishing it.

One night I sank into a short sleep on the wicker sofa. I heard a muffled shout. I jumped up and ran into the kitchen. Christiane was nervously beating out the smouldering blanket which had caught fire on the electric stove.

"Why did you not call me?" I asked her.

"I was afraid you would notice!"

She completed one of the larger doll paintings every two months. She was desperate over our quarrels. She told me jokingly that she had tried to hang herself with one of my ties from a bannister in our stairway. The tie did not hold her up. Her attempt was serious enough for her to have found out that the tie

316

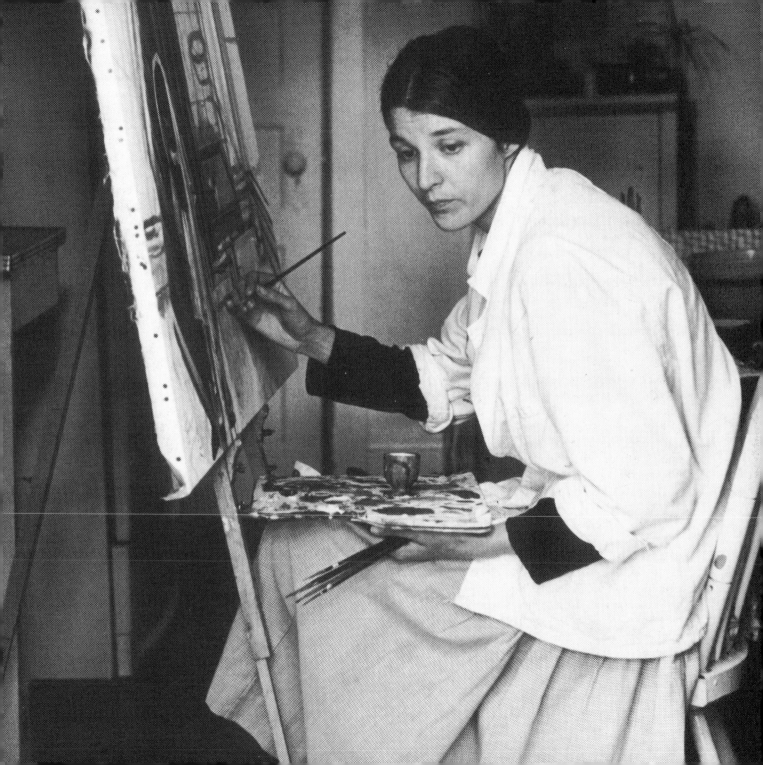

would not hold her. It added to my fear of leaving her alone, or of seeing her leave the house after a quarrel. Whenever she did, I went after her and led her home.

The next painting was a winter painting. The black doll on the balcony stared through the window panes holding one of its hands against the glass, behind it a wintry garden and the view through the now-bare trees to the horizon. In the distance one saw the sky-line. The night painting and this winter painting were full in tone and colour. She kept up with the seasons. During a grey and rainy March, she painted the Shirley Temple doll through the panes of the closed kitchen door, sitting on the small white stool, leaning to the left as if leaning with the wind. The door was painted in a heavier grey than on the two previous paintings. The landscape outside was grey and brown, with soggy grass in the garden, and a few patches of snow. The branches of the trees spread under a grey, rain-swept sky. We called the painting "With the Last Snow."

Each of these paintings was preceded with a small sketch. The large and accomplished canvasses gave Christiane more confidence in her work, the security of progressing step by step with the seasons. She ran into difficulties towards the end of each painting, and into phases of exhaustion in the last week or so as she finished off details.

By May 1964 she had completed eight paintings. The Isaacs Gallery gave her her second exhibition. It consisted of the last landscapes from the railroad yard, the still-lifes of wilted flowers from the winter of 1962, the first small doll paintings on postcard-sized canvasses, the dolls on the black chair and the larger doll paintings and their sketches.

Christiane left arrangements for the exhibition to me. I carried the paintings to Isaacs for framing. My mother warned us not place too many hopes in this exhibition. I answered that we could not place enough

hopes in it. Painting was our life.

The exhibition filled the second and smaller room of the gallery. There were more people at the opening than ever before. Christiane's family was there. Anton came with several friends. Dr. Fitzgerald, a neurologist from St. Joseph's, bought one of the small sketches. Anton busied himself with Mrs. Fitzgerald's poodle. Christiane enjoyed the exhibition, the support of friends and family and the beginning recognition. The critics were supportive. Neither they nor the audience understood much of the intense feelings and struggles that produced these paintings. All her paintings sold.

The completion of the last painting, finished in time for the show and carried to the gallery while still wet, brought a release from the strain under which she had worked. She enjoyed one of the short periods, in which she had a little more time. She started to draw out of our windows. As it got warmer outside, she made drawings in the Rosedale ravine and in Winston Churchill Park. She drew brick buildings behind trees at Ramsden Park.

In summer she started a painting of one of the black dolls standing on the balcony, facing the garden. The doll, in a red dress with printed flowers in black and white, was painted sharply. The dense black hair is parted in two braids. The doll holds its arms up towards the garden. The foliage was painted in a more angry green than in the earlier summer painting. Over the roof of a house on Walker Avenue a white pigeon flies up towards the sky. Five birds are hidden among the leaves and the twigs of the trees, some of them seen from the side as a silhouette, others seen from the front. The wires of the balcony railing are painted in detail, with their surfaces changing from dark to light, depending on how they caught the light and twisted around each other.

Christiane spent three months on this complex painting. A green apple on the balcony floor and a few fallen leaves were added as the summer passed. There is a harsh light on the drying leaves. The doll is seen in great clarity, not that of photo-realist painters, but that of the penetrating and sharp luminosity of the Mannerist painters. The light is not the milky light of a summer noon, but a light as from a distant lightning, shed on a summer landscape under a grey sky. The symbolism of the black doll reaching out into the garden, or reaching towards the closed door and looking blindly into the room, was obvious, though in her mind not as literal as people interpreted it.

And so everything passes, the sadness about what was lost, and what one never had, is sometimes so violent and unreasonable. I mean against all reason and what one could possibly expect. Always one wants to lift the day beyond itself into something marvellously festive, dream-like and beautiful. Stella and Morris Louis succeeded. Compared to that, what one does oneself looks cramped and detailed, but I can't do anything else. The sun shines on the small houses, through the twigs of the trees one sees cars standing in front of each other. Covered with snow, the car roofs are set off from each other, here and there a red or blue one, which I am just painting. I love to paint again. I'm not so impatient any more. Sometimes it seems to me as if the mass of different elements produces an effect which puts it into relation to the complexity and confusion of life. Then again, one would like to take a broom and create space for clear pure forms and colours. And so it goes on, with the restlessness that eats one and hollows one out, a kind of constant battle. One doesn't want to imagine that one could fail.

Christiane Pflug

SARAH SHEARD

Song of Departure

hree events within the last five months have rocked my friends in the writing community. In September 1988, Barrie Nichol, an editor at Coach House Press, a personal friend and widely loved poet, died suddenly while undergoing an operation to remove a tumour from his spine. He was forty-four.

In February, Ken Adachi, book reviewer for the *Toronto Star* and considered by many to be the best in Canada, died. This came as a complete shock to us all.

A fortnight after Ken's death, the Ayatollah Khomeini ordered Salman Rushdie to be "sent to hell" because certain passages in his novel *Satanic Verses* were considered blasphemous to Muslims and the "Rushdie Affair" escalated into an international incident which still shows no signs of abating.

Back in September, when Barrie died, I counselled myself to accept it as *something that happens* as one gets older. Death comes to people one knows. Ken's suicide a few short months later was harder to accept as *something that happens*. The death threat to Salman

Rushdie, hitting the papers only a couple of weeks later, felt like the third aftershock in possibly a series as though we'd been straddling a hidden fault line that had begun to shift — first, the shock that Monday morning when I was called out of the shower to be told that Barrie had just died. I had refused to anticipate the possibility of his death and so was immediately knotted up with regret that I hadn't called him in the hospital before his operation, had squandered my last opportunity to talk to him, jolly him up, let him know how I felt about him. Driving around town the next few days, I kept spotting his old jeep, that turquoise trademark junker he'd actually recently traded in for something kinder to his back — death skews chronology. Passing certain landmarks reminded me of how long I'd known him, various streets he'd lived on, or the former Therafields Centre, once Barrie's second home, the corner I'd let him off at, not a month before his death, and the conversation we'd had in the car on the way, about shuffle dancing — all ghosts now, like the emotions themselves, of grief and confusion that drifted downwind from that initial moment of shock.

The power of death to purge what is trivial from what isn't dissipated eventually, but it left behind a kind of halo around Barrie's life, enhancing its edges, illuminating even minor details in my recollection of him.

I ran into Ken Adachi a few days after Barrie's wake and thanked him for the sensitive obituary he had run in a town not always known, shall we say, for its handling of literary obits. I liked the way Ken had paid tribute to the affection people felt for bp, as well as to his professional achievements. He confessed that he was one of the few people in the Toronto literary community who hadn't personally known Barrie. I was startled but covered with a little joke — To know, know, know him was to love, love, love him.

That was around the end of September.

And then Ken.

In another of those trivial discoveries, I was cleaning out my wallet and found a folded receipt from the lunch I'd had with him, last April. We'd eaten Japanese food and talked book business and then, as we were leaving, he had broken down and confessed with that short, embarrassed laugh of his that he usually never ate lunch. I saw then that he'd agreed to a lunch meeting and had eaten everything just to be polite. A moment later I wondered why he had told me. His uncomfortable honesty informed the nature of most of our encounters, usually crowded literary events which he dutifully attended but admitted he never enjoyed. I think he would have been made most uncomfortable by the publicity that his passing has brought to his life's work.

Cause and Effect. I want to take responsibility for not being a person he might have approached before taking his own life, for falling into the other camp, of colleagues whose imagined reproach must have fuelled his desperation. A terrible lesson has been taught all of us, especially the people who worked with him.

Predicting cause and effect around the Rushdie affair has been a new experience for everyone, certainly for governments. Ours has reacted slowly, dreamily almost. Governments prefer to follow precedents rather than set them. I am free to say that. But the act of picking up my pen to comment has been charged with self-consciousness, to say the least. How close is the danger? The darker possibilities of Rushdie's predicament multiply logarithmically with the thump of each morning's paper on the porch. Even in clear-our-throats-primly Toronto, a mob of fifteen hundred marched down University Avenue, burning books and chanting death threats. Last week I visited Pages, one of several independent bookstores receiving recorded death threats, glanced over my shoulder and ordered a copy of *Satanic Verses* for myself, amused at my own uneasiness that my name, address and phone number were being recorded together with my request on the back-order card. That done, I drifted over to the coolly rational shelf of Zen Buddhist books, searching, as is my wont, for fresh goodies. I came upon *Moon in a Dewdrop,* a revised translation of texts and poems by Dogen, the Zen patriarch, a very contemporary ancient mind. I had once visited a grave containing some, but not all, of his ashes in Kyoto. (A guy that good they tend to spread around.) When I opened the book my eyes fell on a quote to the effect that insight is inflexible, although intellect is not. The quote as well as the manner of finding it seemed profoundly appropriate to my thinking on death and oppression, although I couldn't say why, which of course intensified my belief in its wisdom. So I bought the book and took it home, searching in vain for the quote and, less directly, for peace of mind.

A couple of nights later, coming home after a party with old friends who'd talked on and off all night about Rushdie and Ken, I felt steeped, despite the warmth and candlelight, in the combined sadness and despondency of our times, if that doesn't sound impossibly grandiose. I felt our best intentions clouded over by the unresolved nature of all this bad news, jangling against the six o'clock reports that, almost daily, present us with catastrophes we would have thought fantastical if they'd occurred, say, once in a lifetime — nine sucked out of a jumbo jet over Honolulu, twelve killed in a riot over Rushdie's novel in Pakistan, a professor at the University of Western Ontario debates his theory of racial superiority using comparisons of cranial dimensions, IQ tests, "litter size," etc.

I paid the babysitter, locked up and was about to punch off the set when I saw it was the funeral procession of the late emperor of Japan, his palanquin borne by grey-robed Shinto priests accompanied by the eerie keening of the *sho* pipes, astringent music of mourning that mingled with the rain, the hushed commentary and the slurry of feet over the river-washed gravel specially laid along the processional path. I found the formal presentation of bereavement compelling and watched the repeated footage until early morning.

The next day (risking the ridicule of the entire community on whose behalf I was consulting), I took out the Buddhist *I Ching* by Chih-hsu Ou-i, and threw the coins, ten-yen pieces left over from that trip, so long ago. I concentrated in turn on death, loss, fearfulness, isolation, confusion and direction to resolution and drew the resulting trigram Li Ken (36) and its corollary trigram Tui K'un (19). The reading concerned itself with illumination through use of darkness. It advised that "afflictions, bad habits, illnesses, bedevilments,

conceits and false views are excellent subjects for the exercise of complete all-at-once cessations of confusion and seeing the truth."

I haven't come any closer yet to an explanation for the loss of two irreplaceable friends and colleagues, as well as the loss of those certainties I had carefully constructed around love, friendship, and in the case of Rushdie, unvanquishable freedom of literary expression in the western world, right over might. With such losses — and particularly ones falling so close together — I felt this huge desire to shore myself up with evidence of some larger purpose. When I discover what that is, I'll probably have transcended the desire to know. But the act itself of searching — which Barrie's life was devoted to and probably Ken's as well — has begun to cut across the need to come up with answers.

In the meantime, there's always that piece of paper, curled over from moisture, pinned to the back of the bathroom door long before these things happened, which my eye falls on every time I step out of the shower, including that great big morning I heard the news about Barrie:

Great is the problem of birth and death.
Impermanence surrounds us.
Be awake every moment.
Do not waste your life.

322

MICHAEL DAVIDSON

Robert Duncan 1919–1988

"It is toward the old poets / we go, to their faltering,
their unaltering wrongness that has style, / their variable truth ..."

 suspect that for many members of my generation the first image we had of a poet was a tweedy gentleman standing in front of a classroom discussing symbolism in Donne or Keats. Poetry was presented as serious business, not to be taken lightly. Levity was to be tempered with irony, passion with personae and intellect with discretion. What a revelation, then, to encounter Robert Duncan in person, a poet whose hypnotic, nonstop talk shattered all preconceptions of literary decorum.

The first time I saw Duncan read was in Buffalo, New York, at the height of the Viet Nam War. He swept into the auditorium wearing a full-length cape, underneath which he wore a velvet jacket covered with elaborate embroidery. He wore his hair long, in the fashion of the day, and sported thick, fluffy sideburns that exploded on either side of his broad forehead. And when he began to talk, his voice seemed to explode as well. It was as though he had already been talking to us on the way to the podium so that when he reached it, he was already fully engaged.

And that conversation was really unbelievable — full of literary gossip, pronouncements on the escalating war, esoteric bits of information, catty asides and brilliant observations about literary figures. He seldom completed a thought but moved on to something else according to an associative logic of formidable complexity. One would "get" the point long after he had moved on to other subjects, so that listening became somewhat of a retrospective process. And when he finally read a poem, it appeared as a rhythmic and highly inflected lacuna in a much larger, oceanic discussion. He punctuated his pauses with his hand, as though conducting from a score, and his body swayed to cadences of Mahlerian grandeur.

Now Johnson would go up to join the great
    simulcra of men,
Hitler and Stalin, to work his fame
with planes roaring out from Guam over Asia,

all America become a sea of toiling men

Clearly, my English department exposure to poetry had not prepared me for such a spectacle.

Having seen Duncan on the public stage in this fashion, I was surprised to find later that he was incredibly generous in private conversation. Not that he didn't keep on talking, but that he remained acutely aware of what his interlocuter was saying. At times, after trying to drive a wedge into his conversation, I would give up in despair, feeling that any dialogue was hopeless — at which moment he would connect what he had been saying with a whole series of things that I had said some time ago, weaving them back into his conversation as though I had been talking the whole time. Since his sight was impaired, one of eyes was always roaming around the room while the other was pinned on me. And, although he kindly explained which eye saw the near and which the far, I still had the uncanny feeling of being both present and absent at the same time.

I stress these impressions because they are among the most vivid images I have of Robert Duncan, but also because they are part of the participatory poetics that he encouraged. He wanted the audience to have as powerful a sense of his experience as he himself did — to take you up, as he said in one of his Dante sonnets, in a "sorcery" of excited talk and testimony. He willingly accepted the romantic projection of the poet as *vates,* as seer, as one who testifies to the aura surrounding natural phenomenon. At times this role conflicted with daily reality; he would lose his keys, misplace a book on the bus stop, forget someone's name, turn abruptly away from one conversation to begin another. But, in the poems, this distraction reflects his impatience to confront a dream:

in which all things are living

I return to, leaving my self.
I am beside myself with this
thought of the One in the World-Egg

He often figured this dualism in terms of his eyesight: "Gladly the cross-eyed bear," a joke that he played against himself that he might become the witness of his experience. He was unwilling to be Emerson's transparent eyeball, floating passively over a world of inert matter — he had more of Whitman's need to be in the crowd, moving in a phantasmagoria of sensations. That dazzling world was made out of words.

"I have more of being in the magic of the language and in the dreams of poets than I have in my personal existence." For a generation of poets fiercely attempting to reclaim the personal and confessional such remarks must have seemed to avoid the hard reality of daily suffering. And for a generation of poets acutely aware of the social obligations of the poet in the wake of nuclear holocaust, such remarks might have seemed an elegant irrelevance. Yet Duncan was articulating in 1963 what we have come, painfully, to realize: that we live in and through an inherited language, that we do not make up our speech out of whole cloth, that we are spoken through. Duncan's rhetoric was much more vatic, perhaps, but he insisted on the life of and in the sign. Moreover, that sign never manifested itself as a transparent embodiment of some prior reality but brought with it a kind of semiotic surplus, a residue of its origins in human speech. The poet could attempt to expunge or efface that surplus in an ethos of the rhetorically balanced, well-made poem — or he could, as Duncan did, incorporate the unwanted, unexpected or otherwise "inappropriate" word into the ever-expanding structure. A slightly awkward figure, a childlike expostulation, a line by Pindar in a Victorian translation — those elements we were taught to eliminate from our verse — Duncan made the "lures," as he liked to say, for more intense feeling. Hence, in a paradox at the heart of his poetics, he made language his own by relinquishing control over it.

In memorial tributes of this sort, one must finally come to grips with what his loss will mean, and for me that loss involves the model of the poet for whom all reality can enter the poem. Duncan's "permission" to exercise his faculties at large was not another word for supreme egoism but a challenge for all of us to live as though language mattered, as though speech were our last fatal pact with significant action. The end of such a stance is political, since it recognizes the relation between language and power — that if we don't treat words as the site of authority, someone else will speak for us, and we will truly become victims of the news instead of actors *within* it. Duncan's talk may not have been everyone's model for a daily social discourse, but it was a map for resistance. And in resistance, we most accept his legacy.

bpNICHOL

JOHN BERGER

Keeping a Rendez-Vous

he photographs came from Warsaw, Leipzig, Budapest, Bratislava, Riga, Sofia. Each nation has a slightly different way of physically standing shoulder to shoulder during mass demonstrations. But what interests me in all the photos is something that is invisible.

Like most moments of great happiness, the recent events in Eastern Europe were unforeseeable. Yet is happiness the right word to describe the emotion shared by millions this winter? Was not something graver than happiness involved?

Just as the events were unforeseeable, so now is the future. Would it not be more apt to talk of concern, confusion, relief? Why insist upon happiness? The faces in the photos are tense, drawn, pensive. Yet smiles are not obligatory for happiness. Happiness occurs when people can give the whole of themselves to the moment being lived, when being and becoming are the same thing.

As I write, I remember leaving Prague by train twenty years ago. It was as if we were leaving a city in which every stone of every building was black. I hear again the words of a student leader, who stayed behind, as he addressed the last meeting. "What are the plans of my generation for this year of 1969? To pursue a current of political thought opposed to all forms of Stalinism, and yet not to indulge in dreams. To reject the utopia of the New Left, for with such dreams we could be buried. To maintain somehow our links with the trade unions, to continue to work for and prepare an alternative model of socialism. It may take us one year, it may take us ten...." Now the student leader is middle-aged. And Alexander Dubcek is the Chair of the National Parliament of his country.

Many refer to what is happening as a revolution. Power has changed hands as a result of political pressure from below. States are being transformed — economically, politically, juridically. Governing élites are being chased from office. What more is needed to make a revolution? Nothing. Yet this one is unlike any other in modern times.

First, because the ruling élite (except in the case of Romania) did not fight back, but abdicated or reneged, although the revolutionaries were unarmed. And second, because it is being made without Utopian illusions. Made step by step, with an awareness that speed is necessary, yet without the dreaded, classic exhortation of FORWARD!

Rather, the hope of a return. To the past, to the time before all the previous revolutions? Impossible. And it is only small minorities who demand the impossible. These are spontaneous mass demonstrations. People of every generation, muffled up against the cold, their faces grave, happy, keeping a rendezvous. With whom?

Before answering, we have to ask, What is it that has just ended? The Berlin Wall, the one-party system, in many countries the Communist Party, the Red Army occupation, the Cold War? Something else that was older than these and less easy to name has also ended. Voices are not lacking to tell us what it is. History! Ideology! Socialism! Such answers are unconvincing for they are made by wishful thinkers. Nevertheless something vast has ended.

Occasionally history seems to be oddly mathematical. 1989 — as we were often reminded — was the two-hundredth anniversary of the French Revolution, which, although not the first, became the classic model for all other modern revolutions. 1789–1989. It is sufficient to write down these dates to ask whether they do not constitute a period. Is it this that has ended? If so, what made this a period? What was its distinguishing historical feature?

During these two centuries the world was opened up, unified, modernized, created, destroyed and transformed on a scale such as had never occurred before. The energy for these transformations was generated by capitalism. It was the period when self-interest, instead of being seen as a daily human temptation, was made heroic. Many opposed the new Promethean energy in the name of the General Good, of Reason and of Justice. But the Prometheans and their opponents had certain beliefs in common. Both believed in Progress, Science and a new future for Man. Everyone had a

personal set of beliefs (one reason why so many novels could be written), but in their practice, their traffic with the world, their exchanges, all were subject to systems based exclusively on a materialist interpretation of life.

Capitalism, following the doctrines of its philosophers — Adam Smith, David Ricardo, Herbert Spencer — installed a practice in which only materialist considerations and values counted. Thus the spiritual was marginalized; its prohibitions and pleas were ruled out of court by the priority given to economic laws, laws given the authority (as they still have today) of natural laws.

Official religion became an evasive theatre, turning its back on real consequences and blessing principally the powerful. And in the face of capitalism's "creative destruction" — as Joseph Schumpeter, one of its own eminent theorists, defined it — the modern rhetoric of bourgeois politics developed so as to hide the pitiless logic of the underlying practice.

The socialist opposition, undeceived by the rhetoric and hypocrisy, insisted upon the practice. This insistence was Marx's genius. Nothing diverted him. He unveiled the practice layer by layer until it stood exposed once and for all. The shocking vastness of the revelation gave prophetic authority to historical materialism. Here was the secret of history and all its sufferings! Everything in the universe could now be explained (and resolved!) on a material basis, open to human reason. Egoism itself would eventually become outdated.

The human imagination, however, has great difficulty in living strictly within the confines of a materialist practice or philosophy. It dreams, like a dog in its basket, of hares in the open. And so, during these two centuries the spiritual persisted, but in marginalized, new forms.

Take Giacomo Leopardi, who was born when our period opened. He was to become Italy's greatest

modern lyric poet. As a child of his time, he was a rationalist of the existent and studied the universe as a materialist. Nevertheless, his sadness and the stoicism with which he bore it became, within his poetry, even larger than the universe. The more he insisted on the materialist reality surrounding him, the more transcendent became his melancholy.

Likewise, people who were not poets tried to make exceptions to the materialism that dominated their epoch. They created enclaves of the beyond, of what did not fit into materialist explanations. These enclaves resembled hiding places; they were often kept private. Visited at night. Thought of with bated breath. Sometimes transformed into theatres of madness. Sometimes walled in like gardens.

What they contained, the forms of the beyond stored away in these enclaves, varied enormously according to period, social class, personal choice, fashion. Romanticism, the Gothic revival, vegetarianism, Rudolf Steiner, theosophy, art for art's sake, sport, nudism ... each movement saved for its adepts fragments of the spiritual that had been banished.

The question of fascism, of course, cannot be avoided here. It did the same thing. Nobody should presume that evil has no spiritual power. Indeed, one of the principal errors of the two centuries concerned evil. For the philosophical materialists the category was banished, and for the rhetoricians of the establishment, evil became Marxist materialism! This left the field wide open for what Kierkegaard called the prattle of the Devil, the prattle that erects a terrible screen between name and thing, act and consequence.

Yet the most original marginalized spiritual form of the period was the transcendent yet secular faith of those struggling for social justice against the greed of the rich. This struggle extended from the Club des Cordeliers of the French Revolution to the sailors in Kronstadt to my student friends at the University of Prague. It included members of all classes, illiterate peasants and professors of etymology. Their faith was mute in the sense that it lacked ritual declaration. Its spirituality was implicit, not explicit. It probably produced more acts of willing self-sacrifice, of nobility (a word from which some might have shrunk), than any other historical movement of the period. The explanations and strategies of the men and women concerned were materialist, yet their hopes and the unexpected tranquillity they sometimes found in their hearts were the stuff of transcendent visionaries.

To say, as is often said, that communism was a religion, is to understand nothing. What counted was that the material forces in the world carried for millions — in a way such as had never happened before — a promise of universal salvation. Even if Nietzsche had announced that God was dead, these millions felt that He was hiding in History and that, if together they could carry the full weight of the material world, souls would again be given wings. Their faith marked a road for humankind across the usual darkness of the planet.

Yet in their sociopolitical analyses there was no space for such faith, so they treated it as an illegitimate but loved child, who was never given a name. And here the tragedy began. Since their faith was unnamed, it could easily be usurped. It was in the name of their determination and their solidarity that the party machines justified the first crimes and, later, the crimes to cover up further crimes, until finally there was no faith left anywhere.

Sometimes, because of its immediacy, television produces a kind of electronic parable. Berlin, for instance, on the day the wall was opened. Rostropovich was playing his cello by the wall that no longer cast a shadow, and a million East Berliners were thronging to the West to shop with an allowance given them by West German banks! At that moment the whole world saw how materialism had lost its awesome historic power and become a shopping list!

A shopping list implies consumers. And this is why capitalism believes it has won the world. Chunks of the Berlin Wall are now being sold across the world. Forty marks for a large piece from the western side, ten marks for a piece from the eastern side. On January 31 the first McDonald's opened in Moscow; three years ago the first Kentucky Fried Chicken opened near Tiananmen Square. The multinationals have become global in the sense that they are more powerful than any single nation-state. The free market is to be installed everywhere.

Yet if the materialist philosophy of the past two centuries has run out, what is to happen to the materialist fantasy on which consumerism and therefore global capitalism are now utterly dependent?

Marketing punctuates our lives as regularly and systematically as any prayer cycle in a seminary. It transfigures the product or package being sold so that it gains an aura, wins a radiance, that promises a kind of temporary immunity from suffering, a sort of provisional salvation; the salutary act always being the same one of buying. Thus any commodity becomes a way of dreaming, but, more important, the imagination itself becomes acquisitive, accepting the credo of Ivan Boesky addressing students at the University of California's school of business administration: "I think greed is healthy. You can be greedy and still feel good about yourself."

According to the eminent economic historian Immanuel Wallerstein, the majority of the human race is probably worse off today than it was five centuries ago. The poverty of our century is unlike that of any other. It is not, as poverty was before, the result of natural scarcity, but of a set of priorities imposed upon the rest of the world by the rich. Consequently the modern poor are not pitied — except by individuals — but written off as trash. The twentieth-century consumer economy has produced the first culture for which a beggar is a reminder of nothing.

Most commentators on the events in Eastern Europe emphasize the return to religion and nationalism. This is part of a worldwide tendency, yet the word "return" may be misleading. For the religious organizations in question are not the same as they previously were, and the people who make up this return are living, with transistors, at the end of the twentieth century, not the eighteenth.

For example, in Latin America it is a branch of the Catholic Church (much to the Pope's embarrassment) that today leads the revolutionary struggle for social justice and offers means of survival to those being treated as historical trash. In many parts of the Middle East the growing appeal of Islam is inseparable from the social conscience it promises on behalf of the poor, or (as with the Palestinians) the landless and the exiled, up against the remorseless economic and military machinery of the West.

The resurgent nationalisms reflect a similar tendency. All independence movements make economic and territorial demands, but their first claim is of a spiritual order. The Irish, the Basques, the Corsicans, the Kurds, the Kosovans, the Azerbaijanis, the Puerto Ricans, the Latvians have little in common culturally or historically, but all of them want to be free from distant, foreign centres that, through long, bitter experience, they have come to know as soulless.

All nationalisms are at heart deeply concerned with names: with the most immaterial and original human invention. Those who dismiss names as a detail have never been displaced; but the peoples on the peripheries are always being displaced. That is why they insist upon their identity being recognized, insist upon their continuity — their links with their dead and the unborn.

If the "return" to religion is in part a protest against the heartlessness of the materialist systems, the resurgence of nationalism is in part a protest against the anonymity of those systems, their reduction of everything and everybody to statistics and ephemerality.

Democracy is a political demand. But it is something more. It is a moral demand for the individual's right to decide by what criteria an action is called right or wrong. Democracy was born of the principle of conscience. Not, as the free market today would have us believe, of the principle of choice, which, if it is a principle at all, is a relatively trivial one.

The spiritual — marginalized, driven into the corners — is beginning to reclaim its lost terrain. Above all, this is happening in people's minds. The old reasoning, the old common sense, even old forms of courage have been abandoned, and unfamiliar recognitions and hopes, long banished to the peripheries, are returning to claim their own. This is where the happiness behind the faces in the photos starts. But it does not end there.

A reunion has occurred. The separated — those separated by frontiers and by centuries — are meeting. Throughout the period that is ending, daily life, with all its harshness, was continually justified by promises of a radiant future: promises of the new Communist Man, for whom the living were ceaselessly sacrificed; the promise of science forever rolling back the frontiers of ignorance and prejudice; and more recently, the promise of credit cards buying the next instant happiness.

This excessive need of a radiant future separated the present from all past epochs and past experience. Those who had lived before were further away than they had ever been in history. Their lives became remote from the unique exception of the present. Thus for two centuries the future "promise" of history assured an unprecedented solitude for the living.

Today the living are re-meeting the dead, even the dead of long ago, sharing their pain and their hope. And, curiously, this too is part of the happiness behind the faces in the photos.

How long can this moment last? All the imaginable dangers of history are waiting in the wings: bigotry, fanaticism, racism. The colossal economic difficulties of everyday survival are, in theory, going to be solved by the free market. With such a market comes the risk of new ravenous appetites for money, and with their voraciousness comes the law of the jungle. But nothing is finally determined. The soul and the operator have come out of hiding together. We are back in the human condition.

Against all the unanswered questions, I insist upon the grave happiness recorded in these photos — a happiness such as I never thought to live to see, a happiness that carries the hope of our century, so heavy with its unique experience.

Russell Banks's generous introduction moves me to admit a few truths about the actual process of making *Brick,* which does, in fact, live in a garage. Three times a year, though, at random intervals, Gord Robertson, David McFadden, Michael and I haul the paraphernalia of a paste-up into Coach House Printing, where we huddle around a Macintosh and the light table, chosing pictures and pasting up text until we run out of space or arguments. This usually takes two nights of working until two in the morning and involves much eating of pizza, drinking of coffee and loss of temper and dignity. One of our sessions occurred after Coach House had been vandalized. The person responsible appears every year or so to even up a grudge against the press for rejecting a manuscript in 1968. His revenge always takes the same form: he cuts electric wires and erects pyramids of books on the floor, on tables and desks. The electric wires in this old building are as numerous as the books it has stored for years. I remember David on his knees, pulling severed wires out from under pieces of furniture and equipment and re-connecting them with black electrical tape. At one point he connected the aquarium pump to the laser printer. The pyramids were left in place. The rejected poet was found asleep in Michael's car. Several police officers climbed the steep, wooden steps to the second floor at the same time as a pizza arrived. I remember the sight of their caps ascending, seeing them from above. And the smell of the pizza. Another *Brick* about to be born.

Linda Spalding

Contributors

Russell Banks is the author of ten books, including *Continental Drift* and *Affliction*. He lives and teaches in Princeton, New Jersey.

John Berger is the author of *G.*; *Ways of Seeing*; a trilogy that includes *Pig Earth*, *Once in Europa* and *Lilac and Flag*; and a forthcoming book of essays, *Keeping a Rendez-Vous*. He lives in France.

Eavan Boland's two most recent books of poetry are *Outside History: Poems 1980–1990* and *Selected Poems,* published in 1989.

David Bolduc is a Toronto artist.

George Bowering is the author of more than 30 books of poetry, fiction and criticism. He teaches at Simon Fraser University in Vancouver. He is working on a new book of poems, titled *Urban Snow*.

Derek Cohen grew up in South Africa and now teaches at York University in Toronto. He has written two books on Shakespeare and writes regularly on South African literature and art.

Kevin Connolly is a poet, critic and editor of *WHAT!* magazine. His writing has appeared in *The Second Macmillan Anthology*, and numerous journals including *Rampike*, *Border/Lines* and *West Coast Line*.

Michael Davidson teaches at the University of California, San Diego. He is the author of several books of poetry and a critical book, *The San Francisco Renaissance*.

Hillman Dickinson is a retired U.S. Army general now living in Arlington, Virginia. His article was written in 1967 and appeared in *Army* magazine.

Stan Dragland teaches at the University of Western Ontario. He is the author of *Peckertracks*, *Journeys Through Bookland* and *Simon Jesse's Journey*. His *The Bees of the Invisible: Essays in Contemporary English Canadian Literature* appeared this year.

Joe Fafard is a sculptor who lives in Regina, Saskatchewan.

Richard Ford is the author of *A Piece of My Heart*, *The Sportswriter* and *Wild Life,* as well as a collection of short stories, *Rock Springs*. He lives in Montana.

Lawrence Garber lives in London, Ontario, where he teaches at the University of Western Ontario. He is the author of three works of fiction, *Tales From the Quarter*, *Circuit* and *Sirens and Graces*. He is currently at work on a new novel.

Victoria Glendinning has written several bestselling

and prize-winning biographies, including *Edith Sitwell: A Unicorn Among Lions* and *Vita*, a life of Vita Sackville-West. She has recently completed biographies of Rebecca West and Anthony Trollope. Her first novel, *The Grownups*, was published in 1989. She lives in London.

Diana Hartog lives and writes in the Slocan Valley in British Columbia. She has published two volumes of poetry, *Matinee Light* and *Candy From Strangers*, and is presently completing works of fiction and poetry.

Vaclav Havel is a playwright and author and the President of Czechoslovakia.

Russell Hoban was born in Pennsylvania and has lived in London since 1969. His novels are *The Mouse and His Child*, *The Lion of Boaz-Jachin and Jachin-Boaz*, *Kleinzeit*, *Turtle Diary*, *Riddley Walker*, *Pilgerman* and *The Medusa Frequency*.

Linda Hutcheon's books include *The Canadian Postmodern*, *Splitting Images: Contemporary Canadian Ironies* and *The Politics of Postmodernism*. She teaches at the University of Toronto.

Suanne Kelman is a Toronto freelance writer and broadcaster.

Robert Kroetsch is a novelist and poet whose seven novels include *The Studhorse Man*, *Badlands* and *Alibi*. His poetry includes *Completed Field Notes*.

Alberto Manguel is an author, editor, translator and critic. His first novel is *News From a Foreign Country Came*. He is this year's editor of *Soho Square*.

Joyce Marshall is the author of *Presently Tomorrow*,

Lovers and Strangers and *A Private Place*. She has translated several books from French, including *The Road Past Altamont, Windflower* and Gabrielle Roy's *Enchanted Summer*. A book of short stories will be published in 1992.

Mary Meigs is the author of *Lily Briscoe: A Self-Portrait, The Medusa Head* and *The Box Closet*. *Interval* is a chapter of her new book, *In "The Company of Strangers,"* published in 1991.

Rohinton Mistry is the author of a novel, *Such a Long Journey*, and a collection of short stories, *Tales From Firozsha Baag*.

bpNichol wrote eleven books of poetry, four novels, several children's books and one collection of short fiction. *The Martyrology*, his lifework, is recognized internationally as a major poetic achievement. He was a member of the sound poetry ensemble The Four Horsemen. bpNichol died in 1988.

P.K. Page is the author of several books of poetry, including *Evening Dance of the Grey Flies* and *The Glass Air*. She is also the author of the novel, *The Sun and the Moon*, a memoir, *Brazilian Journal*, and two children's books. She lives in Victoria, British Columbia.

Christiane Pflug was born in Berlin. She lived and painted in Toronto from 1960 until her death in 1972 on the Toronto Islands.

Michael Pflug is a rheumatologist and painter in West Hill, Ontario.

Marilynne Robinson grew up in Idaho. She is the author of *Housekeeping*, a novel, and *Mother Country*, a non-fiction book about England.

Leon Rooke is an author, playwright and editor. His books include *The Happiness of Others, A Good Baby, Shakespeare's Dog* and *A Bolt of White Cloth*.

Joe Rosenblatt is a poet and the author of two books of fiction: *The Kissing Goldfish of Siam* and *Escape From the Glue Factory*. A work of mysticism, *Beds and Consenting Dreamers,* is forthcoming.

Holley Rubinsky is the author of *Rapid Transits and Other Stories*. She is working on a collection of stories.

Hector de Saint-Denis Garneau was a Quebec poet, artist and critic. He died in 1943.

John Ralston Saul's last novel was *The Paradise Eater*. His next book is a political essay — *Voltaire's Bastards: The Dictatorship of Reason in the West*.

Sarah Sheard is author of a novel, *Almost Japanese*. She is on the editorial board of Coach House Press and lives in Toronto.

Robert Stone is the author of *A Hall of Mirrors, Dog Soldiers, A Flag for Sunrise and Children of Light*. He lives in Connecticut.

Rosemary Sullivan is the author of two books of poetry, *The Space A Name Makes* and *Blue Panic*, and of *By Heart: Elizabeth Smart/A Life*. She lives in Toronto.

Colin Taylor is a Toronto-based playwright and director, and Artistic Director of Theatre WUM.

Sharon Thesen is a poet, editor and critic. Her most-recent books are her selected poems, *The Pangs of Sunday*, and *The New Long Poem Anthology,* which she edited.

Lola Lemire Tostevin has published four collections of poems; her first novel, *Frog Moon*, will appear in 1992. She teaches at York University in Toronto.

Jane Urquhart is the author of one collection of short stories, two novels — *The Whirlpool* and *Changing Heaven* — and three books of poetry.

Eleanor Wachtel is a writer and broadcaster living in Toronto. She is host of CBC Stereo's "Writers & Company." She co-edited *Language In Her Eye* and *The Expo Story*. Her interviews with Grace Paley and Alice Munro were originally aired on "The Arts Tonight" and "Writers & Company," respectively.

Edmund White is the author of *A Boy's Own Story* and *The Beautiful Room Is Empty*. He lives in Paris.

Paul Wilson is Associate Editor of *The Idler* magazine in Toronto. He has translated many novels by Joseph Skvorecky and several books by Vaclav Havel. Most recently he has edited an anthology of Havel's prose titled *Open Letters: Selected Writings 1965-1990*.

C.D. Wright grew up in Arkansas and is the author of *Further Adventures With You, Translations of the Gospel Back into Tongues,* and *String Light. Just Whistle* is forthcoming. She teaches at Brown University and, with Forrest Gander, runs Lost Roads Publishers.

Geoffrey York is a parliamentary correspondent for *The Globe and Mail*. He has reported on aboriginal issues for the past eight years. He is the author of *The Dispossessed: Life and Death in Native Canada* and the co-author of *People of the Pines: The Warriors and the Legacy of Oka*.

Linda Spalding is the author of *Daughters of Captain Cook*, a novel. She is editor of *Brick* magazine and lives in Toronto.

Michael Ondaatje is a poet, novelist and filmmaker who lives in Toronto and teaches at Glendon College, York University. His most-recent books are *In the Skin of a Lion* and, as editor, *From Ink Lake,* an anthology of Canadian stories. He is contributing editor of *Brick* Magazine. Most of the photographs in this book were taken by Michael Ondaatje.

Editor for the Press: Leon Rooke
Design: Gordon Robertson
Illustrations: David Bolduc

Coach House Press
401 (rear) Huron Street
Toronto, Canada M5S 2G5

Brick: A Literary Journal comes out three times a year.
To subscribe, send $22.00 for two years or $29.00 for three years,
to *Brick*, Box 537, Station Q, Toronto, Canada M4T 2M5.
Prices include GST.

The Writers in Prison Committee of the Canadian
Centre of International PEN works on behalf of writers in prison,
under house arrest, banned from publication, or who have
"been disappeared." Their crimes are to have peacefully
exercised their freedom of expression.